Understanding English Grammar

Why Do You Need This New Edition?

Why Should You Buy This New Edition?

If you're wondering why you should buy this new edition of *Understanding English Grammar*, here are seven good reasons!

- A new section (Ch. 1) highlights **the diversity of English as a world language**, showing you the importance of understanding English in a new "global" culture.
- **"An introduction to Words and Phrases,"** expanded from a section to a complete chapter, offers a complete review of nouns, verbs, adjectives, adverbs, and prepositional phrases and introduces the concepts of noun phrase and verb phrase in clear, jargon-free language.
- **A brief summary of sentence types** has been added to the discussion of sentence patterns in Chapter 3.
- **A new chapter, "Changing Sentence Focus,"** (Ch. 5) focuses in greater detail on the often misunderstood structure and rhetorical effects of the passive voice, the *there*-transformation, and cleft sentences.
- **New sections on "Future Tense"** (Ch. 4) and **"Antithesis"** (Ch. 15), and **an enhanced explanation of punctuation** (Ch. 16), provide new help with difficult constructions and mechanics.
- **An Appendix on Diagramming** offers explanations of the strengths and weaknesses of this visual method of examining sentence structure.
- **Updated exercises and activities,** along with streamlined discussions throughout the chapters, result in an even more accessible, student friendly text.

PEARSO
Longma

Understanding English Grammar

EIGHTH EDITION

Martha Kolln

The Pennsylvania State University

Robert Funk

Eastern Illinois University

Longman

New York San Francisco Boston
London Toronto Sydney Tokyo Singapore Madrid
Mexico City Munich Paris Cape Town Hong Kong Montreal

Senior Sponsoring Editor: Virginia Blanford
Senior Supplements Editor: Donna Campion
Senior Marketing Manager: Sandra McGuire
Production Manager: Ellen MacElree
Project Coordination, Text Design, and Electronic Page Makeup:
  Electronic Publishing Services Inc., NYC
Cover Design Manager: Wendy Ann Fredericks
Cover Designer: Susan Koski Zucker
Cover Art: Grenados/Gomez/Art Box Images/Getty Images
Manufacturing Manager: Mary Fischer
Printer and Binder: R. R. Donnelley & Sons/Harrisonburg
Cover Printer: Lehigh–Phoenix Color/Hagerstown

Library of Congress Cataloging-in-Publication Data

Kolln, Martha.
  Understanding English grammar / Martha Kolln, Robert Funk.—Eighth ed.
    p. cm.
  Includes bibliographical references and index.
  ISBN 13 978-0-205-62690-8
  ISBN 0-205-62690-4
  1. English language—Grammar. I. Funk, Robert. II. Title.
  PE1112.K64 2008
  428.2—dc22

                                                        2008031526

Longman
is an imprint of

ISBN 13: 978-0-205-62690-8
ISBN 10:   0-205-62690-4

2 3 4 5 6 7 8 9 10—DOH—11 10 09
                        Please visit our website at
                        http://www.ablongman.com

Contents

Chapter 4
Expanding the Main Verb   67

Chapter 5
Changing Sentence Focus   90

PART III
Expanding the Sentence   109

Chapter 6
Modifiers of the Verb: Adverbials   112

Chapter 7
Modifiers of the Noun: Adjectivals   132

Chapter 8
The Noun Phrase Functions: Nominals   *168*

Chapter 9
Sentence Modifiers   *193*

Chapter 10
Coordination   *213*

PART IV
Words and Word Classes   **229**

Chapter 11
Morphemes   *231*

Chapter 12
The Form Classes   *243*

Chapter 13
The Structure Classes   268

Chapter 14
Pronouns   293

PART V
Grammar for Writers   *311*

Chapter 15
Rhetorical Grammar   *313*

Preface

The central purpose of this eighth edition of *Understanding English Grammar* remains the same as it has always been: to help students understand the systematic nature of language and to appreciate their own language expertise.

We recognize that most people who use this book are speakers of English who already know English grammar, intuitively and unconsciously. But we also realize that many of them don't *understand* what they know: They're unable to describe what they do when they string words together, and they don't know what has happened when they encounter or produce unclear, imprecise, or ineffective speech and writing. Their grammatical ability is extraordinary, but knowing how to control and improve it is a conscious process that requires analysis and study.

In recent years, the widespread institution of state-mandated standards, the growth of high-stakes testing, and the increased use of diagnostic writing samples make it clear that today's students—and those who are preparing to teach them—must both *know* and *understand* grammar.

While *Understanding English Grammar* assumes no prior knowledge on the readers' part beyond, perhaps, vague recollections of long-ago grammar lessons, we do assume that, as language users, students will learn to draw on their subconscious linguistic knowledge as they learn about the structure of English in a conscious way.

We help students tap into their subconscious grammar knowledge with a new chapter on words and phrases, laying the groundwork for the study of sentence patterns and their expansion. Our focus on syntax begins where the students' own language strengths lie: in their sentence-producing ability. With a few helpful guidelines, the basic sentence patterns become familiar very quickly and provide a framework for further grammatical and rhetorical investigations. English language learners too will appreciate the detailed step-by-step approach, along with highlighted discussions of

ELL issues. The thorough study of sentence patterns in Chapter 3 builds the foundation for the rest of the chapters.

The study of grammar, of course, is not just for English majors or for future teachers: It is for people in business and industry, in science and engineering, in law and politics, in the arts and social services. Every user of the language, in fact, will benefit from the consciousness-raising that results from the study of grammar. The more that speakers and writers know consciously about their language, the more power they have over it and the better they can make it serve their needs.

Teachers familiar with the previous editions of *Understanding English Grammar* will find the same progression of topics in this new one:

Part I: The Study of Grammar: An Overview
Part II: The Grammar of Basic Sentences
Part III: Expanding the Sentence
Part IV: Words and Word Classes
Part V: Grammar for Writers

In this revision we have tried to improve on our approach with the following changes and additions:

- A new section in Chapter 1 on the diversity of the English language
- A new Chapter 2, "An Introduction to Words and Phrases," with basic explanations and exercises to prepare students for the study of sentence patterns
- A brief summary of sentence types to round out the discussion of sentence patterns in Chapter 3
- A new Chapter 5, "Changing Sentence Focus," focusing on the structure and rhetorical effects of the passive voice, the *there* transformation, and cleft sentences
- New sections on future tense in Chapter 4 and antithesis in Chapter 15, along with enhanced explanations of punctuation in Chapter 16
- New and updated exercises and discussion questions
- An Appendix on diagramming

Exercises throughout the chapters reinforce the principles of grammar as they are introduced. Answers to the exercises, which are provided at the end of the book, give the book a strong self-instructional quality. Other exercises, called "Investigating Language," will stimulate class discussion, calling on students to tap into their innate language ability.

Each chapter ends with a list of key terms, a section of practice sentences (for which answers are provided only in the *Instructor's Manual*), a series of questions for discussion that go beyond the concepts covered in the text, and several classroom applications that can be used in your college classes as well as in the future classrooms of your students. The students will also find the Glossary of Grammatical Terms and the Index extremely helpful.

Supplementing the eighth edition of the text, the *Instructor's Manual* (ISBN 0-205-62687-4) includes analyses of the practice sentences, suggested answers for the discussion questions, and suggestions for using the book. The *Instructor's Manual* is available from your Longman/Pearson representative.

Another supplement to the text is the new edition of *Exercises for Understanding English Grammar* (ISBN 0-205-62688-2), with exercises that go beyond those found in the text, many of which call for the students to compose sentences. To keep the self-instructional quality that teachers appreciate, answers for half of the items are included, where answers are appropriate. In addition, there are chapter-ending "test exercises" without answers, which can be used for testing and review. An Answer Key to *Exercises for Understanding English Grammar* (ISBN 0-205-68830-6) is also available from your Longman/Pearson representative.

ACKNOWLEDGMENTS

Understanding English Grammar has once again been revised, corrected, and shaped by the questions and comments of students and colleagues who use the book. We are particularly grateful to the following reviewers for their thoughtful assessments of the previous edition and their recommendations for revision:

Mary Blockley, University of Texas at Austin
Lars Hinrichs, University of Texas at Austin
Brett McInelly, Brigham Young University
Mimi Rosenbush, University of Illinois at Chicago
Duangrudi Suksang, Eastern Illinois University
Nanette Tamer, Villa Julie College

Finally, our special thanks goes to our editor and friend Ginny Blanford.

Martha Kolln

Robert Funk

Understanding English Grammar

Introduction

The subject of English grammar differs markedly from every other subject in the curriculum—far different from history or math or biology or technical drawing. What makes it different? If your native language is English, you do. As a native speaker, you're already an expert. You bring to the study of grammar a lifetime of "knowing" it—except for your first year or two, a lifetime of producing grammatical sentences.

Modern scholars call this expertise your "language competence." Unlike the competence you may have in other subjects, your grammar competence is innate. Although you weren't born with a vocabulary (it took a year or so before you began to perform), you were born with a language potential just waiting to be triggered. By the age of two you were putting words together into sentences, following your own system of rules: "Cookie all gone"; "Go bye-bye." Before long, your sentences began to resemble those of adults. And by the time you started school, you were an expert in your native language.

Well, almost an expert. There were still a few gaps in your system. For example, you didn't start using verb phrases as direct objects (I like *reading books*) until perhaps second grade; and not until third or fourth grade did you use *although* or *even if* to introduce clauses (I'm going home *even if you're not*). But for the most part, your grammar system was in place on your first day of kindergarten.

At this point you may be wondering why you're here—in this class, reading this textbook—if you're already an expert. The answer to that question is important: You're here to learn in a conscious way the grammar that you use, expertly but subconsciously, every day. You'll learn to think about language and to talk about it, to understand and sharpen your own reading and writing skills and, if your plans for the future include teaching, to help others understand and sharpen theirs.

For those of you whose mother tongue is a language other than English, you will have the opportunity to compare the underlying structure of your first language as you add the vocabulary and structure of English grammar to your language awareness.

This chapter of Part I begins by recognizing English as a world language. We then take up the ways in which it has been studied through the years, along with the issues of correctness and standards and language change. In all of these discussions, a key word is *awareness*. The goal of *Understanding English Grammar* is to help you become consciously aware of your innate language competence.

CHAPTER 1

The Study of Grammar: An Overview

ENGLISH: A WORLD LANGUAGE

All over the world every day, there are people, young and old, doing what you're doing now: studying English. Some are college students in China and Korea and Tunisia preparing for the proficiency test required for admission to graduate school in America. Some are businessmen and women in Germany and Poland learning to communicate with their European Union colleagues. Others are adults here in the United States studying for the written test that leads to citizenship. And in the fifty or more countries where English is either the first language or an official second language, great numbers of students are in elementary and secondary classrooms like those you inhabited during your K–12 years.

As the authors of *The Story of English* make clear, English is indeed a world language:

> The figures tell their own story. According to the best estimates available, English is now the mother tongue of about 380 million people in traditionally English-speaking countries such as Britain, Australia and the United States. Add to this the 350 million "second-language" English speakers in countries like India, Nigeria and Singapore, and a staggering further 500 to 1000 million people in countries like China, Japan and Russia that acknowledge the importance of global English as an agent of global capitalism, and you arrive at a total of nearly 2000 million, or at least a third of the world's population.[1]

---

[1] McCrum *et al.*, *The Story of English*, p. xviii. [See reference list, page 14.]

For the PBS documentary series *The Story of English*, first broadcast in 1986, Robert MacNeil traveled the world to interview native speakers of English: among them, speakers of Indian English in Delhi and Calcutta, of Scots English in the Highlands of Scotland, of Pidgin in Papua New Guinea, and of Gullah in the Sea Islands of Georgia. In many of his conversations, the language he heard included vocabulary, pronunciation, and sentence structure far removed from what we think of as mainstream English.

The theme of the documentary was clear: The story of English—or Englishes—is diversity. There is no one "correct"—no one "proper"— version of the English language: There are many.

Even the version we call American English has a wide variety of **dialects**.[2] Different parts of the country, different levels of education, different ethnic backgrounds, different settlement histories—all of these factors produce differences in language communities. Modern linguists recognize that every variety of English is equally grammatical. We could cite many examples (and so could you!) of language structures that vary from one region of the country to another. There's a word for this phenomenon: We call these variations **regionalisms**. For instance, in Central and Western Pennsylvania you will hear "The car needs washed," while in Eastern Pennsylvania (and most other parts of the country) dirty cars "need washing" or "need to be washed." Clearly, there is no one "exact rule" for the form that follows the verb *need* in this context.

Another example is the well-known *you all* or *y'all* of Southern dialects; in both Midwestern and Appalachian regions you will hear *you'uns* or *y'uns*; in parts of Philadelphia you will hear *youse*. These are all methods of pluralizing the pronoun *you*. It's probably accurate to say that the majority of speech communities in this country have no separate form for *you* when it's plural. But obviously, some do. And while they may not appear in grammar textbooks, these plurals are part of the grammar of many regions.

It will be useful, before looking further at various grammatical issues, to consider more carefully the meaning of *grammar*.

THREE DEFINITIONS OF *GRAMMAR*

Grammar is certainly a common word. You've been hearing it for most of your life, at least during most of your school life, probably from third or fourth grade on. However, there are many different meanings, or different nuances of meaning, in connection with *grammar*. The three we will discuss here are fairly broad definitions that will provide a framework for

---

[2] Words in boldface type are defined in the Glossary of Grammatical Terms, beginning on page 357.

thinking about the various language issues you will be studying in these chapters:

Grammar 1: The system of rules in our heads. As you learned in the Introduction, on page 1, you bring to the study of grammar a lifetime of "knowing" how to produce sentences. This subconscious system of rules is your "language competence." It's important to recognize that these internalized rules vary from one language community to another, as you read in connection with the plural forms of *you.*

Grammar 2: The formal description of the rules. This definition refers to the branch of linguistic science concerned with the formal description of language, the subject matter of books like this one, which identify in an objective way the form and structure, the syntax, of sentences. This is the definition that applies when you say, "I'm studying grammar this semester."

Grammar 3: The social implications of usage, sometimes called "linguistic etiquette." This definition could be called do's and don't's of usage, rather than grammar. For example, using certain words may be thought of as bad manners in particular contexts. This defnition also applies when people use terms like "poor grammar" or "good grammar."

TRADITIONAL SCHOOL GRAMMAR

In grammar books and grammar classes, past and present, the lessons tend to focus on parts of speech, their definitions, rules for combining them into phrases and clauses, and sentence exercises demonstrating grammatical errors to avoid. This model, based on Latin's eight parts of speech, goes as far back as the Middle Ages, when Latin was the language of culture and enlightenment, of literature and religion—when Latin was considered the ideal language. English vernacular, the language that people actually spoke, was considered inferior, almost primitive by comparison. So it was only natural that when scholars began to write grammars of English in the seventeenth century they looked to Latin for their model.

In 1693 the English philosopher John Locke declared that the purpose of teaching grammar was "to teach Men not to speak, but to speak correctly and according to the exact Rules of the Tongue." These words of Locke define the concept that today we call **prescriptive grammar.**[3] Grammar books have traditionally been guided by normative principles, that is, for the purpose of establishing norms, or standards, to prescribe "the exact rules of the tongue."

Much of what we call traditional grammar—sometimes called "school grammar"—is the direct descendent of those early Latin-based books. Its

---

[3.] From *Some Thoughts Concerning Education*, quoted in Baron, *Grammar and Good Taste*, p. 121. [See reference list, page 13.]

purpose is to teach literacy, the skills of reading and writing, continuing the normative tradition. And most language arts textbooks today continue to be based on Latin's eight parts of speech.

A more modern approach to language education, however, is guided by the work of linguists, who look at the way the language is actually used. Rather than *pre*scribing how language should be used, an accurate **descriptive grammar** *de*scribes the way people speak in everyday situations. Such a description recognizes a wide variety of grammatical forms. The standard of formal written English is, of course, one of them.

MODERN LINGUISTICS

The twentieth century witnessed important new developments in linguistics, the scientific study of language. One important difference from traditional school grammar was the emphasis on objectivity in describing the language and its word classes, together with a rejection of prescriptivism.

In the 1920s a great deal of linguistic research was carried out by anthropologists studying Native American languages, many of which were in danger of being lost. It was not unusual for a few elders to be the only remaining speakers of a tribe's language. When they died, the language would die with them.

To understand the structure underlying languages unknown to them, researchers could not rely on their knowledge of Western languages: They could not assume that the language they were hearing was related either to Latin or to the Germanic roots of English. Nor could they assume that word classes like adjective and pronoun and preposition were part of the sentences they were hearing. To be objective in their description, they had to start from scratch in their thinking about word categories and sentence structure.

Structural Grammar. The same kind of objectivity needed to study the grammar of an unknown language was applied to English grammar by a group of linguists who came to be known as structuralists. Their description of grammar is called **structuralism.** Like the anthropologists studying the speech of Native Americans, the structuralists too recognized the importance of describing language on its own terms. Instead of assuming that English words could fit into the traditional eight word groups of Latin, the structuralists examined sentences objectively, paying particular attention to how words change in sound and spelling (their form) and how they are used in sentences (their function).

You will see the result of that examination in the next chapter, where a clear distinction is drawn between the large open **form classes** (nouns, verbs, adjectives, and adverbs) and the small closed **structure classes,** such as prepositions and conjunctions.

Another important feature of structuralism, which came to be called "new grammar," is its emphasis on the systematic nature of English. The description of the form classes is a good case in point. Their formal nature is systematic; for example, words that have a plural and possessive form are nouns; words that have an *-ed* form (past tense) and an *-ing* form are verbs. For the structuralists, this systematic description of the language includes an analysis of the sound system (**phonology**), then the systematic combination of sounds into meaningful units and words (**morphology**), and, finally, the systematic combination of words into meaningful phrase structures and sentence patterns (**syntax**).

Transformational Grammar. In the late 1950s, at a time when structuralism was beginning to have an influence on textbooks, a new approach came into prominence. Called transformational generative grammar, this new linguistic theory, along with changes in the language arts curriculum, finally led to the diminishing influence of structuralism. Linguistic research today carries forward what can only be called a linguistic revolution.

The new linguistics, which began in 1957 with the publication of Noam Chomsky's *Syntactic Structures*, deserves the label "revolutionary." After 1957, the study of grammar would no longer be limited to what is said and how it is interpreted. In fact, the word *grammar* itself took on a new meaning, the definition we are calling Grammar 1: our innate, subconscious ability to generate language, an internal system of rules that constitutes our human language capacity. The goal of the new linguistics was to describe this internal grammar.

Unlike the structuralists, whose goal was to examine the sentences we actually speak and to describe their systematic nature (our Grammar 2), the transformationalists wanted to unlock the secrets of language: to build a model of our internal rules, a model that would produce all of the grammatical—and no ungrammatical—sentences. It might be useful to think of our built-in language system as a computer program. The transformationalists are trying to describe that program.

For example, transformational linguists want to know how our internal linguistic computer can interpret a sentence such as

I enjoy visiting relatives

as ambiguous—that is, as having more than one possible meaning. (To figure out the two meanings, think about who is doing the visiting.) In *Syntactic Structures*, Chomsky distinguished between "deep" and "surface" structure, a concept that may hold the key to ambiguity. This feature is also the basis for the label *transformational*, the idea that meaning, generated in the deep structure, can be *transformed* into a variety of surface structures, the sentences we actually speak. During the past four decades the theory has undergone, and continues to undergo, evolutionary changes.

Although these linguistic theories reach far beyond the scope of classroom grammar, there are several important concepts of transformational grammar that you will be studying in these chapters. One is the recognition that a basic sentence can be transformed into a variety of forms, depending on intent or emphasis, while retaining its essential meaning—for example, questions and exclamations and passive sentences. Another major adoption from transformational grammar is the description of our system for expanding the verb in Chapter 4.

THE ISSUE OF CORRECTNESS

The structural linguists, who had as their goal the objective description of language, recognized that no one variety of English can lay claim to the label "best" or "correct," that the dialects of all native speakers are equally grammatical.

You won't be surprised to learn that the structuralists, after describing the language of all native speakers as grammatical, were themselves called "permissive," charged with advocating a policy of "anything goes." After all, for three hundred years an important goal of school grammar lessons and textbooks had been to teach "proper" grammar. Proper grammar implies standards of correctness, and the structuralists appeared to be rejecting standards and ignoring rules. But what the structural linguists were actually doing was making a distinction between Grammar 2 and Grammar 3: the formal language patterns and "linguistic etiquette."

In his textbook *English Sentences* (Harcourt, 1962), Paul Roberts labeled the following sentences, which represent two dialects of English, equally grammatical:

1. Henry brought his mother some flowers.
2. Henry brung his mother some flowers.

Roberts explains that if we prefer sentence 1,

> we do so simply because in some sense we prefer the people who say sentence 1 to those who say sentence 2. We associate sentence 1 with educated people and sentence 2 with uneducated people. . . . But mark this well: educated people do not say sentence 1 . . . because it is better than 2. Educated people say it, *and that makes it better.* That's all there is to it.(p.7)

The well-known issue of *ain't* provides another illustration of the difference between our internal rules of grammar and our external, social rules of usage, between our Grammar 1 and Grammar 3. You may have assumed that pronouncements about *ain't* have something to do with incorrect or ungrammatical English—but they don't. The word itself, the contraction of *am not*, is produced by an internal rule, the same rule that gives us *aren't* and *isn't*. Any negative bias you may have against *ain't* is strictly a matter of linguistic etiquette. And, as you can hear for yourself, many speakers of English harbor no such bias.

Written texts from the seventeenth and eighteenth centuries show that *ain't* was once a part of conversational English of educated people in England and America. It was sometime during the nineteenth century that the word became stigmatized for public speech and marked a speaker as uneducated or ignorant. It's still possible to hear *ain't* in public speech, but only as an attention-getter:

If it ain't broke, don't fix it.

You ain't seen nothin' yet.

And of course it occurs in written dialogue and in written and spoken humor. But despite the fact that the grammar rules of millions of people produce *ain't* as part of their native language, for many others it carries a stigma.

Investigating Language   1.1

The stigma attached to *ain't* has left a void in our language: We now have no first-person equivalent of the negative questions *Isn't it?* and *Aren't they?* You will discover how we have filled the void when you add the appropriate tag questions to three sentences. The tag question is a common way we have of turning a statement into a question. Two examples will illustrate the structure:

Your mother is a nice person, isn't she?

Your brother is still in high school, isn't he?

Now write the tag for these three sentences:

1. The weather is nice today, _____?
2. You are my friend, _____?
3. I am your friend, _____?

You'll notice that you can turn those tag questions into statements by reversing them. Here are the examples:

She isn't.

He isn't.

Now reverse the three that you wrote:

1. _____ .
2. _____ .
3. _____ .

In trying to reverse the third tag, you have probably discovered the problem that the banishment of *ain't* has produced. It has left us with something that sounds like an ungrammatical structure. Given the linguists' definition of *ungrammatical,* something that a native speaker wouldn't say, would you call *"Aren't I?"* ungrammatical? Explain.

In summary, then, our attitude toward *ain't* is an issue about status, not grammar. We don't hear *ain't,* nor do we hear regionalisms like *I might could go* and *the car needs washed,* in formal speeches or on the nightly news because they are not part of what has come to be called "standard English."

Modern linguists may find the word *standard* objectionable when applied to a particular dialect, given that every dialect is standard within its own speech community. To label Roberts's sentence 1 as standard may seem to imply that others are somehow inferior, or substandard. Here, however, we are using *standard* as the label for the majority dialect—or, perhaps more accurately, the status dialect—the one that is used in newscasts, in formal business transactions, in courtrooms, in all sorts of public discourse. If the network newscasters and the president of the United States and your teachers began to use *ain't* or *brung* on a regular basis, its status too would soon change.

LANGUAGE VARIETY

All of us have a wide range of language varieties available to us. The words we choose and the way in which we say them are determined to a great extent by the speech situation. The way we speak with friends at the pizza parlor is quite different from the conversation we carry on at a formal banquet. "Is it correct?" is probably the wrong question to ask about a particular word or phrase. A more accurate question would be "Is it correct for this situation?" or "Is it appropriate?"

In the written language, too, what is appropriate or effective in one situation may be inappropriate or ineffective in another. The language you use in letters to your family and friends is noticeably different from the language you use in a letter when applying for a job. Even the writing you do in school varies, depending on the situation. The language of the personal essay you write for your composition class has an informality that would be inappropriate for a business report or a history research paper. As with speech, the purpose and the audience make all the difference.

Edited American English is the version of our language that has come to be the standard for written public discourse—for newspapers and books and for most of the writing you do in school and on the job. It is the version of our language that this book describes, the written version of the status dialect as it has evolved through the centuries and continues to evolve.

What we think of as the "rules" of Edited American English have come to us from many sources: Some are the judgments of long-ago printers; others come from those early grammarians who looked to Latin for guidance. Most grammar books and dictionaries now and in the past describe—and sometimes prescribe—the version of English used by influential writers and speakers of their day. Today we don't hear those writers and speakers say "I don't have no money" and "He don't like me" and "I ain't going"—at least not in their public discourse. They say, instead, "I don't have any money" and "He doesn't like me" and "I'm not going," so these are the forms that get included in modern grammar books and usage manuals as the standard.

LANGUAGE CHANGE

Another important aspect of our language that is closely related to the issue of correctness and standards is language change. Change is inevitable in a living organism like language. The change is obvious, of course, when we compare the English of Shakespeare or the King James Bible to our modern version. But we certainly don't have to go back that far to see differences. The following passages are from two different translations of *Pinocchio*, the Italian children's book written in the 1880s by Carlo Collodi. The two versions were published almost sixty years apart. You'll have no trouble distinguishing the translation of 1925 from the one published in 1983:

1a. Fancy the happiness of Pinocchio on finding himself free!
1b. Imagine Pinocchio's joy when he felt himself free.

2a. Gallop on, gallop on, my pretty steed.
2b. Gallop, gallop, little horse.

3a. But whom shall I ask?
3b. But who can I possibly ask?

4a. Woe betide the lazy fellow.
4b. Woe to those who yield to idleness.

5a.   Hasten, Pinocchio.

5b.   Hurry, Pinocchio.

6a.   Without adding another word, the marionette bade the good
      Fairy good-by.

6b.   Without adding another word, the puppet said good-bye to his
      good fairy.

In both cases the translators are writing the English version of 1880 Italian, so the language is not necessarily conversational 1925 or 1983 English. In spite of that constraint, we can recognize—as you've probably figured out—that the first item in each pair is the 1925 translation. Those sentences include words that we simply don't have occasion to use anymore, words that would sound out of place today in a conversation, or even in a fairy tale: *betide, hasten, bade.* The language of 1925 is simply not our language. In truth, the language of 1983 is not our language either. We can see and hear change happening all around us, especially if we consider the new words required for such fields as medicine, space science, and e-commerce.

Investigating Language   1.2

The difference between the two translations in the first pair of *Pinocchio* sentences is connected to the word *fancy,* a word that is still common today. Why did the 1983 translator use *imagine* instead? What has happened to *fancy* in the intervening decades?

The third pair involves a difference in grammar rather than vocabulary, the change from *whom* to *who.* What do you suppose today's language critics would have to say about the 1983 translation?

The last pair includes a spelling change. Check the dictionary to see which is "correct"—or is *correct* the right word? The dictionary includes many words that have more than one spelling. How do you know which one to use?

Finally, provide examples to demonstrate the accuracy of the assertion that the language of 1983 is not our language.

LANGUAGE IN THE CLASSROOM

How about the classroom? Should teachers call attention to the dialect differences in their students' speech? Should teachers "correct" them? These are questions that the National Council of Teachers of English has addressed in a document called "Students' Right to Their Own Language."

The NCTE has taken the position that teachers should respect the dialects of their students. But teachers also have an obligation to teach students to read and write standard English, the language of public discourse and of the workplace that those students are preparing to join. There are ways of doing so without making students feel that the language spoken in their home, the language produced by their own internal grammar rules, is somehow inferior. Certainly one way is to study language differences in an objective, nonjudgmental way, to discuss individual and regional and ethnic differences. The community, the schoolyard, even the individual classroom can serve as the laboratory for examining language in an objective way.

In 1994 the NCTE passed a resolution that encourages the integration of language awareness into classroom instruction and teacher preparation programs. Language awareness includes examining how language varies in a range of social and cultural settings; how people's attitudes towards language vary across cultures, classes, genders, and generations; how oral and written language affects listeners and readers; how "correctness" in language reflects social, political, and economic values; and how first and second languages are acquired. Language awareness also includes the teaching of grammar from a descriptive, rather than a prescriptive, perspective.

CHAPTER *1*
Key Terms

Correctness	Linguistic etiquette
Descriptive grammar	Nonstandard dialect
Dialect	Prescriptive grammar
Edited American English	Regionalisms
Grammar rules	Structuralism
Grammatical	Transformational grammar
Language change	Ungrammatical
Language variety	Usage rules

For Further Reading on Topics in This Chapter

Baron, Dennis E. *Grammar and Good Taste: Reforming the American Language.* New Haven, CT: Yale University Press, 1982.

Crystal, David. *The Cambridge Encyclopedia of Language.* Cambridge, England: Cambridge University Press, 1987.

Haussamen, Brock. *Revising the Rules: Traditional Grammar and Modern Linguistics.* 2nd ed. Dubuque, IA: Kendall-Hunt, 1997.

Hunter, Susan, and Ray Wallace, eds. *The Place of Grammar in Writing Instruction: Past, Present, Future.* Portsmouth, NH: Boynton/Cook, 1995.

Joos, Martin. *The Five Clocks.* New York: Harcourt Brace Jovanovich, 1967.

Kutz, Eleanor. *Language and Literacy: Studying Discourse in Communities and Classrooms.* Portsmouth, NH: Boynton/Cook, 1997.

McCrum, Robert, Robert MacNeil, and William Cran. *The Story of English.* 3rd rev. ed. New York: Penguin Books, 2003.

Pinker, Steven. *The Language Instinct.* New York: William Morrow, 1994.

Pinker, Steven. *The Stuff of Thought: Language as a Window into Human Nature.* New York: Viking, 2007.

Schuster, Edgar H. *Breaking the Rules: Liberating Writers through Innovative Grammar Instruction.* Portsmouth, NH: Heinemann, 2003.

Wolfram, Walt. *Dialects and American English.* Washington, DC: Center for Applied Linguistics, 1991.

QUESTIONS ? for DISCUSSION

1. In *Breaking the Rules*, Edgar H. Schuster labels some of the usage rules we describe as part of Grammar 3 (see page 5) as "mythrules"—prescriptive rules that have no basis in actual usage. One of the best known is the rule against splitting the infinitive—in other words, placing an adverb between *to* and the infinitive verb. A famous example of such "rule breaking" can be found in the opening words of *Star Trek*, where the mission was "to *boldly* go where no man has gone before." Schuster challenges the so-called rule with this little "test": Insert the word given in brackets into the sentences in the place that sounds the most natural:

   I want you *to tell* it like it is. [really]

   I'd like *to know* an opera star. [actually]

   He's the last person *to consider* being dishonest. [ever]

   How many infinitives did you split?

2. Following are the opening paragraphs from two short stories, one written by Nathaniel Hawthorne in 1864 and the other by John Updike in 1962. You'll have no trouble figuring out which is which. Cite specific details that enable you to do the figuring.

> In the latter part of the last century, there lived a man of science—an eminent proficient in every branch of natural philosophy—who, not long before our story opens, had made experience of a spiritual affinity, more attractive than any chemical one. He had left his laboratory to the care of an assistant, cleared his fine countenance from the furnace-smoke, washed the stain of acids from his fingers, and persuaded a beautiful woman to become his wife. ("The Birthmark")

> In walks these three girls in nothing but bathing suits. I'm in the third checkout slot, with my back to the door, so I don't see them until they're over by the bread. The one that caught my eye first was the one with the plaid green two-piece. ("A & P")

CLASSROOM APPLICATIONS

1. Do you use words or phrases that your parents and others of their generation do not? As a class project, compile your own dictionary of slang. Each contribution should include synonyms and context, as dictionary entries generally do. Check a current dictionary. Are your entries already labeled as slang?

   Share the list with the older generation. Which expressions do they recognize? What terms did they use to express the same or similar ideas when they were your age? What other slang expressions did they use? What has happened to them? Have any of them become part of our everyday vocabulary? Are any now labeled as slang in the dictionary?

2. One characteristic of modern "youthspeak" is the frequent, and tiresome, use of *like*. While it may seem that *like* gets added randomly for no particular purpose, some linguists have observed that it seems to function as an opening quotation mark. Play the role of linguist by transcribing actual conversations. Are those observations about the function of *like* accurate? If so, is there a closing mark as well?

3. The origins of many stock phrases in our language are lost in history. Perhaps you can figure out, or find out, where these phrases came from:

acid test	fall guy
against the grain	greenhorn
bank teller	pass the buck
bring home the bacon	rank and file
by and large	sleep like a top

You may not find the origins of these phrases in the dictionary, so check the reference section of your library for specialized usage dictionaries.

The Grammar of Basic Sentences

You might have been surprised to learn, when you read the introduction to Part I, that you're already an expert in grammar—and have been since before you started school. Indeed, you're such an expert that you can generate completely original sentences with those internal grammar rules of yours, sentences that have never before been spoken or written. Here's one to get you started:

> At this very moment, I, [Insert your name], am reading page 17 of the eighth edition of *Understanding English Grammar*.

Surely the occasion for that sentence has never happened before; you can be quite sure that it's original. Perhaps even more surprising is the fact that the number of such sentences you can produce is infinite.

When you study the grammar of your native language, then, you are studying a subject you already "know"; so rather than *learning* grammar, you will be "learning about" grammar. If you're not a native speaker, you will probably be learning both grammar and "about" grammar; the mix will depend on your background and experience. It's important that you understand what you are bringing to this course—even though you may have forgotten all those "parts of speech" labels and definitions you once consciously learned. The unconscious, or subconscious, knowledge that you have can help you if you will let it. The discussions and the exercises in this book are designed to help you put your intuition to work, to help you bring to a conscious level and use that grammar expertise of yours.

We will begin the study of grammar by examining words and phrases in Chapter 2. Then in Chapter 3 we take up basic sentence patterns, the underlying framework of sentences, looking for both their common and their distinguishing features. A conscious knowledge of the basic patterns will provide a foundation for understanding the sentence expansions and variations that come later. In Chapter 4 we will examine the expanded verb, the system of auxiliaries that makes our verbs so versatile. In Chapter 5 we will look at the ways we have of changing sentence focus for a variety of purposes.

CHAPTER
2

An Introduction to Words and Phrases

CHAPTER PREVIEW

The purpose of this chapter is really to *review* words and phrases rather than to introduce them; we assume that most of you have met them before. But even if you haven't, or even if you've forgotten those long-ago lessons, you'll discover that you know more about words and phrases than you suspect—as you read in the previous Introduction.

As with every subject in your curriculum, the discussion of sentence structure requires a special vocabulary—in this case, a language for discussing language. For the most part that language uses the terms of traditional grammar, many of which may already be familiar to you. However, instead of the traditional eight parts of speech, we will introduce the word categories of the structural linguists, who classified words in two broad groups: **form classes** and **structure classes**. And we will help you mine your internal grammar expertise to assist you in bringing your subconscious grammar knowledge to a conscious level.

Pay special attention to the terms in bold type; they constitute your grammar vocabulary. They are defined in the Glossary, beginning on page 357. You will find the location of further information about these and many other topics by checking the Index.

This review will lay the groundwork for the study of the sentence patterns and their expansions in the chapters that follow.

FORM CLASSES

In the middle of the twentieth century, linguists recognized that the traditional classification of words—eight parts of speech based on Latin—did not accurately describe the way words functioned in English. For example, they emphasized that content words—our **nouns, verbs, adjectives**, and **adverbs**—have special qualities that the other word classes do not have. Their numbers alone make them special: These four word classes constitute over 99 percent of our vocabulary. They are also different from other word classes in that they can be identified by their forms. Each of them has, or can have, particular endings, or **suffixes**. And that, of course, is the reason for the label "form classes."

We will begin by looking at nouns and verbs, our two largest word categories—and put them into our simplest kind of sentence:

> Cats fight.
>
> Mary laughed.

You're probably familiar with the traditional definition of a noun, such as *cats* or *Mary*, a definition based on meaning: "the name of a person, place, or thing." Verbs, too, are traditionally defined according to meaning: "words expressing action, being, or state of being." However, instead of these definitions based on meaning, let's look at their forms. Our two sample sentences illustrate one suffix for nouns and one for verbs: the **plural** marker, *-s*, on the noun *cat*; the **past tense** marker, *-ed*, on the verb *laugh*. As you'll see, we can use these "formal" characteristics as criteria in our definitions of "noun" and "verb."

NOUNS

The **plural** *-s* is one of two noun endings that we call **inflections**; the other noun inflection is the **possessive case** ending, the apostrophe plus *-s*—or, in the case of most plural nouns, just the apostrophe. Most nouns will fit into the following framework:[1]

SINGULAR	PLURAL	SINGULAR POSSESSIVE	PLURAL POSSESSIVE
cat	cats	cat's	cats'
horse	horses	horse's	horses'

We now have a simple definition of *noun* based on form:

> **A noun is a word that can be made plural and/or possessive.**

We will enhance this simple definition after describing the noun phrase.

---

[1] In words where the plural noun has no *-s*, as in the case of irregular plurals such as *men* and *women*, both the singular and the plural possessive forms take the apostrophe plus *-s*:

man	men	man's	men's
woman	women	woman's	women's

THE NOUN PHRASE

The term **noun phrase** may be new to you, although you're probably familiar with the word **phrase**, which traditionally refers to any group of words that functions as a unit within the sentence. But sometimes a single word will function as a unit by itself, as in our two earlier examples, where *cats* and *Mary* function as subjects in their sentences. For this reason, we are going to alter that traditional definition of *phrase* to include single words:

> ***A phrase is a word or group of words that functions as a unit within the sentence.***

A phrase will always have a head, or **headword**; and as you might expect, the headword of the noun phrase is a noun. Most noun phrases (NPs) also include a noun signaler, or marker, called a **determiner**. Here are three NPs you have seen in this chapter, with their headwords underlined and their determiners shown in italics:

the <u>headword</u>

a single <u>word</u>

the traditional <u>definition</u>

As the examples illustrate, the headword may be preceded by a modifier. The most common modifier in preheadword position is the adjective, such as *single* and *traditional*. You will be studying about many other structures as well that function the way adjectives function, as modifiers of nouns.

As you may have noticed in the three examples, the opening determiners are the **articles** *a* and *the*. While they are our most common determiners, other word groups also function as determiners, signaling noun phrases. For example, the function of possessive nouns and possessive pronouns is almost always that of determiner:

Mary's boyfriend

his apartment

Another common word category in the determiner slot is the **demonstrative pronoun**—*this, that, these, those*:

this old house

these expensive sneakers

Because noun phrases can be single words, as we saw in our earlier examples (*Cats fight, Mary laughed*), it follows that not all noun phrases will have determiners. **Proper nouns**, such as the names of people and places

(*Mary*) and certain plural nouns (*cats*), are among the most common that appear without a noun signaler.

In spite of these exceptions, however, it is accurate to say that most noun phrases do begin with determiners. Likewise, it's accurate to say—and important to recognize—that whenever you encounter a determiner *you can be sure you are at the beginning of a noun phrase*. In other words, articles (*a, an, the*) and certain other words, such as possessive nouns and pronouns, demonstrative pronouns, numbers, and another subclass of pronouns called **indefinite pronouns** (e.g., *some, many, both, each, every*), tell you that a noun headword is on the way.

We can now identify three defining characteristics of nouns:

> *A noun is a word that can be made plural and/or possessive; it occupies the headword position in the noun phrase; it is usually signaled by a determiner.*

In the study of syntax, which you are now undertaking, you can't help but notice the prevalence of noun phrases and their signalers, the determiners.

Exercise 1

The following six sentences include 16 noun phrases. Your job is to identify their determiners and headwords.
Note: Answers to the exercises are provided, beginning on page 377.

1. The students rested after their long trip.
2. Our new neighbors across the hall became our best friends.
3. Mickey's roommate studies in the library every evening.
4. A huge crowd lined the streets for the big parade.
5. This new lasagna recipe feeds an enormous crowd.
6. Jessica made her new boyfriend some cookies.

VERBS

When the dictionary identifies a word as a verb, it lists three forms: the **base form** (*laugh*), the **past tense** (*laughed*), and the **past participle** (*laughed*). These three forms are traditionally referred to as the verb's "three principal parts." The base form is also known as the infinitive; it is often written with *to* (*to laugh*). All verbs also have two more forms: the **third-person singular,** which adds an *-s* to the base form, and the **present participle**, which has an *-ing* ending.

Base form (also called present tense)	laugh
Third person singular (*-s* form)	laughs
Past tense (*-ed* form)	laughed
Past participle (*-en* form)	laughed
Present participle (*-ing* form)	laughing

All verbs have these five forms. The verb *be*, our only verb with more than five, has eight forms: *am, are, is, was, were, been, being,* along with *be,* the infinitive form. *Be* is our only verb that has an infinitive form that is separate from the present tense. (You'll read about verbs in detail in Chapter 4.)

The point to be made here is that in using your knowledge of verb inflections you can use the criterion of form to define *verb*, just as you did with *noun*:

> *A verb is a word that can be used in present and past tenses; it has both an -s form and an -ing form.*

THE VERB PHRASE

As you would expect, the headword of a verb phrase, or VP, is the verb; the other components, if any, will depend in part on whether the verb is **transitive** (*The cat chased the mouse*) or **intransitive** (*Cats fight*). In most sentences, the verb phrase will include **adverbials** (*Mary laughed loudly*). In Chapter 3 you will be studying verb phrases in detail because it is the variations in the verb phrases, the sentence **predicates**, that differentiate the sentence patterns.

As we saw with the noun phrase, it is also possible for a verb phrase to be complete with only the headword. Our two earlier examples—*Cats fight; Mary laughed*—illustrate instances of single-word noun phrases, which are fairly common in most written work, as well as single-word verb phrases, which are not common at all. In fact, single-word verb phrases as predicates are very rare. So far in this chapter, none of the verb phrases we have used come close to the brevity of those two sample sentences.

NP + VP = S

This formula—NP + VP = S—is another way of saying "Subject plus Predicate equals Sentence." Our formula with the labels NP and VP simply emphasizes the form of those two sentence parts. The following diagram includes both labels, and their form and function:

SENTENCE

Noun Phrase
(Subject)

Verb Phrase
(Predicate)

Using what you have learned so far about noun phrases and verb phrases—as well as your intuition—you should have no trouble recognizing the two parts of the following sentences. You'll notice right away that the first word of the subject noun phrase in all of the sentences is a determiner.

> Our county commissioners passed a new ordinance.
>
> The mayor's husband spoke against the ordinance.
>
> The mayor was upset with her husband.
>
> Some residents of the community spoke passionately for the ordinance.
>
> The merchants in town are unhappy.
>
> This new law prohibits billboards on major highways.

As a quick review of noun phrases, identify the headwords of the subject noun phrases in the six sentences just listed:

——————————   ——————————   ——————————

——————————   ——————————   ——————————

Given your understanding of noun phrases, you probably had no difficulty identifying those headwords: *commissioners, husband, mayor, residents, merchants, law.* In the exercise that follows, you are instructed to identify the two parts of those six sentences to determine where the subject noun phrase ends. This time you'll be using your subconscious knowledge of pronouns.

Exercise 2

You have at your disposal a wonderful tool for figuring out the line between the subject and the predicate: Simply substitute a **personal pronoun** *(I, you, he, she, it, they)* for the subject. You saw these example sentences in Exercise 1:

Examples:

> <u>This new lasagna recipe</u> feeds an enormous crowd.
>
> **It**   feeds an enormous crowd.
>
> <u>Our new neighbors across the hall</u> became our best friends.
>
> **They**   became our best friends.

Now substitute a pronoun for the subject of these sentences you read in the previous discussion:

1. Our county commissioners passed a new ordinance.

    _____

2. The mayor's husband spoke against the ordinance.

    _____

3. The mayor was upset with her husband.

    _____

4. Some residents of the community spoke passionately for the ordinance.

    _____

5. The merchants in town are unhappy.

    _____

6. This new law prohibits billboards on major highways.

    _____

As your answers no doubt show, the personal pronoun stands in for the entire noun phrase, not just the noun headword. Making that substitution, which you do automatically in speech, can help you recognize not only the subject-predicate boundary but the boundaries of noun phrases throughout the sentence.

Recognition of this subject-predicate relationship, the common element in all of our sentences, is the first step in the study of sentence structure. Equally important for the classification of sentences into sentence patterns is the concept of the verb as the central, pivotal slot in the sentence. Before moving on to the sentence patterns, however, we will look briefly at the other two word classes, adjectives and adverbs, which, like nouns and verbs, can often be identified by their forms. We will then describe the prepositional phrase, perhaps our most common modifier, one that adds information to both the noun phrase and the verb phrase.

ADJECTIVES AND ADVERBS

The other two form classes, **adjectives** and **adverbs**, like nouns and verbs, can usually be recognized by their form and/or by their position in the sentence.

The inflectional endings that identify adjectives and some adverbs are the **comparative** suffix -*er* and the **superlative** -*est*:

Adjective	*Adverb*
big	near
bigger	nearer
biggest	nearest

When the word has two or more syllables, the comparative and superlative markers are generally *more* and *most* rather than the suffixes:

beautiful   quickly

more beautiful   more quickly

most beautiful   most quickly

Another test of whether a word is an adjective or adverb, as opposed to noun or verb, is its ability to pattern with a **qualifier**, such as *very*:

very beautiful   very quickly

You'll notice that these tests (the inflectional endings and *very*) can help you differentiate adjectives and adverbs from the other two form classes, nouns and verbs, but they do not help you distinguish the two word classes from each other.

There is one special clue about word form that we use to help us identify adverbs: the -*ly* ending. However, this is not an inflectional suffix like —*er* or -*est*: When we add one of these to an adjective—*happier, happiest*— the word remains an adjective (just as a noun with the plural inflection added is still a noun). In contrast, the -*ly* ending that makes adverbs so visible is actually added to adjectives to turn them into adverbs:

Adjective				*Adverb*
quick	+	ly	=	quickly
pleasant	+	ly	=	pleasantly
happy	+	ly	=	happily

Rather than inflectional, the -*ly* is a **derivational suffix**: It enables us to *derive* adverbs from adjectives. Incidentally, the -*ly* means "like": quickly = quick-like; happily = happy-like. And because we have so many adjectives that can morph into adverbs in this way—many thousands, in fact—we are not often mistaken when we assume that an -*ly* word is an adverb. (In Chapter 12 you will read about derivational suffixes for all four form classes.)

In addition to these "adverbs of manner," as the -*ly* adverbs are called, we have a selection of other adverbs that have no clue of form; among them are *then, now, soon, here, there, everywhere, afterward, often, sometimes, seldom, always.* Often the best way to identify an adverb is by the kind of information it supplies to the sentence—information of time, place, manner, frequency, and the like; in other words, an adverb answers such questions as where, when, why, how, and how often. Adverbs can also be identified on the basis of their position in the predicate and their movability.

As you read in the discussion of noun phrases, the slot between the determiner and the headword is where we find adjectives:

this <u>new</u> recipe   an <u>enormous</u> crowd

Adverbs, on the other hand, modify verbs and, as such, will be part of the predicate:

>Some residents spoke <u>passionately</u> for the ordinance.

>Mario <u>suddenly</u> hit the brakes.

However, unlike adjectives, one of the features of adverbs that makes them so versatile for writers and speakers is their movability: They can often be moved to a different place in the predicate—and they can even leave the predicate and open the sentence:

>Mario hit the brakes <u>suddenly</u>.

>><u>Suddenly</u> Mario hit the brakes.

Bear in mind, however, that some adverbs are more movable than others. We probably don't want to move *passionately* to the beginning of its sentence. And in making the decision to move the adverb, we also want to consider the context, the relation of the sentence to the others around it.

Investigating Language   2.1

Your job in this exercise is to experiment with the underlined adverbs to discover how movable they are. Do you and your classmates agree?

1. I have <u>finally</u> finished my report.
2. Maria has <u>now</u> accumulated sixty credits towards her degree.
3. The hunters moved <u>stealthily</u> through the woods.
4. The kindergartners giggled <u>quietly</u> in the corner.
5. My parents <u>occasionally</u> surprise me with a visit.
6. Our soccer coach will <u>undoubtedly</u> expect us to practice <u>tomorrow</u>.
7. I <u>occasionally</u> jog <u>nowadays</u>.
8. The wind <u>often</u> blows <u>furiously</u> in January.

PREPOSITIONAL PHRASES

Before going on to sentence patterns, let's take a quick look at the **prepositional phrase**, a two-part structure consisting of a **preposition** followed by an object, which is usually a noun phrase. Prepositions are among the most common words in our language. In fact, the paragraph you are now reading includes nine different prepositions: *before, to, at, of* (three times), *by, among, in, throughout,* and *as* (twice). Prepositional phrases show up throughout our sentences, sometimes as part of a noun phrase and sometimes as a modifier of the verb.

In a noun phrase, the prepositional phrase adds a detail or makes clear the identity of the noun, which it follows in postheadword position. Several of the sentences you saw in Exercise 1 included prepositional phrases:

Our new neighbors <u>across the hall</u> became our best friends.

Here the *across* phrase is part of the subject noun phrase, functioning like an adjective, so we call it an **adjectival** prepositional phrase:

They became our best friends.

This *across* phrase tells "which neighbors." In a different sentence that same phrase could function adverbially:

Our good friends live <u>across the hall</u>.

Here the purpose of the *across* phrase is to tell "where" the good friends live.

Here's another sentence from Exercise 1:

The students rested <u>after their long trip</u>.

Here the *after* phrase in the predicate functions like an adverb, telling "when"—so we refer to its function as **adverbial**. Another good clue that the phrase is adverbial is its movability; it could open the sentence:

<u>After their long trip</u>, the students rested.

Remember that the nouns *adjective* and *adverb* name word classes: They name forms. When we add that *-al* or *-ial* suffix—*adjectival* and *adverbial*—they become the names of functions—functions that adjectives and adverbs normally perform. In other words, the terms *adjectival* and *adverbial* can apply to structures other than adjectives and adverbs—such as prepositional phrases, as we have just seen:

Modifiers of nouns are called adjectivals, ***no matter what their form.***

Modifiers of verbs are called adverbials, ***no matter what their form.***

Exercise 3

In the following sentences, most of which you have seen before, identify the underlined prepositional phrases as either adjectival or adverbial:

1. A huge crowd lined the streets <u>for the big parade</u>.
2. Mickey's roommate studies <u>in the library</u> every evening.
3. Some residents <u>of the community</u> spoke passionately <u>for the ordinance</u>.
4. The merchants <u>in town</u> are unhappy.
5. I googled his blog <u>on my BlackBerry</u>.

Unlike the form classes, prepositions cannot be distinguished by their form; that is, there are no endings that identify them, as nouns and verbs often have. Prepositions are one of the word classes called **structure classes**. Other structure classes include determiners, auxiliaries, qualifiers (such as *very*, which you saw in the discussion of adjectives and adverbs), and **conjunctions** (connecting words like *and*, *or*, and *but*).

Because prepositional phrases are such common structures in our language, you might find it helpful to review the lists of **simple** and **phrasal prepositions** in Chapter 13. You'll find them on pages 278 and 279–280.

CHAPTER 2
Key Terms

In this chapter you've been introduced to many basic terms that describe sentence grammar. This list may look formidable, but some of the terms were probably familiar already; those that are new will become more familiar as you continue the study of sentences.

Adjectival	Indefinite pronoun	Preposition
Adjective	Inflection	Prepositional phrase
Adverb	Noun	Pronoun
Adverbial	Noun phrase	Qualifier
Article	Past tense	Subject
Comparative degree	Personal pronoun	Superlative degree
Demonstrative pronoun	Phrase	Verb
Determiner	Plural	Verb phrase
Form classes	Possessive case	
Headword	Predicate	

QUESTIONS
?
for DISCUSSION

1. When a banner was hung across a city's main street to recognize the local bus company's service to the community, some of the citizens objected to the wording. The banner was printed with the company's name, followed by the verb phrase "serving our community" and, in bold print, these three words: SAFELY ECONOMICALLY FRIENDLY. To discover the problem, check out those three *-ly* words.

2. *Bully, belly,* and *silly* all look a great deal alike. Consider what you know about *-ly* and about the inflectional endings on nouns and verbs. How can you show what word classes these three belong to? Do any of them fit in more than one class?

CLASSROOM APPLICATIONS

A. Make each list of words into a noun phrase and then use the phrase in a sentence. Compare your answers with your classmates': The NPs should all be the same (with one exception); the sentences will vary.

1. table, the, small, wooden
2. my, sneakers, roommate's, new
3. cotton, white, t-shirts, the, other, all
4. gentle, a, on the head, tap
5. books, those, moldy, in the basement
6. the, with green eyes, girl

Did you discover the item with two possibilities?

B. Add modifiers to the noun phrases in these sentences: Put an adjective before each noun and a prepositional phrase after:

Example:

Pipes caused contamination.
Rusty pipes *under the sink* caused *serious* contamination *of our water.*

1. The tulips are blooming at last.
2. The children annoyed the neighbors.
3. The drapes match the furniture.

4. The water glistened in the light.
5. Thunderstorms frightened the residents.

C. Proper nouns refer to unique or specific people, places, or things and are usually capitalized. Common nouns name general classes and are not capitalized. In the following sentences, revise the underlined nouns, changing the common nouns to proper and proper nouns to common.

Example:

I created a profile on <u>a social network on the Web</u>.
I created a profile on <u>MySpace</u>.

1. Bill bought a new <u>MacBook Air</u>.
2. <u>Our dormitory</u> is just across the quad.
3. We plan to visit <u>a foreign country</u> this summer.
4. My sister works for <u>IBM</u>.
5. They gave <u>a gift</u> to <u>Dr. McMahan</u>.
6. <u>Dustin Hoffman</u> won <u>an award</u> for his role in <u>that movie</u>.

D. Many words in English can serve as either nouns or verbs. Here are some examples:

> I made a *promise* to my boss. (noun)
> I *promised* to be on time for work. (verb)

> He *offered* to help us. (verb)
> We accepted his *offer*. (noun)

Write a pair of short sentences for each of the following words, demonstrating that they can be either nouns or verbs.

> visit   plant   point   feature   audition

CHAPTER
3

Sentence Patterns

CHAPTER PREVIEW

To understand grammar is to understand sentence structure—and vice versa: To understand sentence structure is to understand grammar. You began the study of sentence structure in the previous chapter when you focused on the noun phrase and the verb phrase and learned to recognize them by their form. In this chapter we will extend the discussion of form to that of whole sentences.

The study of sentences may at first seem like a formidable, if not impossible, task when you consider that the potential number of sentences a speaker can produce is infinite. But of course it's not impossible. What makes it possible is the systematic nature of sentence structure and the limited number of elements that make up sentences. So despite the infinite possibilities, the number of basic sentence forms, or patterns, is decidedly finite—in fact, the total is very small: Ten **sentence patterns** account for the underlying skeletal structure of almost all the possible grammatical sentences in English. And the sentences in all those patterns share a great many common elements.

The ten patterns you will study in this chapter will give you a solid framework for understanding the expanded sentences in the chapters that follow. So take your time as you study them; notice what they have in common and recognize what makes them different.

Each of the ten patterns is introduced with a traditional diagram of its basic structure, a visual aid to help you picture the pattern and the relationship of its parts. On page 59, all ten patterns and their diagrams are shown together as a kind of summary of the chapter. It is a page you will find yourself referring to frequently as you work with sentences throughout the book. Further details of diagramming are explained in Appendix A, pages 373–376.

SUBJECTS AND PREDICATES

The first step in understanding the skeletal structure of the sentence patterns is to recognize the two parts they all have in common, the **subject** and the **predicate**:

The subject of the sentence, as its name suggests, is generally what the sentence is about—its topic. The predicate is what is said about the subject.

The terms *subject* and *predicate* refer to sentence functions, or roles. But we can also describe those sentence functions in terms of form:

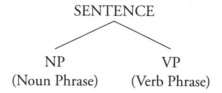

In other words, the subject slot is generally filled by a noun phrase, the predicate slot by a verb phrase. In later chapters we will see sentences in which structures other than noun phrases fill the subject slot; however, the predicate slot is *always* filled by a verb phrase.

Recognizing this subject–predicate relationship, the common element in all of our sentences, is the first step in the study of sentence structure. Equally important for the classification of sentences into sentence patterns is the concept of the verb as the central, pivotal slot in the sentence. In the following list of the ten patterns, the subjects are identical (*The students*) to emphasize that the ten categories are determined by variations in the predicates, variations in the verb headword and in the structures following the verb. So although we call these basic forms *sentence* patterns, a more accurate label might be *predicate* patterns.

We should note that this list of patterns is not the only way to organize the verb classes: Some descriptions include fifteen or more patterns. However, rather than adding more patterns to our list, we account for the sentences that vary somewhat from the general pattern by considering them exceptions.

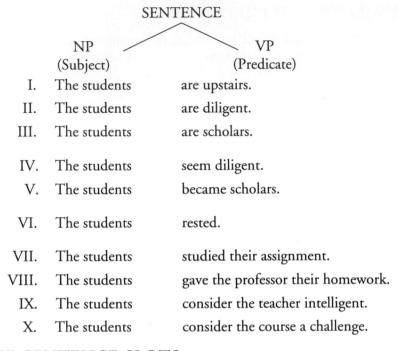

SENTENCE

	NP (Subject)	VP (Predicate)
I.	The students	are upstairs.
II.	The students	are diligent.
III.	The students	are scholars.
IV.	The students	seem diligent.
V.	The students	became scholars.
VI.	The students	rested.
VII.	The students	studied their assignment.
VIII.	The students	gave the professor their homework.
IX.	The students	consider the teacher intelligent.
X.	The students	consider the course a challenge.

THE SENTENCE SLOTS

One way to think about a sentence is to picture it as a series of slots. In the following chart, where all the slots are labeled, you'll see that the first one in every pattern is the subject, and the second—the first slot in the predicate—is the **predicating verb.**

Because the variations among the sentence patterns are in the predicates, we group the ten patterns according to their verb types: the *be* **patterns,** the **linking verb** patterns, the **intransitive verb** pattern, and the **transitive verb** patterns. You'll notice that the number of slots in the predicate varies: Six of the patterns have two, but Pattern VI has only one slot, and three of the transitive patterns, VIII to X, each have three. The label in parentheses names the function, the role, that the slot performs in the sentence.

The subscript numbers you see in some of the patterns in the chart that follows show the relationship between noun phrases: Identical numbers—such as those in Patterns III and V, where both numbers are 1—mean that the two noun phrases have the same referent; different numbers—such as those in Pattern VII, where the numbers are 1 and 2—denote different referents. **Referent** means the thing (or person, event, concept, and so on) that the noun or noun phrase stands for. You'll come to understand noun phrase referents in the discussions of the separate patterns.

This list of patterns, with each slot labeled according to its form and to its role in the sentence, may look formidable at the moment. But don't worry—and don't try to memorize all this detail. It will fall into place as you come to understand the separate patterns.

The be *Patterns*

I	NP	*be*	ADV/TP
	(subject)	(predicating verb)	(adverbial of time or place)
	The students	*are*	*upstairs*
II	NP	*be*	ADJ
	(subj)	(pred vb)	(subject complement)
	The students	*are*	*diligent*
III	NP_1	*be*	NP_1
	(subj)	(pred vb)	(subj comp)
	The students	*are*	*scholars*

The Linking Verb Patterns

IV	NP	linking verb	ADJ
	(subj)	(pred vb)	(subj comp)
	The students	*seem*	*diligent*
V	NP_1	lnk verb	NP_1
	(subj)	(pred vb)	(subj comp)
	The students	*became*	*scholars*

The Intransitive Verb Pattern

VI	NP	intransitive verb
	(subj)	(pred vb)
	The students	*rested*

The Transitive Verb Patterns

VII	NP_1	transitive verb	NP_2	
	(subj)	(pred vb)	(direct object)	
	The students	*studied*	*their assignment*	
VIII	NP_1	trans verb	NP_2	NP_3
	(subj)	(pred vb)	(indirect object)	(dir obj)
	The students	*gave*	*the professor*	*their homework*
IX	NP_1	trans verb	NP_2	ADJ
	(subj)	(pred vb)	(dir obj)	(obj comp)
	The students	*consider*	*the teacher*	*intelligent*
X	NP_1	trans verb	NP_2	NP_2
	(subj)	(pred vb)	(dir obj)	(obj comp)
	The students	*consider*	*the course*	*a challenge*

THE *BE* PATTERNS

The first three formulas state that when a form of *be* serves as the main, or predicating, verb, an adverbial of time or place (Pattern I), or an adjectival (Pattern II), or a noun phrase (Pattern III) will follow it. The one exception to this rule—and, by the way, we can think of the sentence patterns as descriptions of the rules that our internal computer is programmed to follow—is a statement simply affirming existence, such as "I am." Aside from this exception, Patterns I through III describe all the sentences in which a form of *be* is the predicating verb. (Other one-word forms of *be* are *am, is, are, was, were, being,* and *been;* the expanded forms, described in Chapter 4, include *have been, was being, might be,* and *will be.*)

Pattern I: NP *be* ADV/TP

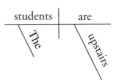

The students are upstairs.

The teacher is here.

The last performance was yesterday.

The ADV in the formula stands for adverbial, a modifier of the verb. The ADV that follows *be* is, with certain exceptions, limited to when and where information, so in the formula for Pattern I we identify the slot as ADV/TP, meaning "adverbial of time or place."[1] In the sample sentences *upstairs* and *here* designate place; *yesterday* designates time. The diagram of Pattern I shows the adverb below the verb, which is where all adverbials are diagrammed.

In the following Pattern I sentences, the adverbials of time and place are prepositional phrases in form:

The next performance is on Monday.
The students are in the library.

The diagram for the adverbial prepositional phrase is a two-part framework with a slanted line for the preposition and a horizontal line for the object:

---

[1] See Question 4 at the end of this chapter for examples of these exceptions.

Notice that the object of the preposition is a noun phrase, so it is diagrammed just as the subject noun phrase is—with the headword on the horizontal line and the determiner below it.

Pattern II: NP *be* ADJ

The students are diligent.

The price of gasoline is ridiculous.

The play was very dull.

students | are \ diligent / The

In this pattern the complement that follows *be* is an adjectival. In the language of traditional grammar, this slot is the **subject complement,** which both completes the verb and modifies or describes the subject.[2] The word *complement* refers to a "completer" of the verb. On the diagram the subject complement follows a diagonal line that slants toward the subject to show their relationship.

In the three sample sentences the subject complements are adjectives in form, as they usually are, but sometimes a prepositional phrase will fill the slot. These are set phrases, or idiomatic expressions, that name an attribute of the subject:

Henry is <u>under the weather</u>.

Kim is <u>in a bad mood</u>.

Although these sentences may look like those you saw in Pattern I, you can figure out that they belong in Pattern II because you can usually think of an adjective, a single descriptive word, that could substitute for the phrase:

Henry is <u>ill</u>.

Kim is <u>cranky</u>.

You can also rule out Pattern I because "under the weather" and "in a bad mood" do not supply information of time or place.

The diagram for the prepositional phrase in a complement position has the same two-part framework that we saw before:

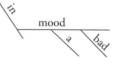

---

[2]More specifically, the traditional label for the subject complement in Pattern II (and IV) is **predicate adjective**; the traditional label for the NP in Pattern III (and V) is **predicate nominative.** We will use the more general term *subject complement* for both adjectives and noun phrases.

We attach that frame to the main line by means of a pedestal. In this way the structure is immediately identifiable in terms of both form (prepositional phrase) and function (subject complement):

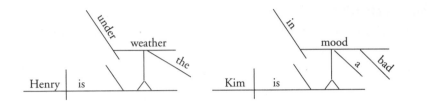

Pattern III: NP$_1$ *be* NP$_1$

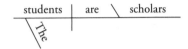

The students are scholars.

Professor Mendez is my math teacher.

The tournament was an exciting event.

The NP, of course, fills the subject slot in all of the patterns; in Pattern III a noun phrase following *be* fills the subject complement slot as well. The numbers that mark the NPs indicate that the two noun phrases have the same referent. For example, when we say "Professor Mendez is my math teacher," the two NPs, "Professor Mendez" and "my math teacher," refer to the same person. The subject complement renames the subject; *be*, the main verb, acts as an "equal sign," connecting the subject with its complement.

Exercise 4

Draw vertical lines to isolate the slots in the following sentences; identify each slot according to its form and function, as the example shows. Then identify the sentence pattern.

Example:

1. Brian's problem is serious. (Pattern _____)
2. The workers are on the roof. (Pattern _____)
3. The excitement of the fans is really contagious. (Pattern _____)
4. Brevity is the soul of wit. [Shakespeare] (Pattern _____)
5. The final exam was at four o'clock. (Pattern _____)

6. The kids are very silly. (Pattern _____)
7. The Bunkers were noisy neighbors. (Pattern _____)
8. Those joggers are out of shape. (Pattern _____)
9. The basketball team is on a roll. (Pattern _____)
10. A foolish consistency is the hobgoblin of little minds. [Ralph Waldo Emerson] (Pattern _____)

Now do a traditional diagram of each sentence, like those you have seen next to the patterns. (See pages 60–62 for notes on the diagrams.)

THE LINKING VERB PATTERNS

The term *linking verb* applies to all verbs other than *be* completed by a subject complement—an adjectival or a noun phrase that describes, characterizes, or identifies the subject. Although many grammar books include *be* among the linking verbs, we have separated it from the linking verb category in order to emphasize its special qualities—variations of both form and function that other verbs do not have. However, it is certainly accurate to think of Patterns II and III as the "linking *be*."

Pattern IV: NP V-lnk ADJ

The students seem diligent.

I grew sleepy.

The soup tastes salty.

students | seem \ diligent (diagram: The)

In these sentences an adjectival fills the subject complement slot; it describes or names an attribute of the subject, just as in Pattern II. In many cases, a form of *be* can be substituted for the Pattern IV linking verb with a minimal change in meaning: *I grew sleepy* and *I was sleepy* are certainly close in meaning. On the other hand, sentences with *be* and *seem* could have significant differences in meaning.

Pattern IV is a common category for verbs of the senses; besides *taste*, the verbs *smell, feel, sound,* and *look* often link an adjective to the subject:

The soup smells good.

The dog looks sick.

Again, as with Pattern II, an adjectival prepositional phrase sometimes fills the subject complement slot:

The piano sounds <u>out of tune</u>.

The fighter seems <u>out of shape</u>.

A complete list of all the verbs that pattern with subject complements would be fairly short. Besides *seem* and the verbs of the senses, others on the list are *appear, become, get, prove, remain,* and *turn.* But just because the list is short, don't try to memorize it. All of these verbs, with the possible exception of *seem,* hold membership in other verb classes too—transitive or intransitive or both. The way to recognize linking verbs is to understand the role of the subject complement, to recognize the form of the structure following the verb and its relationship to the subject.

Pattern V: NP$_1$ V-lnk NP$_1$

The students became scholars.

My uncle remained a bachelor.

In this pattern a noun phrase fills the subject complement slot following the linking verb. As the formula shows, the two noun phrases have the same referent, just as they do in Pattern III. We should note, too, that very few linking verbs will fit in Pattern V; most of them take only adjectivals, not noun phrases, as subject complements. The two verbs used in the examples, *become* and *remain,* are the most common. On rare occasions *seem* also takes a noun phrase rather than its usual adjective:

That seemed a good idea.

He seemed a nice person.

But in the case of these sentences, a prepositional phrase with the preposition *like* is more common:

That seemed like a good idea.

He seemed like a nice person.

The subject complement here is an adjectival prepositional phrase, so these two sentences with *like* are Pattern IV.

Again, we should remember that the most common link between two noun phrases with the same referent is *be* (Pattern III). And often the substitution of *be* for the linking verb in Pattern V makes little difference in meaning:

The students became scholars. (Pattern V)

The students are scholars. (Pattern III)

Exercise 5

Draw vertical lines to identify the sentence slots, as in Exercise 4. Then label them according to their form and function. Identify the sentence pattern. Diagram each sentence.

1. The baby looks healthy.
2. Our new neighbors became our best friends.
3. The piano sounds out of tune.
4. Ryan looks like his older brother.
5. You look a mess!
6. That spaghetti smells wonderful.
7. Your idea seems sensible.
8. Cyberspace remains a complete mystery.
9. The monkeys acted silly.
10. The discussion was over my head.

THE OPTIONAL SLOTS

Before looking at the last five patterns, we will examine an **optional slot**, the adverbial slot, which can appear in every sentence pattern. It is useful to think of the two or three or four slots in the basic patterns as sentence "requirements," the elements needed for sentence completeness. But it's obvious that most sentences include information beyond the basic requirements—words or phrases that answer such questions as *where, when, why, how,* and *how often.* Because sentences are grammatical without them, we consider the elements filling these adverbial slots as "optional." You'll recall that in the case of Pattern I, however, the ADV/TP slot is required. But a Pattern I sentence can include optional adverbials, too, along with its required time and/or place adverbial:

> The fans were in line *(where?)* for tickets to the play-offs *(why?)*.

> The plane was on the runway *(where?)* for an hour *(how long?)*.

All ten sentence patterns can include optional adverbials, which come at the beginning or end of the sentence or even in the middle. And a sentence can have any number of adverbials, providing information about time, place, manner, reason, and the like.

> I stopped <u>at the deli</u> *(where?)* <u>for some bagels</u> *(why?)*. (Pattern VI)
> <u>On Saturday night</u> *(when?)* the library was almost deserted. (Pattern II)
> Mario <u>suddenly</u> *(how?)* hit the brakes. (Pattern VII)

Our most common adverbials are simple adverbs (*suddenly, quickly, here, soon, always, sometimes*) and prepositional phrases (*at the deli, on Saturday night, for some bagels*). In Chapter 6 you will study other forms that add adverbial information.

No matter where they occur in the sentence, all adverbials are diagrammed as modifiers of the verb; the adverbs go on diagonal lines and prepositional phrases on a two-part line below the verb:

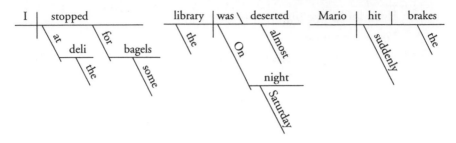

As you saw in Chapter 2, adverbs can be modified with words like *very,* known as **qualifiers**.

She walked very fast.

A qualified adverb is called an **adverb phrase**.

THE INTRANSITIVE VERB PATTERN

Pattern VI: NP V-int

The students rested.

Mary laughed.

The visitors from El Paso arrived.

This formula describes the pattern of intransitive verb sentences. An **intransitive verb** has no complement—no noun phrase or adjectival—in the slot following the verb. Such skeletal sentences, however, are rare in both speech and writing; most Pattern VI sentences contain more than the simple subject and verb. You're likely to find adverbial information added:

The students rested <u>after their long trip</u>.

Mary laughed <u>loudly</u>.

The visitors from El Paso <u>finally</u> arrived <u>at the airport</u>.

You may have noticed that the diagram of this pattern looks a great deal like that of Pattern I, with no complement following the verb on the main line. But there is a difference: The adverbial in Pattern I is not optional; it is required. Another important difference between Patterns I and VI is in the kind of adverbials the sentences include. Pattern I nearly always has a structure that tells where or when. The optional adverbials of Pattern VI, however, are not restricted to time and place information; they can answer other questions, such as *why* or *how* or *how long*. We can say, "John *slept* soundly" or "John *slept* for an hour" (Pattern VI), but we cannot say, "John *was* soundly" or "John *was* for an hour."

Exceptions to the Intransitive Pattern. Unlike the linking verb patterns, with their handful of verbs, the intransitive category has thousands of members. And among them are a few verbs that require an adverbial to make them complete (much like the required adverbial in Pattern I). For example, the following sentences would be ungrammatical without the adverbial:

> My best friend resides in Northridge.
>
> The boys sneaked past the watchman.
>
> She glanced at her watch.

Reside and *sneak* and *glance* are intransitive verbs that require an adverbial of place. We could provide a new sentence pattern for this category of intransitive verbs, but since the number is so small, we will simply consider them exceptions to the usual Pattern VI formula.

<hr>

Exercise   6

In Chapter 2 you learned that prepositional phrases can be adverbial (modifying verbs) or adjectival (modifying nouns). In isolation, however, the two look exactly alike. You need context in order to identify the function.

Here are two sentences with identical prepositional phrases—identical in form only:

> 1. The puppy <u>on the porch</u> is sleeping.
> 2. The puppy is sleeping <u>on the porch</u>.

In sentence (1) the phrase "on the porch" tells "which puppy"; in (2) it tells where the puppy is sleeping. Of course, the position in each case also provides a good clue. In (1) it's part of the subject noun phrase. If we substituted the pronoun *she*, it would take the place of the whole NP—"the puppy on the porch":

> She is sleeping.

In (2) "on the porch" fills the optional adverbial slot.

In this exercise you are to identify each prepositional phrase in the following sentences as either adjectival or adverbial. Underline each one, then indicate the noun or verb it modifies.

Example:

The children <u>in the park</u> are playing <u>on the swing</u>.
ADJ   ADV

1. The rug in the dining room is dirty.
2. On sunny days we lounge on the lawn between classes.
3. The break between classes seems very short on sunny days.
4. At the diner on Water Street, we chatted aimlessly until midnight.
5. Daylilies grow wild in our backyard.
6. In 1638 a young philanthropist of Puritan background became the founder of the oldest university in the United States.
7. The name of that young man was John Harvard.
8. My cousin from Iowa City works for a family with seven children.

For added practice with sentence patterns I through VI, rewrite each of those sentences without their adverbial and adjectival modifiers to clarify the underlying skeletal patterns; then identify the patterns by number.

Intransitive Phrasal Verbs. **Phrasal verbs** are common structures in English. They consist of a verb combined with a preposition-like word, known as a **particle**; together they form an **idiom**. The term *idiom* refers to a combination of words whose meaning cannot be predicted from the meaning of its parts; it is a set expression that acts as a unit. In the following sentence, the meaning of the underlined phrasal verb is not the meaning of *up* added to the meaning of *made:*

We <u>made up</u>.

Rather, *made up* means "reconciled our differences."

In the following sentence, however, *up* is not part of a phrasal verb:

We jumped up.

Here *up* is simply an adverb modifying *jumped*. The meaning of *jumped up* is the meaning of the adverb *up* added to *jumped*. The two diagrams demonstrate the difference:

Another way to demonstrate the properties of verbs such as *made up* and *jumped up* is to test variations of the sentences for parallel results. For example, adverbs can often be shifted to opening position without a change in meaning:

Up we jumped.

But in applying this movability test to the verb *made up*, we produce an ungrammatical sentence:

*Up we made.[3]

Here are some other Pattern VI sentences with phrasal verbs. Note that the first two include adverbial prepositional phrases. You'll discover that all five fail the movability test, just as *made up* did.

We <u>turned in</u> at midnight.

The union finally <u>gave in</u> to the company demands.

Tony will <u>pull through</u>.

My favorite slippers <u>wore out</u>.

The party <u>broke up</u>.

Another test you can apply is that of meaning. In each case the phrasal verb has a special meaning that is different from the combined meaning of its parts: Here *gave in* means "capitulated"; *pull through* means "recover"; *broke up* means "ended." This meaning test is often the clearest indication that the word following the verb is indeed a particle producing a phrasal verb.

Exercise 7

Before diagramming these sentences, decide whether the word following the verb is an *adverb* or a *particle* or a *preposition*. Try both the movability test and the meaning test to help you determine the slot boundaries. Then diagram the sentences.

1. The car turned in a complete circle.
2. The boys turned in at midnight.
3. The baby turned over by himself.
4. The students turned around in their seats.
5. A big crowd turned out for the parade.
6. The fighter passed out in the first round.
7. He came to after thirty seconds.
8. Susan came to the party late.

---

[3]An asterisk (*) marks a sentence that is ungrammatical or questionable.

THE TRANSITIVE VERB PATTERNS

Unlike intransitive verbs, all **transitive verbs** take one or more complements. The last four formulas classify transitive verbs according to the kinds and number of complements they take. All transitive verbs have one complement in common: the **direct object**. Pattern VII, which has only that one complement, can be thought of as the basic transitive verb pattern.

Pattern VII: NP_1 V-tr NP_2

The students studied their
  assignment.

The lead-off batter hit a home run.

Amy's car needs four new tires.

In these sentences the noun phrase following the verb, the **direct object**, has a referent different from that of the subject, as indicated by the different numbers in the formula. Traditionally, we think of the transitive verb as an action word: Its subject is considered the doer and its object the receiver of the action. In many Pattern VII sentences this meaning-based definition applies fairly accurately. In our Pattern VII sample sentences, for instance, we can think of *their assignment* as the receiver of the action *studied* and *a home run* as a receiver of the action *hit*. But sometimes the idea of *receiver of the action* doesn't apply at all:

Our team won the game.

We enjoyed the game.

It hardly seems accurate to say that *game* "receives the action." And in

Red spots covered her neck and face.

the verb indicates a condition rather than an action. So although it is true that many transitive verbs are action words and many direct objects are receivers of the action, this meaning-based way of analyzing the sentence doesn't always work.

We can also think of the direct object as the answer to a *what* or *whom* question:

The students studied (*what?*) geometry.

Devon helped (*whom?*) her little brother.

However, the question will not differentiate transitive verbs from linking verbs; the subject complements in Patterns III and V also tell *what*:

Pat is a doctor. (Pat is *what?*)

Pat became a doctor. (Pat became *what?*)

The one method of distinguishing transitive verbs that works almost every time is the recognition that the two noun phrases have different referents. We don't have to know that *study* and *hit* and *need* are transitive verbs in order to classify the sentences as Pattern VII; we simply recognize that the two noun phrases, the one before the verb and the one following, do not refer to the same thing. Then we know that the second noun phrase is the direct object.

An exception occurs when the direct object is either a **reflexive pronoun** (John cut *himself*) or a **reciprocal pronoun** (John and Mary love *each other*). In sentences with reflexive and reciprocal pronouns, the two NPs, the subject and the direct object, have the same referent, so the numbers 1 and 2 in the formula are inaccurate. In terms of the referents of the NPs, these sentences actually resemble Pattern V, the linking verb pattern. But clearly the purpose and sense of the verbs—*cut* and *love* in the case of these examples—are not like those of the linking verbs. We include these exceptions, where the difference is not in the verbs, in Pattern VII, simply recognizing that when the direct object is a reciprocal or reflexive pronoun the referent numbers are inaccurate.

Note: In Chapter 5 you will see another way of testing whether or not a verb is transitive. Can the sentence be turned into the passive voice? If the answer is yes, the verb is transitive.

Transitive Phrasal Verbs. Many of the idiomatic phrasal verbs belong to the transitive verb category, and like other transitive verbs they take direct objects. Compare the meaning of *came by* in the following sentences:

> He came by his fortune in an unusual way.

> He came by the office in a big hurry.

In the first sentence, *came by* means "acquired"; in the second, *by the office* is a prepositional phrase that modifies the intransitive verb *came*, telling where:

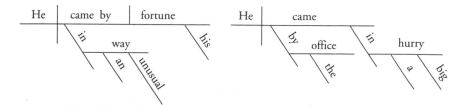

You can also demonstrate the difference between these two sentences by transforming them:

> By which office did he come?

> *By which fortune did he come?

It is clear that *by* functions differently in the two sentences.

The transitive phrasal verbs include both two- and three-word strings:

I don't <u>go in for</u> horse racing.   ⸻

I won't <u>put up with</u> your nonsense.   ⸻

The dog suddenly <u>turned on</u> its trainer.   ⸻

The principal <u>passed out</u> the new regulations.   ⸻

I finally <u>found out</u> the truth.   ⸻

I <u>came across</u> a first edition of Hemingway
    at a garage sale.   ⸻

You can test these as you did the intransitive phrasal verbs, by finding a single word that has the same general meaning. On the blank lines write the one-word substitutes.

Exercise 8

Identify the form and function of the sentence slots; then identify the sentence pattern. (Remember to be on the lookout for phrasal verbs.) Diagram each sentence.

1. The boys prepared a terrific spaghetti dinner.
2. An old jalopy turned into our driveway.
3. The ugly duckling turned into a beautiful swan.
4. The fog comes on little cat feet. [Carl Sandburg]
5. On Sundays the neighbor across the hall walks his dog at 6:00 A.M.
6. Betsy often jogs with her dog.
7. After two months the teachers called off their strike.
8. The whole gang reminisced at our class reunion about the good old days.
9. My best friend from high school arrived on Friday for the weekend.
10. The mass of men lead lives of quiet desperation. [Thoreau]

The Indirect Object Pattern. We are distinguishing among the transitive verb sentences on the basis of verb subclasses—in this case, those verbs with a second object, in addition to the direct object, called the **indirect object**.

PATTERN VIII: NP₁ V-tr NP₂ NP₃

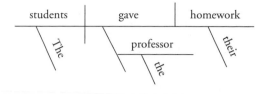

The students gave the professor their homework.

The judges awarded Mary the prize.

The clerk handed me the wrong package.

In this pattern, *two* slots follow the verb, both of them filled by noun phrases. Note that there are three different subscript numbers on the three NPs, indicating that the three noun phrases all have different referents. (When the referents are the same, the numbers are the same, as in Patterns III and V.) The first slot following the verb is the indirect object; the second is the direct object. Even though both Patterns VII and VIII use transitive verbs, they are easily distinguished, since Pattern VII has only one NP following the verb and Pattern VIII has two.

We traditionally define **indirect object** as the recipient of the direct object, the beneficiary of an act. In most cases this definition applies accurately. A Pattern VIII verb—and this is a limited group—usually has a meaning like "give," and the indirect object usually names a person who is the receiver of whatever the subject, NP₁, gives. As with Pattern VII, however, the most accurate way to distinguish this pattern is simply to recognize that all three noun phrases have different referents: In the first sample sentence, *the students, the professor,* and *their homework* all refer to different people or things. Incidentally, in the third Pattern VIII sample sentence, a pronoun rather than a noun phrase fills the indirect object slot.

An important characteristic of the Pattern VIII sentence is the option we have of shifting the indirect object to a position following the direct object, where it will be the object of a preposition:

The students gave their homework <u>to the professor</u>.

The judges awarded the prize <u>to Mary</u>.

The clerk handed the wrong package <u>to me</u>.

With some Pattern VIII verbs the preposition will be *for* rather than *to*:

Jim's father bought him a new car.

Jim's father bought a new car <u>for him</u>.

When the direct object is a pronoun rather than a noun phrase, the shift is required; without the prepositional phrase, the sentence would be ungrammatical:

> The students gave it to the professor.
>
> *The students gave the professor it.
>
> Jim's father bought it for him.
>
> *Jim's father bought him it.

You'll notice that the shift will not alter the diagram—except for the added word. The indirect object is diagrammed as if it were the object in an adverbial prepositional phrase—even when there is no preposition:

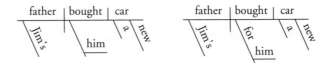

Shifting of the indirect object from the slot following the verb to that of object of the preposition does not mean that the sentence pattern changes: It is still Pattern VIII. Remember that the sentence patterns represent verb categories. Pattern VIII covers the "give" group of verbs, those that include both a direct object and a "recipient" of that object. In other words, there are two possible slots for that recipient, the indirect object, in the Pattern VIII sentence.

In most Pattern VIII sentences, all three NPs have different referents, represented by the numbers 1, 2, and 3. But when the indirect object is a reflexive or reciprocal pronoun (*myself, themselves, each other*, etc.), its referent is identical to that of the subject:

> Jill gave *herself* a haircut.
>
> We gave *each other* identical Hanukkah gifts.

Exercise 9

Identify the form and function of the sentence slots. Identify the sentence patterns and diagram the sentences.

Note: Remember that Pattern VIII is the first sentence pattern you have studied in which *two* required slots follow the verb. In most cases they can be thought of as *someone* (the indirect object) and *something* (the direct object). Remember, too, that all of the sentence patterns can include optional slots—i.e., adverbial information (where, when, how, why)—in addition to their required slots.

1. Jessica made her new boyfriend some cookies.
2. I made an A on my research paper.
3. For lunch Manny made himself a humongous sandwich.
4. The kids made up a story about Pokemon monsters.
5. The teacher wrote a lot of comments in the margins.
6. My advisor wrote a letter of recommendation for me.
7. I wrote down the assignment very carefully.
8. My roommate always writes in her diary after dinner.
9. I saw myself in the mirror.
10. Shirl gave herself a pat on the back.

The Object Complement Patterns. The final category of verbs, those that take an **object complement** following the direct object, is divided into two groups, depending on the form of the object complement: either an adjective or a noun phrase. This is a fairly small class, with relatively few verbs, most of which appear equally often in Pattern VII, where they take the direct object only.

PATTERN IX: NP₁ V-tr NP₂ ADJ

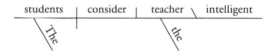

The students consider the teacher intelligent.

The teacher made the test easy.

The boys painted their hockey sticks blue.

In this pattern the object complement is an adjective that modifies or describes the direct object. The relationship between the direct object and the object complement is the same as the relationship between the subject and the subject complement in Patterns II and IV. In Patterns II and IV the subject complement describes the subject; in Pattern IX the object complement describes the direct object. We could say, in fact,

The teacher is intelligent.

The test is easy.

The hockey sticks are blue.

The function of the object complement is twofold: (1) It completes the meaning of the verb; and (2) it describes the direct object.

When we remove the object complement from a Pattern IX sentence, we are sometimes left with a grammatical and meaningful sentence: "The boys painted their hockey sticks." (This is now Pattern VII.) However, most Pattern IX sentences require the object complement; the meaning of the first two examples under the Pattern IX formula would change without it:

The students consider the teacher.

The teacher made the test.

Other verbs commonly found in this pattern are *prefer, like,* and *find.* Some Pattern IX verbs, such as *consider* and *make,* also commonly appear in Pattern X.

PATTERN X: NP$_1$ V-tr NP$_2$ NP$_2$

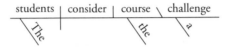

The students consider the course a challenge.

The students elected Emma chairperson.

Barrie named his pug Jill.

Just as both adjectives and noun phrases can be subject complements, both adjectives and noun phrases also serve as object complements. In Pattern X the object complement is a noun phrase, one with the same referent as the direct object, as indicated by the numbers in the formula. Its twofold purpose is much the same as that of the adjectival object complement in Pattern IX: (1) It completes the meaning of the verb; and (2) it renames the direct object. And, again, we can compare the relationship of the two noun phrases to that of the subject and subject complement in Pattern III:

The course is a challenge.

Emma is the chairperson.

In fact, the possibility of actually inserting the words *to be* between the direct object and the following slot can serve as a test for Patterns IX and X. That is, if *to be* is possible, then what follows is an object complement. Which of the following sentences will pass the "to be" test?

Taro finds his job easy.

Taro found his job easily.

Pam found her job the hard way.

Pam finds her job a challenge.

If you have decided that the first and last sentences in the list could include *to be*, you have identified object complements. The other two, you'll discover, end with adverbials that tell "how" about the verb.

Sometimes the object complement is signaled by *as*, which we call an **expletive**:

> We elected Tom *as* our secretary.
>
> We refer to him *as* "Mr. Secretary."
>
> I know him *as* a good friend.
>
> The witness identified the defendant *as* the burglar.

In some cases, the *as* is optional; in other cases, it is required. With the verbs *refer to* and *know*, for example, we cannot add the object complement without *as*:

> *We refer to him "Mr. Secretary."
>
> *I know her a good friend.

The expletive is diagrammed just before the object complement but above the line:

This use of *as* is discussed further on pages 286–287.

COMPOUND STRUCTURES

Every slot in the sentence patterns can be expanded in many ways, as you'll learn in the chapters to come. We'll introduce one common expansion here—that of **coordination**, turning a single structure into a compound structure. Coordination is accomplished with another of the structure classes, the **conjunctions**, the most common of which are the **coordinating conjunctions** *and*, *or*, and *but*. The **correlative conjunctions** are two-part connectors: *both–and*, *not only–but also*, *either–or*, and *neither–nor*.

Every slot in the sentence patterns can be filled by a compound structure:

> Cats *and* dogs fight. (compound subject)
>
> They *either* drove *or* took the bus. (compound predicate)
>
> The teacher was tough *but* fair. (compound subject complement)
>
> We drove over the river *and* through the woods. (compound adverbial prepositional phrase)
>
> I finished *both* my biology project *and* my history paper. (compound direct object)

To diagram compound structures, we simply double the line and connect the two parts with a dotted line. The conjunction goes on the dotted line.

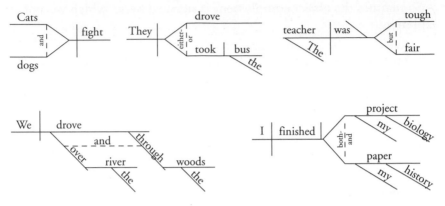

In Chapter 10 we will take up the coordination of full sentences.

Exercise 10

First identify the sentence slots according to their form and function to help you identify sentence patterns. Then diagram the sentences. (Note: The list includes sentences representing all four verb classes: *be*, linking, intransitive, and transitive.)

1. The kids on our block and their dogs drive my mother crazy.
2. She calls them a menace to the neighborhood.
3. On Friday the weather suddenly turned cold and blustery.
4. Yesterday Luis bought himself an expensive leather coat at Nordstrom.
5. England's soccer fans have a reputation for wild behavior.
6. My boss at the pizza parlor promised me a raise.
7. Hector's party broke up at midnight.
8. Eventually the citizens grew lazy and apathetic.
9. Joe cut himself a huge piece of cake.
10. Alaska became the forty-ninth state in 1959.
11. According to the latest census, Wyoming is our least populous state.
12. Some people consider Minnesota's winters excessively long.
13. Our team plays Indiana in the Holiday Invitational Tournament on Saturday night.

14. I ordered you a large Coke and a cheeseburger with onions.

15. Emily selected peach and lavender as the color scheme for her wedding.

EXCEPTIONS TO THE TEN SENTENCE PATTERNS

The ten sentence patterns described here represent the skeletal structure of most English sentences—at least 95 percent, if not more. However, some sentences can be thought of as exceptions to a particular pattern. For example, certain intransitive verbs, such as *reside, sneak,* and *glance,* would be ungrammatical without an adverbial—as we saw on page 43. Certain transitive verbs also differ from the majority because they require adverbials to be complete:

> We *placed* an ad in the paper.

> Joe *put* the groceries away.

To be accurate, the formulas for these sentences would have to include ADV as a requirement, not just an optional slot. However, because the number of these exceptions is small, we will simply include them as variations of Pattern VI or Pattern VII.

Another group of verbs, sometimes called "midverbs," include characteristics of both transitive and intransitive verbs: They require a complement, as transitive verbs do, but the complement differs from mainstream direct objects. For example, rather than telling "what" or "whom," the complements following the verbs *weigh* and *cost* provide information of amount, or measure; they have almost an adverbial sense:

> The roast weighs five pounds.

> The roast cost twenty dollars.

Even though *weigh* and *cost* are different from the exceptional intransitive and transitive verbs cited earlier (which take straightforward adverbials of place), we will consider these uses of *weigh* and *cost* as Pattern VI, rather than add a new sentence pattern, recognizing that for them too the "optional slot" is not optional.

SENTENCE TYPES

The ten sentence pattern formulas in this chapter describe the basic structure of statements, or **declarative** sentences. The purpose of such sentences is to state, or declare, a fact or an opinion. But we don't always make straightforward statements. Sometimes we alter the formula to ask questions (**interrogative sentences**), give commands (**imperative sentences**), and express strong feelings (**exclamatory sentences**):

Declarative:	He talks on his cell phone all day long.
Interrogative:	Is he talking on his cell phone now?
	Why does he talk on his cell phone so much?
Imperative:	Turn that cell phone off.
Exclamatory:	What a lot of time he spends on his cell phone!

INTERROGATIVE SENTENCES (QUESTIONS)

The two most common interrogative patterns in English are the **yes/no question** and the *wh*-**question**, or interrogative-word question. Both kinds of questions alter the basic declarative word order by putting the verb, or part of the verb, in front of the subject:

They are going to the movies. (declarative)

Are they going to the movies? (yes/no question)

Where are they going? (*wh*-question)

In these examples, the first part of the verb *are going* is placed ahead of the subject; it is called an **auxiliary**. You'll learn a lot more about auxiliaries in the next chapter.

As their label suggests, yes/no questions permit "yes" or "no" as appropriate answers, although other responses are possible:

Q: May I go with you?   A. We'll see.

Wh-questions, also called *information questions*, use interrogative words, such as *why, where, when, who, what,* or *how*, to elicit specific details. In the question "Where are they going?" the interrogative word comes first and fills the optional adverbial slot in a Pattern VI sentence:

Where are they going?

They are going <u>where</u>.

The interrogative can also fill an NP slot:

What have you been reading?

You have been reading <u>what</u>. (Pattern VII)

Some interrogatives act as determiners:

Whose car are you taking?

You are taking <u>whose</u> car.

As the preceding examples show, the slots of the basic declarative pattern will be out of order because the interrogative word always comes first, no matter what grammatical function it has. However, when the information being elicited is a *who* or *what* that fills the subject slot, then the usual word order of subject-verb-object is maintained and the auxiliary is not shifted:

> <u>Who</u> broke the window?
>
> <u>What</u> is making that noise?

IMPERATIVE SENTENCES (COMMANDS)

The sentences described so far in this chapter have been two-part structures consisting of a subject and a predicate. However, in the case of **imperative sentences**, or **commands**, the subject is unstated, although clearly understood:

Subject	*Predicate*
(you)	Sit down.
(you)	Take your time.
(you)	Tell us a story.

Commands are fairly common in casual speech. They are not as common in writing, although you've seen them several times in this chapter in the directions for the exercises:

> Draw vertical lines to identify the sentence slots.
>
> Diagram each sentence.

EXCLAMATORY SENTENCES

We usually think of the **exclamatory sentence**, or exclamation, as any sentence spoken with heightened emotion, written with an exclamation point:

> I love your new house!
>
> Wipe that grin off your face!
>
> Are you kidding me!

But in terms of form, the first sentence immediately preceding is *declarative*, a straightforward statement; the second sentence is an *imperative;* and the third one looks like a yes/no question. By contrast, a formal exclamatory sentence involves a shift in word order that focuses special attention on a complement:

> What a lovely house you have!
>
> How proud you must be!
>
> What a piece of work is man! [Shakespeare]

The *what* or *how* that introduces the emphasized element is added to the underlying declarative sentence pattern:

> You have a lovely house. (Pattern VII)
>
> You must be proud. (Pattern II)
>
> Man is a piece of work. (Pattern III)

PUNCTUATION AND THE SENTENCE PATTERNS

There is an easy punctuation lesson to be learned from the sentence patterns with their two or three or four slots:

DO NOT PUT SINGLE COMMAS BETWEEN THE REQUIRED SLOTS.

That is, never separate

- the subject from the verb.
- the verb from the direct object.
- the direct object from the object complement.
- the indirect object from the direct object.
- the verb from the subject complement.

For example, in this sentence there is no place for commas:

> All of the discussion groups and counseling sessions I took part in during Orientation Week were extremely helpful for the incoming freshmen.

Even though the noun phrases that fill the slots may be long, the slots are never separated by commas. A pause for breath does not signal a comma. Sometimes punctuation is called for *within* a noun phrase slot, but even then the rule applies: no single commas between the required slots.

The one exception to this rule occurs when the direct object is a direct quotation following a verb like *say*. Here the punctuation convention calls for a comma before the quoted words:

> He said, "I love you."

DIAGRAMMING THE SENTENCE PATTERNS

The traditional sentence diagram is a visual aid to help you learn the patterns, to understand their common features, and to distinguish their differences. On page 59, where all ten diagrams are shown together, you can see the relationships among them. For example, the two linking verb patterns closely resemble the two *be* patterns, II and III, above them.

Likewise, the intransitive verb pattern, VI, placed at the left of the page, looks exactly like the main line of Pattern I. Finally, the slanted line that separates the subject complement from the verb in the *be* and linking verb patterns, II through V, depicts a relationship similar to that of the object complement and object in Patterns IX and X, which are also separated by a slanted line. All the NP and ADJ slots on the diagrams are labeled according to their functions: subject (S), subject complement (SC), direct object (DO), indirect object (IO), and object complement (OC).

The be *Patterns*

I. NP *be* ADV/TP

S

II. NP *be* ADJ

S \ SC

III. NP$_1$ *be* NP$_1$

S \ SC

The Linking Verb Patterns

IV. NP V-lnk ADJ

S \ SC

V. NP$_1$ V-lnk NP$_1$

S \ SC

The Intransitive Verb Pattern

VI. NP V-int

S

The Transitive Verb Patterns

VII. NP$_1$ V-tr NP$_2$

S | DO

VIII. NP$_1$ V-tr NP$_2$ NP$_3$

S | DO

IO

IX. NP$_1$ V-tr NP$_2$ ADJ

S | DO \ OC

X. NP$_1$ V-tr NP$_2$ NP$_2$

S | DO \ OC

NOTES ON THE DIAGRAMS

The Main Line. The positions on the main horizontal line of a diagram represent the slots in the sentence pattern formulas. Only two required slots are not included on the main line: the adverbial (see Pattern I) and the indirect object (see Pattern VIII). The vertical line that bisects the main line separates the subject and the predicate, showing the binary nature of the sentence. The other vertical and diagonal lines stop at the horizontal line:

The Noun Phrase. The noun phrases we have used so far are fairly simple; in Chapter 7 we identify a wide variety of structures that can modify and expand the noun. But now we will simply recognize the feature that all noun phrases have in common—the noun head, or headword. This is the single word that fills the various NP slots of the diagrams; it always occupies a horizontal line. The modifiers slant down from the noun headword:

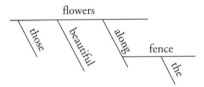

Qualifiers of adjectives are placed on diagonal lines attached to and parallel with the adjective:

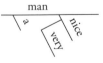

The Verb Phrase.

1. The verb and its auxiliaries go on the main line. In the case of negative verbs, the *not* is usually placed on a diagonal line below the verb. If if is contracted, it can remain attached to the verb:

2. The subject complement follows a diagonal line. The line slants toward the subject to show their relationship:

3. The direct object always follows a vertical line:

Note that only Patterns VII through X have this vertical line following the verb: the only patterns with a direct object.

4. The object complement is set off from the direct object by a line that slants toward the object:

$$I \mid consider \mid zinnias \setminus beautiful$$

5. The indirect object is placed below the verb. We can understand the logic of this treatment of the indirect object when we realize that it can be expressed by a prepositional phrase without changing the meaning or the pattern of the sentence. Both of these sentences are Pattern VIII:

> The students gave <u>the teacher</u> an apple.
> The students gave an apple <u>to the teacher</u>.

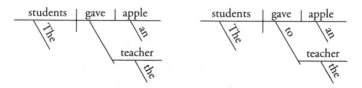

6. Adverbs are placed on slanted lines below the verb; they are modifiers of the verb:

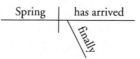

7. Like the qualifiers of adjectives, qualifiers of adverbs are placed on diagonal lines attached to the adverb:

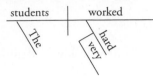

The Prepositional Phrase. The preposition is placed on a diagonal line, its object on a horizontal line attached to it. The prepositional phrase slants down from the noun or verb it modifies. When the prepositional phrase fills the subject complement slot, it is attached to the main line by means of a pedestal:

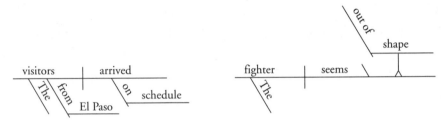

Compound Structures. The two (or more) parts of a compound structure are connected by a dotted line, which holds the conjunction. If a modifier applies to both (or all) parts of the compound structure, it is attached to a line common to them:

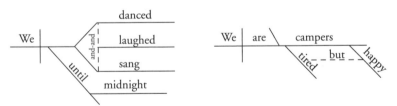

Punctuation. There are no punctuation marks of any kind in the diagram, other than apostrophes.

For further details of diagramming, see the Appendix, pages 373–376.

CHAPTER 3

Key Terms

In this chapter you've been introduced to the basic vocabulary of sentence grammar. Even though this list of key terms may look formidable, some of the terms are already familiar, and those that are new will become more familiar as you continue the study of sentences. You'll discover too that the patterns and their diagrams, as shown on page 59, provide a framework for helping you organize many of these concepts.

Article	Object complement
Auxiliary	Optional slot
Be patterns	Particle
Command	Phrasal verb
Complement	Predicate
Compound structure	Predicating verb
Coordinating conjunction	Question
Correlative conjunction	Reciprocal pronoun
Declarative sentence	Referent
Direct object	Reflexive pronoun
Exclamatory sentence	Sentence pattern
Imperative sentence	Subject
Indirect object	Subject complement
Interrogative sentence	Transitive verb
Intransitive verb	Verb phrase
Linking verb	*Wh*-question
Noun phrase	Yes/no question

Sentences
for PRACTICE

Identify the form and function of the sentence slots; identify the sentence pattern; and diagram each sentence.

1. My boss at the pizza parlor gave everyone a raise.
2. Uncle Fred recently moved to Arizona for his health.
3. Typhoons and hurricanes are identical storms.
4. They simply occur in different parts of the world.
5. Hank's strange behavior was out of character.
6. Grow old along with me. [Robert Browning]
   [Note: *Along with* can be diagrammed as a phrasal preposition.]

7. Some people find modern art very depressing.

8. According to the afternoon paper, the police looked into the sources of the reporter's information.

9. Our art class was at the museum and the botanical gardens on Tuesday afternoon.

10. Is our plan workable?

11. In 2005 the Senate confirmed John Roberts as the seventeenth chief justice of the United States.

12. On Saturday night we left the waitress a generous tip for her splendid service.

13. At age 23, the founder and CEO of Facebook became the youngest self-made billionaire in history.

14. Yesterday my landlord was in a state of panic.

15. According to the latest UN statistics, Norway is now the world's largest exporter of seafood.

QUESTIONS for DISCUSSION

1. Here are some pairs of sentences that look alike. Think about their sentence patterns; label the form and function of their slots and discuss the problems you encounter; diagram the sentences to demonstrate their differences.

    The teacher made the test hard.

    The batter hit the ball hard.

    My husband made me a chocolate cake.

    My husband made me a happy woman.

    We set off through the woods at dawn.

    We set off the firecrackers at dawn.

2. The following sentences are either Pattern I or Pattern II; in other words, the prepositional phrases following *be* are either adverbial or adjectival. What test can you use to distinguish between them?

    The mechanic is under the car.

    The mechanic is under the weather.

The teacher is in a bad mood.

The teacher is in the cafeteria.

3. Very few verbs are restricted to a single category. Verbs like *taste* and *feel* commonly act as linking verbs, but they can fit into other classes as well. Identify the patterns of the following sentences:

    The cook tasted the soup.

    The soup tasted good.

    I felt the kitten's fur.

    The fur feels soft.

    The farmers in Iowa grow a lot of wheat.

    The wheat grows fast in July.

    We grew weary in the hot sun.

    She appeared tired.

    Black clouds appeared suddenly on the horizon.

4. Some sentences in English are not represented by one of the ten patterns described in this chapter. Among those that don't fit very well are certain sentences with *be* as the main verb:

    The book is about black holes.

    The potato salad is for the picnic.

    I am from San Francisco.

    I am in favor of the amendment.

    The misunderstanding was over a scheduling conflict.

    Pat and Jen are among the most popular students in our class.

    The prepositional phrases in these sentences are different from those we saw in Patterns I and II. How would you characterize the difference? A paraphrase of the sentence might help you to determine a possible pattern. And in the following *be* sentences, the noun phrase in subject complement position is different from those we saw in Pattern III. Do these sentences belong in Pattern III? If not, where do they belong?

    My shoes are the wrong color.

    This new wallpaper is an odd pattern.

In what way does the following sentence change our understanding of the *be* patterns?

The time is now.

5. People commonly say "I feel badly" when discussing their physical or mental condition. Using your understanding of sentence patterns, explain why this is sometimes considered an ungrammatical sentence. Assuming that "I feel badly" is indeed questionable, how do you explain the acceptance of "I feel strongly about that"?

6. What is unusual about the following sentence? Think about the sentence pattern:

The waitress served me my coffee black.

7. We have seen sentences in which prepositional phrases function as subject complements. Can they be object complements as well?

8. A sentence is **ambiguous** when it has more than one possible meaning. You can illustrate the two meanings of the following sentences by diagramming each in two different ways. Think about sentence patterns and the referents of the noun phrases.

Herbert found his new bride a good cook.

Rosa called her mother.

CLASSROOM APPLICATIONS

Some of the following activities could be organized as either oral or written activities, perhaps as timed group competitions:

1. Write four sentences about summer (winter, fall, spring) in which each sentence uses a different verb category: *be*, linking, intransitive, and transitive.

2. Write ten sentences about your favorite sport or hobby, using all ten patterns.

3. Drawing on your own internal dictionary, write down as many two-word (verb + particle) idioms as you can, using the particles *up, down, in, out, on, off,* and *over*. Here are some verbs to get you started, but don't limit yourself to these: *break, take, look, run*. (Note: The resulting idioms will include both nouns and verbs—e.g., [*the*] *break-in,* [*to*] *break up*.)

4. Collect newspaper or magazine headlines that represent all ten sentence patterns. Note that in the case of the *be* patterns, the verb itself might be missing, simply understood.

CHAPTER
4

Expanding the Main Verb

CHAPTER PREVIEW

In Chapter 2 we applied the term *form classes* to nouns, verbs, adjectives, and adverbs, the content words of the language, all of which have endings, or forms, that help us identify them. This chapter examines verbs, the most systematic of the four form classes. In this examination of verbs and their auxiliaries, you will be introduced to the discovery method of the transformational linguists, whose goal is to understand how our internal rules generate, or produce, grammatical sentences—or, in this case, grammatical verb strings.

We will analyze the underlying rules that enable us to come up with the wide variety of auxiliary + verb combinations that we use every day. This analysis of our verb expertise, in fact, probably illustrates better than any other part of the grammar what we mean by the word *system.*

In this chapter you will see two highlighted sections called "ELL Issues," which add information that English language learners (nonnative speakers) will find helpful.

THE FIVE VERB FORMS

Before analyzing the system for adding auxiliaries, we will review the five forms that all of our verbs have so that we can conveniently discuss them, using labels that reflect our emphasis on form rather than meaning. Here again is the **regular** verb *laugh*, which we looked at in Chapter 2, along with the **irregular** verb *eat*:

	Regular	*Irregular*
base form (present tense)	laugh	eat
-*s* form (present, 3rd person, singular)	laughs	eats
-*ed* form (past tense)	laughed	ate
-*ing* form (present participle)	laughing	eating
-*en* form (past participle)	laughed	eaten

Most of our verbs—all except 150 or so—are regular, as are all the new verbs that we acquire. For example, here are two recent acquisitions:

I <u>faxed</u> a letter to you yesterday.

I have <u>e-mailed</u> the invitations to our reunion.

As the verb *laugh* and these two new ones illustrate, regular verbs are those in which the past tense and the past participle are formed by adding the **suffix** -*ed* (or, in a few cases, -*t*) to the base form. Among the irregular verbs, there are many patterns of irregularity, but the deviations from regular verbs show up only in these two forms, the past and the past participle. All verbs, with minor exceptions, have regular -*s* and -*ing* forms. (The exceptions are detailed in "ELL Issues" on page 70.)

In our discussion of verbs, we will use the label -*ed* to denote the past tense form and -*en* to denote the past participle form. The past of regular verbs provides the -*ed* label; the past participle of irregular verbs like *eat* (as well as our most common verb, *be*, and about fifteen others, including *drive, give, break,* and *speak*) provides the label for the past participle, which we call the -*en* form. This means that the -*en* form of *laugh* is *laughed;* the -*ed* form of *eat* is *ate.*

Anyone familiar with a foreign language will appreciate the simplicity of our small set of only five verb forms. Instead of adding auxiliaries to express differences as we do in English, a speaker of French or Spanish must add a different suffix to the verb. French verbs, for instance, have more than seventy different forms to express variations in person, number, tense, and mood.

A speaker of English uses only two different forms (*eat, eats*) to express the present tense in first, second, and third **person**, both singular and plural; the speaker of French uses five:

	Singular	*Plural*
1st person	I eat (*je mange*)	we eat (*nous mangeons*)
2nd person	you eat (*tu manges*)	you eat (*vous mangez*)
3rd person	he eats (*il mange*)	they eat (*ils mangent*)

The speaker of English uses only one form (*ate*) to express the simple past tense in all three persons, both singular and plural. Again, the French speaker uses five, all different from the first set. In fact, for the various tenses and moods, the speaker of French uses fourteen such sets, or conjugations, all with different verb endings.

The Irregular *Be*. The only English verb with more than five forms is *be*, the most irregular of our irregular verbs. It is also the only verb with a separate form for the **infinitive**, or base (*be*); it is the only one with three forms for present tense (*am, is, are*) and two for past tense (*was, were*); and of course it has an *-en* form (*been*) and an *-ing* (*being*)—eight forms in all. In addition to its status as a main verb, *be* also serves as an auxiliary in our verb-expansion rule and as the auxiliary that turns the active voice to passive, as you will learn in Chapter 5.

Exercise 11

Fill the blanks with the four additional forms of the verbs listed on the left. If you have a problem figuring out the *-ed* form, simply use it in a sentence with *yesterday:* "Yesterday I _____." If you have trouble figuring out the *-en* form, use it in a sentence with *have:* "I have _____."

BASE	-s FORM	-ed FORM	-ing FORM	-en FORM
1. have				
2. do				
3. say				
4. make				
5. go				
6. take				
7. come				
8. see				
9. get				
10. move				
11. prove				
12. put				
13. think				
14. beat				
15. meet				

The first nine verbs in this exercise, along with *be*, make up a list of the ten most frequently used verbs in English.

    Q. What do these ten have in common?

    A. They are all irregular!

ELL Issues   **The Systematic Verb Forms**

Only two verbs have an irregular *-s* form: *be* (*is*) and *have* (*has*). In two others, the vowel sound changes for the *-s* form: *do* (*does*), *say* (*says*). And one verb, *beware*, has only one form—the infinitive; it's the only verb without an *-s* form or an *-ing* form. So with only these minor deviations, we can certainly say that from the standpoint of form, notably the *-s* and the *-ing* forms, English verbs are highly systematic. It would be hard to find a rule in all of our grammar with fewer exceptions.

AUXILIARY-VERB COMBINATIONS

You learned in Chapter 3 that the predicating verb is the central, or pivotal, slot in the sentence. It is the verb that determines the slots that follow. The predicating verbs we have used in sentence examples so far have been one-word forms, the simple present or past tense, such as *are, were, studied, became, consider.* In our everyday speech and writing, of course, we are just as likely to use expanded forms that include one or more **auxiliaries**, also called **helping verbs**:

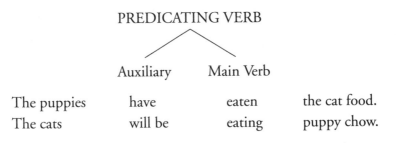

PREDICATING VERB

             Auxiliary   Main Verb

| The puppies | have | eaten | the cat food. |
| The cats | will be | eating | puppy chow. |

As this branching diagram shows, we are using the term *predicating verb* as a label for the entire string that fills the verb slot in the sentence patterns, including auxiliaries and the main verb.

    To discover how our auxiliary system works, we will examine a dozen sentences, all of which have a form of *eat* as the main verb, beginning with the two we have just seen:

1.   The puppies <u>have eaten</u> the cat food.
2.   The cats <u>will be eating</u> puppy chow.

3. I <u>eat</u> an apple every day.
4. I <u>ate</u> one this morning.
5. My sister <u>eats</u> a banana every day.
6. I <u>should eat</u> bananas for their potassium.
7. I <u>am eating</u> healthy these days.
8. We <u>were eating</u> popcorn throughout the movie.
9. We <u>may eat</u> out on Saturday night.
10. I <u>had eaten</u> all the chips by the time the guests arrived.
11. I <u>could have eaten</u> even more.
12. We <u>have been eating</u> junk food all evening.

What is the system underlying these one- and two- and three-word verb strings? How many more variations are there? If we were going to write a computer program to generate all the possible variations, what rules and restrictions would have to be included?

To answer these questions, we will make some observations about the verb strings in our twelve sentences:

1. The base form, *eat*, is used both by itself [3] and with *should* [6] and *may* [9].
2. The *-ed* and *-s* forms of *eat* [4 and 5] are used only by themselves, never with an auxiliary word.
3. An *-en* form, *eaten* or *been*, is used after a form of *have: have* [1, 11, and 12] and *had* [10].
4. The *-ing* form, *eating*, is used after a form of *be: be* [2], *am* [7], *were* [8], and *been* [12].
5. A form of *eat*, the main verb (MV), is always the last word in the string.

We will represent these last three observations by means of a formula:

$$\textbf{(have + -en) (be + -ing) MV}$$

The parentheses in the formula mean "optional." Both *have* and *be* are optional auxiliaries: A grammatical verb string does not require either or both of them. As the formula indicates, however, when we do choose *have* as an auxiliary, we are also choosing *-en*; that is, the *-en* suffix will attach itself to the following word. And when we choose *be*, the *-ing* suffix will attach itself to the following word. In the formula the main verb is shown without parentheses because it is not optional; it is always a component of the predicating verb.

We can derive two further observations from the twelve sentences:

6. Besides *have* and *be*, the sentences illustrate another kind of auxiliary—*will* [2], *should* [6], *may* [9], and *could* [11], called **modal auxiliaries (M)**.
7. When a modal is selected, it is always first in line.

Now we can add another element, (M), to the formula:

(M) (have + -en) (be + -ing) MV

The formula reads as follows:

- In generating a verb string, we can use a modal auxiliary if we choose; when we do, it comes first.
- We can also choose the auxiliary *have;* when we do, an *-en* form follows it.
- We can also choose the auxiliary *be;* when we do, an *-ing* form follows.
- When we use more than one auxiliary, they appear in the order given: modal, *have, be.*
- The last word in the string is the main verb.

To demonstrate how the formula works, let's look at the verbs in three of our twelve *eat* sentences:

Sentence 1: **The puppies <u>have eaten</u> the cat food.**

Here we passed up (M) and chose *have + -en* as the auxiliary. The *-en* will be attached to the following word:

$$\text{have} + \text{-en} + \text{eat} \; = \; \textit{have eaten}$$

Sentence 2: **The cats <u>will be eating</u> puppy chow.**

Here we chose (M), the modal auxiliary *will;* we skipped (*have + -en*) and chose *be + -ing:*

$$\text{will} + \text{be} + \text{-ing} + \text{eat} \; = \; \textit{will be eating}$$

Sentence 12: **We <u>have been eating</u> junk food all evening**.

In this sentence we skipped (M) and chose both *have + -en* and *be + -ing*:

have + -en + be + -ing + eat   =   *have been eating*

So far we have a simple but powerful formula, capable of generating a great many variations of the verb. But something is missing. How did we generate *were eating* in sentence 8 and *had eaten* in sentence 10? What is different about them? The difference is **tense**, which refers to time: *had* and *were* are past tense, the *-ed* forms of *have* and *be*. This means we have to add one more component to the formula: **T**, for tense. Among the five forms of the verb, you will recall, the present and past forms are the only tenses, so in the formula, **T** will represent either present or past tense.

Here, then, is the complete formula for what is known as the **verb-expansion rule**:

T (M) (have + -en) (be + -ing) MV

Notice in the following strings how the tense, either present or past, applies to the first word in the string. Note in the third example that the first word is sometimes the main verb.

I **should have taken** the bus to class this morning.

past + shall + have + -en+ take

The autumn leaves **are making** the sidewalk slippery.

past + be + ing + make

My roommate **worked** on her project until 4:00 A.M.

past + work

You might find the branching diagram helpful for visualizing the rule:

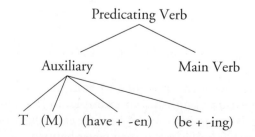

Investigating Language 4.1

The branching diagram illustrates the predicating verb as a two-part structure: an auxiliary and a main verb. Those two parts are obvious in a sentence such as

We *had eaten* by the time you arrived.

or

I *was eating* when you arrived.

Sometimes the two parts of the predicating verbs are not as obvious:

He *eats* too fast.

Beth already *ate.*

Look again at the formula, and remember that parentheses mean "optional." The components of the verb that are shown without parentheses are required.

In sentences with *eats* and *ate*, then, what does the auxiliary consist of?

Look again at the second observation we made on page 71 about our list of twelve sentences: "The *-ed* and *-s* forms of *eat* are used only by themselves, never with an auxiliary word." It's clear then that the auxiliary component of the verbs in sentences with *ate* or *eats* is simply T.

THE MODAL AUXILIARIES

We have six major modals in English, four of which have different forms for present and past:

Present	*Past*
will	would
shall	should
can	could
may	might

Two modals have no past form:

must

ought to

Although we call these forms present and past, that meaning is not really accurate in present-day English. For example, in "I may eat" (present), the act of eating is not going on; in "I might eat" (past) the act of eating is not over; in fact, in both cases it may never happen.

Only in a few instances do the modals indicate actual time. In the company of a time adverbial, *can* and *could* will designate present or past:

> *This morning* the groundhog <u>can</u> see his shadow.
>
> *Yesterday* the groundhog <u>could</u> see his shadow.

However, because we want to emphasize the concept of the predicating verb as a "tensed verb," we will recognize that the position following T carries the tense marker, no matter what occupies that position, whether a modal, the auxiliary *have*, the auxiliary *be*, or the main verb.

The modals differ from the auxiliaries *have* and *be*, both of which can fill the role of main verb in addition to their auxiliary role. The modals never fill the main verb slot, nor do they have all five forms that verbs have.[1] They are so named because they affect what is called the mood of the verb. **Mood** refers to the manner in which a verb is expressed, such as a fact, a desire, a possibility, or a command. **Indicative mood** refers to a sentence dealing with a fact or a question about a fact. The modals convey conditions of probability, possibility, obligation, or necessity: *I may eat; I could eat; I should eat; I must eat.* These are known as the **conditional mood**. We should note also that the modals *will* and *shall* produce what traditional grammarians call the future tense: *will eat* and *shall eat*. (Future time is also commonly expressed with the semiauxiliary *be* + *-ing* + *go*—"I'm going to eat soon"—and with present tense and an adverbial—"The bus leaves at noon.") Modals and modal-like verbs are discussed further in "Auxiliaries" on pages 273–275.

Exercise   12

A. What is the expanded verb that each of the following strings will produce? (Assume in each case that the subject is Fred.)

Example:

past + have + -en + help = *had helped*

1. pres + have + -en + work
2. past + be + -ing + work
3. pres + will + be + -ing + play
4. past + be + -ing + be
5. pres + be + -ing + have
6. past + shall + have + -en + have

---

[1] Sometimes modals appear without verbs in **elliptical clauses**, where the main verb is understood but not expressed:

> Who'll cook the spaghetti? I *will*.
>
> May I join you? Yes, you *may*.

7. past + have + -en + have
8. past + can + have + -en + be
9. pres + may + have + -en + be + -ing + try
10. past + may + have + -en + be + -ing + be

B. Identify the components of the predicating verb in each of the following sentences. Your answers will look like the strings given in Part A.

Example:

Mike was having a bad day = *past + be + -ing + have*

1. The students were studying in the library.
2. I have finally found my lost scarf. [Note: Adverbs, such as *finally*, should not appear in your verb string.]
3. I lost it on the first day of classes.
4. Mickey has been skipping classes lately.
5. He could be in big trouble.
6. My hard drive crashed yesterday.
7. Joanie certainly seems happy in her new apartment.
8. She will probably be having a party this weekend.
9. My roommate may be graduating after only three years.
10. I should have studied harder for this test.

THE SUBJUNCTIVE MOOD

Unlike the conditional mood, the **subjunctive mood** does not involve modal auxiliaries. Rather, it is simply a variation of the verb that we use in special circumstances:

1. In *that* clauses after verbs conveying a strong suggestion or recommendation, we use the base form of the verb:

    We suggested that Mary go with us.

    Kathy insisted that Bill consult the doctor.

    I move that the meeting be adjourned.

Even for third-person singular subjects, which would normally take the *-s* form, we use the base form in these clauses: Mary *go*; Bill *consult*; the meeting *be*. Other verbs that commonly take clauses in the subjunctive mood are *command, demand, ask, require, order, recommend,* and *propose.* A subjunctive *that* clause also follows certain nouns and adjectives related to commands and suggestions:

The suggestion <u>that Bill see the doctor</u> was a good one.

It is advisable <u>that he get a thorough checkup</u>.

2. In *if* clauses that express a wish or a condition contrary to fact, we use *were* as the standard form of *be*, no matter what the subject:

<u>If I were you</u>, I'd be careful.

<u>If Joe weren't so lazy</u>, he'd probably be a millionaire.

The use of *was* is also fairly common in sentences like the second example:

<u>If Joe was here</u>, he'd agree with me.

In writing, however, the subjunctive *were* is the standard form.

In Chapter 9 we will see *if* clauses that discuss a possible condition rather than a wish or a condition contrary to fact:

<u>If it is cold tomorrow</u>, we'll cancel the picnic.

Here we do not use the infinitive form of *be* as we do in the subjunctive mood.

TENSE AND ASPECT

At the opening of this chapter you learned that French verbs have more than seventy different forms—in contrast to the mere five we have in English. Does that mean that our language is less expressive? Not at all. Instead of expressing concepts of time and duration and completion by adding inflectional endings to our verbs, as the French do, we use auxiliaries, either singly or in combination. The verb-expansion rule that you learned, with its tense marker and optional auxiliaries, describes our system for doing so.

The auxiliaries *be* and *have* contribute to what is called **aspect**, referring to whether an action is in progress or completed. In traditional terminology, verbs in the *-ing* form with the auxiliary *be* are called "progressive" or "continuous"; those in the *-en*, or past participle, form with the auxiliary *have* are called "perfect" tenses. The term "perfect" comes to us from Latin grammar, where it refers to "action that is completed before the present moment." However, in English our present perfect,

Bill has lived in Florida since 1992,

while referring to past, includes a connection to the present. This sentence tells us that Bill still lives in Florida. That present connection of one kind or another is implicit in the perfect tenses with *have*. And, as the examples in the following section show, verb strings with *had* refer to a point of time in the past connected to a more recent past time.

The tense marker, T, in our verb-expansion rule, however, is limited to only two tenses: present and past. These are the only two tenses represented by the form of the verb itself. Following are illustrations of our common tenses and auxiliary-verb combinations.

USING THE VERB FORMS

The traditional labels of these common verb forms are shown in parentheses.[2]

Base form and -s form (SIMPLE PRESENT)

I <u>live</u> in Omaha.

The news <u>comes on</u> at six.

Milton's poetry <u>speaks</u> to everyone.   *Historical, habitual, propensity, or timeless present*

Spiders <u>spin</u> webs.

I <u>understand</u> your position.   *Present point in time*

Pres + be + -ing + MV (PRESENT PROGRESSIVE)

I <u>am working</u> at Wal-Mart.   *Present action of*

John <u>is taking</u> philosophy this term.   *limited duration*

Past + MV (SIMPLE PAST)

I <u>moved</u> to Omaha last March.   *Specific point in time*

A virus <u>erased</u> all of my data.

Note that with an appropriate adverbial, this form can indicate an extended period of time in the past, not a specific point:

I <u>studied</u> Spanish *for three years in high school.*

Past + be + -ing + MV (PAST PROGRESSIVE)

A baby <u>was crying</u> during the entire   *Past action of limited*
ceremony this morning.   *duration (often to show*

I <u>was trying</u> to sleep last night during   *one particular action*
the party, but it was no use.   *during a larger span of time)*

---

[2] These traditional labels are called tenses. However, given our use of *tense* in the verb-expansion rule—that is, our restriction of T to present and past—we will adopt the linguist's term *aspect* in reference to the verb strings that are expanded with the perfect (*have* + *-en*) and progressive (*be* + *-ing*) auxiliaries.

Pres + have + -en + MV (PRESENT PERFECT)

> The leaves <u>have turned</u> yellow
>   already.
>
> I <u>have finished</u> my work.
>
> I <u>have memorized</u> several of Frost's
>   poems.

*A completed action
extending from a point
in the past to either the
present or the near pre-
sent—an action with
relevance to the pre-
sent—or occurring at an
unspecified past time*

Past + have + -en + MV (PAST PERFECT)

> The hikers <u>had used up</u> all their water,
>   when finally they found a
>   hidden spring.
>
> The students <u>had finished</u> only the
>   first page of the test by the time
>   the bell rang.

*Past action completed
before another action in
the past*

Pres + have + -en + be + -ing + MV (PRESENT PERFECT PROGRESSIVE)

> The authorities <u>have been looking</u> for
>   the arson suspect since last Sunday.

*Past action continuing
into the present*

Past + have + -en + be + -ing + MV (PAST PERFECT PROGRESSIVE)

> The authorities <u>had been looking</u> for
>   the suspect even before the fire
>   broke out.

*Continuing past action
completed before another
action in the past*

THE "FUTURE TENSE"

As we saw in our discussion of the verb-expansion rule, our five verb forms include only two tenses: present and past. We're quite capable of discussing future time, of course, but we do so using means other than a special verb form. In the traditional description of verb tenses, the addition of the modal auxiliary *will* to denote a future action is called the "future tense":

> I <u>will finish</u> my project later.

When *have + -en* is added, the result is called "future perfect," denoting a future action before another future action:

> I <u>will have finished</u> it by Friday.

However, one of our most common ways of expressing future is with the semi-auxiliary *be + going to*:

> I'<u>m going to finish</u> my project this afternoon.

And both the simple present and the present progressive can express future time with the addition of an appropriate adverbial:

>The bus <u>leaves</u> at 7:00.

>We<u>'re having</u> pizza tonight.

   We should also note that the modal *will* is not used exclusively for future time. In his "Language Log" posted on the Internet in March 2008, British linguist Geoffrey K. Pullum estimates that perhaps 20 percent of the occurrences of *will* do not express the future. Here are a few of his many examples:

>Step this way, if you will, sir. (Means "if you wish to". . . .)

>That will be Mike. (Uttered when the doorbell rings. . . .)

>Metallic potassium will explode on contact with water. (Means potassium already does explode on contact with water. . . .)

>The reason that Warren Buffet has made so much money in his life is that he will not invest in fly-by-night operations. (Means that he has a firm policy of not investing, exemplified by his past practice. . . .)

So even though we use the term *future tense*, we recognize that it does not designate a particular verb form, one with a special ending, as *past tense* does. It can refer to any of our various ways of discussing future time.

EXCEPTIONS TO THE RULE

The verb-expansion rule is simple, but it is powerful. With it we can expand the verb slot in all the sentence patterns to express a great many variations in meaning. Given the variety of modals we have, which we can use with or without *have* + *-en* and *be* + *-ing*, the number of possible variations adds up to fifty or more for most verbs. However, we rarely use all the possibilities for any given verb. Our system restricts the use of some, and others we simply have no occasion to use.

   Although we may say,

>He seems grumpy.

>>and

>They have remained friends.

We would probably never say,

>*He is seeming grumpy.

>>or

>*They have been remaining friends.

Most of the exceptions involve the restriction of *be* + *-ing* with certain linking verbs, with *be* as main verb, and with a small number of transitive verbs that refer to mental processes, such as *prefer*, *know*, and *like*, or states, such as *own*, *resemble*, and *weigh*.

ELL Issues   Special Rules for -ing Verbs

The restriction that applies to the auxiliary *be + -ing* is rooted in the "continuous" or "progressive" meaning that *-ing* gives the verb; that "movement through time" is not logical with verbs like *prefer* and *know*. The restriction also applies to Pattern I, where *be* is the main verb followed by a time or place adverbial. We can use *have + -en* or a modal auxiliary with a time adverbial in Pattern I to describe an extended time in a particular place:

> The students *have been* in the library <u>since noon</u>.

> The students *will be* in the library <u>until this afternoon</u>.

But *be + -ing*, with its progressive meaning, simply doesn't work:

> *The students *are being* in the library.

The Pattern I sentence "The students *are* in the library" simply identifies the present existence of the students in a particular place, not a progressive or continuous state. The same restriction on *be + -ing* applies to Patterns II and III when the subject complement names a permanent, unchanging trait:

> *He is being tall.

> *He is being African-American.

See also the #2 Question for Discussion, on page 86.

THE STAND-IN AUXILIARY *DO*

You may have noticed that one common auxiliary does not appear in our verb-expansion rule (even though it appears in this sentence)—the auxiliary *do*, along with its *-s* and *-ed* forms, *does* and *did*. Why have we left those forms out of the discussion of auxiliaries? Don't they belong in our list, as modals perhaps or as alternatives to *have + -en* and *be + -ing*?

No, they don't. Even though most grammar books include the forms of *do* in their auxiliary lists along with modals and *have* and *be*, they don't really belong there. The auxiliary role played by *do* and *does* and *did* in the predicating verb is very different from that of the others. They belong in a list by themselves.

Consider which of the following sentences sound grammatical to you and which do not:

1. Boris may not work today.
2. Boris worked not yesterday.
3. Amy is not living here.
4. Amy lives not here.
5. Amy is not here.

You may have noticed that all five sentences, including the two that are ungrammatical, have something in common: They are all negative. And it's that negative marker *not* that makes sentences 2 and 4 ungrammatical. Without it, there would be no problem:

> Boris worked yesterday.
>
> Amy lives here.

What do the other three have that those two don't? Sentences 1 and 3 have auxiliaries; 5 has a form of *be* as the main verb. In order to make sentences 2 and 4 grammatical, we have to add an auxiliary. Here's where *do* comes into our grammar:

> Boris didn't work yesterday.
>
> Amy doesn't live here.

Here are two more sentences about Amy that are ungrammatical:

> *Where lives Amy?
>
> *Lives Amy in Austin?

As with negative sentences, both kinds of questions—yes/no questions and *wh*-questions—also require auxiliaries:

> Where does Amy live?
>
> Does Amy live in Austin?

When an auxiliary is required for a sentence variation, including negative sentences and questions, and there is no auxiliary, then *do* comes to the rescue—it stands in as a kind of dummy auxiliary. Linguists have a more formal name for this operation: They call it **do support**.

There is one more occasion that calls for the assistance of *do* support: the **emphatic sentence**.

> Amy does expect to graduate in four years.
>
> Do come in.
>
> We did enjoy our holiday in the mountains.

These three sentences would be grammatical without a form of *do*, but they would lose their emphatic quality. In speech we can make our sentences emphatic simply by adding volume to either an auxiliary or to the verb itself. In writing we could put the verb in capital letters,

> I LOVE holidays in the mountains

—but of course it's not standard procedure. When the sentence has an auxiliary, we can show the emphasis with italics or possibly an adverb:

> I *have* finished my homework.

I certainly have finished my homework.

The emphatic *do* allows us to show the emphasis without any special gimmicks:

I did finish my homework.

The purpose of this discussion of *do* is twofold: (1) to help you understand the distinction between *do* and the other auxiliaries; (2) to help you appreciate how your grammar expertise automatically calls on *do* whenever you need an auxiliary.

Investigating Language 4.2

One way to think about the tricky verbs *lie* and *lay* is in terms of their sentence patterns: One is intransitive (Pattern VI) and one is transitive (Pattern VII). Read the following information adapted from *Webster's Ninth New Collegiate Dictionary*, then fill in the blanks with their various forms.

lie/ (intran) **lay**/; **lain**/; **lying** 1 a. to be or to stay at rest in a horizontal position; be prostrate: REST, RECLINE (~motionless) (~asleep) b. to assume a horizontal position—often used with *down*.

lay/ (tran) **laid**/; **laid**/; **laying** 1: to beat or strike down with force 2 a: to put or set down b: to place for rest or sleep; esp: BURY 3: to bring forth and deposit (an egg).

BASE	-S FORM	-ED FORM	-ING FORM	-EN FORM
1. lie	_____	_____	_____	_____
2. lay	_____	_____	_____	_____

Now identify the verbs in the following sentences as transitive or intransitive and indicate the base form of the verb: Is it *lie* or *lay?*

1. I should lay the papers in neat piles on the table. _____
2. The cat has never lain so still before. _____
3. Yesterday he lay very still. _____
4. I laid the baby on the bed for her nap. _____
5. I lay on the beach for two hours yesterday. _____

If you are accustomed to hearing people say "I'm going to lay down for a nap" or commanding their dogs to "lay down," you may think that the last sentence in the list sounds wrong. It's not unusual to hear people say "I laid on the beach." In fact, it is so common that at the end of the definition for *lay*, just quoted, the dictionary includes *lie* as an intransitive synonym—and labels it "nonstandard." In other words, when you say "lay down," you are using *lay* as a synonym for the intransitive *lie*. (If your dog responds only to standard usage, you'll have to say "lie down.") The reason for the common nonstandard usage becomes clear when you examine the five forms of the two verbs: Both sets include *lay*.

The confusion arising with two other pairs of tricky verbs—*rise/raise* and *sit/set*—can be resolved in the same way as with *lie/lay*, that is, in terms of their sentence pattern category. The dictionary will identify them as transitive or intransitive and list their *-ed*, *-en*, and *-ing* forms.

THE VERB SYSTEM OF AFRICAN AMERICAN VERNACULAR ENGLISH

One of the most noticeable differences between Edited American English (EAE) and African American Vernacular English (AAVE) occurs with the verb-expansion rule.[3] In this chapter we have seen how *have* and *be* function systematically as auxiliaries to designate the perfect (*Mary has worked*) and the progressive (*Mary is working*) forms of the verb. We have also noted that *do* kicks in for questions (*Did Mary eat?*), negative sentences (*Mary didn't eat*), and emphasis (*Mary did eat*) when no other auxiliary is available.

The AAVE system calls for these same auxiliaries, but combines them in different ways. Here is a partial list of AAVE verb strings along with the EAE equivalent for each:

1. He eat. (present) "He is eating."
2. He be eating. (habitual) "He is usually eating."
3. He been eating. (remote past) "He has been eating for a long time."
4. He been ate. (remote past) "He ate a long time ago."
5. He done ate. (completive) "He has already eaten."
6. He been done ate. (remote past completive) "He finished eating a long time ago."
7. He had done ate. (completive) "He had already eaten."

We would need more data, of course, to come up with an accurate verb-expansion rule for AAVE. However, we can recognize certain regular features of the system from this small sample:

1. The auxiliary *done* appears in all the "completive" forms. Note that the adverb *already* or the verb *finished* is required to express the EAE equivalent.

[3.] This description is adapted from an article by Lisa Green: "Study of Verb Classes in African American English," *Linguistics and Education* 7 (1994): 65–81.

2. The auxiliary *been* (pronounced "bin" and spoken with strong stress) carries the meaning of "remote" time. The EAE equivalent requires "a long time" or "a long time ago" to make this remote past distinction.

In terms of form, the fact that the auxiliary *done* appears in the string with other auxiliaries clearly sets this system apart from EAE, where *do* is not part of the verb-expansion rule, but, as mentioned earlier, occurs only as a stand-in auxiliary. (It should be noted that in AAVE a form of *do* also kicks in for some questions and negatives, as in EAE.) Another distinguishing feature of AAVE is the "habitual" *be*, shown in the second example. It includes the meaning "usually" or "habitually," whereas in EAE the adverb must be supplied.

It should be obvious from this brief description that the verb forms of AAVE, although different from those of EAE, are generated by a highly systematized set of rules. This recognition should also illustrate an important lesson that the linguists have contributed to language education: that all dialects of English are equally grammatical.

CHAPTER 4
Key Terms

African American Vernacular English
Auxiliary
Conditional mood
Do support
Emphatic sentence
Helping verb
Indicative mood
Infinitive
Irregular verb
Main verb

Modal auxiliary
Mood
Negative sentence
Person
Regular verb
Stand-in auxiliary
Subjunctive mood
Tense
Verb-expansion rule

Sentences
for PRACTICE

Identify the components of the main verb in each of the following sentences. Your answers will be in the form of verb strings, such as those given in Exercise 12.

1. The press has recently labeled our new senator a radical on domestic issues.
2. The teacher should have given the class more information about the exam.
3. According to the students, their teacher was being downright secretive.
4. In Florida the Coast Guard is now confiscating the boats of drug runners.
5. The president may soon name three women to top posts in the Department of State.
6. Our company will try a new vacation schedule in the summer.
7. All the workers are taking their two-week vacations at the same time.
8. Pat has been jogging regularly for six years.
9. Until last week, Mario had never told me his middle name.
10. The suspect's alibi may have been a lie.
11. I should have been studying on a regular basis throughout the semester.
12. Writers have produced almost 2,500 works about the *Bounty* mutiny during the past 200 years.

QUESTIONS ? for DISCUSSION

1. "I've already ate" is a fairly common nonstandard usage in our country. Explain how it deviates from the standard usage described by the verb-expansion rule. Compare it with "I've already tried"; can you discover a logical reason for the nonstandard usage? Does that particular nonstandard form ever occur with regular verbs?

2. The difference between two such sentences as

   He is tall.   *and*   He is silly.

   is obviously in the adjective that fills the subject complement slot. We cannot say

   *He is being tall.

but we can say

   He is being silly.

so there must be a fundamental difference between the two adjectives.

The contrast is between **stative** and **dynamic** qualities—the one describing a state, usually permanent, and the other a changing quality. What is there about *be* + *-ing* that makes this restriction seem logical? Can you think of other stative adjectives (other than *tall*) that are restricted from the subject complement slot with *be* + *-ing*?

Perhaps a better way of describing the contrast between *silly* and *tall*—between silliness and height—concerns the presence or absence of volition, the power of choice. Which of the following adjectives describe characteristics that are willed: *young, tough, nice, red, absorbent, reckless, round?* Can these adjectives serve as subject complements with *be* + *-ing*?

3. Consider further restrictions on *be* + *-ing*:

   *Mary is resembling her mother.

   *The blue dress is fitting you.

   Can we speak of dynamic and stative or willed and nonwilled qualities of verbs as well as of adjectives? Consider the following verbs: *assume, suit, equal, enjoy, desire, agree with, mean, know, contain, lack, like.* Do any of these have restrictions? Why?

4. Do nouns carry such distinctions, too? Try the following nouns in the subject complement slot of Pattern III: *a doctor, a nuisance, a hero, a nice person, a gentleman, a hard worker, a construction worker.* Here is the slot: "He is being _____." Can all of them be used with *be* + *-ing?* What conclusions can you draw about NPs? Does volition, or the power of choice, make a difference?

5. In the following sentences, what does *'s* stand for?

   He's had enough.

   Mary's not here.

   She's already gone.

   She's already left.

   He's finished.

6. We usually think of contractions (*doesn't, shouldn't, I'll, he'd,* etc.) as optional, informal variations of verbs. And we generally think of them as forms that are best avoided in formal writing. Consider the following sentences in this light. Are the foregoing assumptions true?

> Can't you come with me?
>
> Doesn't the sunset look beatuiful this evening?
>
> Hasn't everyone tried to conserve energy?
>
> Are you sure he'll try hard enough to win?
>
> I'm very hungry.

7. You can demonstrate the ambiguity of the following negative sentences by adding two possible follow-up sentences to each:

> I'm not taking Math 10 because it's so easy.
>
> He did not kill his wife because he loved her.

8. The following aphorism is ambiguous too:

> No news is good news.

Restate the sentence in two ways to demonstrate its two meanings.

9. Why do the following sentences from Shakespeare and the King James Bible sound strange to our twenty-first-century ears? What particular change that has taken place in the language do these sentences illustrate?

> Let not your heart be troubled.
>
> Know you where you are?
>
> Wherefore weep you?
>
> Revolt our subjects?
>
> What means this shouting?

CLASSROOM APPLICATIONS

1. In this chapter we looked briefly at our system for turning sentences into questions, a process that sometimes requires *do*. The tag question is another method for turning statements into questions:

> John is washing his car, <u>isn't he</u>?
>
> Perry should wash his too, <u>shouldn't he</u>?

Add the tags that turn the following statements into questions:

> Harold has finally stopped smoking,————?
>
> The students are not studying Latin,————?
>
> Bev finished her book on schedule,————?
>
> Tim and Joe are good carpenters,————?

    Kris is a good carpenter, too,————?

    She builds beautiful cabinets,————?

Now look at the system you followed for adding these questions. How many steps are involved? Imagine writing a computer program so that it, too, could generate tag questions. What are the steps you would have to include?

    Here are three more tags to supply:

    Harold should stop smoking,————?

    Harold ought to stop smoking,————?

    Harold may stop smoking soon,————?

Take a poll among your friends to get their responses to these three. Do all the respondents agree? Do they follow the procedure you described in the first set? What do these tags tell you about the changing nature of the language?

2. About fifty years ago, David Bourland, a semanticist, invented a writing system that he labeled "E-prime," a version of English without the verb *be*. He rejected all of its forms (*be, am, is, are, was, were, been, being*), including its use as both the main verb and auxiliary and its use in contractions (*I'm, it's, there's, we're,* etc.). As Bourland and others have noted, *be* outdistances all other verbs in frequency of use—and overuse. In fact, your own writing teachers may have advised you to look for alternatives to some of the *be* sentences in your essays.

    To practice your E-prime skills, turn to Chapter 1 and find the second paragraph of the section titled "The Issue of Correctness" on page 8. You'll discover six forms of *be* in the first four sentences. Rewrite those sentences without *be*. Remember that when you eliminate *be*, you also eliminate all main verbs in the -*ing* form.

    Some E-prime users also take pride in speaking without *be*. As a class exercise, see if you can avoid all forms of *be* in your next class discussion.

    You'll find further information about E-prime in Cullen Murphy's article "'To Be' in Their Bonnets," *Atlantic* (February 1992) and on the Web.

(Note: Unlike the paragraph in Chapter 1 referred to, this Classroom Application contains no instances of *be* in a predicating verb, either as an auxiliary or as the main verb.)

Changing Sentence Focus

CHAPTER PREVIEW

The ten sentence-pattern formulas described in Chapter 3 represent the underlying framework of almost all the sentences we speak and write. For example, underlying the sentence you just read, the first one in this paragraph, is a basic Pattern VII sentence:

The formulas	represent	the framework
NP_1	V-tr	NP_2

The two NP slots have been expanded with a variety of phrases and clauses, but the underlying subject and verb and direct object are there, in order, just as the formula describes them; you can pick out the basic skeleton with little trouble. When you read that first sentence, either silently or aloud, you probably put the main stress on "the underlying framework," the direct object. In most of our sentences, the predicate slot following the main verb commands attention; it usually is the peak in the rhythm pattern, the place where we focus on the new information, the reason for the sentence.

In this chapter we will examine the concept of sentence focus, with special attention to the changes in the **active voice** that produce the **passive voice**. We will also examine two other common ways of re-arranging sentence patterns to change their focus: the ***there* transformation** and **cleft sentences**.

THE PASSIVE VOICE

The "voice" of a sentence concerns the relationship of the subject to the verb. You're probably familiar with the definition of verbs as "action words," a description commonly applied to both intransitive and transitive verbs:

> Mary laughed. (Pattern VI)

> The boys ate every piece of pizza. (Pattern VII)

In these sentences the subjects are performing the action; they are making something happen. Linguists use the term **agent** for this "doer" of the verbal action. Another term that describes this relationship of the subject to the verb is **active voice.**

What happens when we turn the Pattern VII sentence around, when we remove the agent from the subject slot and give that role to *every piece of pizza*, the original direct object?

> Every piece of pizza was eaten by the boys.

This reversal changes the sentence from active to **passive voice.** The diagrams clearly illustrate the changed roles:

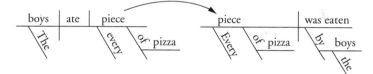

To understand the primary distinction between active and passive voice, it is important to recognize what happens to the subject-verb relationship. In our example, even though *the boys* is no longer the sentence subject, or topic, it is still the agent, or actor; and *every piece of pizza* is still the so-called "receiver of the action," still getting acted upon—still getting eaten! Only their roles in the sentence, their functions, have changed—not their relationship to each other. The passive voice simply describes the event from a different perspective.

In the active voice, while the subject is the sentence topic, the slot that follows the verb, the direct object, is the focus of the sentence—and generally the new information. In other words, what is said about the topic is generally the reason for the sentence. The passive transformation enables the direct object to shift from the focus position to that of sentence topic, or subject. We will see some examples of why that shift occurs in the next section. First, however, we will look at the changes to the verb string that occur in the passive voice.

The passive transformation involves three steps, all of which are fairly easy to see in the diagrams of the pizza sentences:

1. The original direct object becomes the subject.

2. A form of *be* is added as an auxiliary (in this case the past form, *was*, because *ate* is past); it teams with the past participle, the *-en*

form of the verb. In other words, we add *be* + *-en* to the active verb string.

3. The original agent, if mentioned, becomes the object of the preposition *by* (or, in some cases, *for*). This third step is often missing; it is not required. Many, if not most, passive sentences do not include the active agent.

If you think about the first step in the list, you'll understand why we are not using the other example of an action verb, *Mary laughed,* to illustrate the passive voice: Intransitive verbs cannot be made passive because they have no direct object. That's why you read this statement in the discussion of Pattern VII, back in Chapter 3 (page 47):

> In Chapter 5 you will see another way of testing whether or not a verb is transitive. Can the sentence be turned into the passive voice? If the answer is yes, the verb is transitive.

As you learned in Chapter 4, the verb-expansion rule applies to all of the sentence patterns. We can think of it as the active-verb rule:

Active: T (M) (have + -en) (be + -ing) MV

As the formula shows, when we choose *be* as an auxiliary in the active voice, the main verb will be the *-ing* form. But according to Step 2 in our description of the passive transformation, the auxiliary *be* is teamed with the past participle, the *-en* form of the verb:

Every piece of pizza <u>was eaten</u> by the boys.

The passive formula shows this feature as a requirement of the passive voice; you'll note that, unlike the optional *be* + *-ing* in the active rule, the *be* + *-en* is not in parentheses:

Passive: T (M) (have + -en) (be + -ing) **be** + **-en** MV

This formula tells us that a passive verb has three requirements: (1) tense, (2) the auxiliary *be*, together with (3) the past participle form of the main verb. Here are the components of the passive verb in our pizza example:

past + be +-en + eat = was eaten

The formula also shows that a passive sentence can include optional auxiliaries, along with the required *be + -en*:

The work <u>will be finished</u> soon.

The work <u>should have been finished</u> yesterday.

We know these sentences are passive because the auxiliary *be* is not followed by the *-ing* form of the verb.

Exercise 13

Transform the active sentences into the passive by following these steps:
1. Identify the components of the verb string;
2. Add *be + -en*;
3. Shift the direct object to subject position.
4. Include the active subject in a *by* phrase. (Note: This step is optional.)

Example:

The Red Cross is sending aid to the hurricane victims in Florida.

    Active verb: pres + be + -ing + send

    Passive: pres + be + -ing + be + -en + send = *is being sent*

    Aid is being sent to the hurricane victims in Florida by the Red Cross.

1. President Lincoln signed the Emancipation Proclamation in 1862.
2. The campus paper has published several sensational news stories this semester.
3. The student government will hold a run-off election in two weeks.
4. Volunteer searchers found the victim's remains in the woods.
5. The police are keeping the suspect in solitary confinement.
6. The county commissioners will discuss a new tax collection system at their next meeting.
7. Your positive attitude pleases me.
8. Bill's fraternity brothers were teasing him about his new mustache.
9. You should clean your room at least once a week.
10. Heavy thunderstorms have knocked down power lines in three counties.

The Passive *Get*. It's certainly accurate to recognize *be* as the auxiliary that signals the passive voice—but *be* is not the only one. On some occasions we call on the verb *get* to team up with the *-en* form of the verb to form the passive. Such occasions are informal ones; rarely do we see sentences like these in formal writing:

> My sister gets teased about her freckles.
>
> Dave got fired yesterday.
>
> Our basement got flooded during Hurricane Charley.

And here's a sentence you may recognize from the earlier passive discussion:

> The pizza is still getting eaten!

Formality—or its lack—is not the only reason that *get* falls short as an auxiliary, whether active or passive. Unlike other auxiliaries, *get* requires *do* support for negatives and questions:

> My sister doesn't get teased about her freckles.
>
> Did Dave get fired yesterday?

Some of our *get* sentences that look like passives are more accurately identified as linking verb patterns:

> I got tired of waiting.
>
> Hansel and Gretel got lost in the woods.

In these sentences, *tired* and *lost* are filling the subject complement slot. And in contrast to the first group of sentences, these two do not have an understood agent; there's no "by" phrase that's been deleted. So, in contrast to the passive sentences, here *get* is the main verb, not an auxiliary.

The Transitive-Passive Relationship. The ties between the transitive verb and the passive voice are so strong—there are so few exceptions—that we can almost define "transitive verb" in terms of this relationship. In other words, a transitive verb is a verb that can undergo the passive transformation. There are a few exceptions, including *have*, one of our most common verbs. In only a few colloquial expressions does *have* appear in the passive voice: "A good time was had by all," "I've been had." But in most cases *have* sentences cannot be transformed:

> I had a cold.
>
> *A cold was had by me.
>
> Juan has a new car.
>
> *A new car is had by Juan.

Other verbs that fit Pattern VII but are rarely transformed into passive are *lack* ("He lacks skill in debate") and *resemble* ("Mary resembles her mother"). Linguists sometimes classify these as "midverbs" and assign them to a separate sentence pattern. But on the basis of form (NP_1 V NP_2), we will classify these sentences as Pattern VII and simply look on them as exceptions to the passive rule.

Patterns VIII to X in Passive Voice. The passive examples we have seen so far are all Pattern VII. But of course, all of our transitive patterns can be transformed into the passive voice. In the case of Pattern VIII, which has an indirect object in addition to the direct object, we have two options: Either of the two objects can serve as the subject of the passive:

> *Active:* The judge awarded Prudence first prize.
>
> *Passive:* Prudence was awarded first prize.

or

> *Passive:* First prize was awarded to Prudence.

When we diagram the version with *Prudence* as subject, the result looks exactly like an active Pattern VII:

Here, where we have two objects, we have retained the direct object in the passive; in traditional grammar this slot is called the **retained object**.

In order to identify the sentence pattern, to distinguish it from Pattern VII, we have to recognize the sentence as passive, and we do that by noting that the verb *was awarded* cannot be active (otherwise, the auxiliary *be* would be followed by *-ing*).

The diagram of the other version of Pattern VIII, with *First prize* as subject, looks exactly like Pattern VI:

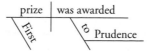

Again, the only way to identify it as a transitive verb is to recognize that the verb is passive: The auxiliary *be* <u>without</u>-*ing* following is the clue.

When we transform Patterns IX and X, which also have two slots following the verb, we have only one choice for the passive: Only the direct object can serve as the subject in the passive voice:

> *Active:* The teacher considers Elizabeth bright. (Pattern IX)
>
> They named their dog Sandy. (Pattern X)

In the passive voice, the active object complement becomes a subject complement. This transformation occurs because the original object becomes the subject:

Note that we have not included a *by* phrase—that is, the active subject—in these passive versions. They could, of course, be added.

Again, in order to identify these last two sentences as Patterns IX and X, it is important to recognize the verbs as passive. Otherwise, they will be mistaken for linking verbs. The simple fact that the verbs are passive, however, immediately sends the message that they are transitive patterns—only the transitive patterns can be transformed into the passive voice.

Exercise 14

Transform the following active sentences into the passive voice, retaining the same verb tense and aspect.

1. Many movie critics gave *No Country for Old Men* rave reviews.
2. Certain parts of the Patriot Act make some citizens nervous.
3. The teacher is giving the third graders too much homework.
4. The judges have chosen three finalists for the science award.
5. These colorful murals have turned the staircase walls into an art museum.
6. Fans and sports writers often refer to Roger Federer as the greatest tennis player of all time.
7. I should paint our kitchen cupboards bright red.
8. Bach composed some of our most intricate fugues.

Changing Passive Voice to Active. To transform a passive sentence into active voice, you need to perform three operations that essentially undo the three steps that produce the passive voice:

1. First, identify the agent, or actor—the doer of the verbal action. If the agent is named, you'll usually find it in a *by* prepositional phrase. If it's not there, just add "someone":

    > A party is being planned by the film club. [Agent: the film club]

    > The work should be finished by Friday. [Agent: someone]

2. Next, delete *be + -en* from the verb string:

    is being planned = pres + be + ing + ~~be~~ + ~~en~~ + plan

    should be finished = past + shall + ~~be~~ + ~~en~~ + finish

3. Rewrite the sentence with the agent in subject position, the revised verb in place, and the passive subject shifted to the direct object slot:

    > The film club is planning a party.

    > Someone should finish the work by Friday.

Exercise 15

Change these passive sentences to the active voice. Remember that in some cases the agent may be missing, so you will have to supply a subject for the active, such as "someone." Identify the sentence patterns for the active sentences you have produced.

1. The football team was led onto the field by the cheerleading squad.
2. The cheerleaders are chosen by a committee in the spring.
3. The new reporters had been warned by the managing editor about late submissions.
4. Several apartments in our building have been burglarized recently.
5. Our neighbor's new computer was stolen last weekend.
6. Dental floss was manufactured for the first time in 1882.
7. The possibility of recession is being talked about in financial circles.
8. Gabrielle must have been granted an extension on her loan payment.
9. The play was called a smashing success.
10. The poison has been rendered harmless.

THE PASSIVE VOICE IN PROSE

It's possible that everything you've heard or read about the passive voice has been negative. Sometimes English teachers even declare it out of bounds. This edict comes about because passive sentences sometimes have a stilted quality; and, yes, ineffective passives can often be improved by being changed to active voice. But often the reason for the problem is not the passive voice itself; the reason lies elsewhere. It's possible that an ineffective passive has the wrong subject, the wrong topic. In such cases, it's the focus that's the problem—not the mere fact that the sentence is passive.

The passive voice has an important job: It enables the writer to shift emphasis in the sentence so that the reader will put the focus where it should be—on the new information. That passive shift enables the writer to provide transition between sentences. Here, for example, is the beginning of a paragraph from the discussion of verbs in Chapter 2. Note how the direct object slot in the first sentence, the new information (underlined), becomes the topic, the subject, of the three following sentences. It has gone from being the focus in the opening sentence to being the old, or known, information—the topic under discussion—in the others. Because that subject is not the agent, the doer of the action, we make use of the passive voice. The passive verbs are shown in bold type.

> When the dictionary identifies a word as a verb, it lists <u>three forms</u>: the base form *(laugh)*, the past tense *(laughed)*, and the past participle *(laughed)*. <u>These three forms</u> **are** traditionally **referred to** as the verb's "three principal parts." <u>The base form</u> **is** also **known** as the infinitive; <u>it</u> **is** often **written** with *to* (*to laugh*). (p. 22)

Other Passive Purposes. The passive voice may also be appropriate if the identity of the agent is obscured in history or simply has no bearing on the discussion:

> In 1905 the streets of Patterson, California, were laid out in the shape of a wheel.

> Oregon's economy is closely tied to the lumber industry.

The passive voice is especially common—and deliberate—in technical and scientific writing, in legal documents, and in lab reports, where the researcher is the agent but to say so would be inappropriate:

> I increased the temperature to 450° for one hour. (*Active*)

> The temperature was increased to 450° for one hour. (*Passive*)

In some instances the passive voice is simply more straightforward:

> Joe was wounded in Iraq.

In many situations, of course, the purpose of the passive is simply to avoid mentioning the agent:

> It was reported today that the federal funds to be allocated for the power plant would not be forthcoming as early as had been anticipated. Some contracts on the preliminary work have been canceled and others renegotiated.

Such "officialese" or "bureaucratese" takes on a nonhuman quality because the agent role has completely disappeared from the sentences. In the foregoing example the reader does not know who is reporting, allocating, anticipating, canceling, or renegotiating.

This kind of agentless passive is especially common in official news conferences, where press secretaries and other government officials explain what is happening without revealing who is responsible for making it happen. The faceless passive does an efficient job of obscuring responsibility, but it is neither efficient nor graceful for the writing that most of us do in school and on the job.

Sometimes student writers resort to the passive voice in order to avoid using *I*, perhaps because the paper has too many of them already or because the teacher has ruled out the first-person point of view:

> The incessant sound of foghorns could be heard along the waterfront.

But English is a versatile language: First person is not the only alternative. Here's a version of the sentence using *sound* as the verb:

> The foghorns sounded along the waterfront.

Here's one that describes the movement of the sound:

> The incessant sound of foghorns floated across the water.

Many times, of course, the writer simply doesn't realize that the passive voice may be the culprit producing the vagueness or wordiness of that first draft. For example, the writer of the following sentence ended a family Christmas story with no awareness of voice at all:

> That visit from Santa was an occurrence that would never be forgotten by the family.

The active version produces a tight, straightforward sentence:

> The family would never forget that visit from Santa.

The writer could also have found an active sentence that retains *visit* as the subject:

> That visit from Santa became part of our family legend.

The passive voice certainly has a place in every kind of prose. To avoid it simply for the sake of avoiding it often results in a stilted, unnatural voice.

THE *THERE* TRANSFORMATION

Like the passive voice, the *there* transformation provides the writer a way of changing sentence focus by altering the word order—in this case, by opening the sentence with the unstressed *there*, known as an **expletive**; the subject of the sentence follows *be:*

> There's a fly in my soup.

> There is an error message on the computer screen.

To diagram a *there* transformation, we must identify the underlying pattern. As the diagram shows, *there* has no grammatical function in the basic sentence:

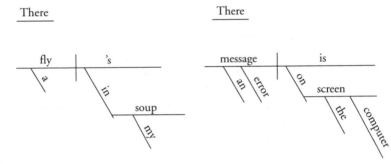

When we use the *there* transformation, we are taking advantage of the natural rhythm of language. In general, our language is a series of valleys and peaks, a fairly regular pattern of unstressed and stressed syllables:

Sentences usually begin with an unstressed valley. And more often than not, that first, unstressed slot is the subject. But the *there* transformation changes that usual word order: When the unstressed *there* fills the opening slot, it delays the subject until that first peak position of stress.

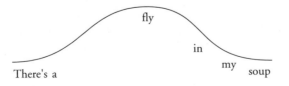

The *there* transformation applies when the subject of the sentence is indefinite: "*a* fly" or "*an* error message" rather than "*the* fly" or "*the* error message." The **indefinite article** is a signal that the subject of the *there* transformation is new information; we use the **definite article**, *the*, for old, or known, information. We might have occasion to say,

> There's the fly I told you about.

if a particular fly under discussion lands in the soup. But clearly this is a known fly, so this is not the unstressed *there*. The stress it carries marks it as an adverb providing information of place (it's called the "locative" adverb, from the word *location*). The same is true of

> There's that error message again.

In these sentences with definite subjects, we have simply shifted the order of the basic sentence pattern, as we sometimes do to emphasize adverbials:

> Here's your book.

> Right off the end of the pier plunged the getaway car.

The expletive *there* is always unstressed; the adverb *there*, when it opens a sentence, is nearly always stressed, providing an exception to the normal rhythm pattern of that opening unstressed valley we just saw. The adverb *there*, besides providing information of place, often acts as a kind of pointer. For example, read the following pair of sentences aloud and notice the difference in meaning and stress of the two *theres*:

> There's a piece of the jigsaw puzzle missing.

> There it is, on the floor.

You can almost see the finger pointing in the case of the second *there*.

In addition to the indefinite subject, the *there* transformation usually has a form of *be* either as the main verb or, in the case of the transitive and intransitive patterns, as an auxiliary. Pattern I (NP *be* ADV/TP) is the most common pattern we transform with *there;* Patterns II and III, in which *be* acts as a linking verb, will not accept the *there* transformation.

The form of *be* will, of course, depend on the tense and on the number of the subject, whether singular or plural:

> There *were* some problems with the heat in our new apartment.

> There *has* been a problem with the plumbing, too.

But an exception to the general rule of **subject-verb agreement** occurs with the *there* transformation. A compound subject, which we usually treat as plural, may take the *-s* form of *be* under some circumstances:

> There *was* some great blocking and some fine running and passing in Saturday's game.

In this sentence "there were" would be awkward, even though the subject is compound.

The *there* transformation without a form of *be* is also possible, but such sentences are not very common:

> There came from the alley a low moaning sound.
>
> There followed a series of unexplained phenomena.
>
> There remains an unanswered question.

Listen to the difference between these sentences and those with *be*. These have a tight, controlled quality about them. Notice also that when a verb other than *be* follows *there* it shares the stress with the subject.

You will read more about the rhythm of sentences and about the *there* transformation as a tool for the writer in Chapter 15.

ELL Issues   a(n)/the

The distinction between the indefinite article, *a* (or its variation *an*), and the definite *the* is a critical one, not only in the selection of the *there* transformation but in other contexts as well. We select the indefinite *a* at the first mention of a noun, when the specific referent of the noun has not yet been established; but for subsequent mentions, the definite *the* takes over:

> I read a good book last weekend. I bought the book for only a
>   quarter at a garage sale. The sale was just down the block.

Notice that at their second mention, the referents of those nouns have become specific, particular.

Exercise   16

Identify the function of *there* in the following sentences. Is it the expletive or is it the locative adverb? Also identify the sentence patterns.

1. There's often a flock of blackbirds lining the telephone wire in our neighborhood.
2. There they are now.
3. There's nothing to do tonight.
4. There's always TV to watch.
5. There's Henry across the street.
6. There he goes.

7. Isn't there a spelling checker on your word processor?
8. There but for the grace of God go I.

CLEFT SENTENCES

Another sentence variation that provides a way to shift the focus of attention is the cleft transformation, so called because it divides a clause into two parts: It cleaves it. The **cleft sentence** allows a writer to accomplish by means of word order what a speaker can do by varying the point of main stress or loudness. The following variations show how a speaker can change the focus or meaning of a sentence simply by putting stress on different words, that is, by saying certain words louder:

MARY wrecked her motorcycle in Phoenix during the Christmas break. (It wasn't Diane who did it.)

Mary wrecked her MOTORCYCLE in Phoenix during the Christmas break. (Not her car.)

Mary wrecked her motorcycle in PHOENIX during the Christmas break. (Not in Albuquerque.)

Mary wrecked her motorcycle in Phoenix during the CHRISTMAS break. (Not Thanksgiving.)

Because the conventions of writing do not include capital letters for words that should get main stress, as shown in the preceding sentences, the writer's intended emphasis may not always be clear. The cleft transformation solves the problem. In one kind of cleft sentence the main subject is *it* with a form of *be* as the main verb. In reading the following sentences aloud, you'll notice that you automatically stress the word or phrase following *was:*

It was <u>Mary</u> who wrecked her motorcycle in Phoenix during the Christmas break.

It was <u>her motorcycle</u> that Mary wrecked in Phoenix during the Christmas break.

It was <u>in Phoenix</u> that Mary wrecked her motorcycle during the Christmas break.

It was <u>during the Christmas break</u> that Mary wrecked her motorcycle.

Another kind of cleft sentence uses a *what* clause in subject position. Note that the added *was* separates the original sentence into two parts:

Mary wrecked her motorcycle.

What Mary wrecked <u>was</u> her motorcycle.

Sometimes *what* shifts the original verb phrase into subject position. Again, a form of *be* is added as the main verb:

A branch in the road <u>caused the accident</u>.

<u>What caused the accident</u> was a branch in the road.

Thick fog <u>reduced the visibility to zero</u>.

<u>What reduced the visibility to zero</u> was the thick fog.

You'll notice in both the *it* and *what* clefts that the sentence pattern of the main clause has changed, a change that does not occur with the other transformations. The Appendix includes a diagram of the *what* cleft (p. 375).

The cleft transformations produce sentences that are quite complicated structurally, with clauses filling certain slots in the patterns. You'll learn about these structures in later chapters. We will not be concerned here with their diagrams.

Given that the sentence variations we have seen in this chapter are important structures for writers, why do handbooks sometimes warn against using the passive voice and against starting sentences with *it* and *there* constructions? You'll find that these warnings generally appear in discussions of wordiness and/or brevity, with advice about deleting extra words. And while it's true that "it is" and "there are" and the passive do add a word or two, when these constructions are used in the right place and for the right reason, they provide the writer with valuable tools for controlling sentence rhythm and focus. It's also true, of course, that you won't want to overuse these transformations. You will want to consider the larger context, to pay attention to how many other *it* or *what* or *there* sentences occur in proximity. But certainly these kinds of sentence manipulations are valuable tools for the right occasion.

CHAPTER 5
Key Terms

Active voice	Indefinite article
Agent	*It* cleft
Case	Objective case
Cleft sentence	Passive voice
Definite article	Subject-verb agreement
Expletive *there*	*There* transformation
	What cleft

Sentences
for PRACTICE

Shift the focus of the following sentences by using the structural variations you have studied in this chapter: the passive voice, the *there* transformation, and the cleft transformations. Write as many variations as you can.

1. The press has recently labeled our new senator a radical on domestic issues.
2. During the primary campaign, everyone was calling him a reactionary.
3. Some sports reporters have called Oriole Park in Baltimore the architecture of nostalgia.
4. Many large firms are now hiring liberal arts majors for management positions.
5. Employers value liberal arts majors for their analytical ability.
6. People are constantly teasing me about my southern accent.
7. Apparently they have never heard a southern accent around here before.
8. Myrtle's special marinated mushrooms added a festive touch to the salad.
9. The destruction of the Amazon rain forest alarms a great many environmentalists.
10. A month of unseasonably warm weather almost ruined the ski season last winter.
11. Several gangs of kids in the neighborhood are cleaning up the empty lot on the corner.
12. The student government is holding the election of officers next Wednesday.

QUESTIONS
?
for DISCUSSION

1. Do we ever need the stand-in auxiliary *do* for a passive sentence? Why or why not?

2. What do you know about a verb when it has two forms of *be* as auxiliaries?

3. In the Classroom Applications section of Chapter 4, you read about turning statements into questions using what we call tag questions. Do the same with the following sentences—that is, add tag questions:

> There's a good movie on television tonight,_____ ?
>
> There were a lot of students absent today,_____ ?

Now explain why some linguists prefer to call *there* the subject of the sentence rather than an expletive. Give other evidence to support or refute that position.

4. In Chapter 3 we looked briefly at sentence variations that help us distinguish verb-particle combinations (phrasal verbs) from verb–adverb combinations:

> We jumped up. → Up we jumped.
>
> We made up. → *Up we made.

The cleft transformation, introduced in this chapter, can also be useful in identifying properties of verbs:

> He came by the office in a big hurry.
>
> He came by his fortune in an unusual manner.
>
> Where he came was by the office.
>
> *Where he came was by his fortune.
>
> Joe turned on the bridge and looked around.
>
> Joe turned on the light and looked around.
>
> It was on the bridge that Joe turned and looked around.
>
> *It was on the light that Joe turned and looked around.

Here are some other pairs that look alike. Use transformations to demonstrate their differences:

> The student looked up the word.
>
> The teacher looked up the hall.
>
> Sharon called up the stairs.
>
> Karen called up the club members.
>
> An old jalopy turned into the driveway.
>
> Cinderella's coach turned into a pumpkin.

CLASSROOM APPLICATIONS

1. Examine the following headlines, copied from a daily newspaper. You'll notice that some have incomplete verb phrases. Rewrite the headlines to complete the incomplete verbs, then identify their sentence patterns. (Note: You'll have to pay attention to voice—active or passive—in identifying the patterns.)

> Dissidents form action committee. (Pattern _____)
>
> Hurricane kills seven. (Pattern _____)
>
> Six found guilty of extortion. (Pattern _____)
>
> Team vies for championship. (Pattern _____)
>
> Battle of Verdun remembered in ceremony.
> (Pattern _____)
>
> Candidates ready for runoff election. (Pattern _____)
>
> New city planner named. (Pattern _____)
>
> Woman injured in crash. (Pattern _____)
>
> Fulbright scholarships awarded to two. (Pattern _____)

Check the headlines of your local paper. Which patterns do you find? Do you find any difference in the patterns used for sports headlines and those heading general news?

2. The following passage is the second paragraph of a seven-paragraph article on the songs of humpback whales titled "Songs from the Deep," part of a longer article on whales by Virginia Morell in the February 2008 issue of *Smithsonian*:

> The humpback's haunting songs are among the most complex animal vocalizations. They have a hierarchical syntax, one of the basic elements of language, according to recent studies. That is, they sing units of sound that together form a phrase. <u>The phrases *are repeated* in patterns known as themes. Each song *is composed* of anywhere from two to nine themes, and the themes *are sung* in a specific order.</u> Some phrases sound like the low moan of a cello, while others are more like the chirp of a songbird. (p. 62)

Note the three underlined clauses. In each case, the passive voice has enabled the writer to use a known element in subject position, with the new information—the reason for the sentence—in the predicate, the position of main focus.

Is there a way the author could have been just as effective without using the passive voice? Imagine that you are the author—and your teacher has asked you to revise the paragraph, declaring the passive voice out of bounds. Working in groups, see if you and your classmates can improve on the original author's version, using only the active voice.

Expanding the Sentence

I n this section we will take up three methods of expanding sentences: modification, noun phrase substitution, and coordination. You first learned about modification in Chapter 2, when you added adverbs to verb phrases and adjectives to noun phrases and prepositional phrases to both. In Chapters 6 and 7 you'll see other structures, as well as these, that function as adverbials and adjectivals. In Chapter 8 you'll see verb phrases and clauses that fill noun phrase slots; in Chapter 9, modifiers of the sentence as a whole; and in Chapter 10, the expansion of the sentence and its parts by means of coordination.

FORM AND FUNCTION

One way to organize all of these new details of sentence structure is to think in terms of form and function. The labels designating **form** that you have learned include the names of word classes such as noun, verb, adjective, adverb, preposition, and conjunction; the various phrases you have come to recognize—noun phrase, verb phrase, prepositional phrase—are also form designations. We recognize, and can label, the form of a structure like *the puppy* as a noun phrase and *on the porch* as a prepositional phrase on the basis of their forms. That is, we need not see these structures in sentences in order to recognize their forms. Until we give those structures a context, however, we have no way of discussing their **functions**. In Chapter 3, you'll recall, we saw a prepositional phrase functioning in two ways, as both an adjectival and an adverbial:

The puppy <u>on the porch</u> is sleeping.

The puppy is sleeping <u>on the porch</u>.

Only when it's in a larger structure can we discuss a word or a phrase in terms of both form and function. In the chapters that follow, the sentence expansions include verb phrases and clauses functioning as adverbials and adjectivals and nominals.

The following outline will be helpful to you in understanding the two-sided analysis of form and function and in organizing the details of sentence expansions.

FORM	FUNCTION
Word	*Adverbial*
noun	modifier of verb
verb	
adjective	*Adjectival*
adverb	subject complement
	object complement
Phrase	modifier of noun
noun phrase	
verb phrase	*Nominal*
gerund	subject
infinitive	subject complement
participle	direct object
prepositional phrase	indirect object
	object complement
Clause	object of preposition
independent clause (sentence)	appositive
dependent clause	
nominal	*Sentence Modifier*
adverbial (subordinate)	
adjectival (relative)	

You'll discover that all of the general functions listed on the right—adverbial, adjectival, nominal, and sentence modifier—can be carried out by all of the general forms listed on the left—words, phrases, and clauses. As an illustration of this principle, turn to the table of contents and read the headings for Chapter 6. You will see that the chapter title names and defines a function: "Modifiers of the Verb: Adverbials." The major subheadings name the five forms that carry out that function: Adverbs, Prepositional Phrases, Noun Phrases, Verb Phrases, and Clauses.

In this section of the book we will again use the sentence diagram to illustrate the various ways of expanding sentences, first with adverbials, then with adjectivals, nominals, and coordinated structures. The sentences are beginning to get long and complex, it's true; however, if you remember to consider the two-sided analysis of form and function, the diagrams will enhance your understanding. Each of the various forms we have discussed—noun phrase, prepositional phrase, verb phrase, clause—has a particular diagram, no matter what its function in the sentence. For example, a prepositional phrase is always diagrammed as a two-part structure, with the preposition on the diagonal line and the object of the preposition on the attached horizontal line; a noun phrase is always diagrammed with the headword on the horizontal line and its modifiers attached below it.

Always begin your analysis of a sentence by identifying the underlying pattern, one of the ten basic sentences you diagrammed in Chapter 3. Then analyze each of the slots to see how it has been expanded. If you take these expansions one step at a time, asking yourself questions about form and function, you'll come to understand the system that produces the sentences of your language.

In these five chapters on sentence expansion, you will be building on your knowledge of the basic sentence patterns. It might be a good idea at this point to revisit Chapter 3, to review the sentence patterns and their slots.

CHAPTER 6

Modifiers of the Verb: Adverbials

CHAPTER PREVIEW

When you studied the sentence patterns in Chapter 3, you learned that in addition to their various required slots all ten patterns can include "optional slots," where we add adverbial information: details of time, place, reason, manner, purpose, and so on. Except for Pattern I and a few other verbs where the adverbial of time or place is required, the sentence patterns are grammatical without that information; that's what we mean by "optional." But of course that doesn't mean that the adverbial information isn't important. There are, in fact, times when that information is the very reason for the sentence.

In the discussion of "Form and Function" in the introduction to Part III, you learned that the term "adverbial" names a function. And as this chapter title announces, that function is defined as "modifier of the verb." In the pages that follow, you will learn that five different structures— different forms—do the job of adding adverbial information. You have already worked with two of those in previous chapters: adverbs and prepositional phrases. In this chapter we will add three more forms to your repertoire of adverbials, all of which are familiar to you: noun phrases, verb phrases, and clauses.

THE MOVABLE ADVERBIALS

In the following sentence, each of the underlined structures—an adverb, a prepositional phrase, and a clause—adds adverbial information to the verb *gasped:*

> The audience gasped <u>nervously</u> <u>throughout the theater</u> <u>when the magician thrust his sword into the box.</u>

The audience gasped *(How?)* nervously.

The audience gasped *(Where?)* throughout the theater.

The audience gasped *(When?)* when the magician thrust his sword into the box.

Even though all the adverbials in the preceding sentence follow the verb, there is really no fixed slot for most adverbials; in fact, movability is one of their most telling characteristics, and, for the writer, one of the most useful. In the preceding sentence, for example, there are several possibilities for ordering the three adverbials:

When the magician thrust his sword into the box, the audience nervously gasped throughout the theater.

Throughout the theater the audience gasped nervously when the magician thrust his sword into the box.

The position may depend on the writer's emphasis, on the rhythm of the sentence, on its relation to the previous sentence, or simply on the desire for sentence variety. Other structures that provide adverbial information are noun phrases and verb phrases. In this chapter we will take up each of these forms in its role as adverbial.

ADVERBS

The words we recognize as adverbs most readily are the **adverbs of manner**— the *-ly* words, such as *nervously, quietly,* and *suddenly.* These adverbs, derived from adjectives, usually tell "how" or "in what manner" about verbs:

They gasped nervously	=	in a nervous manner
They talked quietly	=	in a quiet manner
It stopped suddenly	=	in a sudden manner

The manner adverbs are probably the most movable of all the adverbials; they can appear before or after the verb, as well as at the beginning or end of the sentence:

<u>Suddenly</u> the wind shifted.

The wind <u>suddenly</u> shifted.

The wind shifted <u>suddenly</u>.

Notice that all three versions of the sentence are diagrammed the same; the only clue to word order is capitalization:

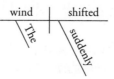

A single-word adverb can even come within the verb string, between the auxiliary word and the main verb:

The roof was <u>suddenly</u> blown off by a strong gust of wind.

Or between auxiliaries:

I have <u>actually</u> been working on my term project.

In all positions the manner adverbs can be marked by qualifiers, words such as *very, quite, so,* and *rather:*

<u>Quite suddenly</u> the crowd grew restless.

The old woman crooned <u>very softly</u>.

The airline employees handled our luggage <u>rather carelessly</u>.

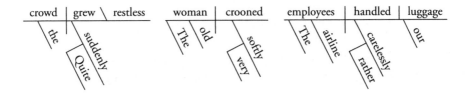

Like the adjectives they are derived from, these adverbs can be made comparative and superlative with *more* and *most:*

<u>More suddenly</u> than the police expected, the crowd grew restless.

The sails flapped <u>more and more furiously</u> as the wind grew stronger.

Besides the *-ly* adverbs, many other single-word adverbs provide information of time, place, frequency, and the like: *now, then, nowadays, today, often, always, sometimes, seldom, never, here, there, everywhere,* and many others.

I <u>still</u> jog <u>here</u> <u>sometimes</u>.

<u>Nowadays</u> I <u>seldom</u> swim.

Some of these, like the manner adverbs, can be compared and qualified:

I should jog <u>more often</u>.

Nowadays Judd and Betty jog <u>quite often</u>.

Although movability is a characteristic of all single-word adverbs, the various subclasses are bound by certain restrictions as to order. For example, in the following sentence, the adverbials of place and time cannot be reversed:

I am going <u>there</u> <u>now</u>.

*I am going <u>now</u> <u>there</u>.

<u>Now</u> I am going <u>there</u>.

*<u>There</u> I am going <u>now</u>.

The rules governing the order and movement of adverbs are quite complex, but as native speakers we are unaware of that complexity; our linguistic computers are programmed to follow the rules automatically.

ELL Issues   Always

The adverb *always* isn't quite as movable as some of the other time adverbials: It doesn't fit comfortably at the beginning or the end of the sentence. It likes the preverb position, where it may be given a beat of stress and has the meaning of *habitually*:

I always order a medium pizza.

Joe always works late on Fridays.

Sometimes in that position it is given extra heavy stress—and when it is, the speaker is probably expressing annoyance rather than explaining someone's habitual behavior:

Mac ALWAYS orders the extra large pizza.

Joe ALWAYS works late on Fridays.

Investigating Language   6.1

The adverbs of frequency, such as those in these six sentences, are among our most movable. In terms of meaning, some are positive and some negative.

1. My friends and I have pizza <u>frequently</u>.
2. <u>Occasionally</u> I order mushrooms.
3. <u>Sometimes</u> I order extra cheese.
4. <u>Seldom</u> do I order hot sausage.
5. <u>Never</u> will I order anchovies.
6. I <u>rarely</u> finish the whole thing.

The movability of these adverbs enables us to change the emphasis in subtle ways. Interestingly, however, the six adverbs in this list don't always behave alike. Notice what has happened in sentences 4 and 5: How do the auxiliaries in those two differ? What rule goes into effect with these "negative" adverbs? What will happen to sentence 6 when you attempt a shift to the opening position?

PREPOSITIONAL PHRASES

The **prepositional phrase** is our most common structure of modification, appearing regularly as a modifier of both nouns and verbs, as we have seen in our sample sentences throughout the chapters.

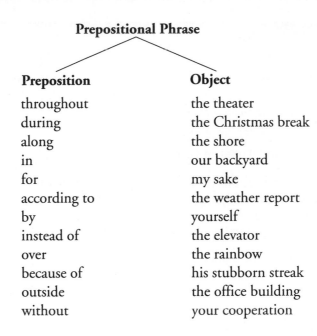

Prepositional Phrase

Preposition	Object
throughout	the theater
during	the Christmas break
along	the shore
in	our backyard
for	my sake
according to	the weather report
by	yourself
instead of	the elevator
over	the rainbow
because of	his stubborn streak
outside	the office building
without	your cooperation

As you learned in Chapter 3, the diagram for the adverbial prepositional phrase is always attached to the verb:

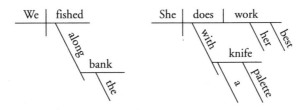

Some prepositional phrases have modifiers that qualify or intensify them, just as adjectives and adverbs do:

He arrived <u>shortly</u> before noon.

The house was built <u>directly</u> over the water.

In the diagram the modifier will be attached to the preposition:

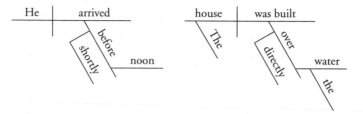

Sentences often have more than one adverbial prepositional phrase:

We hiked <u>in the woods</u> <u>for several hours</u> <u>on Saturday</u>.

And like adverbs, adverbial prepositional phrases can occupy several positions, with those referring to time often more movable than those referring to place, especially when both appear in the same sentence:

<u>For several hours</u> <u>on Saturday</u> we hiked in the woods.

<u>On Saturday</u> we hiked <u>in the woods</u> <u>for several hours</u>.

We are less likely to say:

<u>In the woods</u> we hiked <u>on Saturday</u> <u>for several hours</u>.

In general, an adverbial with main focus will occupy a slot at or near the end of the sentence. But no matter where in the sentence they appear—whether at the beginning, the middle, or the end—in the diagram the adverbial prepositional phrases will be attached to the verb:

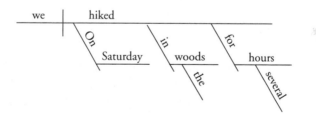

Exercise 17

Diagram the following sentences, paying particular attention to the adverbials. Your first step should be to identify the sentence pattern.

1. In winter we burn wood for our heat.
2. We can heat our house very efficiently in cold weather because of its good insulation.
3. My roommate just went to the store for a loaf of bread.
4. She'll be here in a minute.

5. In an interview on CNN, the chairman of the Federal Reserve discussed his views on both fiscal and monetary policy.

6. Computers throughout the world are constantly being invaded by viruses.

7. During an election year, the state of the economy inevitably becomes big news.

8. Man is by nature a political animal. [Aristotle]

Because prepositional phrases can modify both verbs and nouns, ambiguity is fairly common. The prepositional phrase in the following sentence, for example, could be interpreted as meaning either "with whom" or "which problems":

They discussed their problems <u>with the teacher</u>.

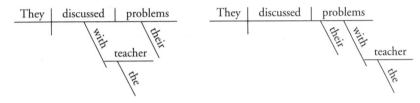

In speech, meaning is rarely a problem, and when it is, the listener can ask for clarification. But the solitary reader has no one to ask, "What do you mean?" or "How's that again?" So the writer has an obligation to make such questions unnecessary. Understanding when modifiers are ambiguous is important for writers; avoiding ambiguity is a requirement of clear writing.

Exercise 18

Rewrite each of the following sentences in two ways to show its two possible meanings:

1. I'm going to wax the car in the garage.

2. We watched the game on the porch.

3. Fred tripped his teammate with the bat.

4. Susan washed the stones she found in the river.

NOUNS AND NOUN PHRASES

Nouns and noun phrases that function adverbially form a fairly short list designating time, place, manner, and quantity. Here are some of them:

We walked <u>home</u>. _____

I'm leaving <u>Monday morning</u>. _____

I'm going <u>your way</u>. _____

<u>Every day</u> he studied <u>two hours</u>. _____

I travel <u>a great deal</u>. _____

We are flying <u>tourist class</u>. _____

I sent the package <u>airmail</u>. _____

The Boy Scouts hiked <u>single file</u> down the trail. _____

He arrived <u>this evening</u>. _____

These noun phrases may look suspiciously like direct objects or subject complements, but if you remember to think about the kind of information that adverbials contribute to the sentence, you should have no trouble in recognizing them as adverbials. In the blank following each sentence, write the adverbial question that the noun phrase answers.

These noun phrases work like prepositional phrases—like prepositional phrases with missing prepositions. The traditional grammarian labels them **adverbial objectives** and diagrams them as though they were the objects in prepositional phrases:

In some of these sentences the preposition is optional: (*on*) Monday morning, (*for*) two hours, (*by*) airmail, (*in*) single file. This method of diagramming the adverbial noun phrase acknowledges both its *form*—a noun headword on a horizontal line with or without modifiers—and its *function*—a modifier of the verb.

6.2

In Chapter 3, when you first studied the sentence patterns, you were advised to think in terms of the referents of the NPs in determining the sentence patterns. For example, you can distinguish Pattern V,

Carmen became a doctor [NP$_1$ V NP$_1$]

from Pattern VII,

Carmen called a doctor [NP$_1$ V NP$_2$]

by recognizing the relationship that the two NPs have to each other. That is, when the NP that follows the verb has a referent different from that of the subject, you can assume that it's a direct object and that the verb is transitive.

In Chapter 5, you learned about another test for determining if a verb is transitive: Can you make the sentence passive? Can you say "A doctor was called (by Carmen)"? In this case, the answer is yes. This means that the verb is transitive and the sentence is Pattern VII.

Now we come to a complication of sorts—sentences that look like Pattern VII:

We arrived home.

I work Sundays.

In both cases the verb is followed by an NP with a referent different from that of the subject. What test can you apply to show that *arrived* and *work* are not transitive verbs?

Here's a pair that might fool you. How can you show that they belong to different patterns? What tests can you apply?

Terry is flying the plane.

Terry is flying first class.

You'll want to bear in mind the kind of information that adverbials and direct objects contribute, the kinds of questions that they answer. Consider also the possibility of an optional preposition.

Exercise 19

Underline the adverbials in the following sentences and identify their forms. Then identify the sentence patterns. In making your judgments, you'll want to think about the kind of information that each slot contributes to the sentence.

1. Pete is working nights this week.
2. I was awake the whole night.
3. I'll see you soon.
4. This morning Pam threw away the leftover spaghetti.
5. George will do dishes next time.
6. I love weekends.
7. Bill works weekends.
8. At the first sign of winter the birds flew south.

VERB PHRASES

The most common form of the verb in an adverbial role is the **infinitive**, the base form of the verb with *to:*

>Mom cashed a check <u>to give Jody her allowance</u>.

>I went home early <u>to relax before the party</u>.

>Jennifer took on two paper routes <u>to earn money for camp</u>.

Remember that the infinitives—*to give, to relax,* and *to earn*—are not simply verbs with *to;* they are entire verb phrases, complete with complements and modifiers.

Underlying the first infinitive phrase is a Pattern VIII sentence:

>Mom gave Jody her allowance.

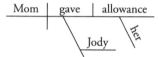

When we turn that predicate into an infinitive, the relationship of the complements and the verb stays the same, as the diagram of the infinitive shows. We have a Pattern VIII infinitive, an adverbial that tells why, in a Pattern VII sentence:

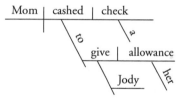

At first glance you may confuse the infinitive with a prepositional phrase, such as *to school* or *to the store; to* appears in both constructions, and the traditional diagrams are similar. But there is an important difference in form: In the prepositional phrase, a noun phrase follows *to;* in the infinitive, a verb phrase follows *to.*

Underlying the *relax* infinitive phrase in the second example is a Pattern VI sentence; underlying the *earn* phrase in the third example is a Pattern VII sentence:

Jennifer earned money for camp.   I relaxed before the party.

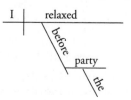

The Pattern VI sentence is now a Pattern VI infinitive phrase; the Pattern VII sentence is now a Pattern VII infinitive phrase. The *relax* phrase has been added to a Pattern VI sentence (*I went home early*), the *earn* phrase to a Pattern VII (*Jennifer took on two paper routes*):

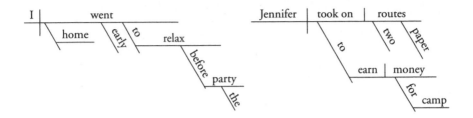

Note, too, that the subjects of the sentences are also the subjects of the infinitives.

In the first and third sentences, where the infinitive phrases follow nouns, *check* and *routes*, they may appear to modify those nouns. The clue that says otherwise is the meaning "in order to" that underlies almost all adverbial infinitives; they answer the question *why:*

> Mom cashed a check **in order to** give Jody her allowance.
>
> I went home early **in order to** relax before the party.
>
> Jennifer took on two paper routes **in order to** earn money for camp.

In fact, we often include *in order,* especially in the introductory position:

> In order to earn money for camp, Jennifer took on two paper routes.

In diagramming the expanded version, you can treat it like a phrasal preposition, with "in order to" on the diagonal line.

There are exceptions. Occasionally an infinitive functions adverbially without the meaning of "in order to," but such sentences are uncommon in speech:

> The detective glanced out the window only to see the suspect slip around the corner.
>
> I arrived at the auditorium only to find every seat taken.

These infinitives have an almost main-verb rather than adverbial quality. We could, and probably would, more often say:

> The detective glanced out the window and saw the suspect slip around the corner.
>
> I arrived at the auditorium and found every seat taken.

Other exceptions, which are fairly common idioms, occur with the verbs *come* and *live*. Here too the infinitive has main-verb status:

I've <u>come to believe</u> in UFOs.

I've <u>come to understand</u> your point of view.

You'll <u>live to regret</u> that remark.

Dangling Infinitives. We noted that the subject of the sentence is also the subject of the adverbial infinitive. When this is not the case, the infinitive is said to "dangle." In the following sentences, the infinitive phrases have no stated subject:

<u>To keep farm machinery in good repair</u>, a regular maintenance schedule is necessary.

For decades the Superstition Mountains in Arizona have been explored in order <u>to find the fabled Lost Dutchman Mine</u>.

Certainly the problem with these sentences is not a problem of communication; the reader is not likely to misinterpret their meaning. But in both cases a kind of fuzziness exists that can be cleared up with the addition of a subject for the infinitive:

<u>A farmer</u> needs a regular maintenance schedule <u>to keep the farm machinery in good repair</u>.

For decades <u>people</u> [or <u>adventurers</u> or <u>prospectors</u>] have explored the Superstition Mountains in Arizona <u>to find the fabled Lost Dutchman Mine</u>.

Exercise 20

Underline all the adverbial modifiers in the following sentences. Identify the sentence pattern of the main clause and any adverbial phrases. After doing that analysis, you should have no trouble diagramming the sentences.

1. Our cat often jumps up on the roof to reach the attic window.
2. Sometimes she even climbs the ladder to get there.
3. Last night my computer blinked ominously during an electrical storm.
4. I immediately turned it off.
5. We went to the mall last Saturday to check out the big sales.
6. Afterwards we stayed home to watch the playoff game with Uncle Dick.

CLAUSES

What is a **clause**? When is a clause adverbial?

The label *clause* denotes a form: a group of words with a subject and a predicate. The ten sentence patterns described in Chapter 3 have this form. The branching diagram, you'll recall, illustrates the two parts:

In other words, the ten sentence patterns are essentially clause patterns.

From the standpoint of mechanical conventions, we can define **sentence** as a word or group of words that begins with a capital letter and ends with a period or other terminal punctuation. A more complete definition would read as follows:

> A *sentence* is a word or group of words based on one or more subject–predicate, or clause, patterns; the written sentence begins with a capital letter and ends with terminal punctuation.

This definition eliminates "Wow!" and "The very idea!" and "Rats!" as sentences, but it includes commands, such as "Help!" with its underlying subject-predicate "You help me." All sentences, then, are clauses, *but not all clauses are sentences.*

At the opening of this chapter we saw a *when* clause in the sentence about the magician:

> The audience gasped nervously throughout the theater <u>when the magician thrust his sword into the box</u>.

Without the word *when*, this clause would be a complete sentence. The subordinator *when*, however, turns it into a **dependent clause**—in this case, a dependent clause functioning as an adverbial.

The term *dependent clause*, in contrast to **independent clause,** refers to any clause that is not itself a complete sentence. In later chapters we will see other dependent clauses, some that function as adjectivals, modifying nouns, and others as nominals, filling NP slots. In traditional terms, any sentence that includes a dependent clause of any kind is known as a **complex sentence**. A sentence with two or more independent clauses is a **compound sentence**. And one with a dependent clause and more than one independent clause is called **compound-complex**.

Another set of contrasting labels traditionally given to clauses (in addition to *independent* and *dependent*) is *main* and *subordinate*. It's accurate to say that the terms *main clause* and *independent clause* are synonymous—and, in fact, are used interchangeably. With their counterparts, however, there is a difference: *Dependent* and *subordinate* are not generally used interchangeably.

The term **subordinate clause** is often restricted to those dependent clauses that are introduced by subordinating conjunctions—words like *since* and *if* and *because* and *when*. That definition rules out the nominal clauses, which are introduced by expletives and interrogatives. It also rules out the adjectival clauses, which are introduced by relative pronouns and relative adverbs. We will see these other dependent clauses in the next two chapters.

The most common subordinators that introduce adverbial clauses are *if, after, because, before, since, so, until, when,* and *while.* Here in the adverbial chapter you will see examples of clauses that answer such adverbial questions as *when* and *why,* as you'll see in the following sentences:

> You should eat some breakfast <u>before you take that exam</u>.
>
> Pay close attention to your e-mail <u>because a virus could be lurking there</u>.

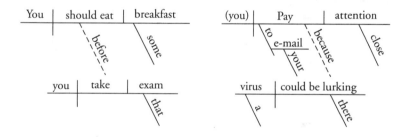

At first glance these sentence diagrams may look complicated, but as you can see, they are simply two sentence patterns connected by the subordinator that introduces the adverbial clause. Note too that the adverbial *because* clause itself includes an adverbial—the adverb *there.*

Exercise 21

Diagram the sentences, paying particular attention to all the sentence patterns, those of adverbial verb phrases and clauses, as well as of main clauses. Remember, too, that any adverbial that includes a verb (as clauses and verb phrases do) can also include other adverbials.

1. We will be visiting Yellowstone Park this summer, when we drive across the country in our new hybrid.

2. Last year we stayed at Silver Falls State Park for three days during our vacation in Oregon.

3. Whenever our dog sees lightning or hears thunder, he scratches frantically at the door to get our attention.

4. Is Mike really moving to Memphis to look for a job after he graduates?

5. I never take the subway home at night because my family worries about me.

6. After our building was burglarized twice in one month, we searched the ads to find a new apartment.

PUNCTUATION OF ADVERBIALS

You may have noticed in the examples that some opening adverbials are set off by commas and some are not. Their punctuation is sometimes a matter of choice, especially in the case of phrases. Generally a short prepositional phrase or noun phrase or an adverb will not be set off:

> Saturday morning we all pitched in and cleaned the garage.

> By noon we were exhausted.

> Hastily they gathered their books and left the room.

With longer prepositional phrases there is a choice:

> At the top of the hill the hikers sat down to rest.

> At the end of a long and exhausting morning, we all collapsed.

When the end of the adverbial slot is not readily apparent, the comma will be needed to prevent misreading:

> During the winter, vacation days are especially welcome.

> In the middle of the night, winds from the north brought subzero temperatures and the end of Indian summer.

The two opening adverbial structures that are *always* set off by commas are verb phrases and clauses—no matter what their length:

> To earn money for camp, Jennifer took on two paper routes.

> To succeed, you'll need self-discipline.

> When the speech finally ended, the audience broke into applause.

When an adverbial interrupts the verb phrase for a special effect, it will be set off by commas:

> I finally bought, on my birthday, a brand new car.

> The stranger asked me, quite openly, for my credit card number.

When the opening phrase is parenthetical—more clearly a comment on the whole sentence than a straightforward adverbial—then a comma is called for:

> According to all the polls, the incumbent was expected to win.

> On the other hand, not everyone was surprised at the outcome of the election.

> Luckily, no one was hurt.

The punctuation of sentence modifiers is discussed in Chapter 9.

Investigating Language 6.3

It's not at all unusual for inexperienced writers to punctuate subordinate clauses as complete sentences. It's probably the most common sentence fragment that teachers encounter:

> The children have been quite bored this summer. Because the swimming pool has been closed since July.

> Although we had a lot of rain last spring. Apparently the drought is not over yet.

Given what you know about sentence slots, can you explain why writers would make that mistake? In the second example, what's the difference between *although* and *apparently?*

If you listen carefully to the intonation of subordinate clauses and complete sentences, you will hear the difference. Read the clauses aloud:

> because you were here

> since Joe went away

> if he knows the truth

Now read them without the subordinator:

> You were here.

> Joe went away.

> He knows the truth.

You can probably hear the pitch of your voice dropping at the end of the last three. In the set with subordinators, your pitch would normally stay more level on the last word. (Even if you didn't read them with that contrast, you probably could do so to illustrate the difference.)

There's another way of reading that first group: as if they were answers to questions. In fact, such sentence fragments are common in conversation:

Q. Why did you come back?   A. Because you were here.

Q. How long have you lived alone? A. Since Joe went away.

Q. Will Mike ever forgive you?   A. If he knows the truth.

Does this reading help explain why writers make punctuation errors? What can a writing teacher do to help students understand and correct their punctuation?

CHAPTER 6
Key Terms

Adverb   Independent clause

Adverbial   Infinitive

Adverbial clause   Main clause

Adverbial infinitive   Movability

Adverbial noun phrase   Prepositional phrase

Adverbial prepositional phrase   Sentence

Ambiguity   Sentence fragment

Clause   Subordinate clause

Dangling infinitive   Subordinating conjunction

Dependent clause

Sentences
for PRACTICE

Underline the adverbials in the following sentences and identify their forms. For additional practice, identify the sentence patterns and diagram the sentences. Remember also to identify the sentence patterns of the adverbial verb phrases and clauses.

1. By the end of the fifth inning, the playoff game had already become boring.

2. When the fall foliage shows its colors in New England, thousands of tourists go there to enjoy nature's astonishing display.

3. On Halloween night the neighborhood children rang every doorbell on the block to fill their bags with goodies.

4. The recent crisis in mortgage foreclosures may have occurred because most home loans these days pass through a nationwide chain of brokers, lenders, and investors.

5. According to the National Highway Traffic Safety Administration, almost 80 percent of crashes and 65 percent of near crashes involve some form of driver inattention.

6. When Hurricane Katrina struck New Orleans in 2005, many sections of the city were completely wiped out.

7. The myth of the "sugar high" may finally be laid to rest by a new scientific study, according to a report in the *Los Angeles Times*.

8. Because of a lyme disease outbreak in several counties, fewer hunters applied for licenses last fall.

9. Cowards die many times before their death. [Shakespeare]

10. Be silent always when you doubt your sense. [Alexander Pope]

11. Diane must take 19 credits to graduate this semester.

12. Susan plans to stay home on Friday to fix a special gourmet dinner for her roommates.

13. During the month of December there will be dozens of holiday specials on television.

14. Where were you when I needed a shove to get my car to the garage for repairs?

15. Never in the field of human conflict was so much owed by so many to so few. [Winston Churchill]

QUESTIONS
?
for DISCUSSION

1. How would you analyze the following sentences, which were spoken in a television interview by an attorney whose client had been accused of murder?

> You're not talking a traffic ticket here. You're talking somebody's life.

In considering the sentence patterns and the referents of the noun phrases, you might think that *talking* is a transitive verb. Is it?

2. How do you account for the difference in meaning of the following sentences? Why is "in the mountains" so important?

> After his retirement, Professor Jones lived for six months in the mountains.

> After his retirement, Professor Jones lived for six months.

3. As you know, single-word adverbs are often movable, producing a number of variations in a sentence. How many acceptable variations can you produce by adding the adverb *frequently* to the following sentence?

> I have had colds this year.

Are there any slots in the sentence where *frequently* is clearly unacceptable?

CLASSROOM APPLICATIONS

1. Compose a cinquain (pronounced "sin-cane")—a five-line poem in which the number of syllables increases with each line—about an action or feeling; in other words, your topic is a verb. For the five lines, use the five forms of adverbials you studied in this chapter: adverb, prepositional phrase, noun phrase, verb phrase, and clause—preferably in that order. The title of your poem will be the verb (or, possibly, a verb + direct object or a verb + subject complement) that you're expanding with the five adverbials. Here is an example:

> **Waiting**
>
> Here
>
> For you
>
> One last time
>
> To plead my case
>
> Because you promised to listen

Here are some possible titles for you to try: Sleeping, Studying Grammar, Worrying, Playing Soccer, Feeling Special, Making Friends, Skiing, Thinking.

2. Shifting the position of certain adverbs—such as *only, almost, simply,* and *merely*—can alter the meaning in a sentence. The following sentences differ in meaning because of the different locations of *only:*

> Only Rupert crammed for the final exam. [Others did not cram.]
>
> Rupert only crammed for the final exam. [He didn't prepare in any other way.]
>
> Rupert crammed for the final exam only. [He didn't cram for quizzes or other tests.]

Shift the position of *only* in the following sentence; you should be able to put it in five different places.

> Adults may swim in the lake after 4 P.M.

Does the position of *only* change the meaning?

CHAPTER 7

Modifiers of the Noun: Adjectivals

CHAPTER PREVIEW

The traditional definition of *adjective* is "a word that modifies a noun." Like the word *adverb*, however, *adjective* refers to a word class with particular characteristics, not to a grammatical function. That traditional definition, then, turns out to be a definition not of *adjective* but rather of **adjectival**, the topic of this chapter. By now you've probably come to realize that the adjective is only one of many structures that modify nouns. (You've been seeing adjectival prepositional phrases since Chapter 2.) In addition to adjectives and prepositional phrases, you'll learn that verb phrases and clauses—and even other nouns—also modify nouns. Because of their frequency in the sentence and the variety of structures we use to expand them, noun phrases provide a remarkable range of possibilities for putting ideas into words. In this chapter the description of noun modification provides further evidence that our grammar is highly systematic.

As you know, a noun phrase occupies at least one slot in every sentence pattern—that of subject. In six of the ten patterns, noun phrases occupy one or more slots in the predicate as well: direct object, indirect object, subject complement, and object complement; the noun phrase also serves as the object of the preposition. Most of the NPs used in the sample sentences have been simple two-word phrases: determiner + headword *(the students, a scholar, an apple, their homework)*. But in the sentences we actually speak and write, the noun phrases are frequently expanded with modifiers—not only with adjectives, the basic noun modifier, but with other forms as well. In preheadword position we use nouns as well as adjectives—and, as we'll see later in the chapter, single-word participles:

> We live next door to an *orange* house.
>
> My cousin lives in a *brick* house.

In postheadword position we use prepositional phrases, participial phrases, and relative clauses:

> The house *on the corner* is new. (prepositional phrase)
>
> That house *covered with ivy* looks haunted. (verb phrase)
>
> This is the house *that Jack built*. (clause)

We can think of the noun phrase as a series of slots (in much the same way as we looked at the expanded verb), with the determiner and noun headword as the required slots and the modifiers before and after the headword as optional:

$$\text{NP} = \underline{\text{Det}} \quad (\underline{\ \ }) \quad (\underline{\ \ }) \quad \underline{\text{HEAD-}} \quad (\underline{\ \ }) \quad (\underline{\ \ }) \quad (\underline{\ \ })$$
$$\text{NOUN}$$
$$\text{WORD}$$

Filling the **headword** slot in the noun phrase is, of course, the noun, the word signaled by the determiner. (In the previous list of sample sentences, the word *house* fills the headword slot of the underlined noun phrases.) Traditional grammarians define noun as "the name of a person, place, or thing"—a definition based on meaning. That definition works in a limited way. But a better way to identify nouns, as you learned in Chapter 2, is to put your innate language ability to work: Is the word signaled by a determiner—or could it be? Can you make it plural? Also, an understanding of the system of pre- and postnoun modifiers in the noun phrase will make the identification of the noun headword an easy matter.

Recognition of the headword of the noun phrase can also help in preventing problems of subject–verb agreement. Such problems can arise when a postheadword modifier includes a noun itself:

> *The stack of instruction <u>forms</u> were misplaced.

> *The complicated instructions on the new income tax
> <u>form</u> really confuses me.

With just a few exceptions, it is the number, either singular or plural, of the headword in the subject noun phrase that dictates the form of the verb in the present tense. In the preceding sentences, the writer has used the wrong noun in making the verb selection. *Stack* and *instructions* are the headwords; *forms* and *form* are simply parts of postnoun modifiers.

The <u>stack</u> was misplaced.

The <u>stack of instruction forms</u> was misplaced.

The <u>instructions</u> really confuse me.

The <u>complicated instructions on the new income
tax form</u> really confuse me.

The exceptions to this system involve noun phrases with certain **collective nouns** and pronouns in which the modifier rather than the headword determines the verb:

<u>A bunch</u> of my friends <u>are</u> coming over for dinner.

<u>Some</u> of the cookies <u>are</u> missing.

<u>Some</u> of the cake <u>is</u> missing.

This topic, along with other details of determiners, is discussed further in the "Determiner" section of Chapter 13.

THE DETERMINER

The determiner, one of the structure classes, is the word class that signals nouns. This class includes *articles, possessive nouns, possessive pronouns, demonstrative pronouns,* and *numbers,* as well as a variety of other common words. When you see one of these words, you can be fairly sure you're at the beginning of a noun phrase.

The native speaker rarely thinks about determiners; they are automatic in speech. But for the writer, the determiner's role is something to think about. For example, as the first word of the noun phrase, and thus frequently the first word of the sentence and even of the paragraph, the determiner can provide a bridge, or transition, between ideas. The selection of that bridge can make subtle but important differences in emphasis:

<u>This</u> attempt at reconciliation proved futile.

<u>The</u> attempt at reconciliation . . .

<u>Their</u> attempt . . .

<u>One such</u> attempt . . .

<u>All their</u> attempts . . .

<u>Those</u> attempts . . .

In selecting determiners, writers have the opportunity not only to make such distinctions but also to help their readers move easily from one idea to the next in a meaningful way.

Some nouns, of course, are used without determiners: proper nouns (*John, Berkeley*), noncountable nouns (*salt, water*), abstract nouns (*justice, grief*), and sometimes plural count nouns (*apples, students*). You will read more about these categories in Chapter 12.

ADJECTIVES AND NOUNS

These two word classes generally fill the slots between the determiner and the headword. When the noun phrase includes both an adjective and a noun as modifiers, they appear in that order; they cannot be reversed:

DETERMINER	ADJECTIVE	NOUN	HEADWORD
the	beautiful		house
the		brick	house
our	little	neighbor	boy
an	ancient	marble	bathtub
that	nervous	test	pilot
Bill's	new	kitchen	table

We do not say, "Bill's kitchen new table" or "Our neighbor little boy."

It's fairly common in traditional descriptions of grammar to see these preheadword nouns labeled as adjectives. However, it is only their function that undergoes a change, not their form. Instead, we recognize what is called **functional shift**. This is the same phenomenon described in the previous chapter, where we saw nouns modifying verbs—in other words, functioning as adverbs do. They retain their identity as nouns while functioning adverbially.

The adjective slot frequently includes more than one adjective; all of them modify the headword:

the funny brown monkey

the little old man

You'll notice that there are no commas in the preceding noun phrases, even though there are several modifiers before the noun. But sometimes commas are called for. A good rule of thumb is to use a comma if it is possible to insert *and* between the modifiers. We would not talk about "a little and old man" or "a funny and brown monkey." However, we would say "a strange and wonderful experience," so in using these two adjectives without *and*, we would use a comma:

a strange, wonderful experience

That comma represents juncture in speech—a pause and slight upward shift in pitch. Read the following pair of sentences aloud and listen to the difference in your voice:

> On the table stood a little black suitcase.
>
> On the table stood an ugly, misshapen suitcase.

In general, the system calls for a comma between two adjectives when they are of the same class—for instance, when they are both abstract qualities such as "strange" and "wonderful" or "ugly" and "misshapen." However, in the earlier example—*funny brown monkey*—the adjectives *funny* and *brown* are not alike: "funny" is an abstract, changeable quality, a subjective quality; "brown" is a concrete, permanent quality.

The adjective can also be qualified or intensified:

the extremely bright young lady

a really important career decision

Prenoun Participles.   We can also use participles to fill the adjective slot between the determiner and the headword:

> Our <u>snoring</u> visitor kept the household awake.
>
> The <u>barking</u> dog across the street drives us crazy.
>
> A <u>rolling</u> stone gathers no moss.

Because participles are verbs, they are also commonly modified by adverbs:

> Our <u>loudly snoring</u> visitor kept the household awake.
>
> The <u>peacefully sleeping</u> baby was a joy to watch.
>
> We submitted a <u>carefully conceived</u> plan to the administration.

Sometimes we have occasion to use a hyphen to make it clear that the adverbial modifies the prenoun participle, not the headword:

> a half-baked idea
>
> the Spanish-speaking community
>
> a well-developed paragraph
>
> the fast-moving train

The hyphen rule here is fairly straightforward: The *-ly* adverbs (such as *loudly, peacefully,* and *carefully*) do not take hyphens; other adverbs (such as *well* and *fast*) do take hyphens.

Other classes of words also need hyphens when the first modifier applies not to the headword but to the second modifier:

high-technology industries

two-word verbs

all-around athletes

free-form sculpture

Another occasion for hyphens in the preheadword position occurs when we use a complete phrase in the adjective slot:

an off-the-wall idea

the end-of-the-term party

a middle-of-the-road policy

my back-to-back exams

When a phrasal modifier fills the subject complement or an ending adverbial slot in the sentence pattern, however, the hyphens are generally omitted:

Our party will be <u>at the end of the term</u>.

My exams during finals week are <u>back to back</u>.

In certain idioms they would probably be retained:

Her idea seemed off-the-wall to me.

The policy he subscribes to is strictly middle-of-the-road.

The position in the sentence can also affect the earlier hyphenated examples:

The paragraph was well developed.

The industry did research in high technology.

Investigating Language **7.1**

Both hyphens and commas can make an important difference in meaning.

A. You can hyphenate the following sentence in two ways to show two different meanings:

1. The researchers studied ten year old children.
2. The researchers studied ten year old children.

Hyphenate sentence 1 to make clear that the children are of school age. In sentence 2 use the hyphen to show that the children are still babies.

B. Explain the difference the comma makes in terms of both meaning and word function:

Becky is a pretty, intelligent student.

Diagram the sentence in two ways, showing the meaning with and without the comma.

Exercise 22

A. Label the determiner (D) and headword (H) in each underlined noun phrase in the following paragraph. Identify the form (adjective, noun, participle) of any modifiers that fill the slots between the determiner and headword.

> Born in England, Joshua Abraham Norton migrated to San Francisco in 1849, where he became <u>a highly successful land speculator</u>. By 1853, he was worth an estimated quarter of a million dollars—a wealthy man, even by <u>today's standards</u>. But when he attempted to corner the market on rice, he lost <u>his entire fortune</u>. <u>This financial disaster</u> affected his mind, and on September 17, 1859, he sent to <u>a local newspaper</u> an announcement that he had been chosen the Emperor of the United States. The city was amused and accepted <u>their newly discovered eccentric</u>; he ate without paying in restaurants, and theaters reserved special seats for him. Wearing <u>an old blue military uniform</u> with epaulets and a hat with feathers, he attended <u>every public function and meeting</u>. <u>A large upholstered chair</u> was always reserved for him in <u>the state legislature</u>. Norton even issued <u>his own imperial bonds</u>, <u>each note</u> granting the bearer <u>the face value</u> plus seven percent interest at maturity, apparently in 1900. But Emperor Norton died on January 8, 1880, on his way to <u>a scientific conference</u>. <u>His lavish funeral</u> was attended by a reported thirty thousand people.

B. Underline the determiner and headword of each noun phrase in the following sentences. Identify the form of any modifiers that fill slots between them. Punctuate the noun phrases with commas and hyphens, if necessary.

1. The department's personnel committee met in the main office this morning.

2. Our whole family is impressed with the new Sunday brunch menu at the cafeteria.

3. Serena's daughter found an expensive looking copper colored bracelet in the subway station.

4. The bicycle safety commission will discuss the new regulations at their regular meeting this noon.

5. Her lovely gracious manner was apparent from the start.

6. Any mother could easily perform the job of several air traffic controllers.

7. The rising interest rates should be a serious concern for every cost conscious citizen.

The postheadword position in the noun phrase may contain modifiers of many forms; when there is more than one, they appear in this order:

		Prepositional	Participial	Relative
Det	HEADWORD	Phrase	Phrase	Clause
the	airplane	on the far runway		
			waiting to take off	
				which was hijacked by terrorists

In this section we will look at all of these structures that follow the headword, beginning with the most common postnoun modifier, the prepositional phrase.

PREPOSITIONAL PHRASES

The adjectival prepositional phrase, which modifies a noun, is in form identical to the adverbial prepositional phrase described in Chapter 6. In its adjectival role the prepositional phrase identifies the noun headword in relation to time, place, direction, purpose, origin, and the like:

The *house* <u>on the corner</u> is new.

The security *guard* <u>in our building</u> knows every tenant personally.

I have always admired the lovely *homes* <u>along Sparks Street</u>.

The *meeting* <u>during our lunch hour</u> was a waste of time.

Jack is a *man* <u>of many talents</u>.

An adjectival prepositional phrase helps to identify a noun or pronoun by answering the questions "Which one?" or "What kind of?" Which house is new? The one *on the corner*. Jack is what kind of man? One *of many talents*.

Because the prepositional phrase itself includes a noun phrase, the adjectival prepositional phrase demonstrates the recursiveness of the language—the embedding of one structure in another of the same kind. Such recursiveness occurs in many parts of the sentence: a clause within a clause, a noun phrase within a noun phrase, a verb phrase within a verb phrase. In the case of the adjectival prepositional phrase, we nearly always have a noun phrase within a noun phrase. And we needn't stop with one embedding; we could continue branching that NP at the bottom of the diagram with another Det + N + PP, which would produce yet another NP:

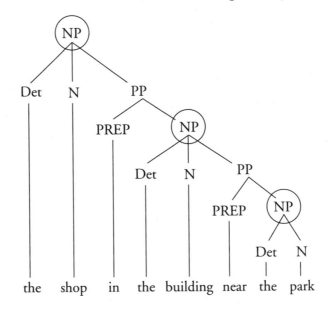

Such strings, though fairly common, especially at the end of the sentence, are sometimes open to ambiguity:

> My sister manages the flower shop in the new brick
> building near the park on Center Street.

Our linguistic computer most readily associates a modifier with the nearest possible referent:

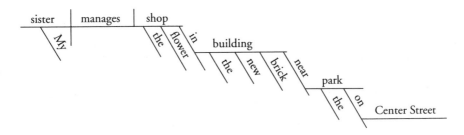

If a different meaning is intended—if, for example, it is the building rather than the park that is on Center Street—the writer must make that clear: "the flower shop in the brick building on Center Street that is near the park."

Exercise 23

Underline the adjectival prepositional phrases in the following sentences. If any of them are ambiguous, rewrite them in two ways to show their two possible meanings unambiguously.

1. A young man with a cast on his left foot hobbled down the street.
2. I will meet you in the lobby of the museum near the visitors' information booth.
3. The party after the game at Bob's house must have been a riot.
4. The threat of computer viruses is causing concern among scientists.
5. The computer world is being threatened by an enemy from within.
6. The textbook for my science course was written by a Nobel laureate from Stanford.
7. The bank will make loans to businesses of any size.
8. The candidates with the weakest qualifications usually have the most complaints about the selection process.

RELATIVE CLAUSES

Like the adverbial clause that modifies verbs, the **relative clause** (also called the **adjectival clause**) is a dependent clause. In its adjectival function, the relative clause identifies the noun or pronoun it modifies—and almost always appears immediately after that noun or pronoun:

> The arrow <u>that has left the bow</u> never returns.

> Relatives are persons <u>who live too near and visit too often</u>.

Like adjectival prepositional phrases, relative clauses answer the questions "Which one?" or "What kind of?" Which arrow? The one *that has left the bow*. What kind of persons? Those *who live too near and visit too often*.

In form, a relative clause is a sentence pattern, complete with a subject and a predicate. The only difference between a relative clause and a complete sentence is the introductory word, the relative pronoun (*who, whose, whom, which*, or *that*). Like other pronouns, the relative pronoun has an **antecedent**, the noun that it refers to and replaces. The traditional diagram clearly shows the relationship of the clause to the noun it modifies:

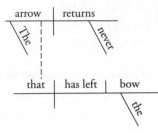

Three features of the relative pronoun will help you to recognize the relative clause: (1) The relative pronoun renames the headword of the noun phrase in which it appears; in our example, *arrow* is the antecedent of *that*. (2) The relative pronoun fills a sentence slot in its own clause; in the example, *that* is in the subject slot. And (3) the relative pronoun introduces the clause, no matter what slot it fills.

Let's look at another example of a relative clause introduced by *that*, perhaps our most common relative pronoun:

This is the house *that Jack built.*

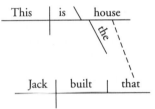

As the diagram shows, *that* opens its clause, even though it functions as the direct object.

In referring to people, we generally use *who* rather than *that* ; and when it functions as an object in its clause, the form we use is *whom*, the **objective case**:

A man <u>whom I knew in the army</u> phoned me this morning.

The clerk at the post office, <u>to whom I complained about our mail service</u>, was very patient with me.

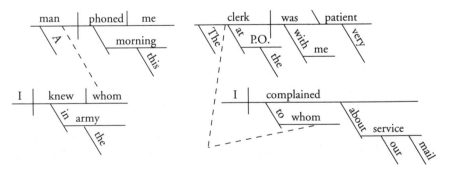

Notice in the second preceding example that *whom* is the object of a preposition. You may have noticed that the preposition, not the relative pronoun, is the first word in the relative clause. This is the only instance where the relative is not the immediate clause opener—that is, when the relative pronoun is the object of a preposition.

The following sentence illustrates the **possessive case** of *who*. Like other possessive pronouns (such as *my, his, their*), *whose* functions as a determiner in its clause:

The student <u>whose notes I borrowed</u> was absent today.

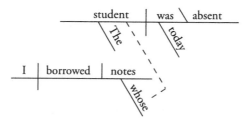

The dotted line connects the pronoun to its antecedent, *the student*; in other words, "whose notes" means "the student's notes."

Another common relative pronoun is *which*:

Huckleberry Finn, <u>which we read in high school</u>, is a classic <u>that often causes controversy</u>.

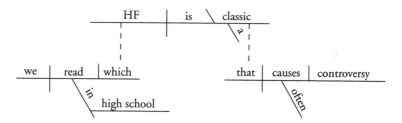

You'll read more about *which* later in the chapter, in connection with punctuation.

The following example illustrates an important feature of sentences in which the relative pronoun *that* is the direct object in its clause:

You can choose a color <u>that you like</u>.

You will note that this sentence would be equally grammatical without *that*:

You can choose a color you like.

The relative *that* is often deleted, but the deletion is possible only when the pronoun functions as an object in its clause, not when it acts as the subject.

The objective case relative, *whom*, like the relative *that,* can often be deleted too:

> A woman [whom] my mother knew in high school has invited me to dinner.

Even though the relative pronoun is deleted, it will have a place on the diagram; it is "understood." The deleted word can be shown in brackets, or it can be replaced by an x:

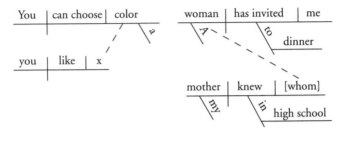

Exercise 24

Underline the relative clauses in the following sentences. Identify (1) the noun that the clause modifies; (2) the role of the relative pronoun in its clause; and (3) the sentence pattern of the clause.

1. A rattlesnake that doesn't bite teaches you nothing. [Jessamyn West]
2. A person who plays alone always wins. [Sicilian proverb]
3. Come with me to the concert that the jazz club is sponsoring.
4. The gift she gave the bride and groom attracted a lot of attention.
5. A weed is a plant whose virtues have not been discovered. [Ralph Waldo Emerson]
6. What do you say about a couple of kids who have everything but good sense?
7. Terry received congratulations from people whom she had not seen in years.
8. I skimmed the last article, in which the connection between automobile exhaust and acid rain is explained.
9. The shed, which was damp and drafty, at least provided shelter from the rain.
10. This is the cat that killed the rat that ate the malt that lay in the house that Jack built.

Note: Your teacher may also want you to diagram these sentences. Having analyzed the clauses, you've done most of the work already!

All the relative pronouns fill slots in the clauses that nouns normally fill. However, some adjectival clauses are introduced not by relative pronouns but by the **relative adverbs** *where, when,* and *why.* In these clauses the relative adverb replaces an adverbial structure in its clause. The relative adverb *where* introduces clauses that modify nouns of place:

Newsworthy events rarely happen in the small *town* <u>where I was born</u>.

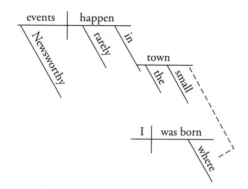

Note in the diagram that the relative adverb *where* modifies the verb *was born* in its own clause; however, the clause itself is adjectival, modifying *town.*

When clauses modify nouns of time:

> I will be nervous until next *Tuesday,* <u>when results of the audition will be posted</u>.

Why clauses modify the noun *reason*:

> I understand the *reason* <u>why Margo got the lead in the spring play</u>.

Where, when, and *why* clauses are often equally acceptable, and sometimes smoother, without the relative adverb:

> I understand the reason <u>Margo got the lead</u>.

> I will be nervous until the day <u>the results are posted</u>.

PARTICIPIAL PHRASES

You'll recall that the formula describing the noun phrase includes three postheadword modifiers:

			(1)	(2)	(3)
			Prepositional	Participial	Relative
<u>Det</u> <u>Adj</u> <u>Noun</u>	<u>HEADWORD</u>		<u>Phrase</u>	<u>Phrase</u>	<u>Clause</u>

You've been seeing the prepositional phrase as an adjectival since Chapter 2:

> the neighbors <u>from Korea</u>

> the president's announcement <u>about the meeting</u>

And in the previous section you studied the relative clause:

the man <u>who lives across the street</u>

If we change the form of the verb in the relative clause by adding *be* + *-ing*,

the man <u>who is living across the street</u>,

we can easily demonstrate that the adjectival **participial phrase** is essentially a reduced relative clause:

the man <u>living across the street</u>

This noun phrase, with its participial phrase as a modifier, will fit in any nominal slot of the sentence:

I know <u>the man living across the street</u>. (direct object)

<u>The man living across the street</u> seems very nice. (subject)

I often visit with <u>the man living across the street</u>. (object of the preposition)

Like the other adjectivals, in the diagram the participial phrase is attached below the noun. The participial phrase begins on a diagonal line, which then bends to become a horizontal line. The horizontal line will accommodate any complements and/or modifiers the participle may have:

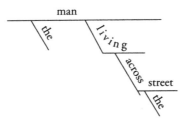

You'll notice that the diagram of the participial phrase looks exactly like the predicate of the sentence (or relative clause) that underlies it:

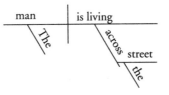

The clause—and the participial phrase—are Pattern VI.

Here are two further examples of participial phrases, the first a transitive verb, the second a linking verb:

The students <u>taking the SAT</u> look nervous.

Do you recognize those boys <u>acting so foolish</u>?

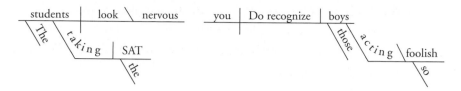

Note that the participles are diagrammed exactly like the predicates of the sentences that underlie them:

Again, you will recognize that the participial phrases are reduced versions of clauses:

> The students <u>who are taking the SAT</u> look nervous.

> Do you recognize the boys <u>who are acting so foolish</u>?

The only difference between the verb in the clause and the verb in the participial phrase is the presence or absence of the auxiliary *be* and tense.

As the examples illustrate, transitive participles will have direct objects (taking *the SAT*), and linking-verb participles will have subject complements (acting *so foolish*). And all participles, just like verbs in all the sentence patterns, may be modified by adverbials of various forms.

In the following sentence, we have added the adverbial noun phrase *this morning*:

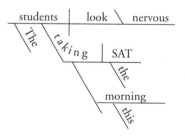

Here are three key points that will help you understand participles:

1. Verbs from all four classes—*be*, linking, intransitive, and transitive—can function as participles.

2. The noun phrases in all the NP slots can include participles (or participial phrases) as modifiers: direct objects, subject complements, object complements, indirect objects, objects of prepositions, as well as subjects.

3. The noun that the participle modifies is its subject; that is, the relationship between the headword of the noun phrase in which the participle is embedded and the participle itself is a subject-verb relationship. In the diagram, the participle is connected to its own subject.

Exercise 25

Turn each of the following sentences into a noun phrase that includes a participial phrase as a postnoun modifier. Use the noun phrase in a sentence.

Example: Two dogs are fighting over the bone.
   NP: two dogs fighting over the bone
   Sentence: I recognize those two dogs fighting over the bone.

1. An expensive sports car is standing in the driveway.
2. The baby is sleeping upstairs in the crib.
3. The fans are lining up at the ticket office.
4. The students are searching the Internet.
5. The fullback was charging through the line.
6. The teachers are walking the picket line.

Passive Participles.   The participles we have seen so far are the *-ing* form of the verb (traditionally called the present participle); as you would expect, the clauses underlying them are also in the active voice. Another common form of the adjectival participle is the *-en* form. This form, which is traditionally called the past participle, might be more accurately called the "passive participle."

The houses <u>designed by Frank Lloyd Wright</u> are national treasures.

The car <u>being driven by the front-runner</u> has developed engine trouble.

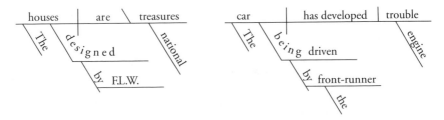

Like the *-ing* participles, the *-en* participles are also reduced clauses:

> The houses <u>that were designed by Frank Lloyd Wright</u> are national treasures.

> That car <u>that is being driven by the front-runner</u> has developed engine trouble.

Both of these underlying relative clauses are in the passive voice. (Note that in the last example, the active voice version of the verb includes *be* + *-ing: is driving.* When *be* + *-en* is added to make it passive, the resulting verb has two forms of *be* as auxiliaries: *is being driven.*)

Remember, we produce a passive sentence by adding *be* + *-en* to the verb, so a passive verb is always the *-en* form. When we turn such sentences into participles, they will automatically have the *-en* form.

The Participle as Object Complement. You'll recall from Chapter 3 that two of the required slots in the sentence patterns, two functions, are filled by adjectivals: the subject complement slot in Patterns II and IV and the object complement slot in Pattern IX. In most cases, these slots are filled by adjectives:

> The teacher seems <u>angry</u>. (subject complement)

> We found the teacher <u>unreasonable</u>. (object complement)

We did see some examples, however, of prepositional phrases as subject complements:

> The teacher was <u>in a bad mood</u> this morning.

> The piano sounds <u>out of tune</u>.

We could easily come up with prepositional phrases as object complements as well:

> We found the teacher <u>in a bad mood</u> this morning.

> I consider your behavior <u>out of line</u>.

The object complement slot can also be filled by a participle:

> I could feel my heart <u>beating faster</u>.

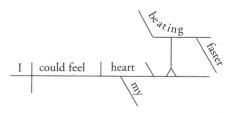

Again, we make use of the pedestal in the diagram to place the participle's characteristic bent line in the object complement slot on the main line.

What this diagram says is that "my heart beating faster" is not a single noun phrase; it is two separate structures. You can test this conclusion by substituting a pronoun for the direct object:

I could feel <u>it</u> beating faster.

Clearly there are two slots following the verb, both of which are required for the sense of the sentence.

The distinction between the participle as object complement—a separate slot—and the participle as a modifier in the direct object slot may be subtle:

The police found the murdered witness.

The police found the witness murdered.

Again, you can determine the number of slots following the verb by substituting pronouns:

The police found him.

The police found him murdered.

A fairly reliable way to determine if the sentence has an object complement is to insert *to be*:

I could feel my heart to be beating faster.

The police found him to be murdered.

The resulting sentences may not be the most natural way of expressing the object complement, but they are certainly grammatical.

Movable Participles.   We can think of the postheadword slot in the noun phrase as the "home base" of the participle, as it is of the relative clause. But unlike the clause, the participial phrase can be shifted to the beginning of the sentence when it modifies the subject:

<u>Built by Frank Lloyd Wright in 1936</u>, the Kauffman house at Fallingwater is one of Western Pennsylvania's most valued architectural treasures.

<u>Carrying heavy packs on their backs</u>, the hikers were exhausted when they reached the summit of Black Butte.

The participial phrase that modifies the subject can also be shifted to the end of the sentence:

The students cheered noisily for the basketball team, <u>standing up throughout the game</u>.

In both of these alternative positions, at the beginning or end of the sentence, the participial phrase gets special emphasis. It is commonly known as a **free modifier**. Clearly, however, it has a connection to its subject.

No matter where it appears in the sentence, the adjectival participial phrase is attached in the diagram to its own subject, the headword of the noun phrase in which it appears:

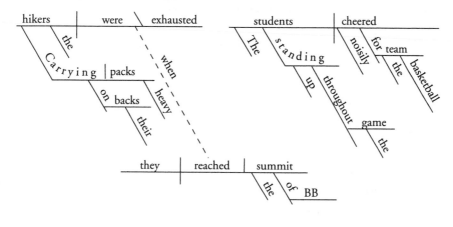

Exercise 26

Underline the participles and participial phrases in the following sentences; identify their sentence patterns. Diagram.

1. The award given every year to the outstanding volunteer has been announced.
2. Being a philosopher, she can propose a problem for every solution.
3. He has all the gall of a shoplifter returning an item for a refund.
4. The hostess gave the departing guests some leftover food for their pets.
5. Finding the price reasonable, they rented the apartment on the spot.
6. Congress shall make no law abridging the freedom of speech or of the press.
7. They planned the class picnic for Saturday, hoping for good weather.
8. The university will not fund research involving genetic manipulation.
9. The special computer workshops held on campus last weekend were designed for students majoring in business.

10. The teachers' union has finally approved the last two disputed
    sections of the contract offered by the school district.

Dangling Participles. The introductory participial phrase provides a
good way to add variety to sentences, to get away from the standard subject opener. But it carries an important restriction:

*The participle can open the sentence only when its subject is also the
subject of the sentence and is located in regular subject position.
Otherwise, the participle dangles.*

A dangling participle, in other words, is a verb in search of a subject:

*Having found the rent reasonable, the apartment turned out to be
    perfect.

(It was not the apartment that found the rent reasonable!)

*Standing nervously on the platform, a barrage of ripe tomatoes
    suddenly pelted the candidate.

(The tomatoes weren't standing on the platform!)
    A common source of the dangling participle is the sentence with a
"delayed subject." Two common delayers are the *there* transformation and
the **anticipatory** *it*:

*Having moved the patio furniture into the garage, there was no
    longer room for the car.

*Knowing how much work I had to do yesterday, it was good of
    you to come and help.

In the last sentence the subject of the participle, *you,* is there, but it appears
in the predicate rather than in the usual subject position. As readers and
listeners, we process sentences with certain built-in expectations. We
expect the subject of an introductory verb to be the first logical noun or
pronoun.
    Incidentally, moving a participle to the end of the sentence will not
solve the problem if the subject has been omitted. Even there, we expect
the subject of the sentence to be the subject of the participle as well:

*There was no longer room for the car, having moved the patio fur-
    niture into the garage.

Often the most efficient way to revise such sentences is to expand the
participial phrase into a complete clause:

After we moved the patio furniture into the garage, there was no
    longer room for the car.

It was good of you to come and help yesterday <u>when you learned how much work I had to do</u>.

Another common source of the dangling participle is the passive sentence:

*Having worked hard since 6:00 A.M., the project was completed before noon.

Here the problem arises because the passive transformation has deleted the agent of the verb *completed*, which is also the subject of the participle. Transforming the sentence into the active voice will solve the problem:

Having worked hard since 6:00 A.M., *we* completed the project before noon.

Exercise 27

Rewrite the following sentences to eliminate the dangling participles.

1. Needing considerable repair, my parents were able to buy the house for little money.
2. Installing a new program, all other applications should be turned off.
3. Having misunderstood the assignment, my paper got a low grade.
4. Covered with the grime of centuries, the archeologists could not decipher the inscription.
5. Searching for change in her purse, the bus left without her.
6. Having spent four hours on the operating table, a double bypass was performed on the patient's severely blocked arteries.
7. Once considered only an average player, Chris's game has improved greatly in the last three months.
8. Breaking in through the window of the girls' dormitory, the dean of men surprised several members of the football team.
9. Pickled, I'll eat anything.
10. Seen from miles away, you might mistake the mountain for a cloud.

Participles as Adverbials. Although we have traditionally thought of the participle as an adjectival (and that is certainly its more common role), some participles and participial phrases clearly have an adverbial function, providing information of time, place, reason, and manner, as other adverbials do:

My uncle made a fortune <u>selling real estate</u>. (*How?*)

The kids came <u>running out of the house</u>. (*How? Where?*)

The adverbial participial phrase is diagrammed below the verb, as other adverbials are:

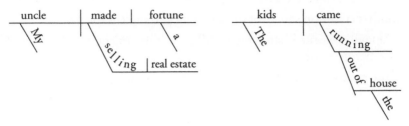

Some participial phrases have characteristics of both adverbials and adjectivals:

<u>Standing near a huge puddle</u>, Jan got thoroughly splashed.

Here the opening verb phrase could be expanded into either an adjectival *who* clause (Jan, *who was standing near a huge puddle*, got thoroughly splashed) or an adverbial *while* clause (*While she was standing near a huge puddle*, Jan got thoroughly spashed). The sentence would be correctly analyzed either way.

PUNCTUATION OF CLAUSES AND PARTICIPLES

The question regarding punctuation of clauses and participles is the question of **restrictive** versus **nonrestrictive modifiers**. Put simply, the question is "Should I set off the phrase or clause with commas?"

In answering this question, the writer must think about the referent of the noun being modified. Is it clear to the reader? In the case of a singular noun, is there only one possible person (or place or thing, etc.) to which the noun can refer? In the case of plurals, are the limits understood? If there is only one, the modifier cannot restrict the noun's meaning any further: The modifier is therefore nonrestrictive and will be set off by commas. It might be useful to think of these commas as parentheses and the modifier as optional; if it's optional, we can assume it's not needed to make the referent of the noun clear.

If the referent of the noun is not clear to the reader—if there is more than one possible referent or if the limits are not known—the purpose of the modifier is quite different: to restrict the meaning of the noun. Thus the modifier in this case is restrictive and is not set off by commas. You may find the terms *defining* and *commenting* easier to understand than *restrictive* and *nonrestrictive*.[1] Does the modifier define (restrict) the noun or does it merely comment on (not restrict) it?

[1.]These terms are used by Francis Christensen in *Notes Toward a New Rhetoric* (New York: Harper & Row, 1967), pp. 95 ff.

Notice the difference in the punctuation of the following pair of sentences:

> The football players wearing shiny orange helmets stood out in the crowd.

> The football players, wearing shiny orange helmets, stood out in the crowd.

In the first sentence the purpose of the participial phrase is to define *which* football players stood out in the crowd. We could illustrate the situation by depicting a crowd of football players on the field, some of whom are wearing *shiny orange helmets*; they are noticeable—they *stand out in the crowd* of football players—because the others are wearing drab, dark helmets or perhaps no helmets at all. In the second sentence the modifier merely comments on the players—it does not define them. An illustration of this situation might show a group of orange-helmeted football players signing autographs in a crowd of children; those players would stand out in that crowd with or without orange helmets. The modifier does *not* tell *which* football players stood out in the crowd; they *all* did. (And, incidentally, they were all wearing orange helmets.)

Context, of course, will make a difference. What does the reader already know? For example, out of context the clause in the following sentence appears to be restrictive:

> The president <u>who was elected in 1932</u> faced problems that would have overwhelmed the average man.

Ordinarily we would say that the noun phrase *the president* has many possible referents; the *who* clause is needed to make the referent clear; it defines and restricts *the president* to a particular man, the one elected in 1932. But what if the reader already knows the referent?

> Franklin Delano Roosevelt took office at a time when the outlook for the nation was bleak indeed. The president, <u>who was elected in 1932</u>, faced decisions that would have overwhelmed the average man.

In this context the clause is simply commenting; the referent of the noun phrase *the president* is already defined by the time the reader gets to it. Many times, however, context alone is an insufficient determinant; only the writer knows if the clause defines or comments. The reader can only take the writer's word—or punctuation—at face value:

> The rain began with the first drumbeat. Only the band members <u>who were wearing rain gear</u> stayed reasonably dry. Everyone else at the parade, spectators and marchers alike, got wet.

Without commas the clause restricts the meaning of the noun phrase *the band members*; it defines those band members who stayed dry. With commas the clause suggests that all the band members were wearing rain gear.

In the case of participial phrases that modify the subject, the writer has a useful test for deciding if they are defining or commenting: Can the modifier be shifted to the beginning or end of the sentence? If that shift does not change the meaning, the modifier is nonrestrictive, simply commenting. The restrictive participial phrase will remain within the noun phrase, whereas the nonrestrictive phrase can introduce the sentence and sometimes follow it:

<u>Wearing rain gear</u>, the band members stayed reasonably dry.

In the case of the relative clause, the relative pronoun provides some clues for punctuation:

1. The adjectival *that* clause is always restrictive; it is never set off by commas.

2. The *which* clause is generally nonrestrictive; it is set off by commas. You can test a *which* clause by substituting *that*. If it works, the clause is restrictive and should not have commas, and if not, it is nonrestrictive. NOTE: There is an exception to this general rule about *that* in restrictive and *which* in nonrestrictive clauses: Only *which* functions as the object of a preposition; *that* does not. So the relative pronoun in that position will be *which* whether the clause is restrictive or nonrestrictive:

    I probably won't get either of the jobs for which I applied.
    Pat got a terrific new job, for which I also applied.

3. If the relative pronoun can be deleted, the clause is restrictive:

    The bus (that) I ride to work is always late.
    The woman (whom) I work with is always early.

The next two rules apply to both clauses and phrases:

1. After any proper noun the modifier will be nonrestrictive.

    Herbert Hoover, elected president in 1928, was the first president born west of the Mississippi River.

2. After any common noun that has only one possible referent, the modifier will be nonrestrictive:

    My youngest sister, who lives in Oregon, is much more domestic than I.

    The highest mountain in the world, which resisted the efforts of climbers until 1953, looks truly forbidding from the air.

Exercise 28

Identify the postheadword modifiers in the following sentences as restrictive or nonrestrictive by adding commas if needed.

1. Samuel Johnson who published his famous dictionary in 1755 defined a lexicographer as "a harmless drudge."
2. The town where I was born which has a population of 3,000 offers very little in the way of entertainment for teenagers.
3. No one could identify the man standing in the hotel window.
4. Naphtha which is highly flammable is no longer used in dry cleaning.
5. As director of personnel you must often make decisions that are painful to you and your employees.
6. Any book printed before 1501 is called an incunabulum which literally means "swaddling clothes."
7. The hurricane bearing down on Florida destroyed the homes of many residents who live along the coast.
8. Those who wish to sing always find a song.
9. Con men can always find people who are trusting, greedy, and foolish.
10. Derek Jeter leaping high in the air speared the line drive that would have won the game.

MULTIPLE MODIFIERS

So far most of the sentences used to illustrate adjectivals have had a single postheadword modifier, either a clause or a phrase. But we often have more than one such modifier, and when we do, the order in which they appear is well defined: prepositional phrase, participial phrase, relative clause:

the security guard [in our building] [who checks out the visitors]

the woman [from London] [staying with the Renfords]

the DC-10 [on the far runway] [being prepared for takeoff] [which was hijacked by a group of terrorists]

In a traditional diagram, all the noun modifiers in both pre-and post-position are attached to the headword:

A change in the order of modifiers would change the meaning:

> the DC-10 being prepared for takeoff, which was hijacked by a
> group of terrorists on the far runway

Here the prepositional phrase no longer specifies *which* DC-10; it has become an adverbial modifier in the relative clause, modifying *was hijacked.* In this version *DC-10* has only two postheadword modifiers, not three:

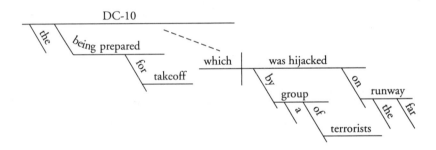

Just as ambiguity may result from a string of prepositional phrases, these multiple modifiers, too, are sometimes open to more than one interpretation:

> the driver of the bus standing on the corner
>
> a friend of my sister who lives in Tampa

In context these noun phrases may or may not be clear to the reader. In any case, the ambiguity is easily avoided:

> the driver of the bus who was standing on the corner
>
> the driver of the bus parked at the corner

> my sister's friend from Tampa
>
> my sister in Tampa's friend (or, my sister in Tampa has a friend who . . .)

OTHER POSTNOUN MODIFIERS

Infinitives. The infinitive—the base form of the verb preceded by *to*—can serve as a modifier in the postheadword position. As a verb, it will have all the attributes of verbs, including complements and modifiers, depending on its underlying sentence pattern:

> the way <u>to be helpful</u>
>
> the time <u>to start</u>
>
> the party after the play <u>to honor the director</u>
>
> the best place in San Francisco <u>to eat seafood</u>

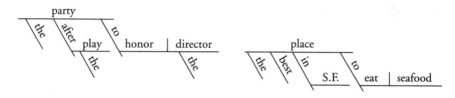

As the last two examples illustrate, the infinitive can be separated from the headword by another modifier. These examples also illustrate another common feature of the adjectival infinitive: Its subject may not be the noun it modifies; its subject is frequently just understood—the object in an understood prepositional phrase:

> That was a nice thing [for you] to do.
>
> Fisherman's Wharf is not necessarily the best place in San Francisco [for one] to eat seafood.

Noun Phrases. Nouns or noun phrases of time and place can follow the headword:

> the party <u>last night</u>
>
> the ride <u>home</u>

These adjectival noun phrases are diagrammed just as the adverbial noun phrases are—on horizontal lines:

Adjectives. Qualified adjectives and compound adjectives, which usually occupy the preheadword position, can follow the headword if they are set off by commas:

> the neighbors, <u>usually quiet</u>

> the neighborhood, <u>quiet and peaceful</u>

Like the nonrestrictive participles, these nonrestrictive adjectives can also introduce the sentence when they modify the subject:

> <u>Usually quiet</u>, the neighbors upstairs are having a regular brawl tonight.

> <u>Quiet and peaceful</u>, the neighborhood slept while the cat burglars made their rounds.

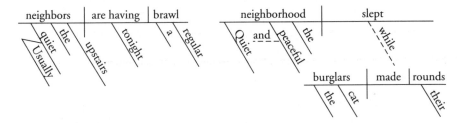

The diagram does not distinguish between pre-and postheadword modifiers—except for the capital letter. But the purpose of the diagram, after all, is to show the structural relationships, not the word order.

Adverbs. Even adverbs can occupy the postheadword position in the noun phrase:

> That was my idea <u>exactly</u>.

> The people <u>here</u> have no idea of conditions <u>there</u>.

Exercise 29

Identify all the postnoun modifiers in the following sentences and label them by form. A sentence may contain more than one postnoun modifier.

1. Curling is a game in which players slide circular, handle-topped granite stones across the ice toward a target.

2. The sport, which originated in Scotland and the Netherlands, combines the skills of bowling and shuffleboard with the strategies of billiards and chess.

3. It is played on an ice rink that is 42 yards long and 10 yards wide, in teams of four players to a side.

4. Each player propels two stones toward a target that is 38 yards away.

5. Curling stones are made from a very special granite called Blue Hone, which is known for its toughness and resiliency.

6. Players "deliver" their stones with a twist of the wrist, imparting the curling action for which the game is named.

7. The third and fourth players on a team look for ways to knock the opponents' stones out of bounds.

8. An important piece of curling equipment is the broom, used by players to melt the ice slightly in the path of a teammate's stone.

9. The winning team is the one whose stones are closest to the center of the target; for each stone that is closer, one point is scored.

10. The sport is extremely popular in Canada, where there are more than a million curlers, who play both at local clubs and on a thriving cash circuit.

Investigating Language   7.2

Grammarians and language experts have been discussing the question of when and whether to use *who* or *whom* for well over two hundred years, with citations that stretch from Shakespeare to the 1996 presidential campaign:

> Who wouldst thou strike? (*The Two Gentlemen of Verona*, 1595)

> Consider who the King your father sends,
> To whom he sends, and what's his embassy. (*Love's Labour's Lost*, 1595)

> It all boils down to who do you trust. (Bob Dole, 1996)

> Who do you trust to select the [pizza] toppings? (Bill Clinton, 1996)

In all four of these examples, the pronoun *who* functions as the direct object in its clause. Countless grammar books, dating as far back as 1762, maintain that *who* is incorrect in that position, that *whom* is called for. Why? Because in Latin grammar, the direct object slot requires the objective case, not the nominative (or subjective). But William Safire, in his *New York Times* column "On Language" (June 30, 1996), contends that

> at the beginning of a sentence, *whom* comes across as an affectation. In politics, formality went out with neckties, and what is comfortable to the listener's ear is to be preferred in address.

Safire agrees with many linguists who recognize that *who* is natural in speech at the beginning of a sentence or clause and that *whom* is natural only after a preposition:

> To whom shall I mail the check?

If the preposition comes at the end of the sentence, however, we will probably hear *who* in speech:

> Who shall I mail the check to?

The written language is a different issue. A writer can usually find a way to avoid both the affectation of *whom* and the "ungrammatical" *who* when the objective case is called for:

> Where shall I mail the check?
> Who should receive the check?

Another usage issue connected with substitutes for *whom* concerns the use of *that* when referring to people:

> A woman that I knew in high school has invited me to lunch.

Most handbooks consider this use of *that* unacceptable for formal writing, prescribing the use of *who* when referring to people. In this sentence, the correct form would be the awkward *whom*. Here the obvious solution is to delete the pronoun:

> A woman I knew in high school has invited me to lunch.

But when the clause is set off by commas, the pronoun cannot be deleted:

> Jane Barnard, whom I knew in high school, has invited me to lunch.

Can you find a way to revise this sentence in order to avoid this awkward use of *whom?*

CHAPTER 7

Key Terms

Adjectival	Adjective
Adjectival clause	Adverbial participle
Adjectival infinitive	Antecedent
Adjectival prepositional phrase	Case

Dangling participle	Participle
Demonstrative pronoun	Passive participle
Determiner	Possessive case
Functional shift	Postheadword modifier
Free modifier	Preheadword modifier
Headword	Relative adverb
Intonation	Relative clause
Nonrestrictive modifier	Relative pronoun
Participial phrase	Restrictive modifier

Sentences
for PRACTICE

Draw vertical lines between the slots of the sentence patterns. Mark the headword of each NP with an X, the determiner with a D; underline the pre- and postheadword modifiers; then label each according to its form. Circle any pronouns that fill NP slots.

For further practice, identify the sentence patterns and diagram the sentences. Remember that all verb phrases and clauses functioning as adverbials and adjectivals also have identifiable sentence patterns.

1. The clown, acting silly to entertain the children, was not very funny.

2. The person who tries something and fails is infinitely better than the person who tries nothing and succeeds.

3. My neighbor's husband, who is a strong union man, would not cross the picket line that the clerical workers organized at the mill where he is a foreman.

4. The company's reorganization plan, voted down last week, called for the removal of all incumbent officers.

5. At midnight Cinderella's beautiful coach, in which she had been driven to the ball, suddenly became a pumpkin again.

6. According to the Sierra Club, the equivalent of eleven barrels of oil is saved for every ton of plastic bags reused or recycled.

7. Drawing on my fine command of the English language, I said nothing. [Robert Benchley]

8. The play's the thing wherein I'll catch the conscience of the king. [Shakespeare]

9. Uneasy lies the head that wears the crown. [Shakespeare]

10. Calling Pearl Harbor Day a day that would live in infamy, President Roosevelt asked Congress for a declaration of war.

11. Having been a police officer in downtown Nashville for thirty years, my neighbor grew restless and bored after he retired from the force.

12. The town in Missouri where I lived until I reached my fifteenth birthday is in the foothills of the beautiful Ozarks.

13. Too many people are spending money they haven't earned to buy things they don't need to impress people they don't like.

14. The newly formed commission on gender equity could not meet on a day when Professor Lang was out of town.

15. People who leave home to set the world on fire often come back for more matches. [Confucius]

16. Those whom the gods would destroy they first make famous.

QUESTIONS
?
for DISCUSSION

1. Generate a noun phrase according to each of the following formulas:

   A. det + adj + HEADWORD + participial phrase

   B. det + adj + noun + HEADWORD + clause

   C. det + adj + HEADWORD + prep phrase + part phrase

   D. det + noun + HEADWORD + part phrase + clause

   Use your NPs in sentences as follows:

   > Use A as the direct object of a Pattern VII sentence.
   >
   > Use B as the object of a preposition.
   >
   > Use C as an indirect object.
   >
   > Use D as the direct object in a relative clause.

2. In our description of the noun phrase, we saw that the headword slot is filled by a word that is a noun in form. Would you consider these underlined noun phrases as exceptions to the rule?

The rich are different from other people.

I was late for our meeting.

You clean the upstairs, and I'll do the downstairs.

3. Explain the source of the ambiguity in the following sentence:

     My brother is considered the area's best foreign car mechanic.

4. In this chapter we discussed the recursive quality of the noun phrase—that is, the embedding of one noun phrase in another. Give a sentence in which a relative clause is embedded in another relative clause; give another in which a participle is embedded in another participial phrase; another with a participle in a relative clause; another with a relative clause in a participial phrase.

5. Linguist Francis Christensen, quoted in the discussion of punctuation, suggests that restrictive modifiers make one statement and imply the opposite. What opposite statements can you infer from the following?

     All the students with an average of 90 or higher will be excused from the final.

     The flight controllers who saw the strange lights in the sky became firm believers in UFOs.

     The customers who witnessed the fight were called to testify.

   How would the meaning of these sentences change if the postnoun modifiers were set off by commas?

6. What is the source of the ambiguity in the following sentences?

     Tony buried the knife he found in the cellar.

     Fred tripped his teammate with the baseball bat.

   Diagram each sentence in two ways to show its two possible meanings.

7. Both of the following sentences include an adjectival infinitive as a modifier of *decision;* and in both, the expletive *as* introduces an object complement. But there's an important difference between them. Diagram both sentences to illustrate the difference.

     The Jaycees are hailing the decision to admit women as a landmark.

     The Jaycees are hailing the decision to admit women as members.

8. In *The Book of Lists* (Morrow, 1977), David Wallechinsky, Irving Wallace, and Amy Wallace describe a comma "that cost the government two million dollars before Congress could rectify the error." Here's the expensive sentence:

All foreign fruit, plants are free from duty.

The clerk who wrote the rule was supposed to use a hyphen instead of a comma. Explain the difference.

CLASSROOM APPLICATIONS

1. There are very few, if any, nouns that cannot function as modifiers of other nouns. Here's a vocabulary exercise to test this statement. Begin with a common noun, such as *light* or *tree* or *house*. Use it as a modifier; then use the noun you modified as a modifier. See how long you can keep the chain going—perhaps around the room at least once. For example,

    tree farm, farm building, building code, code word, word game, game player, player piano, piano bench, bench warmer, warmer oven, oven light . . .

   If you get stuck, you can go back and change a word to start a new path.

2. The term "sentence combining" refers to a popular method of teaching sentence structure in which writers learn to combine short sentences in various ways. This method is based on the work of the transformational linguists, who hold that every modifier in the noun phrase is actually a basic sentence. For example, this sentence,

   The silly, awkward clown is entertaining the children,
   combines three basic sentences:

   The clown is entertaining the children.

   The clown is silly.

   The clown is awkward.

   There are other ways in which these same three sentences could be combined:

   The silly clown entertaining the children is awkward.

   The awkward clown who is entertaining the children is silly.

   Silly and awkward, the clown is entertaining the children.

   The clown, silly and awkward, is entertaining the children.

   The children are being entertained by the silly, awkward clown.

   While entertaining the children, the clown was silly and awkward.

The awkward clown was being silly as he entertained the children.

Using your knowledge of both adverbial and adjectival modifiers, combine the following groups of sentences in as many ways as you can. (Try for at least a dozen!)

Becky stood before the magistrate.

Becky felt nervous.

The dancers kept time to the raucous music.

The dancers wore strange costumes.

The dancers acted crazy.

The young man waited for the train

The train was very late.

The young man looked impatient.

The young man paced back and forth on the station platform.

CHAPTER
8

The Noun Phrase Functions: Nominals

CHAPTER PREVIEW

In the previous two chapters you saw how the basic sentence patterns can be expanded by adding optional modifiers of various kinds—words, phrases, and clauses that function as adverbials and adjectivals. In this chapter you will learn how the NP slots can be expanded by using structures other than noun phrases. We begin this chapter by reviewing the various roles that NPs play in our basic sentence patterns, including an optional NP slot called the **appositive**. Then we examine in detail how to fill these same slots with verb phrases and dependent clauses instead of noun phrases.

THE NOMINAL SLOTS

You have already learned that the terms *adverbial* and *adjectival* denote functions. An *adverbial* is any form—any word, phrase, or clause—that does what an adverb does—that is, modify a verb. *Adjectival* refers to any structure that does what an adjective usually does—modify a noun. But you'll notice that we have not used the parallel *-al* term for noun, **nominal**, until now. Up to this point, all of the required slots in the sentence patterns labeled NP, such as subject and direct object, have been filled with noun phrases (and sometimes with pronouns, which stand in for NPs). We did this mainly for simplicity. But now that we're going to study other forms that fill the required sentence slots, it's time to introduce the term *nominal*.

All of those NP slots you learned about in Chapter 3 are actually nominal slots. Adverbials and adjectivals have only one function each—to modify a verb or modify a noun. But nominals perform a variety of functions, most of which are required to produce a complete grammatical sentence:

168

Subject: <u>My best buddy</u> lives in Iowa.

Direct object: I visited <u>my best buddy</u> last Christmas.

Indirect object: I sent <u>my best buddy</u> a card for his birthday.

Subject complement: The town's new mayor is <u>my best buddy</u>.

Object complement: I consider Rich <u>my best buddy</u>.

Object of a preposition: The town has a lot of respect for <u>my best buddy</u>.

As you will see, these slots can be filled with forms other than NPs—namely, verb phrases and dependent clauses. But before we get to those other forms, let's look at one more nominal function, one that does not show up in the sentence patterns—an optional nominal slot called the **appositive**.

APPOSITIVES

An appositive is a nominal companion, a structure (usually an NP) that adds information to a sentence by renaming another nominal. It is sometimes called "a noun in apposition."

My best buddy, <u>Rich</u>, lives in Iowa.

The prosecutor cross-examined the next witness, <u>the victim's ex-husband</u>.

You can easily understand the optional nature of the appositive: These sentences would be grammatical without the added information. On the diagram the appositive occupies a place right next to the noun, or other nominal structure, that it renames, with the headword in parentheses:

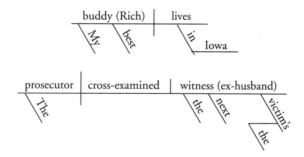

As the diagram clearly illustrates, the appositives add information to the noun phrase, as adjectivals do. But they are different from other adjectivals in that they can substitute for the nouns that they rename:

Rich lives in Iowa.

The prosecutor cross-examined the victim's ex-husband.

If the appositive renames the subject, it can be used to introduce the sentence:

> <u>An ex-Marine who once played professional football</u>, the prosecutor was an intimidating presence in the courtroom.

Punctuation of Appositives. The distinction between restrictive and nonrestrictive modifiers, which you learned in connection with participial phrases and relative clauses, also applies to appositives. When the appositive defines (restricts) the meaning of the nominal it renames, no commas are needed. An altered version of the first example will illustrate the distinction:

> My buddy Rich lives in Iowa.

In the earlier example, the added name simply comments:

> My best buddy, Rich, lives in Iowa.

The adjective *best* makes all the difference. *My best buddy* obviously refers to one specific person, just as *my only buddy* would. *My buddy*, however, has a general reference; the added name makes the referent of the noun phrase specific, actually defining the phrase *my buddy*. You can hear the contrast when you read the two sentences aloud.

Exercise 30

Underline the noun phrases that are functioning as appositives. Remember, an appositive noun phrase has the same referent as the nominal it renames.

1. Folk songs, simple ballads sung to guitar music, became very popular in the 1960s.
2. One of the best-known folk singers of that period was Arlo Guthrie, son of the legendary songwriter Woody Guthrie.
3. An offbeat film about illegal trash dumping, "Alice's Restaurant" was inspired by Arlo's song of the same name.
4. The theme of many Arlo Guthrie songs, the search for personal freedom, is still appealing today.
5. Gillian Welch, a contemporary folk singer and songwriter, combines simple ballad-like melodies with topical lyrics in two very popular CDs, *Soul Journey* and *Time (The Revelator)*.
6. I went to the concert with my friend Casey, who is Gillian Welch's biggest fan.

In Chapter 15, we take up the use of colons and dashes in connection with appositives. And in the following sections of this chapter, we include appositives in forms other than noun phrases—verb phrases and clauses.

NOUN PHRASE SUBSTITUTES

Three other structures can perform the grammatical functions that noun phrases generally perform: the gerund phrase, the infinitive phrase, and the nominal clause. Our study of these nominal forms—these substitutes for NPs—will focus on their five primary functions: subject, direct object, subject complement, object of a preposition, and appositive.

GERUNDS

In Chapter 4 you saw the *-ing* form of the verb combined with a *be* auxiliary functioning as the predicating, or tensed, verb:

The children <u>are running</u> through the woods.

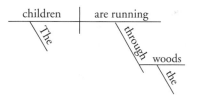

Here the diagram clearly shows the sentence as Pattern VI, with the intransitive verb *are running* modified by an adverbial prepositional phrase.

In the previous chapter you saw the *-ing* verb functioning as a noun modifier, called the participle; and you'll recall that the noun the participle modifies is also the participle's subject:

The children <u>running through the woods</u> look happy.

In this chapter we will use the same *-ing* verb as a nominal to fill an NP slot. In this function, it is called a **gerund**:

<u>Running through the woods</u> is the children's favorite activity.

Here the gerund phrase is the subject of the sentence. We can think of gerunds as names. But rather than naming persons, places, things, and events, as nouns generally do, gerunds name actions or behaviors or states of mind or states of being. And because they are verbs in form, gerunds will also include all the complements and modifiers that tensed verbs include. In our gerund example, *running* is modified by an adverbial prepositional phrase, *through the woods*, just as it was as a main verb.

Even though sentences with gerunds in the NP slots may look more complicated than those you've seen before, the system for analyzing them is the same. You do that by identifying the sentence pattern. The first step is to locate the predicating verb. No matter what structure fills the subject slot, you can determine where it ends by substituting a pronoun, such as *something* or *it*:

Running through the woods is the children's favorite activity.

In other words,

<u>It</u> is the children's favorite activity.

Now you've identified the predicating verb, *is*, a form of *be*. Next you'll see that a noun phrase (*the children's favorite activity*) follows, so you know the sentence is Pattern III.

The next step is to identify the form of the structure filling that "it" slot. You can recognize *Running through the woods* as a gerund because it begins with an *-ing* verb form. (You can usually identify the form of a structure by looking at the first word.)

In diagramming the gerund when it fills a slot in the main clause, we simply attach the phrase to the main line by means of a pedestal, just as we did in Chapter 3 when a prepositional phrase filled the subject complement slot. The line for the gerund itself has a small step at the left, which identifies the *-ing* verb as a gerund:

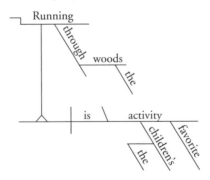

Following are examples of other NP slots occupied by gerund phrases.

Direct object: Both adults and teenagers enjoy playing computer games.

Subject complement: My favorite pastime is playing computer games.

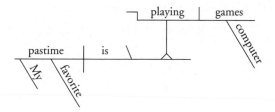

Object of a preposition: I work off a lot of tension by playing computer games.

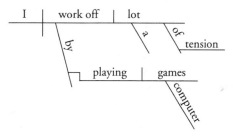

Appositive: My favorite pastime, playing computer games, is inexpensive but time-consuming.

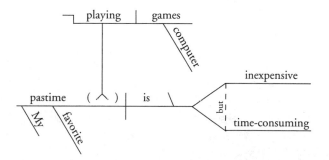

The Pattern of the Gerund. In these sentences with the gerund phrase *playing computer games,* the gerund *playing* has a direct object (*playing what?*), so we can identify the underlying sentence, with its one slot following the verb, as Pattern VII:

X is playing computer games.

The predicating verb in every pattern has the potential for becoming a gerund phrase when it is turned into the *-ing* form:

> Pattern III: My little brother <u>is a pest</u>. (*being a pest*)
>
> Pattern VIII: Tony <u>gave the landlord a bad time</u>. (*giving the landlord a bad time*)
>
> Pattern IX: We <u>painted the bathroom orange</u>. (*painting the bathroom orange*)

In the following sentences, those *-ing* verb phrases have become gerunds filling NP slots:

> My little brother enjoys <u>being a pest</u>. (direct object)
>
> After <u>giving the landlord a bad time</u>, Tony regretted his behavior. (object of a preposition)
>
> Our bright idea, <u>painting the bathroom orange</u>, was a decorating disaster. (appositive)

It's important to note that just because the function of the verb phrase changes—from predicating verb to nominal—its sentence pattern does not change. The three gerunds remain Patterns III, VIII, and IX, respectively.

Exercise 31

A. Identify the gerund phrases in the following sentences, and indicate the function (subject, direct object, subject complement, object of a preposition, appositive) that each one performs in its sentence. Also identify the sentence patterns of the main clause and of the gerund phrase. Diagram the sentences.

1. Flying a supersonic jet has been Sally's dream since childhood.
2. The coach enjoys playing practical jokes on his players.
3. The speaker began by telling a few jokes.
4. My hardest accomplishment last semester was staying awake in my eight o'clock class.
5. Leaving the scene of the accident was not a good idea.
6. Two witnesses reported seeing the suspect near the entrance of the bank.
7. Michael Phelps trained hard to achieve his goal, winning eight gold medals at the Beijing Olympics.
8. He trained by swimming for many hours every day.
9. The cost of going to college has risen dramatically in the last ten years.

10. Thinking a problem through requires time, solitude, and concentration.

B. Compose sentences that include the following verb phrases as gerunds. Try to use each gerund phrase in at least two different functions.

taking grammar tests   giving people a helping hand
being punctual   lying on the beach

Investigating Language   8.1

Compare these pairs of sentences:

Her job was selling computers in a discount store.
She was selling computers in a discount store.

My brother is getting into trouble again.
My problem is getting into law school.

How do the patterns of the two sentences in each pair differ? What are the predicating verbs? Which ones contain gerunds? How would the diagrams for each be different? Marking off the sentence slots with vertical lines will help to show the differences in the sentence patterns. You can also try substituting pronouns to help you see where the NP slots begin and end.

The Subject of the Gerund.   The subject of the gerund—that is, the person or agent performing the action expressed in the gerund—is usually not part of the gerund phrase itself. However, it is often the same as the subject of the sentence, as in item 2 in Exercise 31, where "coach" is the subject of both "enjoys" (the main verb) and "playing" (the gerund). Sometimes the subject can be inferred from another word in the sentence, as in item 4, where "my" indicates who had trouble "staying awake." The subject of the gerund will usually be left unstated when it names a general, rather than a particular, action or behavior, as in items 9 and 10 in Exercise 31.

But sometimes the subject can be expressed in the gerund phrase itself. When it is, it will often be in the possessive case:

His drinking is excessive.

I objected to Jeremy's taking on another part-time job.

Your complaining about the work will not make it any easier.

Although the possessive case may sometimes sound excessively formal or even incorrect, it is the form considered standard in formal writing.

In the diagram, the subject of the gerund is diagrammed like a determiner and attached to the step on the left:

Dangling Gerunds.   The following sentences are likely to elicit an "awk" from your composition teacher. What is it that makes them awkward?

Upon seeing the stop sign, the car screeched to a halt.

By proofreading my papers, my grades improved greatly.

The ingredients should be assembled before starting to bake a cake.

You probably recognized that these sentences aren't strictly logical: They suggest that the car saw the stop sign, the grades proofread the papers, and the ingredients baked the cake. We call that problem the "dangling gerund," a problem that occurs when the subject of the gerund is not stated or clearly implied. These sentences have the same fuzzy quality that dangling participles have.

Dangling gerunds usually turn up when the gerund serves as the object in an opening or closing prepositional phrase. To clear up a dangling gerund, you can revise the sentence in one of two ways:

1. Make sure that the subject of the main clause is also the subject of the gerund:

    Upon seeing the stop sign, I brought the car to a screeching halt.

    By proofreading my papers, I improved my grades greatly.

2. Turn the prepositional phrase with the gerund into an adverbial clause:

    Assemble the ingredients before you start to bake a cake.

Exercise 32

Improve the following sentences by providing a clear subject for the gerund.

1. After finishing the decorations, the ballroom looked beautiful.
2. Your revising time will be reduced by following a few helpful pointers.

3. In making a career decision, your counselor will be a big help.

4. By signing this waiver, no claims against the owner can be made.

5. Our backpacks got really heavy after hiking up that steep mountain trail.

ELL Issues   **Go + -ing verbs**

The verb *go* is used with a great many *-ing* verbs, but, interestingly, those verbs are limited to recreational activities of various kinds:

Let's go hunting (fishing, bowling, swimming, shopping, jogging, etc.).

We don't say "Let's go gardening," "Let's go cooking," or "Let's go doing homework."

This is one of those "why" questions that we have no answer for! Another is what to call that *-ing* verb that follows *Let's go*. Because *go* is nearly always intransitive, the *-ing* activity can probably be interpreted as an adverbial, a participle functioning adverbially. But because that *-ing* verb names an activity, we could also make a case for calling it a gerund. Perhaps the best answer is to recognize its special usage and call it an idiom.

INFINITIVES

Another form of the verb that functions as a nominal is the **infinitive phrase**—the base form of the verb with *to*. Like the gerund, the nominal infinitive names an action or behavior or state of being. In fact, the infinitive closely parallels the gerund and is often an alternative to it:

Gerund: <u>Remaining neutral on this issue</u> is unconscionable.

Nominal infinitive: <u>To remain neutral on this issue</u> is unconscionable.

You have already seen infinitives functioning as modifiers of verbs (Chapter 6, Adverbials) and as modifiers of nouns (Chapter 7, Adjectivals). In this chapter you will see the nominal infinitive functioning as subject, direct object, subject complement, and appositive:

Subject: <u>To be a successful farmer these days</u> requires stamina and perseverance.

Direct object: My cousin wants <u>to be a successful farmer</u>.

Subject complement: My cousin's ambition is <u>to be a successful farmer</u>.

Appositive: My cousin's ambition, <u>to be a successful farmer</u>, requires stamina and perseverance.

As with gerunds, you can substitute a pronoun to help you decide what nominal slot the infinitive phrase fills:

<u>Something</u> requires stamina and perseverance.

My cousin wants <u>something</u>.

My cousin's ambition is <u>this</u>.

Infinitives, like gerunds, are verb forms; they may include complements and/or adverbial modifiers. And like gerunds, infinitive phrases can be derived from all the sentence patterns. Our "farmer" infinitive is Pattern III. In the first example it fills the subject slot in a Pattern VII sentence:

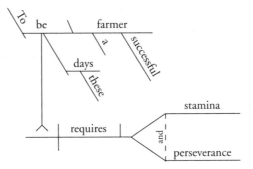

In the diagram, the infinitive phrase, like the gerund, is connected to the main line with a pedestal. The infinitive itself is on a two-part line exactly like that of a prepositional phrase. (It's easy to tell the difference, however: In the infinitive phrase, *to* is followed by a verb, not by a noun phrase.)

In the following sentence, a Pattern VII infinitive phrase functions as an appositive:

My job, to hand out the diplomas, was a last-minute assignment.

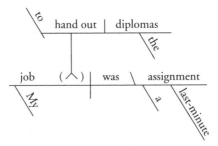

The action expressed in the infinitive phrase renames the subject, *My job*; it tells what the job is.

Exercise 33

Identify the sentence pattern of each infinitive phrase and its function in the sentence. Diagram the sentences.

1. Ruth plans to give her father a necktie for Christmas.
2. To side with the truth is noble.
3. Our only hope is to beg for mercy.
4. To walk across campus alone at night could be dangerous.
5. Both candidates desperately want to become president.
6. Winston Churchill had a rule never to take strong drink before lunch.
7. My friend Renato likes to shock people with his outrageous political views.
8. A mother bird will attempt to distract predators from the nest.
9. The worst solitude is to be destitute of sincere friendship. [Francis Bacon]
10. To know him is to love him.

The Subject of the Infinitive. In most of the infinitive sentences we have seen so far, the subject of the tensed verb is also the subject of the infinitive. For example, in item 7 of the previous exercise, "My friend Renato likes to shock people with his outrageous political views," *friend* is the subject of both *likes* and *to shock*. But when an infinitive has a general meaning, the sentence may not include that infinitive's actual subject, especially if the infinitive occupies the subject slot:

> <u>To listen to Norah Jones</u> is pure delight.

In some cases, however, the subject of the infinitive will be expressed in a prepositional phrase:

> <u>For Conchita to win this match</u> would be a miracle.

> <u>For the district attorney to take part in this discussion</u> is a conflict of interest.

Conchita and *district attorney* are the subjects of the infinitives *to win* and *to take part.*

Prepositional phrases with embedded infinitives also occur in the direct object position after verbs like *hope, like, want,* and *prefer*:

> Conchita's fans would like <u>for her to win this match.</u>

> We are hoping <u>for our legislature to make a wise decision about school taxes.</u>

In the diagram for these sentences, the vertical line between the object of the preposition and the infinitive indicates the subject-verb boundary:

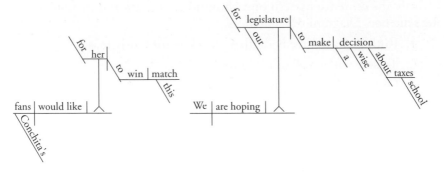

Some verbs that can appear in such sentences are also grammatical without the preposition *for*:

Conchita's fans would like her to win this match.

In these examples we have treated the infinitive and its subject as a single unit filling the direct object slot:

Conchita's fans would like <u>something</u>.

We are hoping <u>something</u>.

But in the following sentence, there are two slots:

We asked <u>the uninvited guests</u> <u>to leave the party</u>.

In this sentence, we have both a "someone" and a "something" following the verb; so rather than analyze the sentence as Pattern VII, we would explain it as Pattern VIII, with the "someone" as an indirect object:

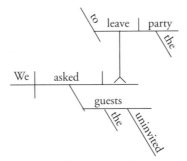

You might argue that the verb *asked* is not a "give" verb, as most Pattern VIII verbs are, and that *uninvited guests* isn't really a "recipient," as most indirect objects are. However, the two slots clearly have different referents, so the Pattern VIII formula, with its NP_2 and NP_3, seems to fit. We can also transform the sentence into passive voice to show that *to leave the party* occupies a separate slot from *the uninvited guests*:

The uninvited guests were asked to leave the party.

Other verbs that follow this pattern include *tell, advise, invite, require, order,* and *expect.*

Underline the nominal verb phrases—both gerunds and infinitives—in the following sentences. Then identify the function of each nominal verb phrase. Finally, diagram the sentences. Be sure to think about sentences patterns.

1. The best thing would be for you to tell the truth.
2. By remaining silent, you are merely making the situation worse.
3. To ignore the judge's order would be foolhardy.
4. Ms. Graham chose to welcome the new investor into the company.
5. This invitation thwarted his latest plan, to buy up a controlling number of stocks.
6. Raising the company's national profile was the new owner's long-term goal.
7. Our composition teacher instructed us to write three drafts of every assignment.
8. I appreciate your proofreading this final version for me.
9. I like to watch the goldfinches at the bird feeder in the morning.
10. The baby's crying upset the rest of the passengers.

NOMINAL CLAUSES

In the preceding sections you have seen examples of verb phrases—gerunds and infinitives—filling NP slots. In this section you will see that nominal clauses can do so as well:

> I understand <u>that several students have launched a protest</u>.
>
> I wonder <u>what prompted their action</u>.

These nominal clauses (also called "noun clauses") are further examples of dependent clauses, just as adverbial and adjectival clauses are: They do not function as complete sentences, as independent clauses do.

The trick of substituting a pronoun to determine the boundaries of the NP slot is especially useful when the nominal slot it filled by a clause, as in the two previous examples:

> I understand <u>something</u>.
>
> I wonder <u>something</u>.

The pronoun substitutes for the entire nominal slot.

These two examples also illustrate the two kinds of introductory words that signal nominal clauses: the **expletive** *that* and **interrogative** words such as *what*. The diagrams will show a basic difference between them:

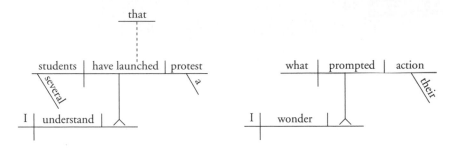

The interrogative *what* fills a grammatical role in the clause it introduces—in this case, that of subject; the expletive does not.

(*Diagramming note:* The pedestal can be attached to the nominal clause wherever it is convenient to do so. The expletive is placed above the clause it introduces and attached with a broken line, again wherever convenient.)

The Expletive *That*.   The term *expletive* refers to a sentence element that plays no grammatical role itself; it's an added element that enables us to manipulate a structure for reasons of emphasis and the like. The expletive *that* makes it possible to embed one sentence as a nominal in another sentence. This use of *that* is sometimes labeled a *nominalizer*. In the previous example, the Pattern VII sentence "Several students have launched a protest" becomes the direct object in another Pattern VII sentence. The diagram illustrates the added-on quality of the expletive.

The expletive *that* can turn any declarative sentence into a nominal clause:

The guests from El Paso ⟶ I hope that the guests from
will arrive soon.   El Paso will arrive soon.

The common cold is ⟶ That the common cold is
caused by a virus.   caused by a virus has been
                           clearly established by science.

When the *that* clause fills the direct object slot, as in the first example, the sentence may be grammatical without the expletive:

I hope the guests from El Paso will arrive soon.

When the clause is in the subject position, however, the expletive is required:

*The common cold is caused by a virus has been clearly established by science.

Nominal *that* clauses can also function as subject complements and appositives, as the following examples illustrate:

> *Subject complement:* Your assumption is <u>that interest rates will remain relatively low</u>.

> *Appositive:* The reviewer's criticism, <u>that the characters lack conviction</u>, is fully justified.

Exercise 35

Create a nominal *that* clause to fill the following slots. Identify the function of the clause that you've added.

1. You should know_____ .

2. _____makes everyone angry.

3. My parents are expecting _____.

4. _____has not occurred to them.

5. The truth is _____

6. The fact _____disturbs me.

Investigating Language 8.2

Nominal clauses that begin with the expletive *that* should not be confused with adjectival clauses that begin with the relative pronoun *that*. Compare the following examples:

> *Nominal clause:* I know <u>that I reminded you about the deadline</u>.

> *Adjectival clause:* You ignored the reminders <u>that I gave you</u>.

Because the expletive *that* plays no grammatical role in its clause, the nominal clause will be a complete sentence without the *that: I reminded you about the deadline*. But the relative pronoun *that* does have a role to play within its clause; if you remove it, the remaining words won't be a complete sentence: **I gave you*.

You can also distinguish between *that* clauses by replacing the *that* with *which*. If the clause is adjectival, the sentence will still be grammatical:

> You ignored the reminders <u>which I gave you</u>.

But if you substitute *which* for the expletive *that* in a nominal clause, the result will be clearly ungrammatical:

> **I know which I reminded you about the deadline*.

Here are some more sentences with clauses introduced by *that*. Decide which clauses are nominal (introduced by an expletive) and which are adjectival (introduced by a relative pronoun):

The color that you chose for the walls doesn't match the rug. _____

Milton suspects that someone has been using his computer.

_____

The books that I need for chemistry class are expensive.

_____

I suppose that the books that I need for art history will be expensive too._____, _____

The idea that I need your help is absurd. _____

The idea that you proposed to the committee is a brilliant one.

_____

He gave her a look that you could have poured on a waffle.
    [Ring Lardner] _____

You can check your answers by doing a diagram to make sure that you've identified the *that* correctly.

Interrogatives. One of the sample sentences we saw earlier included a nominal clause introduced by the interrogative *what*:

I wonder <u>what prompted their action</u>.

Other **interrogatives**, or question words, that introduce nominal clauses are *who, whose, whom, which, where, when, why,* and *how.* Unlike the expletive, the interrogative always plays a grammatical role in its own clause. In the previous example, *what* functions as the subject of *prompted.* In the following sentence, *what* is the direct object in its clause:

I wonder <u>what the students are demanding</u>.

In both of these examples, the *what* clause functions as the direct object. Another common function of nominal clauses introduced by interrogatives is that of subject, as shown in the next two examples:

<u>*Where* you are going</u> is no business of mine.

Where is an interrogative adverb, so it acts as an adverb in its clause. The interrogative pronoun *who* will be the subject in its own clause:

<u>*Who* will be at the party</u> remains a mystery.

Who can also be the subject complement in its clause. Here the clause fills the direct object slot:

I don't know <u>*who* that stranger is</u>.

In the following sentences *which* and *what* function as determiners in their clauses; both clauses fill the direct object slot:

I wonder <u>*which* brand of yogurt has the least fat</u>.

I can't decide <u>*what* brand I should buy</u>.

Nominal clauses introduced by interrogatives can also function as objects of prepositions and as appositives:

Object of a preposition: Clarice knows a lot about <u>how computers work</u>.

Appositive: The dean's question, <u>why the students didn't object sooner</u>, has not been answered.

Exercise 36

Both *when* and *where* hold membership in two word classes. As **subordinators** they introduce adverbial clauses; as **interrogatives** they introduce nominal clauses. Identify the function of the *where* and *when* clauses in the following sentences. Are they adverbial or nominal? If the clause is nominal, identify the NP slot it fills. Also identify the sentence patterns of both the independent and dependent clauses.

1. Julie could not remember where she had left her keys.
2. Rob lost his keys when he misplaced his backpack.
3. When I get in late, my roommate gets upset.
4. When I get home is my own business.
5. The starship *Enterprise* ventures where explorers have never gone before.
6. When you decide where we are having dinner, give me a call.

7. When you don't know where you are going, any road will take you there.

8. They have finally decided where the wedding will be held.

9. When I am an old woman, I shall wear purple. [Jenny Joseph]

10. The police asked where we were when the accident occurred.

Yes/No Interrogatives. In Chapter 3 you read about our two kinds of questions: those that ask for specific information, the so-called *wh-* questions; and yes/no questions. Here we've seen those same interrogative words used to introduce nominal clauses, filling NP slots in sentences. We also have nominal clauses based on yes/no questions, introduced by two expletive-like elements, *if* and *whether (or not)*:

> I can't remember <u>if I turned off the television</u>.
>
> <u>Whether or not I turned it off</u> doesn't really matter.

We consider these introductory words as expletives because, like the expletive *that*, they play no part in the clause; they simply act as operators that allow us to use yes/no questions as nominal clauses:

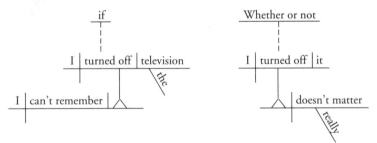

Unlike the expletive *that*, which can sometimes be omitted, these introducers of interrogative clauses will always be included.

Underline the nominal clause in each of the following sentences. Then identify its function in the sentence: What NP slot does it fill? Diagram the sentences.

1. Until yesterday I never realized how awesome a redwood tree could be.

2. The main complaint about his presentation was that it was too short.

3. What Carlos said about his cousin is unfair and inaccurate.

4. Our psychology teacher is writing a book about why people fear intimacy.

5. My sister told her children that they could have a dog.

6. Who invented calculus is a matter of some dispute.

7. We could not tell which twin was Elaine.

8. Percy wondered if we could come for the weekend.

9. I wish he would explain his explanation. [Lord Byron]

10. The decision that they should replay the point upset both contestants.

Punctuation of Nominal Clauses. As many of the previous examples and exercise items illustrate, sentences with nominal clauses can get fairly long. But with one exception, the punctuation of these sentences remains exactly the same as the punctuation of the basic sentence: no single commas between the sentence pattern slots. The exception occurs when the direct object is a direct quotation. The standard convention calls for a comma between a verb like *say* or *reply* and the quotation:

> He said, "I will meet you at the gym at five o'clock."

In this sentence the quoted passage is essentially a nominal clause in direct object position.

Exercise | **38**

Underline the nominal clauses, gerund phrases, and nominal infinitives in the following sentences. Identify the function that each of them performs in its sentence.

1. You can't lose weight by clipping a diet out of a magazine.

2. To search for the causes of lower SAT scores would be an exercise in conjecture.

3. The neighbors never suspected that we had a pet boa constrictor in our house.

4. The guest speaker's e-mail message informed us when he would arrive.

5. The airlines are planning to raise their fares.

6. Several airlines announced recently that they are planning to raise their fares.

7. A major cause of highway accidents is falling asleep at the wheel.

8. Why reality shows are so popular is a mystery to many people.

9. The knowledge that the semester is almost over makes me happy.

10. The instructor asked us to make copies of our poems for everyone in class.

11. Success is getting what you want; happiness is wanting what you get. (Dale Carnegie)
12. When I saw the questions that were on the exam, I realized I had studied the wrong chapters.

NOMINALS AS DELAYED SUBJECTS

We have seen nominal clauses that fill the subject slot, some of which have a formal quality more characteristic of writing than speech; in fact, such sentences are uncommon in speech:

> That the common cold is caused by a virus has been clearly established.
>
> That Sherry left school so suddenly was a shock to us all.

In conversation we are more likely to delay the information in that opening clause, substituting for the subject what is called the **anticipatory *it*:**

> It has been clearly established that the common cold is caused by a virus.
>
> It was a shock to us all that Sherry left school so suddenly.

The infinitive phrase as subject can also be delayed in this way:

> To play computer games is fun. $\longrightarrow$ It is fun to play computer games.
>
> To remain neutral on this issue is unconscionable. $\longrightarrow$ It is unconscionable to remain neutral on this issue.

The anticipatory *it* allows us to change the stress of the sentence, in much the same way that we saw with the cleft sentence in the discussion of sentence transformations in Chapter 5 (pages 103–104). This use of *it* as a tool for writers is discussed in Chapter 15 (pages 320–321).

CHAPTER 8
Key Terms

Anticipatory *it*   Delayed subject
Appositive   Dependent clause
Clause   Direct quotation
Dangling gerund   Expletive *that*

Gerund

Independent clause

Infinitive

Interrogative

Nominal

Nominal clause

Nominal verb phrase

Subordinator

Tensed verb

Sentences

for PRACTICE

Draw vertical lines to show the sentence slots. Label the form of the structure that occupies each slot. Identify the sentence pattern for each verb phrase and clause. Diagram the sentences.

1. I wonder what Jeff's problem is.

2. I think that I know what the solution to Jeff's problem is.

3. Chondra said that she would call me today when she got back home.

4. Speaking on television last week, the president announced that he will propose a tax cut during this session of Congress.

5. Where you will be in ten years is a question you probably think about sometimes.

6. The defendant's claim that he was kidnapped by aliens did not impress the jury.

7. I know how men in exile feed on dreams. [Acschylus]

8. The hen is an egg's way of producing another egg.

9. My roommate, who will graduate this month, wonders why finding a job in his field, business management, is so difficult.

10. I haven't figured out which Shakespeare play is my favorite.

11. According to the U.S. Customs Service, smuggling birds from the Caribbean has become a big business.

12. Our biological rhythms play a crucial role in determining how alert we feel.

13. I remember hearing from my grandmother about how the Great Depression affected her family.

14. The rule that we follow in this organization is that debate should be internal.

15. To know what is right and not to do it is the worst cowardice.

1. Why is the appositive set off with commas in the second of these two sentences?

> Mark's brother George coaches basketball in Indiana.

> Mark's brother, George, coaches basketball in Indiana.

Which sentence tells you that Mark has only one brother? Which sentence implies that Mark has more than one brother? Why does the following sentence need commas?

> The senator's husband, Reuben, accompanied her to Washington.

2. Consider the differences in meaning in these two pairs of sentences. How do you account for these differences? Do the differences involve different sentence patterns?

> Mel stopped to talk to Walt.

> Mel stopped talking to Walt.

> Mel started talking to Walt.

> Mel started to talk to Walt.

3. Show by a diagram how the following two sentences are different. Identify their sentence patterns.

> I went to work.

> I want to work.

4. Your understanding of participles and gerunds will help you understand and explain the ambiguity of these two sentences:

> Flying planes can be dangerous.

> I don't like burping babies.

Diagram each of them in two ways to show their two meanings.

5. What are two possible meanings of the following ambiguous sentence?

> The shooting of the hunters was a wanton act.

In what way is the traditional diagram inadequate to account for that ambiguity?

6. One of the most common roles for nominals is as object of the preposition. In the following sentences, identify the form of that object in the underlined prepositional phrases.

> This afternoon I took a nap <u>after exercising</u>.
>
> <u>Before starting my exercise program</u>, I had a thorough physical examination.
>
> <u>Until recently</u>, I did very little exercise.
>
> <u>After my physical</u>, I began doing calisthenics gradually.
>
> <u>From then on</u>, I began to be careful about my diet, too.
>
> <u>For the truly obese</u>, strenuous exercise can be dangerous.

7. In Chapter 5 we examined the passive voice of predicating verbs. Can gerunds and infinitives be passive?

8. The traditional grammarian would label the *who* clause in this famous line by Shakespeare an adjectival clause. Why? Why is it not nominal? How would you as a twenty-first-century speaker word this statement?

> Who steals my purse steals trash.

9. Perhaps the best way to explain this *that*-filled sentence is to diagram it.

> I know that that *that* that that student wrote is wrong.

CLASSROOM APPLICATIONS

The following can be organized as either oral or written activities, perhaps as timed group competitions:

1. The fact that verb phrases and clauses can fill NP slots gives the language great embedding capabilities. For example, a gerund phrase could easily fill the direct object slot in a nominal clause. Picture the diagram:

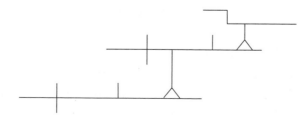

Here's a six-word sentence that would fit:

I know that Joe enjoys swimming.

Now try two other patterns:

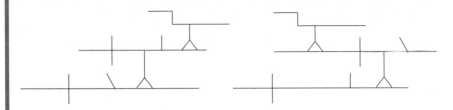

(Hint: Bear in mind that the expletive *that* can turn almost any sentence into a nominal clause. Now write a sentence with a gerund in the position shown—as subject or direct object; then turn that sentence into a nominal clause. In the first example, the sentence "Joe enjoys swimming" has been embedded as the direct object following the verb *know.*)

2. This time your task is the opposite of #1: Write a sentence in which a nominal clause is embedded in a gerund phrase.

3. Write a sentence in which an adjectival clause is embedded in a nominal clause.

4. Write a sentence in which an adverbial infinitive phrase is embedded in a gerund phrase.

5. Write a sentence in which a gerund phrase is embedded in an adverbial clause.

Note: These exercises can be organized for group or individual competition in the class. To add to the challenge, the topic of the sentences can be specified: Write about baseball, summer, winter sports, health, rap music, competition, the election campaign, movies, etc. And, of course, other specific directions could be included: Use a nominal *who* clause; use the passive voice; include two prepositional phrases; include an indirect object, etc.

CHAPTER 9

Sentence Modifiers

CHAPTER PREVIEW

The modifiers and nominals you studied in the three preceding chapters add information that expands units within the sentence: adverbials (Chapter 6), adjectivals (Chapter 7), and noun phrase substitutes (Chapter 8). The structures you will study in this chapter, however, have no clear connection to a particular sentence slot; instead, the information they add relates to the sentence as a whole.

Some of the structures identified here as sentence modifiers are often treated as adverbials. For example, most descriptions of grammar, including traditional grammar, treat all subordinate clauses as verb modifiers. Certainly, the line between the two functions—adverbial and sentence modifier—does become fuzzy at times.

In general this chapter serves as a way of gathering into one place those parts of our grammar that share an "outsider" quality, that lie outside the boundaries of the main sentence. To identify such a quality, however, is not to judge the importance of a structure in terms of meaning. It's true that sentences may be grammatical without a vocative, interjection, absolute phrase, sentence appositive, or the other independent structure described here. That fact does not lessen the impact that such a structure may have on the meaning or intent of the sentence, nor its impact on or connection to the larger text.

Like the modifiers of nouns and verbs, modifiers of the sentence as a whole also come in the form of single words, phrases, and clauses. Because most of the single-word modifiers are adverbs in form, you may be tempted to label them adverbials. However, as the following pair of sentences illustrates, there is a clear contrast in meaning between (1) the adverb as adverbial and (2) the adverb as **sentence modifier**:

1. Mark did not explain the situation <u>clearly</u>.
2. <u>Clearly</u>, Mark did not explain the situation.

The adverbial says something about the verb, about the manner in which Mark did the explaining; -*ly* adverbs are called "manner adverbs." The sentence modifier, on the other hand, indicates the attitude of the writer towards the message stated in the main clause, a signal that provides a guidepost for the reader. This kind of attitude message is called **metadiscourse;** in other words, discourse about the discourse. We will look more closely at the topic of metadiscourse in Chapter 15.

The diagrams make the difference clear:

There are a number of tests you can apply to verify the difference. For example, the adverb in sentence 1 can be moved to the preverb position:

Mark did not clearly explain the situation.

We probably wouldn't make the same change in 2, but if we did, we would have to include the commas, to retain the parenthetical meaning:

Mark did not, clearly, explain the situation.

The commas would also stay if we moved the sentence modifier to the end:

Mark did not explain the situation, clearly.

The substitution of close synonyms would also clarify the difference:

Obviously, Mark did not explain the situation.

*Mark did not explain the situation obviously.

Mark did not explain the situation very well.

*Very well, Mark did not explain the situation.

Not all single-word sentence modifiers are as easy to demonstrate as this one, where a clear contrast in meaning exists between *clearly* in its two roles. But many adverbs do have this same parenthetical quality, this metadiscourse function:

> <u>Invariably</u>, the dress or pair of shoes I like best is the one with the highest price tag.
>
> <u>Luckily</u>, the van didn't get a scratch when it hit the ditch.
>
> <u>Undoubtedly</u>, we will see interest rates gradually rise.
>
> The book you want is out of print, <u>unfortunately</u>.

But not all sentence modifiers are separated by commas:

> <u>Perhaps</u> the entire starting lineup ought to be replaced.

Here it is fairly clear that *perhaps* raises a question about the idea of the sentence as a whole. If it were moved to a position within the sentence, it would probably be set off by commas:

> The entire starting lineup, <u>perhaps</u>, ought to be replaced.

So the absence of a comma after an introductory modifier does not rule it out as a sentence modifier; but neither does the presence of a comma rule it in. As we saw in the earlier chapters on noun and verb modifiers, both adjectivals and adverbials can sometimes be shifted to the opening position. That shift does not in itself make them sentence modifiers. For example, in the following sentences the introductory phrases are adjectival, modifiers of the subject:

> <u>Hot and tired</u>, we loaded the camping gear into the station wagon for the long trip home.
>
> <u>Limping noticeably</u>, the runner rounded third base and managed to beat the throw at home plate.

Verb modifiers in introductory position are somewhat more open to interpretation as sentence modifiers, because adverbials do tend to add information that relates to the whole idea. In Chapter 6 we classified phrases like the following as modifiers of the verb, although admittedly the designation is somewhat arbitrary; a case could be made for such modifiers to be classified as sentence modifiers rather than adverbials:

> <u>To polish his skills for his trip to Las Vegas</u>, Tim plays poker every night.
>
> <u>Almost every Monday morning</u>, I make a vow to start counting calories.
>
> <u>On a day like today</u>, I prefer to stay in bed.

The less clearly a modifier is related to a particular part of the sentence, the more clearly we can classify it as a modifier of the sentence as a whole. English has many idiomatic expressions—unvarying formulas that have an independent or parenthetical quality—that are clearly sentence modifiers. Unlike the previous three adverbial examples, the introductory modifiers in the following sentences are not added for information such as *when* or *where* or *why*:

> <u>Frankly</u>, I didn't expect sailing to be so much work.
>
> <u>To our amazement</u>, the driver of the Corvette walked away from the accident.
>
> <u>To my regret</u>, I've never seen the Grand Canyon.
>
> <u>Speaking of the weather</u>, let's decide on the place for our picnic.
>
> <u>To tell the truth</u>, I have never read *Silas Marner*.

Besides the adverb, these examples include two prepositional phrases, a participial phrase, and an infinitive phrase.

You might think that the last two sentence modifiers in the list, which are verb phrases in form, look suspiciously like the danglers that we have seen in earlier discussions of gerunds and infinitives and participles. But it's probably accurate to say that, in contrast to those earlier examples, *speaking of the weather* and *to tell the truth* have achieved the status of independent idiomatic expressions, or set phrases.

Another set phrase that is becoming fairly common in spoken news reports—*having said that*—has that same almost-dangling effect. Speakers use this phrase as a transition device, usually to an idea in support of the topic under discussion or sometimes to a new topic:

> <u>Having said that</u>, the economic indicators tell us a different story.
>
> <u>Having said that</u>, we can't forget the long-term effects of the deficit.

These set phrases are diagrammed apart from the rest of the sentence with their usual pattern:

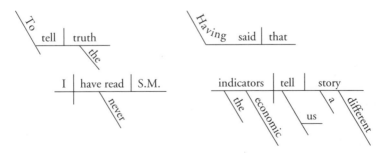

NOUNS OF DIRECT ADDRESS: THE VOCATIVES

Another structure set off by a comma is the noun or noun phrase of direct address, known as a **vocative**:

> Ladies and gentlemen, please be seated.

> Jennifer, your date is here.

Although the vocative is not a modifier in the same sense that other structures are, in that it does not modify the meaning of the sentence, it does have a relationship to the sentence as a whole. And like other modifiers, it can come at the beginning, middle, or end of the sentence:

> We certainly hope, my dear friends, that you will visit again soon.

> I promise you won't see me here in court again, your honor.

> Tell us, Mr. President, how your new tax plan will benefit the economy.

The purpose of the vocative, as the term "direct address" implies, is to direct the writer's or speaker's message to a particular person or group. (In most cases it's the speaker's message: This structure is much more common in speech than in writing.) And, as the foregoing examples illustrate, the vocative can express the attitude of the writer or speaker and reflect the tone, whether formal or informal, serious or light, familiar or distant. In that sense, certainly, the vocative is a "sentence modifier": It can affect the meaning of the words.

The vocatives are diagrammed just as the other sentence modifiers are, on a line set apart from the main clause.

INTERJECTIONS

The **interjection**—usually a single word or short phrase—can also be considered as a modifier of the sentence as a whole:

> Oh, don't frighten me like that!

> Wow! That's not what I expected.

The traditional view of grammar treats the interjection as one of the eight parts of speech, probably because there is no other way to categorize such "nonwords" as *oh* and *ah* and *wow* and *ouch*. However, many words that we recognize as nouns and verbs are also used as exclamatory sentence modifiers of this kind:

> Heavens, I don't know what to say.

> Good grief! Don't confuse me with the facts!

> My word! This will never do.

Like the vocatives, interjections are much more likely to occur in speech than in writing (other than written dialogue).

It might seem logical to consider these actual words as interjections, the same as we treat *oh* and *wow;* however, we do not put all such "interjections" into a single parts-of-speech class, as the traditional grammarians do. Such a classification distorts the principle on which we make judgments about word categories. Except for *oh* and *ah* and *whew* and a few others, we recognize interjections strictly by their exclamatory, or emotional, function in the sentence. It's true, of course, that the familiar definitions given to the traditional eight parts of speech are not necessarily consistent in their criteria; for example, nouns and verbs are defined according to their meaning (as names and as actions) and adjectives and adverbs by their function (as modifiers). Nevertheless, out of all eight traditional "parts of speech," only the interjection category is denoted strictly by sentence function, rather than as a word type; that is, the other seven traditional parts of speech (noun, verb, adjective, adverb, pronoun, preposition, and conjunction) are names of word classes. It is for this reason that the interjection is not included in our inventory of structure words, described in Chapter 13, but, rather, is included here as a function, one kind of sentence modifier.

Interjections, like the other sentence modifiers, are diagrammed on a separate line.

Exercise 39

Underline any sentence modifiers in the following sentences.

1. Amazingly, the money held out until the end of the month.
2. The twins look amazingly alike.
3. Well, I plan to stay, myself.
4. Myself, I plan to stay well.
5. Strangely, he seemed to look right through me.
6. I thought he looked at me strangely.
7. Without a doubt our team will win the league championship.
8. We will no doubt win the league championship.
9. I told my friend I was not interested in her scheme.
10. I told you, my friend, that I am not interested.

SUBORDINATE CLAUSES

In Chapter 6 we looked at the adverbial clauses, recognizing that they, too, often seem to relate to the sentence as a whole rather than to the verb specifically. Those introduced by *where, when, before,* and *after* seem to be the most "adverbial" of all in that they convey information of time and place about the verb; but certainly we could make an equal case for classifying even these as sentence modifiers. **Subordinate clauses** introduced by such subordinators as *if, since, as,* and *although* seem even more clearly to modify the idea of the whole sentence, because the subordinator explains the relationship of one idea to another:

> *If* you promise to be there, I'll go to Sue's party.
>
> I'll go with you, *although* I would rather stay home.

The phrasal subordinators, too, may relate one complete clause to another:

> *Provided that* the moving van arrives on schedule, we'll be ready to leave by three o'clock.
>
> All the members of the city council, *as far as* I know, voted in favor of the new dog ordinance.

(See pages 283–284 for a list of the simple and phrasal subordinators.)

Some of the interrogatives and **indefinite relative pronouns** introduce conditional clauses that are clearly sentence modifiers:

> *Whatever* decision you eventually make, I'll support you.
>
> *Whichever* route we take, there's no way we'll get there on time in this traffic.
>
> *No matter how much* overtime I work, my paycheck never seems to stretch far enough.

The subjunctive *if* clauses that we saw in Chapter 4 can also join this list of clauses that say something about the sentence as a whole:

> If I were you, I'd skip the party.

Punctuation of Subordinate Clauses. In opening position the subordinate clause is always set off by a comma; in closing position, punctuation is related to meaning. As a general rule, when the idea in the main clause is conditional upon or dependent upon the idea in the subordinate clause, there is no comma. For example, the idea of the main clause—the opening clause—in the following sentence will be realized only if the idea in the subordinate clause is carried out; thus here the main clause depends on the *if* clause:

> I'll go to Sue's party *if you promise to be there.*

But in the next sentence the subordinate clause does not affect the fulfillment of the main clause:

> I'm going to the party that Sue's giving on Saturday night, *even though I know I'll be bored.*

The distinction between these two functions is comparable to the restrictive/nonrestrictive distinction we examined in connection with adjectivals in Chapter 7. If the subordinate clause "defines" the situation, it will not be set off from the main clause; if it simply "comments," it will take the comma.

In general *even though* and *although* are preceded by commas; *if* is not. The point to be made here is that the subordinator relates the idea in its clause to the idea in the main clause, so the subordinate clause clearly functions as a modifier of the sentence as a whole—even though it is not preceded by a comma. But in opening position, the clause is always followed by a comma. The use of the comma with final subordinate clauses is probably one of the least standardized of our punctuation rules. The final criteria must be readability and clarity for the reader.

Exercise 40

Add commas to the following sentences, if necessary.

1. We left the party as soon as we politely could.
2. Jim agreed to leave the party early and go bowling with us although he was having a good time.
3. When the storm is over we can head for home.
4. We might as well put on the coffee since we're going to be here for another hour.
5. I know that Jerry and I will never be able to afford that much money for rent even if it does include utilities.
6. I won't be able to stay in this apartment if the rent goes any higher.
7. I won't be able to stay in this apartment even if the rent stays the same.
8. If you can't stand the heat get out of the kitchen. [Harry Truman]

Elliptical Clauses. Many subordinate clauses are **elliptical**—that is, certain understood words are left out:

> <u>While</u> [we were] <u>waiting for the guests to arrive</u>, we ate all the good hors d'oeuvres ourselves.

> <u>When</u> [I am] <u>in doubt about the weather</u>, I always carry an umbrella.

As a reader, you have no problem understanding either of those elliptical clauses: In both cases the missing words, the subject of the elliptical clause, show up as the subject of the main clause.

What would happen if that understood subject did not show up? The result would be a fuzzy sentence, similar to those we have seen with dangling participles and gerunds and infinitives. Like the opening verb phrase, the elliptical element sets up certain expectations in the reader; it's the writer's job to fulfill those expectations. Consider what you expect in the main clause following these elliptical openers:

*When late for work, the subway is better than the bus.

*If kept too long in hot weather, mold will grow on the bread.

*While driving to the game on Saturday, an accident tied up traffic for over an hour.

As with many of the dangling structures we have seen, the message of the sentence may be clear; but there's simply no reason for a writer to set up a situation in which the reader must make the connections—and must do so in a conscious way. Those connections are the writer's job.

In some cases only the elliptical version is grammatical:

I'm a week older than Bob.

My sister isn't as tall as I.

or

I'm a week older than Bob is.

My sister isn't as tall as I am.

We would never include the entire clause:

*I'm a week older than Bob is old.

*My sister isn't as tall as I am tall.

In both of these examples, we are comparing an attribute of the subjects of the two clauses. But the ellipses in such comparisons can produce ambiguity when the main clause has more than one possible noun phrase for the subordinate clause to be compared with:

The Packers beat the Patriots worse than the Panthers.

Joe likes Mary better than Pat.

In these sentences we don't know whether the comparison is between subjects or objects because we don't know what has been left out. We don't know whether

The Packers beat the Patriots worse than }   the Packers beat the Panthers.
or
the Panthers beat the Patriots.

Joe likes Mary better than }   Joe likes Pat.
or
Pat likes Mary.

See the Appendix for diagrams illustrating these clauses (p. 376).

The comparison in the clauses with *as . . . as* can become a problem when an alternative comparison is added. Here is how such comparisons should read:

Our team is <u>as good as</u>, or <u>better than</u>, the Wildcats.

But sometimes the writer (or speaker) omits the second *as*:

*Our team is as good, or better than, the Wildcats.

*My sister is just as strong, or stronger than, you.

These omissions do not result in ambiguity, but the sentences clearly have a grammatical problem—an incomplete comparison.

Incidentally, these clauses of comparison are actually modifying adjectives—*older, tall, worse, better, good,* and *strong*—the qualities that are being compared, rather than modifying the sentence as a whole. We are discussing them here with the sentence modifiers because of the shared elliptical feature.

Exercise 41

A. Rewrite the three sentences on page 201 to include a subject in the elliptical clause. You may have to make changes in the main clause as well.

1. When late for work, the subway is better than the bus.

2. If kept too long in hot weather, mold will grow on the bread.

3. While driving to the game on Saturday, an accident tied up traffic for over an hour.

B. Now rewrite the following sentences, supplying the words missing in the elliptical clauses. Are the sentences clear?

1. I picked up a Midwestern accent while living in Omaha.

2. My accent is not as noticeable as Carlo's.

3. Holmes hit Ali harder than Norton.

4. If necessary, strain the juice before adding the sugar.

5. While waiting at the train station in Lewistown, there was no place to sit.

6. If handed in late, your grade will be lowered 10 percent.

7. Love goes toward love, as schoolboys from their books. But love from love, toward school with heavy looks. [Shakespeare]

8. The weather in Little Rock is not as humid as New Orleans.

ABSOLUTE PHRASES

The absolute phrase (also known as the *nominative absolute*) is a structure independent from the main sentence; in form the absolute phrase is a noun phrase that includes a postnoun modifier. The modifier is commonly an *-en* or *-ing* participle or participial phrase, but it can also be a prepositional phrase, an adjective phrase, or a noun phrase. The absolute phrase introduces an idea related to the sentence as a whole, not to any one of its parts:

> <u>Our car having developed engine trouble</u>, we stopped for the night at a roadside rest area.
>
> <u>The weather being warm and clear</u>, we decided to have a picnic.
>
> <u>Victory assured</u>, the fans stood and cheered during the last five minutes of the game.

Absolute phrases are of two kinds—with different purposes and different effects. (Moreover, both are structures generally used in writing, rather than in speech.) The preceding sentences illustrate the first kind: the absolute that explains a cause or condition. In the first sentence, the absolute phrase could be rewritten as a *because, when,* or *since* clause:

> When our car developed engine trouble,
>
> *or*
>
> Since our car developed engine trouble,   } we stopped for the night. . . .
>
> *or*
>
> Because our car developed engine trouble,

The absolute construction allows the writer to include the information without the explicitness that the complete clause requires. In other words, the absolute phrase can be thought of as containing all the meanings in the three versions shown here rather than any one of them.

In the following sentence the idea in the *because* clause could be interpreted as the only reason for the picnic:

> <u>Because the weather was warm and clear</u>, we decided to have a picnic.

The absolute construction, on the other hand, leaves open the possibility of other reasons for the picnic:

> <u>The weather being warm and clear</u>, we decided to have a picnic.

It also suggests simply an attendant condition rather than a cause.

Perhaps the most famous absolute phrase is the one found in the Second Amendment to the United States Constitution. And, as we know, it is open to more than one interpretation:

> A well-regulated militia, being necessary to the security of a free state, the right of the people to keep and bear arms, shall not be infringed.

The author might have been well advised to use a structure other than the absolute phrase: A full clause or a separate sentence could have forestalled the controversy that surrounds the amendment's meaning. We should note, too, that the convention of comma use has changed in the intervening years; two of those commas are superfluous by today's standards.

In the second kind of absolute phrase, illustrated by the sentences following, a prepositional phrase (*above his head*), adjective phrase (*alert to every passing footstep*), or noun phrase (*a dripping mess*), as well as a participle (*trembling*), may serve as the postnoun modifier. This second kind of absolute adds a detail or point of focus to the idea stated in the main clause:

> Julie tried to fit the key into the rusty lock, her hands trembling.
>
> The old hound stood guard faithfully, his ears alert to every passing footstep.
>
> Hands above his head, the suspect advanced cautiously toward the uniformed officers.
>
> Her hair a dripping mess, she dashed in out of the rain.

This technique of focusing on a detail allows the writer to move the reader in for a close-up view, just as a filmmaker uses the camera. The absolute phrase is especially effective in writing description. Notice how the authors of the following passages use the main clause of the sentence as the wide lens and the absolute phrase as the close-up:

> There was no bus in sight and Julian, his hands still jammed in his pockets and his head thrust forward, scowled down the empty street.
>
> FLANNERY O'CONNOR, *Everything That Rises Must Converge*

> The man stood laughing, his weapons at his hips.
>
> STEPHEN CRANE, *The Bride Comes to Yellow Sky*

> To his right the valley continued in its sleepy beauty, mute and understated, its wildest autumn colors blunted by the distance, placid as a water color by an artist who mixed all his colors with brown.
>
> JOYCE CAROL OATES, *The Secret Marriage*

The traditional diagram of the absolute simply shows the noun phrase on a line separate from the main clause, with the headword on the horizontal:

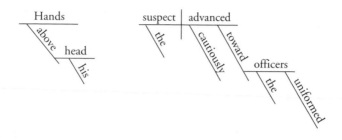

Exercise 42

Underline any absolute phrases in the following sentences. Is the modifier of the headword an adjective, a prepositional phrase, a noun phrase, or a participle?

1. The cat lay by the fire, purring contentedly, her tail moving from side to side like a metronome.

2. Chuck and Margie kicked their way through the fallen leaves, their arms draped across each other's shoulders.

3. The rain having persisted for over an hour, the game was officially stopped in the sixth inning.

4. Michelle lounged in front of the fire, her book open on the floor, her eyes intent on the flames.

5. He saw the city spread below like a glittering golden ocean, the streets tiny ribbons of light, the planet curving away at the edges, the sky a purple hollow extending into infinity. [Anne Tyler]

6. Then the boy was moving, his bunched shirt and the hard, bony hand between his shoulder-blades, his toes just touching the floor, across the room and into the other one, past the sisters sitting with spread heavy thighs in the two chairs over the cold hearth, and to where his mother and aunt sat side by side on the bed, the aunt's arms about his mother's shoulders. [William Faulkner]

APPOSITIVES

You'll recall that one of the nominals described in Chapter 8 is the appositive, a structure that in form is often a noun phrase:

Our visitor, <u>a grey-haired lady of indeterminate age</u>, surprised us all
when she joined in the volleyball game.

In this example, the appositive renames the subject of the sentence. But
sometimes we use a noun phrase to rename or, more accurately, to encap-
sulate the idea in the sentence as a whole. We call these structures sentence
appositives:

He waved his pink right hand in circles, <u>his favorite gesture</u>.

JOHN FOWLES, *The Magus*

We often use a dash to set off the sentence appositive:

The musical opened to rave reviews and standing-room-only
crowds—<u>a smashing success</u>.

A pair of cardinals has set up housekeeping in our pine tree—<u>an
unexpected but welcome event</u>.

Like the absolutes, which are also noun phrases in form, these sentence
appositives are related to the sentence as a whole, but their purpose is
quite different: They simply label, or restate, the idea of the main clause;
they do not introduce a new, subordinate idea, as both kinds of absolute
phrases do.

The rhetorical effects of sentence appositives are discussed further in
Chapter 15.

RELATIVE CLAUSES

Most relative clauses are modifiers of nouns, and most are introduced by
a relative pronoun that refers to that noun:

Joe's car, <u>which he bought just last week</u>, looks like a gas guzzler
to me.

In this sentence the antecedent of *which* is the noun *car*; the noun is
modified by the clause.

But in some sentences *which* refers not to a particular noun but to a
whole idea; it has what we call *broad reference*. In the following sentence,
the antecedent of *which* is the idea of the entire main clause:

Joe bought a gas guzzler, <u>which surprised me</u>.

All such broad-reference clauses are introduced by *which*, never by *who*
or *that*, and all are nonrestrictive—that is, they are set off by commas:

Tom cleaned up the garage without being asked, <u>which made me
suspect that he wanted to borrow the car</u>.

> This summer's heat wave in the Midwest devastated the corn crop,
> <u>which probably means higher meat prices for next year</u>.

Many writers try to avoid the broad-reference relative clause, instead using *which* only in the adjectival clause to refer to a specific noun. In inexperienced hands the broad-reference *which* clause often has the vagueness associated with dangling modifiers:

> I broke out in a rash, <u>which really bothered me</u>.

In this sentence the referent of *which* is unclear; *which* could refer to either the *rash* or the *breaking out*. There are a number of alternatives in which the meaning is clear:

> Breaking out in a rash really bothered me.
>
> The rash I got last week really bothered me.

Even though they are not particularly vague, the earlier examples, too, can be revised in ways that avoid the broad-reference *which:*

> When Tom cleaned up the garage without being asked, I suspected
> that he wanted to borrow the car.
>
> Tom's cleaning up the garage without being asked made me suspect
> that he wanted to borrow the car.
>
> This summer's heat wave in the Midwest, which devastated the
> corn crop, probably means higher meat prices for next year.

Exercise 43

Rewrite the following sentences to eliminate the broad-reference *which*.

1. I had to clean the basement this morning, which wasn't very much fun.
2. Otis didn't want to stay for the second half of the game, which surprised me.
3. The president criticized the Congress rather severely in his press conference, which some observers considered quite inappropriate.
4. The first snowstorm of the season in Denver was both early and severe, which was not what the weather service had predicted.
5. We're having company for dinner three times this week, which probably means hot dogs for the rest of the month.

CHAPTER 9
Key Terms

Absolute phrase

Broad-reference clause

Direct address

Elliptical clause

Idiomatic expression

Independent modifier

Interjection

Metadiscourse

Relative clause

Sentence appositive

Sentence modifier

Subordinate clause

Vocative

Sentences
for PRACTICE

Draw vertical lines to set off sentence modifiers; identify them by form. If the sentence modifier is, or includes, a verb phrase or clause, identify its sentence pattern.

1. My brother will finish basic training next month if everything goes smoothly.
2. Last week stock prices scored surprisingly strong gains as Wall Street experienced one of the busiest periods in the market's history.
3. If you don't mind, I want to be alone.
4. Speaking of travel, would you like to go to Seattle next week to see the Seahawks play?
5. Incidentally, you forgot to pay me for your share of the expenses.
6. The weather being so beautiful last Sunday, we decided to go to Silver Creek Falls for a picnic.
7. The invitations having been sent, we started planning the menu for Maria's birthday party.
8. Jennifer stayed in bed all day, her fever getting worse instead of better.
9. If bread is kept too long in hot weather, mold will begin to grow on it.
10. The giant redwoods loomed majestically, their branches filling the sky above us.

11. It is impossible to enjoy idling thoroughly unless one has plenty of work to do. [Jerome K. Jerome]

12. Luckily, Sunday was a nice day, so we didn't miss our weekly hike.

13. Freddie suggested we take a taxi instead of the subway—a splendid idea.

14. Old Town was festive, indeed—the stores decorated with bright-colored banners, the air alive with music, the streets crowded with people.

15. If I can stop one heart from breaking, I shall not live in vain. [Emily Dickinson]

QUESTIONS
?
for DISCUSSION

1. Many of the simple and phrasal subordinators listed on pages 283–284 introduce clauses that could be interpreted as either sentence modifiers or verb modifiers. How would you classify the underlined clauses in the following sentences—as sentence modifiers or as verb modifiers? Why?

   I'll return your book <u>as soon as I finish it</u>.

   He'll lend me the money <u>provided that I use it for tuition</u>.

   The dog looked at me <u>as if he wanted to tell me something important</u>.

   Nero fiddled <u>while Rome burned</u>.

2. The following sentences are both illogical and ungrammatical. What is the source of the problem?

   The summer temperatures in the Santa Clara Valley are much higher than San Francisco.

   The Pirates' stolen-base record is better than the Cardinals.

3. The following sentence is less elliptical than those you just read, but it's equally fuzzy. What is the source of its problem?

   The people of Atlanta are much friendlier than they are in New York.

4. Consider the pronouns in these elliptical clauses. Are they the correct form? Is it possible that both sentences are correct?

> I think my little sister likes our cat better than me.
>
> I think my little sister likes our cat better than I.

5. A common subject for discussion among people who think about language and usage is the "problem" of *hopefully*. The following sentences are, in fact, avoided by many speakers and writers:

   > Hopefully, we will get to the theater before the play starts.
   >
   > Hopefully, this play will be better than the last one we saw.

   Is the adverb *hopefully* used incorrectly in these sentences? Should it be used only as a manner adverb? Or can it function as a sentence modifier? Make a case for both sides of the issue. (In considering *hopefully*, think also about other adverbs as sentence modifiers, such as c*learly, luckily, confidentially, seriously,* and *admittedly*.)

6. How do you explain the difference in meaning between the following sentences, which appear so similar on the surface? Discuss the effect of the understood elliptical clause in the second sentence. Are both sentences negative?

   > I have never been happy with our living arrangement.
   >
   > I have never been happier with our living arrangement.

7. The little comma can carry a great deal of meaning. Explain why it's so important in this sentence.

   > You should call the boss, Herbert.

   What happens to the meaning of the sentence when the comma is removed? Use your knowledge of sentence patterns in thinking about the two meanings.

8. As you consider the ambiguity of the following sentence, think about two of the topics you have studied in this chapter and in the previous one, vocatives and appositives:

   > I am taking a trip with Mildred, my dear friend.

   Rewrite the sentence in two ways to show its meanings unambiguously.

CLASSROOM APPLICATIONS

1. Combine the following pairs of sentences, reducing one of them to a sentence modifier. Experiment with variations.

Example:

I was lucky. I knew how to swim

<u>Luckily, I knew how to swim</u>.

   1. The door was closed. We climbed in the back window.
   2. The contract is invalid. That's a fact.
   3. The guests departed. We resumed our normal household routine.
   4. Consider the circumstances. He was lucky to escape alive.
   5. Felice is the best tenor in the choir. That's my opinion.
   6. I'll tell you the truth. I don't like your new haircut.
   7. She did not complete her thesis. That is unfortunate.
   8. The copy machine has been malfunctioning. That was apparent.
   9. Our school orchestra is not the best in the world. Everyone is sure of that.
   10. It doesn't matter what you say. Graham is going to quit school.

2. One popular technique for teaching writing, which dates back to the schools of Ancient Greece, is known as modeling. Students learn to write by copying the form of sentences, using the same blueprint while supplying new words. For this exercise, you are to model the following sentences, some of which you saw earlier as examples of absolute phrases. Remember the comparison of the absolute to the close-up view; the main clause provides the wide-angle shot.

Example:

The man stood laughing, his weapon at his hips.

Modeled version:

The woman sat smoking, a black poodle in her lap.

   1. The man stood laughing, his weapon at his hips.
      [Stephen Crane]

2. With a breathy shriek the train pulled away, the crowd cheering, waving at the caboose until it was out of sight. [E. Annie Proulx]

3. There was no bus in sight and Julian, his hands still jammed in his pockets and his head thrust forward, scowled down the empty street. [Flannery O'Connor]

4. He smiled to himself as he ran, holding the ball lightly in front of him with his two hands, his knees pumping high, his hips twisting in the almost girlish run of a back in a broken field. [Irwin Shaw]

5. Soon afterwards they retired, Mama in her big oak bed on one side of the room, Emilio and Rosy in their boxes full of straw and sheepskins on the other side of the room. [John Steinbeck]

6. In the pouring rain, following a muddy, almost invisible path, I finally arrived at the station, my shoes leaving puddles with every step, my clothes and satchel waterlogged. [Devon Riley]

CHAPTER 10

Coordination

CHAPTER PREVIEW

Throughout the previous chapters you have been seeing coordination within sentences, both in the samples for discussion and in the text itself. In fact, the sentence you just read includes one such structure, a compound prepositional phrase connected by the correlative conjunction *both–and*. We make these connections at every level—word, phrase, and clause; in speech we do so automatically.

In this chapter we will take up several features of compound structures within the sentence, including punctuation, ellipsis, subject-verb agreement, and parallelism. Then we will look at the coordination of whole sentences, with special emphasis on the punctuation conventions that apply to them.

COORDINATION WITHIN THE SENTENCE

Punctuation. A simple punctuation rule applies to nearly all the compound pairs of words, phrases, and clauses that occur within the sentence: *We use no comma with the conjunction.* Notice in the following examples that no comma appears even when the two parts being joined are fairly long:

> On Homecoming weekend our frat party <u>started at noon *and* lasted until dawn</u>. (compound verb phrase)
>
> I will buy <u>*either* the blue dress with the long sleeves *or* the green print with a matching jacket</u>. (compound noun phrase)
>
> He said <u>that he would get here sooner or later *and* that I shouldn't start the rehearsal without him</u>. (compound dependent clause)

An exception to the rule against commas with compound elements occurs when the conjunction is *but:*

> I have visited a lot of big cities, <u>but</u> never Los Angeles.
>
> I worked hard all night, <u>but</u> just couldn't finish my project.
>
> My new white dress is beautiful, <u>but</u> not very practical.

There's a clear disjunction with *but*, resulting, of course, from its meaning: It introduces a contrast. Furthermore, the phrase introduced by *but* could almost be thought of as an elliptical clause, another reason that the comma seems logical:

> I worked hard all night, but [I] just couldn't finish my project.
>
> My new white dress is beautiful, but [it is] not very practical.

Another exception to the comma restriction occurs when we want to give special emphasis to the second element in a coordinated pair:

> I didn't believe him, and said so.
>
> My new white dress is beautiful, and expensive.

This emphasis will be even stronger with a dash instead of a comma:

> I didn't believe him—and said so.
>
> My new white dress is beautiful—and expensive.

We also use commas with a series of three or more elements:

> We gossiped, laughed, and sang together at the class reunion, just like old times.

These commas represent the pauses and slight changes of pitch that occur in the production of the series. You can hear the commas in your voice when you compare the two—the series and the pair. Read them aloud:

> We gossiped, laughed, and sang.
>
> We laughed and sang.

You probably noticed a leveling of the pitch in reading the pair, a certain smoothness that the series did not have. In the series with conjunctions instead of commas, you'll notice that same leveling:

> We gossiped <u>and</u> laughed <u>and</u> sang together at the class reunion, just like old times.

When conjunctions connect all the elements, we use no commas.

In the series of three, some writers—and some publications as a matter of policy—use only one comma, leaving out the **serial comma**, the one immediately before *and:*

> We gossiped, laughed <u>and</u> sang together at the class reunion, just like old times.

Perhaps they do so on the assumption that the conjunction substitutes for the comma. But it really does not. In fact, this punctuation misleads the reader in two ways: It implies a closer connection than actually exists between the last two elements of the series, and it ignores the pitch change, however slight, represented by the comma. The main purpose of punctuation, after all, is to represent graphically the meaningful speech signals—pitch, stress (loudness), and juncture (pauses)—that the written language otherwise lacks. That small pitch change represented by the comma can make a difference in emphasis and meaning.

Exercise 44

Punctuate the following sentences.

1. Pete sanded the car on Friday and painted it with undercoating on Saturday.

2. Even though the car's new paint job looks terrific now I suspect it will be covered with rust and scratches and dents before next winter.

3. I spent a fortune on new tires shock absorbers and brake linings for the car last week.

4. The car that my grandfather had back in the 1960s and 1970s a 1959 Chevy required very little maintenance and no major repairs during the ten or more years he drove it.

5. I have decided to park my car until gas prices go down and to ride my bicycle instead.

6. I don't suppose I'll ever be able to afford either the down payment or the insurance on a new Corvette the car of my dreams.

Elliptical Coordinate Structures. Elliptical structures are those in which something has been left out. You'll recall from the discussion in the previous chapter that fuzziness or ambiguity sometimes results when the "understood" element is not, in fact, understood. The same kind of problem can occur with coordinate structures.

One common ellipsis is the elimination of the second determiner in a coordinate noun phrase:

The cat and dog are sleeping on the porch.

A problem can arise when the noun phrase includes modifiers:

Our new cat and dog are sleeping on the porch.

The clear implication of the noun phrase is that both the cat and the dog are new. If that's not the case, then *dog* needs its own determiner:

> Our new cat and our dog are sleeping on the porch.
>
> *or*
>
> Our dog and new cat are sleeping on the porch.

Postnoun modifiers can also be the source of ambiguity in coordinate structures:

> Visitors to this area always admire the flower gardens and stately elms on campus.

Without a determiner for *elms*, the reader is justified in inferring that both the flowers and trees are on the campus, although it's certainly possible that the writer had a different intention. The problem of ambiguity is much more blatant when both noun phrases have determiners:

> Visitors to this area always admire the flower gardens and the stately elms on campus.

Now the reader has no way to decide what *on campus* modifies. If only the elms are on campus, the writer can either reverse the two noun phrases or add another modifier so that both locations are clear:

> . . . the stately elms on campus and the flower gardens.
>
> . . . the flower gardens near City Hall and the stately elms on campus.

Here's a similar problem sentence, one with an ambiguous *by* phrase:

> Penn State's administration building, Old Main, is best known for its presidential portraits and [its] murals by Henry Varnum Poor.

With or without the determiner for *murals*, this sentence is ambiguous. Another problem can occur with numbers as determiners:

> There were six men and women waiting in line.
>
> There were six dogs and cats on the porch.
>
> There were six mothers and daughters at the mother-daughter reception.

We don't, of course, know whether the noun phrases include six or twelve people or animals.

There are many possibilities for structural ambiguity, where the reader simply has no way of knowing the writer's intention. Coordinate structures are especially open to misinterpretation. It's the job of the writer to make sure that the meaning is clear.

Subject–Verb Agreement. When nouns or noun phrases in the subject slot are joined by *and* or by the correlative *both–and*, the subject is plural:

> My roommate and his brother are coming to the wedding.

However, the coordinating conjunction *or* and the correlatives *either-or* and *neither-nor* do not have the additive meaning of *and*; with *or* and *nor* the relationship is called disjunctive. In compound subjects with these conjunctions, the verb will be determined by the closer member of the pair:

> Neither the speaker nor the listeners were intimidated by the protestors.

> Either the class officers or the faculty advisor makes the final decision.

> Do the class officers or the faculty advisor make the final decision?

> Does the faculty advisor or the class officers make the final decision?

If the correct sentence sounds incorrect or awkward because of the verb form, you can simply reverse the compound pair:

> Either the faculty advisor or the class officers make the final decision.

When both members of the pair are alike, of course, there is no question:

> Either the president or the vice-president is going to introduce the speaker.

> Neither the union members nor the management representatives were willing to compromise.

For most verb forms, you'll recall, there is no decision to be made about subject–verb agreement; the issue arises only when the -*s* form of the verb or auxiliary is involved. In the following sentences, there is no -*s* form:

> Either the class officers or the faculty advisor will make the final decision.

> Either the faculty advisor or the class officers will make the final decision.

Another situation that sometimes causes confusion about number—that is, whether the subject is singular or plural—occurs with subjects that include a phrase introduced by *as well as* or *in addition to* or *along with*:

> *The sidewalk, in addition to the driveway, need to be repaired.

> *The piano player, as well as the rest of the group, usually join in the singing.

> *Mike, along with several friends, often help out at the bakery on weekends.

These additions to the subject are parenthetical; they are not treated as part of the subject. To make the subject compound—to include them—the writer should use a coordinating conjunction, such as *and*:

> The sidewalk <u>and</u> the driveway <u>need</u> to be repaired.
>
> The piano player <u>and</u> the rest of the group usually <u>join</u> in the singing.
>
> Mike <u>and</u> several friends often <u>help</u> out at the bakery on weekends.

Parallel Structure. An important requirement for coordinate structures is that they be **parallel**. A structure is parallel when all the coordinate parts are of the same grammatical form. The conjunctions must join comparable structures, such as pairs of noun phrases or verb phrases or adjectives:

> The <u>short blonde woman</u> *and* <u>her apricot poodle</u> seemed to belong together.
>
> The stew <u>smells delicious</u> *and* <u>tastes even better</u>.
>
> The entire cast gave <u>powerful</u> *and* <u>exciting</u> performances.

Unparallel structures occur most commonly with the correlative conjunctions: *both–and, either–or, neither–nor,* and *not only–but also*. For example, in the following sentence, the two coordinators introduce structures of different forms:

> *Either <u>they will fly straight home</u> *or* <u>stop overnight in Dubuque</u>.

Being able to picture the diagram can be helpful in preventing such unparallel structures. With the sentence above, you'll discover that the conjunction line would connect a complete sentence (*they will fly straight home*) and a verb phrase (*stop overnight in Dubuque*). Because the two structures are not parallel, the diagram simply won't work.

A diagram of the following sentence won't work either:

> *I'll *either* <u>take a bus</u> *or* <u>a taxi</u>.

The conjunction line would have to connect a verb phrase and a noun phrase; again the two structures are not parallel.

Such problems are easy to correct. It's just a matter of shifting one part of the correlative pair so that both introduce the same kind of construction:

> They will *either* <u>fly straight home</u> *or* <u>stop overnight in Dubuque</u>.
>
> I'll take *either* <u>a bus</u> *or* <u>a taxi</u>.

Further examples of the correlative conjunctions are given on page 282.

Exercise | **45**

Rewrite the following sentences, paying particular attention to unparallel structures and agreement errors.

1. I can't decide which activity I prefer: to swim at the shore in July, when the sand is warm, or jogging along country roads in October, when the autumn leaves are at their colorful best.

2. I almost never watch television. There is either nothing on that appeals to me or the picture disappears at a crucial moment.

3. I neither enjoy flying across the country nor particularly want to take the train.

4. Either the members of the school board or the superintendent make the final decision.

5. The recipe was either printed wrong, or I misread it.

6. I was unhappy with what he said and the way he said it.

7. The coach announced an extra hour of drill on Saturday and that the practice on Sunday would be canceled.

8. My history class, as well as both English classes, require a term paper.

9. Aunt Rosa has promised to fix her famous lasagna for my birthday dinner and will also bake my favorite cake.

10. For the picnic we brought baskets of chicken and lemonade.

COORDINATING COMPLETE SENTENCES

We have three methods of joining independent clauses to produce **compound sentences**: (1) using coordinating conjunctions; (2) using the semicolon, either with or without conjunctive adverbs; and (3), for limited situations, using the colon.

Conjunctions. The compound sentence with a coordinating conjunction such as *and* shows up at an early stage of the writer's development:

We went to the fair, <u>and</u> we had a good time.

Robby is mean, <u>and</u> I don't like him.

Such sentences can, of course, be effective when they are used sparingly, but they will strike the reader as immature when overused. The compound sentence is most effective when the coordinate ideas have relatively equal importance—when the two ideas contribute equal weight:

> I disapprove of her spending money on lottery tickets, <u>and</u> I told her so.

> The curtain rose to reveal a perfectly bare stage, <u>and</u> a stillness settled over the audience.

> Pete filled the bags with hot roasted peanuts, <u>and</u> I stapled them shut.

Note that the punctuation rule that applies to the compound sentence differs from the rule regarding internal coordinate constructions. Between the sentences in a compound sentence we do use a comma with the conjunction; between the parts of a coordinate structure within the sentence we do not. When the clauses of a compound sentence are quite short and closely connected, however, we sometimes omit the comma. The following sentence, for example, would probably be spoken without the pitch change we associate with commas:

> October came <u>and</u> the tourists left.

The coordinators *and* and *or* can link a series of three or more sentences:

> Pete filled the bags, <u>and</u> I stapled them shut, <u>and</u> Marty packed them in the cartons.

> The kids can wait for me at the pool, <u>or</u> they can go over to the shopping center and catch the bus, <u>or</u> they can even walk home.

In these two sentences, the first conjunction can be replaced by a comma:

> Pete filled the bags, I stapled them shut, <u>and</u> Marty packed them in the cartons.

But usually joins only two clauses:

> Jill wanted me to wait for her, <u>but</u> I refused.

But can introduce the final clause when *and* or *or* joins the first two:

> Pete filled the bags, <u>and</u> I stapled them, <u>but</u> Marty refused to lift a finger.

> The kids can wait for me at the pool, <u>or</u> they can walk to the bus stop, <u>but</u> I really think they ought to walk home.

Semicolons. When a semicolon connects two coordinate clauses, the conjunction can be omitted:

> Pete packed the hot roasted peanuts into bags; I stapled them shut.

> The curtain rose; a stillness settled over the audience.

The semicolon is also used when a **conjunctive adverb** introduces the second clause. Note, too, that the conjunctive adverb is set off by a comma:

> We worked hard for the Consumer Party candidates, ringing doorbells and stuffing envelopes; <u>however</u>, we knew they didn't stand a chance.

> We knew our candidates didn't have a hope of winning; <u>nevertheless</u>, for weeks on end we faithfully rang doorbells and stuffed envelopes.

Of all the adverbial conjunctions, only *yet* and *so* can be used with a comma instead of a semicolon between clauses:

> Several formations of birds were flying northward, <u>so</u> I knew spring was on the way.

> Several formations of birds were flying northward, <u>yet</u> I suspected that winter was far from over.

In both of these sentences, a semicolon could replace the comma, depending on the writer's emphasis. The semicolon would put extra emphasis on the second clause. *So* and *yet* straddle the border between the coordinating conjunctions and the conjunctive adverbs; they are often listed as both. In meaning, *so* is similar to *therefore* and *yet* to *however*; but unlike these conjunctive adverbs, *so* and *yet* always introduce the clause, so in this respect they are perhaps closer to the coordinating conjunctions. Sometimes we use both the conjunction and the adverbial: *and so*; *but yet*.

Because they are also adverbials, most conjunctive adverbs are movable; they can appear in the middle of the clause or at the end, as well as at the beginning:

> We worked hard for the Consumer Party candidates; we knew, <u>however</u>, they didn't stand a chance.
>
> *or*
>
> . . . we knew they didn't stand a chance, <u>however</u>.

Other common conjunctive adverbs are listed on page 283.

Colons. As a sentence connector, the colon is rather specialized. Unlike the semicolon, which connects sentences with the meaning of *and*, the colon makes an announcement of sorts: It means "namely." You're probably familiar with the colon that signals an appositive or a list:

> I'm taking three English courses this semester: advanced grammar, American lit, and Shakespeare.

Here the colon says, "Here it comes, the information I promised." When the colon signals a complete sentence, the message is similar. It promises to complete the idea set up in the first clause:

> We finally made our decision: We would sell the house and move.

> Easton, Pennsylvania, is a most colorful city: It's where Crayolas are made.

> Ideas are like children: There are none so wonderful as your own.

Diagramming the Compound Sentence. In the diagram a broken line connects the two verbs, with the connector on a solid line approximately halfway between the two clauses:

> Pete filled the bags, and I stapled them shut, but Marty refused to lift a finger.

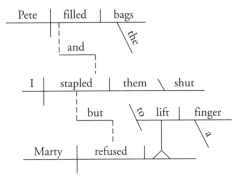

Combine the following groups of sentences into compound sentences, using conjunctions of your choice, including conjunctive adverbs. In each case there are a number of possible ways to combine them, depending on the emphasis.

1. The library closes at noon on Thursdays.
   It is open until 9:00 p.m. on Fridays.

2. The food at the new French restaurant is exceptionally good.
   The prices are exceptionally high.

3. I am going to take piano lessons this fall.
   I may take guitar lessons, too.

4. My first-period students are bright.
   They are wide awake at 8:00 A.M., too.

5. Our trip across Kansas was long and straight and uneventful.
   The trip across Kansas took an entire day.

Now turn your compound sentences into **compound-complex sentences** by adding a dependent clause to each one. The dependent clause can be nominal, adverbial, or adjectival. (You may have to make other changes to accommodate the dependent clauses.)

1. _____

   _____

2. _____

   _____

3. _____

   _____

4. _____

   _____

5 _____

   _____

CHAPTER *10*
Key Terms

Colon	Coordination
Compound sentence	Correlative conjunction
Compound structure	Elliptical coordinate structure
Compound-complex sentence	Parallel structure
Conjunction	Semicolon
Conjunctive adverb	Serial comma
Coordinating conjunction	Subject-verb agreement

Sentences
for PRACTICE

Underline the sentence slots that have coordinate structures; circle the conjunctions. For further practice, identify the sentence patterns and diagram the sentences.

1. The housing market is caught in a cycle of falling prices and surging foreclosures.

2. I lent my son and daughter-in-law a sizable sum of money.

3. They have recently moved to Ohio and will soon be buying a new house.

4. To get your rebate, simply fill out the coupon and mail it to the company's headquarters in Michigan.

5. I have battled beetles and aphids and tent caterpillars for the entire summer.

6. Next month many students and tourists will be going to our nation's capital to visit the historical monuments or perhaps to stroll along the streets and simply enjoy that beautiful city.

7. My friends and I, finding the movie boring, left at intermission and adjourned to our favorite hangout.

8. Hope is the thing with feathers
    That perches in the soul,
    And sings the tune without the words,
    And never stops at all. [Emily Dickinson]

9. Thousands of Americans, united by a deep and urgent concern about the quality of life for themselves and future generations, have given both their money and their time to the environmental movement.

10. The hundreds of separate groups that make up the environmental movement are demonstrating to get the support of their fellow citizens and their legislators.

11. Having found an apartment that was inexpensive, roomy, and close to the subway, we made a split-second decision and rented it on the spot.

12. The woods are lovely, dark, and deep,
    But I have promises to keep,
    And miles to go before I sleep. [Robert Frost]

13. The boom in cosmetic surgery is apparently the result of new, more sophisticated procedures, safer anesthetics, and the desire for self-improvement.

14. Only two knots are required for most fly-fishing situations: a knot for tying on the fly and a knot for joining monofilament.

QUESTIONS ? for DISCUSSION

1. In the following sentences the coordinate ideas are unparallel in form. Do some seem more acceptable than others? Rank them in order of acceptability. Rewrite those that can be improved.

> Almost every lineman on the squad was overweight and out of condition when the season started.
>
> She volunteered her services at the senior citizens' center frequently and with boundless enthusiasm.
>
> The old man, broke and having no friends to turn to, simply disappeared from the neighborhood.
>
> I have always loved sports of all kinds and jog regularly.

2. Consider the following compound sentences. Are they parallel? Can you find a way to improve them? What is their special problem?

> I fixed three bowls of popcorn for the party, but it was eaten up before most of the guests even got there.
>
> Burglars broke into the art museum last night, and three valuable paintings were stolen.
>
> The television lost its sound last week, but luckily it got fixed before the World Series started.

3. Explain the ambiguity of the compound structures in these two sentences.

> Six red and blue banners were hanging from the ceiling.
>
> My uncle sells used cars and motorcylces.

4. Explain why the verbs or auxiliaries in the following sentences would not be the *-s* form even though the subject headwords *crime* and *stamina* are singular.

> Blue collar and white collar crime are on the increase.

> Both physical and mental stamina are required for long-distance running.

5. The following passage commonly appears on labels of movie videos:

> This film has been modified from its original version. It has been formatted to fit your screen.

In what way would the meaning change if, instead of the period, a colon followed the first sentence? In what way is the passage ambiguous as written?

CLASSROOM APPLICATIONS

1. Notice how choppy and repetitious the following passage sounds:

> I know very little about laboratory science. I have the impression that conclusions are supposed to be logical. From a given set of circumstances a predictable result should follow. The trouble is that in human behavior it is impossible to isolate a given set of circumstances. It is also impossible to repeat these circumstances. That is true of history, too. Complex human acts cannot be reproduced. They cannot be deliberately initiated. They cannot be counted upon like the phenomena of nature.

Now read the original of that choppy passage (from an article by Barbara Tuchman, "Is History a Guide to the Future?"). Observe how coordination makes it smoother and more concise. (The coordinating conjunctions and transitional expressions have been italicized.)

> I know very little about laboratory science, *but* I have the impression that conclusions are supposed to be logical; *that is*, from a given set of circumstances a predictable result should follow. The trouble is that in human behavior *and* history it is impossible to isolate *or* repeat a given set of circumstances. Complex human acts cannot be *either* reproduced *or* deliberately initiated—*or* counted upon like the phenomena of nature.

Now revise the following passage (a "de-combined" section from Lewis Thomas's *Lives of a Cell*), using coordination to eliminate choppiness and unnecessary repetition:

> The Iks, a nomadic tribe in northern Uganda, have become celebrities. They have also become literary symbols

for the ultimate fate of disheartened mankind. They are also symbols of heartless mankind at large. Two disastrous things happened to them. They were compelled to give up hunting. They had to become farmers on poor hillside soil. Also, an anthropologist detested them. The anthropologist wrote a book about them.

2. The following is a typical sentence-combining exercise—a list of sentences to be formed into an effective paragraph. As you can see, these sentences include a great deal of repetition, some of which you can eliminate by using coordination. Experiment with both coordination and modification in combining these ideas.

1. The Anza-Borrego Desert State Park is California's largest state park.
2. The Anza-Borrego encompasses 600,000 acres.
3. The park reaches south to within three miles of the border with Mexico.
4. The Santa Rosa Mountains form the western border of the Anza-Borrego.
5. The Santa Rosa Mountains rise to a height of 8,700 feet.
6. The San Ysidro Mountains form the southwestern border of the Anza-Borrego.
7. The Anza-Borrego holds a rich archaeological heritage.
8. Archaeologists have found evidence of early inhabitants.
9. These early people lived in the Anza-Borrego 6,000 years ago.
10. The technology of these people did not yet include pottery.
11. Their technology did not include the bow and arrow.
12. The Anza-Borrego is rich in fossil remains.
13. The extinct North American camel has been uncovered in the Anza-Borrego.
14. This camel is known as Camelops.
15. The age of the camel fossils is estimated to be 800,000 years.

Words and Word Classes

I f you studied traditional grammar in middle school or high school, you may remember learning about the eight "parts of speech": noun, verb, adjective, adverb, pronoun, preposition, conjunction, and interjection. As you may recall from Chapter 1, early grammarians came up with those eight categories in order to make their description of English conform to the word categories of Latin. Scholarly grammarians, however, recognize that the accurate description of a language—any language—requires a framework of its own.

When the structural linguists went about identifying the word categories of English, they did so by examining the language as it is actually used, by reading personal letters and listening to phone conversations. They looked at the words themselves, at their forms, their meanings, and their functions in the sentence, and then established two main categories: the **form classes** and the **structure classes**. We can think of the form-class words as the bricks of the language and the structure words as the mortar that holds them together.

Probably the most striking difference between the form classes and the structure classes is characterized by their numbers. Of the half million or more words in our language, the structure words—with some notable exceptions—can be counted in the hundreds. The form classes, however, are large, open classes; new nouns and verbs and adjectives and adverbs regularly enter the language as new technology and new ideas require them. They are sometimes abandoned, too, as the dictionary's "obsolete" and "archaic" labels testify. The structure classes, on the other hand, remain constant—and limited. It's true that we don't hear *whilst* and *betwixt* and *thy* anymore, nor do we see them in contemporary prose and poetry, but most of our structure words are identical to those that Shakespeare and his contemporaries used.

FORM CLASSES	STRUCTURE CLASSES	
Noun	Determiner	Pronoun
Verb	Auxiliary	Conjunction
Adjective	Qualifier	Interrogative
Adverb	Preposition	Expletive
		Particle

An important difference between the classes has to do with form. As their label suggests, the form classes are those that can undergo changes in form—that are, in fact, distinguishable by their form—whereas the structure classes are not. But, as with almost every "rule" of the language, we will encounter exceptions. For example, auxiliaries are among the structure classes, although some of them, because they are verbs, show form variations; *be, have,* and *do,* as you know, can be both auxiliaries and verbs. Some of the pronouns also have variations in form. On the other hand, there are many words in the form classes that have no distinctions in form and do not undergo change—nouns like *chaos,* adjectives like *main,* and adverbs like *there.*

Another complication in our two-part form/structure division is the inclusion of the determiner and qualifier classes, both of which are more accurately described as *functions,* rather than word classes. The determiner class, as you have seen, includes words from other classes, such as pronouns; the fact that it also includes possessive nouns actually makes it an open class. The qualifier class, too, includes words from other classes, such as adverbs, so that class, also, is open to membership.

Before looking at the classes individually, we need to examine the basic unit of word formation, the morpheme; an understanding of the morpheme is central to the conscious understanding of words. Then we will take up the form classes, the structure classes, and, in a separate chapter, pronouns.

A caveat, a word of caution, is in order here: Don't be intimidated by the amount of detail you find about the word classes in these four chapters. These are not details for you to memorize—not at all. For the most part, in fact, they are simply descriptions of details you already know, not only from your study of grammar but also from your everyday use of the language, even though you may not have thought consciously about them.

Morphemes

CHAPTER PREVIEW

In this chapter, in preparation for the study of word classes, you will learn about morphemes, basic units of meaning that make up words. You'll find that an understanding of morphemes will help to trigger your unconscious language expertise, as you consciously study the form of words. You'll learn that nouns, verbs, adjectives, and adverbs have characteristics that enable you to identify them, not by their meanings but by their forms.

Some of the detail in this chapter may also trigger memories of vocabulary and dictionary lessons from your early grades. When you study morphemes, you are actually studying in a conscious way the lexicon in your head—your internal dictionary. In fact, for this chapter you'll need access to the other kind of dictionary too—the alphabetical kind that sits on your desk.

When we study sentence patterns and their expansions, we are studying **syntax**. The structural linguist, however, begins the study of grammar not with syntax, but with **phonology**, the study of individual sounds. At the next level, before syntax, comes **morphology**, the study of **morphemes,** combinations of sounds with meaning.

This definition of *morpheme* may sound to you like the definition of *word*. Many morphemes are, in fact, complete words; *head* and *act* and *kind* and *walk* (as well as *and*) are words consisting of a single morpheme, a single meaningful combination of sounds. But others, such as *heads* and *actively* and *unkindly* and *walking*, consist of two or more morphemes, each of which has meaning itself. The success you had years ago in learning to read and spell was in part dependent on your awareness of the parts of words. For instance, in spelling a word like *actively*, you probably break it into its three morphemes automatically: Its stem, or **base morpheme**, is the verb *act;* the suffix *-ive* turns it into an adjective; and the suffix *-ly* turns the adjective into an adverb. Each of these three morphemes, the base and the two suffixes, has meaning itself; and each appears in other environments (other words) with the same meaning. These are the two primary criteria that we use to identify the morphemes in a word: They have meaning; they appear with the same meaning in other words.

We should also emphasize that *morpheme* and *syllable* are not synonymous—even though the morphemes discussed so far consist of a single syllable. There are, in fact, many two-syllable words in English that are single morphemes: *carrot, college, jolly, merit, over.* Furthermore, many two-morpheme words are single syllables: *acts, walked, dog's.* So even though it may be understandable to think of syllable boundaries as boundaries for morphemes, it is inaccurate to do so.

The individual morphemes in a word are not always quite as obvious as they are in words like *actively.* In the word *reflections*, for example, we can recognize the verb *reflect,* the *-ion* ending that turns it into a noun, and the *-s* that makes it plural: *reflect + ion + s.* But how about the word *reflect?* Is that a single morpheme, or is it two? Are *re* and *flect* separate morphemes? Do they both have meaning? Do they appear in other environments with the same meaning? Certainly there are many words that begin with the prefix *re-: reverse, rebound, refer.* In all these, *re-* means "back," so *re* passes the morpheme test. How about *flect?* We have *inflect* and *deflect.* The dictionary reveals that all three words with *flect* are based on the Latin verb *flectere,* meaning "to bend." So in the word *reflections* we can identify four morphemes: *re + flect + ion + s.*

Incidentally, it's not unusual to need the dictionary to understand the morpheme structure of a word. The meanings of words often change, and their origins become obscure. Take the word *obscure,* for example. How many morphemes does it have, one or two? What does *scure* mean? Does it appear in other words with the same meaning? Is *ob* the same morpheme we find in *observe?* What does it mean? And how about *observe?* Is that the verb *serve?* Such meanderings into the dictionary in search of clues about morphemes can heighten our awareness of words and appreciation of language. And certainly an awareness of morphemes can enhance the understanding of language essential to both reader and writer. When we study etymology and historical linguistics, we begin to understand the intricacies of morphemes, their changes, and their variations. But our interest in morphemes here is a limited one. We will look mainly at those that signal the form classes, that contribute to our understanding of the parts of speech.

BASES AND AFFIXES

All words, as we have seen, are combinations of morphemes, or, in the case of a word like *act* (as well as the eight words preceding it in this sentence), single morphemes. All morphemes are either **bases** (*act*), which we define as the morpheme that gives the word its primary lexical meaning, or **affixes** (*-ive, -ly*); and all affixes are either **prefixes**, those that precede the base (*re-*), or **suffixes**, those that follow it (*-ion*):

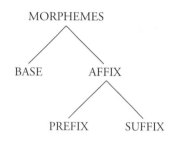

Exercise 46

The following four sets of words illustrate some of the relationships of morphemes. In each set find the common base. What does the base mean? Draw vertical lines in the words to show the separate morphemes.

nova	auditor	durable	conceive
renovation	audience	endure	capable
innovate	inaudible	duration	susceptible
novice	auditorium	during	capture
novelist	audio	endurance	intercept

BOUND AND FREE MORPHEMES

One other feature of morphemes concerns their ability to stand alone. Many cannot. For example, the affixes are **bound**, or attached, to another morpheme rather than **free** to stand alone; that's what *affix* means. In the word *actively*, only the first morpheme is free: *-ive* and *-ly* are bound. In *reflections*, even the base is bound; *flect* is not a word that can stand by itself. We call this a bound base. Other examples of words without free morphemes are *concur, conceive, depict, expel,* and many others with these common prefixes. There are also a few affixes that are free, such as *able, like,* and *less*. A free morpheme is a word; a bound morpheme is not. The solid arrows in the following diagram represent the most common circumstance, the broken ones the less common:

Find a word to fit each of the following formulas. Include only the morphemes called for.

Examples:
   free + bound = **birds**
   bound + free = **rerun**

    1. free + bound
    2. bound + free
    3. free + bound + bound
    4. bound + free + bound
    5. free + free
    6. bound + free + bound + bound
    7. bound + bound
    8. bound + bound + bound

DERIVATIONAL AND INFLECTIONAL MORPHEMES

Another feature of affixes we want to recognize is their classification as either derivational or inflectional. Although we have several hundred suffixes, distinguishing between the derivational and inflectional ones is easy to do. Only eight are **inflectional**. You'll recognize four of them from the discussion of verbs in Chapter 4.

    -s (plural)
    -s (possessive) }   Noun inflections

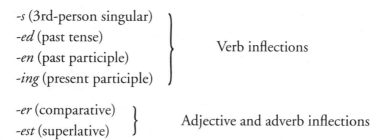

-s (3rd-person singular)
-ed (past tense)
-en (past participle)
-ing (present participle)
} Verb inflections

-er (comparative)
-est (superlative)
} Adjective and adverb inflections

All the other suffixes, as well as all the prefixes, are **derivational**.

As the branching diagram shows, all prefixes are derivational, whereas suffixes are either derivational or inflectional:

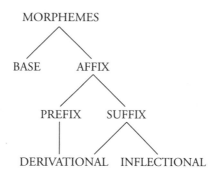

The term *derivational* refers to the change that a word undergoes when a derivational morpheme is added: Either the meaning of the word changes or the class, the part of speech, changes—or both. Take the word *inactivity*, for example. With the derivational morpheme *-ive*, the verb *act* becomes the adjective *active*—that is, we derive one class of word from another. When we add *in-*, the class remains the same—*active* and *inactive* are both adjectives—but the prefix does affect the meaning, as prefixes generally do; in other words, we derive a new meaning. Finally, with the addition of *-ity* the adjective becomes the noun *inactivity*.

The significance, then, of derivational morphemes is this ability they give us to derive new words: *Active* and *inactive* are two different words; so are *active* and *actively;* so are *act* and *action*.

The inflectional affixes also change words, of course, but the changes do not represent new words in the same sense that the changes with derivational morphemes do. It is probably accurate to consider the verb *acting* as simply a variation of *act;* likewise, the inflections we add to nouns—the plural and possessive—produce variations of the singular noun; we think of *dogs* and *dog's* simply as variations of *dog*, rather than as different words.

There are two other attributes of derivational morphemes that distinguish them from the inflectional morphemes:

1. **Derivational morphemes are arbitrary.** Unlike the inflectional morphemes, which apply in a systematic way to all, or at least to a significant number of, the words in a class, the derivational morphemes are quite unsystematic. For example, all verbs—with only two or three exceptions—take the inflectional *-s* and *-ing* endings; and almost all verbs have an *-ed* and *-en* inflection as well. However, there's nothing systematic about the derivational endings that we add to other word classes to form verbs: The adjective *able* becomes a verb with the addition of the prefix *en-* (*enable*); *sweet* takes the suffix *-en* (*sweeten*); *legal* takes *-ize* to become a verb (*legalize*); *active* takes *-ate* (*activate*). For many adjectives, however, we have no derivational morpheme at all for producing verbs; we have no way to turn such adjectives as *big*, *good*, *happy*, and *vicious* into verbs. On the other hand, we can derive nouns from these particular adjectives by adding *-ness*. As you might expect, however, *-ness* is not our only noun-forming suffix: Others include *-ity* (*generosity, activity, creativity*); *-acy* (*supremacy, literacy*); *-er* (*singer, helper*); *-ion, -tion* (*action, preparation*); and *-ment* (*contentment, enlargement*). We have no rules to explain what goes with what, no system to account for these differences; that lack of system is what "arbitrary" means.

2. **Derivational morphemes often change the class of the word.** Most of the time, in fact, that change in class is their very purpose; they produce new words. Inflectional morphemes, on the other hand, never change the class. And, as mentioned earlier, we generally don't even consider the inflected form of a word as a different word.

If all these derivational and inflectional morphemes seem complicated to you, it's probably because you haven't thought about them before. If you're a native speaker, they're really not complicated at all; you use them without even thinking. In fact, there is probably no feature of English that illustrates more clearly the innate ability that native speakers have than this inventory of prefixes and suffixes that gives the language such versatility.

Investigating Language 11.1

Consider the following sets:

A. *X* can dorf; *X* dorfs; *X* is dorfing; *X* has dorfed already.
B. Give me that dorf. No, I mean those dorfs. Where's your dorf's snape?

C. You're pretty dorf, but *X* is dorfer, and *Y* is the dorfest of all.

1. In which set is *dorf* an adjective? What morphological—not syntactic—evidence tells you that?

2. In which set is *dorf* a verb? Again, what morphological evidence tells you that?

3. In which set is *dorf* a noun? Once more, what morphological evidence tells you that?

4. What type of morphemes have you been dealing with in these questions: inflectional or derivational?

5. The traditional definition of *noun* is "the name of a person, place, or thing" and that of *verb* is "a word that denotes action, being, or state of being." Instead of using those criteria of meaning, write your own definitions of *noun* and *verb* that are based on form.

ALLOMORPHS

In Exercise 46 the base morphemes *aud* and *dur* are pronounced and spelled the same in all five words in their lists. However, the morpheme *nov* in that same exercise has two pronunciations; in *nova* and *novelist* the vowel sounds are different, comparable to the difference between *node* and *nod.* In the last group in the exercise, the difference from one word to the next is greater still, with variations in spelling as well as pronunciation. In fact, without the help of a dictionary we would be tempted to label *ceive* and *cap* and *cept* as different morphemes altogether, rather than variations of the same one. Such variations of morphemes, which are extremely common in English, are known as **allomorphs**.

Sometimes the base morphemes have allomorphic variations as the result of suffixes. For example, a word ending in *f* often takes a *v* in the plural:

leaf → leaves   wife → wives   elf → elves

We would call *leav* and *wiv* and *elv* allomorphs of *leaf* and *wife* and *elf.* Here are some other examples in which the pronunciation of the base morpheme changes with the addition of a suffix: *type/typify; please/pleasant; press/pressure; able/ability; oblige/obligation; child/children.* Because these allomorphs of the base are not used without the suffix, we would include them in the category of bound bases.

Prefixes and suffixes, too, undergo such variation; that is, they also have allomorphs. For example, notice the negative prefix we add to these adjectives: *unkind, improper, illegal, irrelevant, ineligible.* All these prefixes mean *not*, so it is probably accurate to consider *im, il, ir,* and *in* as allomorphs of the prefix *un,* the most common among them. At any rate, their sounds are determined by their environment.

Suffixes also have allomorphic variation. Consider, for example, the sound you add to make nouns plural:

cat → cats   dog → dogs   kiss → kisses

Even though the first two are spelled the same, the sounds are different: in *cats* the sound is an *s;* in *dogs,* it's a *z.* And in *kisses,* the *es* represents an unstressed vowel sound followed by *z.*

HOMONYMS

You're probably familiar with homonyms, words with different meanings that happen to have the same spelling and the same sound, such as *saw* (the tool) and *saw* (the past tense verb). The concept refers also to morphemes, in some cases to parts of words that sound the same but have different meanings. Prefixes and suffixes, for example, can be homonyms. The *ex* in *exchange* and the *ex* in *ex-husband* have two different meanings: "from" and "former." So do the *er* in *singer* and the *er* in *brighter:* "one who" and "more." In the case of *er,* one is derivational and one is inflectional. And the *s* endings we add to verbs and nouns also have different meanings. All of these are examples of homonyms.

You might find it useful to think of homonyms as simply accidents of language, mere coincidences. It's coincidence that the word *bell* and the bound morpheme *bell* (in *rebellion*) sound and look alike. The dictionary will show they have no connection: The free morpheme *bell* has its origin in the Old English word meaning roar; *rebellion* comes from the Latin word for war. And certainly it's coincidence that the name of the carpenter's tool sounds the same and shares the same spelling as the past tense form of *see.*

A subclass of homonyms, called **homophones,** includes those words with identical sounds in which both meaning and spelling are different: *to, two, too; sale, sail.*

COMPOUND WORDS

Merriam-Webster's Collegiate Dictionary (eleventh edition) lists three examples in the definition of **compound word**: *rowboat, high school, devil-may-care.* All three of these are combinations of free morphemes, which is the standard definition of the term. Even though the three are connected differently (or not at all, in the case of *high school*), they share one common characteristic, one that helps us to recognize their grammatical framework as compound—their common stress pattern:[1]

---

[1]Linguists generally recognize four degrees of stress in intonation: / (primary), ^ (secondary), \ (tertiary), and ˘ (weak or unstress).

$\overset{/}{\text{row}}\overset{\backslash}{\text{boat}}$ $\overset{/}{\text{high}}\overset{\backslash}{\text{school}}$ $\overset{/}{\text{devil}}\text{-may-}\overset{\backslash}{\text{care}}$

When you read the following compound words aloud, you'll hear their stress pattern in the same way, with primary stress on the first word:

newspaper	snowman	blackboard
girl crazy	blacktop	candlelight
dog house	bag lady	workweek
dog catcher	bagman	storehouse

It's the stress pattern that makes the distinction between a house that is green and a greenhouse; between a teacher from France and a teacher of French, a French teacher; between a big load that's a heavy weight and a boxer who's a heavyweight; between a room that's dark and a photographer's darkroom.

We often have to consult a recent dictionary to find out how a compound word is written: with or without hyphens, as separate words or one word. You might be reluctant to call two separate words a compound word, but in the case of *high school,* the dictionary does! By the time the twelfth edition of Webster's is published, high school may have gained a hyphen, and by the thirteenth, it may be closed up.

What we are distinguishing in the case of $\overset{\wedge}{\text{dark}}\ \overset{/}{\text{room}}$ versus $\overset{/}{\text{dark}}\overset{\backslash}{\text{room}}$ or $\overset{\wedge}{\text{French}}\ \overset{/}{\text{teacher}}\overset{\backslash}{}$ versus $\overset{/}{\text{French}}\ \overset{\wedge}{\text{teacher}}\overset{\backslash}{}$ is the difference between a noun phrase and a compound noun. In a noun phrase with the headword preceded by an adjectival, the main stress in most cases will be on the headword. Intonation can always be altered in speech for a different emphasis, but generally the stress pattern—along with meaning, of course—provides the best clue for recognizing a compound word.

Exercise 48

Draw vertical lines in the following words to indicate their morpheme boundaries. Identify each morpheme as follows: *bound* or *free; base* or *affix.* Identify each affix as *derivational* or *inflectional.* You will probably need to consult your dictionary.

precision	unaware	illegal
candidate	money	wealthy
detoured	sidewalks	television
excessively	promotion	revises

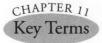

CHAPTER *11*
Key Terms

Affix	Homophones
Allomorph	Inflectional suffix
Base morpheme	Morpheme
Bound morpheme	Morphology
Compound words	Phonology
Derivational morpheme	Prefix
Free morpheme	Suffix
Homonyms	

QUESTIONS ? for DISCUSSION

1. Most morphemes are made up of combinations of sounds. Give some examples of morphemes that are single sounds.

2. Consider how the meaning of a word comes about. Explain the origin of the following words:

ambulance	cohort	fancy	mayhem
budget	daisy	hussy	meal
calculate	dial	infant	money
candidate	easel	lunatic	pilot
cigar	escape	magazine	vaccine

3. What do the following compound words have in common: *fingerprint, sourpuss, overland, walkway?* In what way are they different?

4. Consider the difference between derivational and inflectional suffixes. What can you say about their positions when both appear on the same word? Is the rule fairly constant? Is it possible for more than one derivational and/or inflectional suffix to appear on a single word?

5. Which of the following words appear to violate the system that you described in Question 4?

    inflectional   sportsmanship   microscopy   teaspoonsful

6. How can the awareness of morphemes be of help in spelling problem words, such as the following?

entirely	innovate	disappoint
safety	inaudible	roommate
professor	misspell	vineyard

7. Explain the difference between the words "painful" and "pained." Under what circumstances would the following sentences be accurate?

> He had a pained expression on his face.

> He had a painful expression on his face.

Now think about the difference between "healthy" and "healthful." Would you say that carrots are a healthy food to eat? And what's the difference between "masterly" and "masterful"?

8. Our vocabulary expands in many ways. Sometimes we give new meanings to old words or to their combinations, as in *waterbed, whistle-blower, gridlock,* and *moonshot.* And sometimes we combine two words into a completely new one: We made *brunch* from *breakfast* and *lunch.* What two words do you suppose were combined in the formation of these: *bash, clash, flare, blog,* and *smash?*

CLASSROOM APPLICATIONS

1. Homophones are words with the same pronunciation but with different spellings and different meanings, like *pear* and *pair* or *haul* and *hall.* In his book *A Chocolate Moose for Dinner,* Fred Gwynne plays with homophones, as you can see from the title. Before eating your dessert of chocolate moose, what would you have for your main course? Stake, perhaps? Plan a complete menu for your meal using (misusing!) homophones.

2. Homophones usually occur in pairs. But sometimes there are three or even four words in English that sound alike but differ in meaning and spelling. See how many trios of homophones you can come up with. (For starters, think of another to go with *pair* and *pear.*)

3. Another tricky class of our words is that of **heteronyms**—pairs of words that are spelled alike but differ in both meaning and pronunciation: *bass/bass, sewer/sewer, row/row.* See how many others you can come up with; then try to use both in the same sentence.

4. Among the bound bases of our vocabulary, some are combined with the suffix *-logy,* meaning a science. For example, the

bound base *herpeto*, which means "to creep," when combined with *-logy* means the scientific study of creatures that crawl and creep—reptiles. When we add *-ist*, we get the title of the scientist who studies reptiles: *herpetologist*.

Use your dictionary to figure out the jobs and the job titles that can be produced from the following bound bases:

socio-

bio-

anthropo-

ethno-

cardio-

eco-

patho-

zoo-

geol-

entomo-

CHAPTER
12

The Form Classes

CHAPTER PREVIEW

As you read in the opening of Part IV, an important difference between traditional and structural grammar is in the classification of words. The structuralists' definitions of the form classes—nouns, verbs, adjectives, and adverbs—make use of the native speaker's inherent language ability. For example, does the word have both *-s* and *-ing* forms? Then it's a verb. Can it be made plural or possessive? Then it's a noun. In traditional grammar, the definition of *noun* (the name of a person, place, or thing) and *verb* (a word showing action) are based on meaning.

The new grammarians also differentiate the word itself from its function in the sentence. In addition to a category such as *adjective*, which names the word class, we need the category *adjectival*, which specifies the function of adjectives. The structuralist defines *adjective* as a member of the class that can be qualified *(very big)* and inflected for the comparative and superlative degrees *(bigger, biggest)*. By contrast, the traditional class of *adjective* is defined as "a word that modifies a noun." As a result, in a noun phrase such as "the stone house," both words preceding the headword *house* are labeled as adjectives: They fit that traditional definition.

In this chapter, however, we want to study adjectives—as well as nouns, verbs, and adverbs—in a "formal" way, as classes with certain characteristics of form. We will do so by following up on the study of morphemes, by looking at the derivational and inflectional suffixes that distinguish the four form classes. We will also look at the structure words that signal them.

NOUNS

We traditionally define *noun* on the basis of meaning, as the *name* of a person, place, thing, idea, event, or the like, and that definition works fairly well. After all, we've been learning names since we spoke our first words: *mama, daddy, cookie, baby.* The word *noun,* in fact, comes from *nomen,* the Latin word for "name."

We also get a sense of "nounness" from the words that signal nouns—the determiners. A word such as *the, my,* or *an* tells us a noun will follow, although not necessarily as the next word: *the* books, *my* sister, *an* honest opinion. Determiners are simply not used without nouns.

But certainly the most reliable clue for recognizing nouns is form. We can often differentiate the form classes from one another without reference to either meaning or context, simply on the basis of their derivational and inflectional suffixes.

Noun Derivational Suffixes. Each of the four form classes has its own inventory of derivational suffixes. The ending *-ion,* for example, converts the verb *reflect* into a noun, so we call it—or its variations, *-tion, -sion, -cion,* and *-ation*—a noun-forming suffix. A quick check of the dictionary reveals that all the *-ion* words listed on the first few pages are also nouns formed from verbs:

abbreviation	abstraction	accusation
abolition	accommodation	acquisition
abortion	accumulation	action

Some *-ion* words function as both nouns and verbs: *question, partition, mention,* and, yes, *function;* you may be able to think of others. But you will find few, if any, *-ion* words that are not nouns; *-ion* is a reliable signal. Many other derivational suffixes do the same job, that of converting verbs into nouns:

accomplish<u>ment</u>	break<u>age</u>
accept<u>ance</u>	deliver<u>y</u>
arriv<u>al</u>	depart<u>ure</u>
assist<u>ant</u>	teach<u>er</u>

This variety of noun-forming suffixes that we add to verbs—and, incidentally, there are many more than these—illustrates not only our versatility in changing one part of speech to another but also the arbitrary way in which we do so. Why, for example, do we say "delivery" and "deliverance" but not "deliverment"? Why "departure" rather than "departation"? Why "deportation" rather than "deporture"? There are no good answers to such questions.

The same arbitrariness runs through all the word classes. For example, many adjectives become nouns with the addition of *-ness*: pretti*ness*, lazi*ness*, strange*ness*, happi*ness*, helpless*ness*. But there is a long list of other suffixes that do the same job: tru*th*, wis*dom*, just*ice*, partial*ity*. And a number of suffixes simply alter the meaning of the word without changing the class; for example, we derive the abstract noun *boyhood* from the concrete noun *boy*. Other examples of suffixes that produce new meanings include *kingdom, friendship, Spaniard, gardener, terrorism*.

Finally, the nouns *partiality* and *activation* illustrate another feature of derivational suffixes, where a noun-forming suffix is added to a word that already has one or more derivational suffixes:

part + *-ial* = partial + *-ity* = partiality
(noun)   *(adj)*   *(noun)*

act + *-ive* = active + *-ate* = activate + *-ion* = activation
(verb)   *(adj)*   *(verb)*   *(noun)*

This feature also illustrates another difference between derivational and inflectional suffixes. The inflectional suffixes do not add on in this way. With the exception of the plural and possessive morphemes of nouns, which may appear in combination, the form-class words will have only one inflectional suffix, and it will always come at the end of the word, after any derivational suffixes.

Exercise 49

Transform the following verbs into nouns by adding a derivational suffix. Are there any that have more than one noun form?

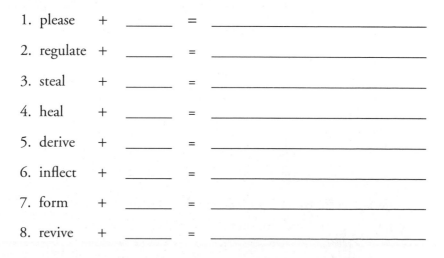

1. please   + _____ = _____

2. regulate + _____ = _____

3. steal   + _____ = _____

4. heal   + _____ = _____

5. derive   + _____ = _____

6. inflect   + _____ = _____

7. form   + _____ = _____

8. revive   + _____ = _____

9. seize   +   _____   =   _____

10. retire   +   _____   =   _____

Noun Inflectional Suffixes. The other aspect of form that differentiates the four form classes both from the structure classes and from one another is the set of inflectional morphemes that each form class has, which we saw in Chapter 2. Our nouns have only two grammatical inflections, one indicating **number (plural)** and one indicating case **(possessive)**:

SINGULAR	PLURAL	SINGULAR POSSESSIVE	PLURAL POSSESSIVE
cat	cats	cat's	cats'
dog	dogs	dog's	dogs'
horse	horses	horse's	horses'
mouse	mice	mouse's	mice's

The nouns *cat* and *dog* and *horse* illustrate that in speech we can't always distinguish among inflected forms of nouns: *Cats, cat's,* and *cats'* are all pronounced exactly the same. Only in writing can we differentiate the plural from the possessive and from the plural possessive. In the case of *mouse,* with its irregular plural, we of course make the distinction in speech as well as in writing.

The preceding examples illustrate another point about noun inflections: Sometimes the plural inflection is not a single /s/ or /z/ sound, as in *cats* and *dogs.* It may be two sounds, an entire syllable, complete with vowel, as in *horses.* The sound we add is determined by the final sound of the noun. With words ending in what is called a sibilant sound—usually spelled with *s, z, sh, ch, dge,* or *ge*—we must add a syllable to pronounce the *-s* plural (as well as the possessive): kiss*es,* maz*es,* sash*es,* church*es,* judg*es,* pag*es.*

Exercise   50

The possessive marks are missing from the following noun phrases. Read each one aloud; then punctuate each phrase in two ways to show its two possible meanings.

all my teachers assignments   the horses sore legs
all my teachers assignments   the horses sore legs

my sisters husbands business   my sons problems
my sisters husbands business   my sons problems

Recognizing whether or not the added sound is a complete syllable can be a useful clue in spelling. Spelling the plural and possessive of words that end in an /s/ or /z/ sound is sometimes confusing; they not only sound strange, they tend to look strange when they're written:

> Mr. and Mrs. Jones are the Joneses. (*Plural*)

> Their cat is the Joneses' cat. (*Possessive*)

To turn *Joneses*, the plural of *Jones*, into the possessive case, we add only the apostrophe, the usual procedure for possessive plurals: cats', horses', leaders'.

According to *The Chicago Manual of Style*, which is generally considered the bible of publishing,

> [t]he question of how to form the possessive of names of more than one syllable ending in the sound of s or z probably occasions more dissension among writers and editors of good will than any other orthographic matter open to disagreement. (p. 162, thirteenth ed.)

The policy of the University of Chicago Press, as the *Manual* puts it, is "essentially a restatement of William Strunk's 'Rule No. 1' in the famous *Elements of Style*." Strunk's rule is, simply,

> Form the possessive singular of nouns by adding *'s*.

In other words, according to the *Manual* (and Strunk), there should be no question with a name like Martinez or Williams, multisyllable names ending with a sibilant (/s/ or /z/) sound. Even though you may not pronounce the extra *s* when you say "Martinez's batting average" or "Mr. Williams's Hummer," you should include the *s* with the apostrophe when you write the possessive case.

However, both Strunk and *The Chicago Manual* list exceptions for certain proper names that have multiple sibilant (/s/ or /z/) sounds, such as Moses' and Jesus'. The *Manual* also makes exceptions for words with an unaccented ending pronounced /eez/, among them Euripedes' plays, Ramses' tomb, Surtees' novels. And Strunk's exceptions include such forms as "for conscience' sake" and "for righteousness' sake." All of these are words in which an added syllable would not be pronounced, so the *s* is not added with the apostrophe. In most of these cases, the final syllable both begins and ends with a sibilant sound.

As the *Chicago Manual* makes clear, however, names ending with a single sibilant follow the basic rule:

> Maria Callas's performance.

> Dylan Thomas's poetry.

> Roy Harris's compositions.

In these cases, the possessive *-s* is an added syllable when pronounced. A word's pronunciation, whether or not you add a syllable in speech, is sometimes used as the guideline for whether to add apostrophe plus *-s* or only the apostrophe; as the *Manual* points out, this issue is a well-known matter of disagreement among editors. However, you won't go wrong if you stick to Strunk's No. 1 rule and add apostrophe plus *-s*.

The plural and possessive inflections provide a test of sorts for "nounness." Can the word be made plural and/or possessive? If so, it's a noun. If not? Well, the possibility for nounness is still there. In applying the inflection test to the nouns in the preceding section on derivational suffixes, we find that all the words on the *-ion* list can take the plural inflection, but most of them will not take the possessive *-s*. With many nouns the *of* prepositional phrase is more common than the possessive *-s* inflection: In general, the more specific or concrete the sense of the noun, the more likely it is that the inflections will be acceptable.

Exercise 51

Transform the *of* possessive phrase into the inflected noun.

1. The son of Mr. Price is Mr. _____ son.
2. The daughter of Ms. Hedges is Ms. _____ daughter.
3. The computer belonging to James is _____ computer.
4. The governor of Massachusetts is _____ governor.
5. The blanket belonging to Linus is _____ blanket.
6. The garden of the neighbor is the _____ garden.
7. The garden of the neighbors is the _____ garden.
8. The curls on the head and tail of Miss Piggy are _____ curls.
9. The club the women belong to is the _____ club.
10. The wisdom of Confucius is _____ wisdom.

The Meaning of the Possessive Case.   In the examples we have seen so far, the relationship between the possessive noun and the headword is actually one of possession, or ownership, but such a relationship is not always the case. As the following examples show, the possessive noun can be simply a description:

> an evening's entertainment
>
> a bachelor's degree
>
> today's news

It can also be a measure of value or time:

<u>a day's</u> wages

<u>a moment's</u> notice

<u>a dollar's</u> worth

It can denote origin:

<u>the teacher's</u> suggestion

<u>Lincoln's</u> Gettysburg Address

Sometimes the actual relationship is unclear, even in context:

We admired <u>Van Gogh's</u> portrait.

This possessive could refer either to a portrait *of* the artist or to a portrait *by* the artist.

Irregular Plural Inflections. Before leaving the noun inflections,we should note the many instances of irregular plurals, such as *mice,* in our lexicon. Some are old forms of English that have resisted becoming regularized: *foot–feet, tooth–teeth, man–men, child–children, ox–oxen.* A number of animal and fish names are irregular in that they have no inflection for the plural: *sheep, deer, bass, salmon, trout.* A large number of borrowed words have retained their foreign plural inflections: *larva–larvae, criterion–criteria, alumnus–alumni, appendix–appendices.* Incidentally, some of these borrowings are now in the process of acquiring regular plurals. *Appendixes* appears along with *appendices; indexes* and *formulas* are even more common than *indices* and *formulae; stadiums* has all but replaced *stadia. Memorandum* is giving way to the shortened *memo,* along with its regular plural, *memos;* and the added complication of gender in *alumnus–alumni* (masculine) and *alumna–alumnae* (feminine) no doubt encourages the use of the simpler, gender-free—and informal—*alum* and *alums.* The borrowed words ending in *-s*—*analysis–analyses, nucleus–nuclei, hypothesis–hypotheses, stimulus–stimuli*—are less likely to lose their foreign inflections; the addition of *-es* to the singular would be cumbersome.

The irregularity of noun inflections, incidentally, applies only to the plural; the possessive follows the regular rule:

SINGULAR	SINGULAR POSSESSIVE	PLURAL	PLURAL POSSESSIVE
man	man's	men	men's
child	child's	children	children's
deer	deer's	deer	deer's
mouse	mouse's	mice	mice's
larva	larva's	larvae	larvae's

Note that these plural possessives look different from regular plural possessives *(dogs')*, only because for regular plural nouns we don't add an *-s* to make the word possessive; the regular plural already has one.

Plural-Only Forms.   Some nouns, even when singular in meaning, are plural in form. One such group refers to things that are in two parts—that are bifurcated, or branching: *scissors, shears, pliers, pants, trousers, slacks, shorts, glasses, spectacles.* As subjects of sentences, these nouns present no problems with subject–verb agreement: They take the same verb form as other plural subjects do. Interestingly, even though a pair of shorts is a single garment and a pair of pliers is a single tool, we use the plural pronoun in reference to them:

> I bought a new pair of shorts today; <u>they</u>'re navy blue.

> I've lost my pliers; have you seen <u>them</u>?

Other plural nouns that have no singular form include *measles, mumps, means, tidings, clothes,* and *athletics.*
    A different situation arises with certain plural-in-form nouns that are sometimes singular in meaning. A noun such as *physics, mathematics,* and *linguistics,* when referring to an academic discipline or course, is treated as singular:

> Physics <u>is</u> my favorite subject.

> Linguistics <u>is</u> the scientific study of language.

But sometimes such nouns as *mathematics* and *statistics* are used with plural meanings:

> The mathematics involved in the experiment <u>are</u> very theoretical.

> The statistics on poverty levels <u>are</u> quite depressing.

These uses also call for plural pronouns.

Collective Nouns.   Nouns such as *family, choir, team, majority, minority*—any noun that names a group of individual members—can be treated as either singular or plural, depending on context and meaning:

> The <u>family</u> *have* all gone their separate ways.

> The whole <u>family</u> *is* celebrating the holidays at home this year.

> The <u>majority</u> of our city council members *are* Republicans.

> The <u>majority</u> always *rules*.

Other singular-in-form nouns, such as *remainder, rest,* and *number,* also have a plural meaning in certain contexts; their number depends on their modifiers:

> <u>The remainder of the job applicants</u> *are* waiting outside.

The rest of the books *are* being donated to the library.

A number of customers *have* come early.

This system also applies to certain indefinite pronouns, such as *some, all,* and *enough:*

Some of the books *were* missing.

All of the cookies *were* eaten.

Notice what happens to the verb in such sentences when the modifier of the subject headword is singular:

The rest of the map *was* found.

Some of the water *is* polluted.

All of the cake *was* eaten.

The remainder of this chapter *is* especially important.

The pronoun to use in reference to these noun phrases will depend on the meaning, and it will usually be obvious:

They (some of the books) *were* missing.

It (some of the water) *is* polluted.

One special problem occurs with the word *none*, which has its origin in the phrase *not one.* Because of that original meaning, many writers insist that *none* always be singular, as *not one* clearly is. However, a more accurate way to assess its meaning is to recognize *none* as the negative, or opposite, of *all* and to treat it in the same way, with its number (whether singular or plural) determined by the number of the modifier or of the referent:

None of the guests *want* to leave.

None of the cookies *were* left.

None of the cake *was* eaten.

All of the guests *are* staying; none of them *are* leaving.

Semantic Features of Nouns. Nouns can be classified according to certain built-in semantic features that affect their distribution. At an early age we begin this process of classification, recognizing, for example, whether a noun can be counted. We can say "one cookie" or "two cookies"; but a noun like *milk* is not countable. This understanding is evident in our selection of determiners:

I want milk.

I want a cookie.

I want some milk.

Within a few short years our linguistic computers have become programmed to make distinctions like this that we are hardly aware of. The nonnative speaker, on the other hand, must work conscientiously to make such distinctions. The person who says "I need a new luggage" or "I have a lot of homeworks" or "I am looking forward to a peace and quiet this weekend" has not distinguished between **countable** and **noncountable nouns**. Linguists have described these features of our nouns in a hierarchy, each level of which has consequences for selecting determiners and other parts of the sentence:

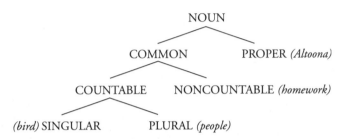

The restrictions built into the word determine its place in the hierarchy; each word carries with it only those features in the higher intersections (or *nodes*) that it is connected with: *Homework* is a noncountable, common noun; *bird* is a singular, countable common noun. Determiners have related built-in features or restrictions; the determiner *a* (or *an*) includes the features "singular" and "countable," so we are restricted from using it with *homework*. It will signal only those nouns that fit in the lowest, left-hand branch, like *bird*. Some nouns appear in both branches of a node, depending on their meaning. For example, some nouns can be both countable and noncountable:

> I had a strange experience yesterday.
>
> I've had experience working with animals.
>
> I baked a cake today.
>
> I'll have some cake.

The term **proper noun** refers to a noun (or noun phrase) with a specific referent—a single meaning: Empire State Building, Grand Canyon, William Shakespeare, London, the *CBS Evening News*, Aunt Mildred, November, Pearl Harbor Day, Thanksgiving. Proper nouns name people, geographic regions and locations, buildings, events, holidays, months, and days of the week; they are usually written with initial capital letters. Although most proper nouns are singular, exceptions occur in the case of mountain ranges and island groups—the Rockies, the Andes, the Falklands—which are plural.

Investigating Language 12.1

A careful writer would avoid writing sentences like these two:

*There have been less accidents in the county this year.

*I have also noticed an increase in the amount of bicycles on the
roads.

But there's no problem with these:

There are fewer students enrolled in the advanced ceramics class
this year.

There is an increase in the number of students enrolled in the
beginning course.

Think about where in the noun hierarchy on page 252 you would find
accidents, bicycles, and *students.* How would a careful writer revise those
first two sentences? If you were helping a nonnative speaker revise those
sentences, how would you explain the changes?

Would that careful writer avoid any of the following sentences?

There were less than a dozen accidents in the county this year.

We had fewer accidents than last year.

We have less dollars than we need.

We have less money than we need.

We have less than ten dollars to last until payday.

You probably gave that nonnative speaker some advice about the use of
less/fewer and *amount of/number of.* Should you revise your explanation?
In what way?

VERBS

The traditional definition of *verb,* like that of *noun,* is based on meaning:
a word denoting action, being, or state of being. When we look for the
verb in a sentence, we look for the word that tells *what is happening,* and
most of the time this method works. But a much more reliable criterion
for defining *verb* is that of form. Some verbs have derivational endings that
signal that they are verbs; and, with only two or three exceptions, all verbs
fit into the verb-expansion rule, the system of adding auxiliaries and inflections described in Chapter 4.

Verb Derivational Affixes. Many of the root words, or bases, that take
noun-forming suffixes are verbs to begin with; for example, most of our

nouns with *-ion* are formed from verbs. The opposite operation—deriving verbs from other form classes—is less common. We are more likely to turn a noun into a verb without changing its form at all, another example of **functional shift**—in other words, shifting the function of the word. We *chair* meetings and *table* motions; the carpenter *roofs* the house; the cook *dishes* up the food; the painter *coats* the wall with paint; the gardener *seeds* the lawn and *weeds* the garden; we *butter* the bread, *bread* the chicken— and who among us hasn't *chickened out* at one time or another?

But we also have a few verb-forming affixes that combine with certain nouns and adjectives:

| typi**fy** | dark**en** | activ**ate** | lega**lize** |

In addition to these suffixes, the prefixes *en-* and *be-* and *de-* and *dis-* can turn nouns and adjectives into verbs and can alter the meaning of other verbs: *enable, enact, enchant, encounter, encourage, encrust, endear, enforce, enlighten, enthrone, bedevil, bewitch, besmirch, dethrone, derail, disable.* But compared with the large number of derivational morphemes that signal nouns, the inventory of verb-forming affixes is fairly small.

Verb Inflectional Suffixes.   The verb-expansion rule describes the system of adding auxiliaries and inflectional suffixes to verbs. So as a clue in identifying the part of speech we call *verb*, the inflectional system is extremely reliable. All verbs, with only one or two exceptions—even those with irregular *-en* and *-ed* forms—have both *-s* and *-ing* forms. This means we can identify a word as a verb simply by noting its *-s* and *-ing* forms. Every verb has the other three forms as well—the base, the *-ed*, and the *-en*—but they may not be as recognizable: Verbs such as *hit* and *put*, for instance, show no changes in form from the base (*hit, put*) to the *-ed* form (*hit, put*) to the *-en* form (*hit, put*); others include *cast, hurt, shut, split,* and *spread.* Yet the *-s* and the *-ing* forms are exactly like those of every other verb: *hits, puts, hitting, putting.* The verb inflectional system is so regular, in fact, that we can define *verb* on that basis alone. A word that doesn't have an *-s* or an *-ing* form is simply not a verb.

Investigating Language   **12.2**

It is easy to demonstrate the "verbness" of *ground, water, air,* and *fire,* even though these words may, at first glance, appear to be nouns. First, add the verb inflections. Then write a sentence for each of the four verbs, using the form called for. Remember that the *-en* form will follow the auxiliary *have;* and if you begin your sentence with *yesterday,* you'll automatically use the *-ed* form.

	BASE	-s FORM	-ed FORM	-ing FORM	-en FORM
1. GROUND	_____	_____	_____	_____
(-ed)	_____
2. WATER	_____	_____	_____	_____
(-s)	_____
3. AIR	_____	_____	_____	_____
(-ing)	_____
4. FIRE	_____	_____	_____	_____
(-en)	_____

Now test the "verbness" of the verbs in the following sentences (*rumor, beware*) by listing their five forms:

It was rumored that Marcus broke his leg.

You should always beware of rumors.

What have you discovered about the reliability of identifying verbs by their inflections? Would a different criterion be more accurate—perhaps one based on the possibility of auxiliaries?

The verbs *rumor* and *beware* are indeed exceptions to the inflectional-suffix rule for identifying verbs. The verb *rumor* is used exclusively in the passive voice, although the dictionary does include the -*ing* form—perhaps used at one time or place in a particular dialect. The verb *beware* is used exclusively with *you*—or, in commands, with the understood *you*. The dictionary lists only the base form for *beware*. But we shouldn't let these two exceptions—and they do appear to be the only two—discourage us from relying on the almost infallible inflection test for identifying verbs.

ADJECTIVES

In terms of form, adjectives are not as easily identifiable in isolation as are nouns and verbs. Often we need either meaning or context for clues. One reliable way to discover if a word is an adjective is this "adjective test frame":

The _____ NOUN is very _____.

Only an adjective will fit into both slots. For example,

The diligent student is very diligent.

The ordinary house is very ordinary.

Because these sentences are grammatical (although perhaps not sentences you'd ever be likely to use), we have shown that the words *diligent* and *ordinary* are adjectives. But in some cases the form of the word also provides clues. A number of derivational suffixes signal adjectives.

Adjective Derivational Suffixes. The most reliable derivational suffix identifying a word as an adjective is *-ous;* we know that *gorgeous, famous, porous, courageous,* and *contagious* are adjectives simply on the basis of form. Here are some other adjective-forming suffixes:

merry, funny	childish, reddish
beautiful, wonderful	fragmentary, complimentary
terrific, ascetic	punitive, active
fortunate, temperate	variable, amenable

As clues to adjectives, these suffixes are not as reliable as *-ous* because they show up occasionally on other form classes too: hand*ful* (noun), pan*ic* (noun, verb), pun*ish* (verb). But it is safe to say that most words with these endings are adjectives.

Adjective Inflectional Suffixes. The inflectional suffixes that pattern with adjectives are *-er*, the sign of the **comparative degree,** and *-est,* the **superlative:**

Positive:	big	young	smart
Comparative:	bigger	younger	smarter
Superlative:	biggest	youngest	smartest

The *-er* form is used in the comparison of two nouns—that's why this form is called the comparative degree:

Pat is younger than Phyllis.

Phyllis is the better student of the two.

The comparative degree with *than* can also be followed by a clause rather than a noun phrase:

Pat is younger than I suspected.

The *-est* form, the superlative degree, is used when singling out one of more than two nouns:

Tom was the oldest person in the room.

Of the three candidates, Sarah is the best campaigner.

For many adjectives the comparative and superlative degrees are not formed with *-er* and *-est* but with *more* and *most,* which we can think of as alternative forms, or allomorphs, of the morphemes *-er* and *-est*. In fact, adjectives of more than one syllable generally pattern with *more* and *most*, with certain exceptions: two-syllable adjectives ending in *-y* or *-ly* (*prettiest, friendlier, lovelier*); some ending in *-le* (*nobler, noblest*), *-ow* (*narrower, narrowest*), and *-er* (*tenderest*).

But *more* and *most* are not exclusive to adjectives either. The *-ly* adverbs, those derived from adjectives, also have comparative and superlative versions: *more quickly, most frequently*. And there are some adjectives, such as *former, main*, and *principal*, that have no comparative and superlative forms.

A small group of words that have comparative and superlative forms can serve as either adjectives or adverbs, so the inflectional test is not completely reliable in identifying a word as an adjective:

early	fast	late	high
earlier	faster	later	higher
earliest	fastest	latest	highest
hard	long	low	deep
harder	longer	lower	deeper
hardest	longest	lowest	deepest

Another word we could add to this list is *near* (*nearer, nearest*), which can serve not only as an adjective and an adverb, but also as a preposition ("Our seats were *near* the fifty-yard line")—the only preposition that takes inflections. In short, the possibility of making a word comparative or superlative is not exclusive to adjectives.

In spite of all these limitations, we have no difficulty distinguishing adjectives in sentences. First, we know the positions they fill in the sentence patterns—as subject and object complements and in noun phrases as prenoun modifiers. And although nouns can also fill all these slots, the differences in the form of nouns and adjectives make it easy to distinguish between them.

On the subject of the comparative and superlative degrees, we should also note that adjectives can be compared in a negative sense with *as, less*, and *least*:

This picnic is not <u>as enjoyable as</u> I thought it would be.

This picnic is <u>less enjoyable than</u> I thought it would be.

This is the <u>least enjoyable</u> picnic I've ever attended.

We should also note some exceptions to the regular comparative and superlative forms:

good	bad	far	far
better	worse	farther	further
best	worst	farthest	furthest

Exercise 52

Fill in the blanks with the comparative and superlative degrees of the adjectives listed. Do any of them require *more* and *most?*

POSITIVE	COMPARATIVE	SUPERLATIVE
friendly	_____	_____
helpful	_____	_____
wise	_____	_____
awful	_____	_____
rich	_____	_____
mellow	_____	_____
expensive	_____	_____
valid	_____	_____
pure	_____	_____
able	_____	_____

Subclasses of Adjectives. The adjective test frame, The _____ NOUN is very _____, is useful in identifying adjectives. It is also useful in helping distinguish subclasses of adjectives: those that are limited to the prenoun slot and those that are limited to the complement slots.

Adjectives actually fill three slots in the sentence patterns: as subject complement and object complement (where they are called **predicative adjectives**) and as modifiers in the noun phrase (where they are called **attributive adjectives**). Most adjectives can fill all three slots; the test frame uses two of them: attributive and subject complement.

But a small number will not fill the complement slots. The following adjectives are attributive only: *main, principal, former, mere, potential, atomic, late* (meaning "dead"), and such technical adjectives as *sulfuric* and *hydrochloric.* These do not serve as either subject or object complements in the verb phrase, nor do they take qualifiers, such as *very:*

He is the former president.

*The president is former.

*My reason is main.

*My main reason is very main.

She is a mere child.

*The child is mere.

Many of the so-called A-adjectives—*ablaze, afraid, aghast, alone, awake*—are predicative only:

The house was ablaze.

*The ablaze house burned down in an hour.

The children were awake.

*The awake children were noisy.

There are a few others—*fond, ready, ill, well*—that rarely appear in attributive position in reference to animate nouns. We may refer to a "ready wit" but rarely to a "ready person." We may talk about an "ill omen" but rarely an "ill person"; we are more likely to say a "sick person."

Incidentally, not all predicative adjectives take *very*, the sample qualifier in the test frame. We usually don't say "very afraid" or "very awake"; we are more likely to say "very much afraid" or "very much awake." But these adjectives do combine with other qualifiers: *quite* afraid, *extremely* afraid, *completely* awake, *wide* awake.

A number of adjectives in predicative position appear frequently with complements in the form of phrases or clauses; some adjectives, such as *fond* and *aware*, are rarely used without them.

The children were <u>afraid that the dog would bite</u>.

The children were <u>aware that the dog would bite</u>.

The dog was <u>fond of biting children</u>.

We were <u>conscious of the problem</u>.

Our team is <u>certain to win</u>.

We call these "complements" rather than, simply, modifiers or qualifiers because they complete the idea expressed by the adjective, in much the same way that direct objects are complements of verbs.

Another subclassification of adjectives relates to their ability to combine with qualifiers. Certain adjectives denote meanings that are considered **absolute** in nature: *unique, round, square, perfect, single, double, fatal, empty, right, wrong, impossible*. These can fill both the attributive and predicate slots, but they generally cannot be qualified or compared. We can, of course, say "almost perfect" or "nearly square," but most writers avoid "more perfect" or "very perfect." For most of these words, however, we recognize more than a single, absolute meaning. In the case of *unique*, it has come to mean "rare" or "unusual," in which case "very unique" would be comparable to "very unusual." However, given the historical meaning "one of a kind," the qualified "very unique" is generally avoided.

Investigating Language   12.3

In discussing word stems and affixes in his book *The Language Instinct* (Morrow, 1994), Steven Pinker makes the following statement:

> [The suffix] *-able* combines with any verb to create an adjective, as in *crunch–crunchable*. The suffix *-er* converts any verb to a noun, as in *crunch–cruncher*, and the suffix *-ness* converts any adjective into a noun, as in *crunchy–crunchiness*. (pp. 133–134)

Test those rules on your own vocabulary to see if you can find exceptions. Can you think of other suffixes or prefixes that have similar powers?

ADVERBS

Of all the form classes, adverbs are the hardest to pin down in terms of both form and position. Many of them have no distinguishing affixes, and except in Pattern I they fill no required slots in the sentence patterns. (We have identified certain verbs in Patterns VI and VII, however— among them, *lay, put, place*, and *set*—that do require adverbials.) The fact that adverbs are often movable is perhaps their most distinguishing characteristic.

The class we are calling "adverb" differs from the class identified as "adverb" in traditional grammar. You'll recall the traditional definition as "a word that modifies a verb, an adjective, or another adverb." This definition includes words that we call "qualifiers," words that intensify or qualify the meaning of adjectives and adverbs: *very* nice, *quite* slow, *rather* quickly. But even when we leave out adjectives and other adverbs from the traditional definition, we are left with a definition of "adverbial"—that is, the definition of a function, not a word class. (Chapter 6 describes many structures—not only adverbs—that function adverbially.) Remember, we are defining the four form classes on the basis of their inflectional and derivational affixes and of the words that signal them—not on the basis of their function in the sentence. You'll read more about the distinction between qualifiers and adverbs in the section on "Qualifiers" in Chapter 13.

Adverb Derivational Suffixes. One common indicator of form we do have is the derivational suffix *-ly*, which we use to derive adverbs of manner from adjectives—adverbs that tell *how* or *in what way* about the verb:

He walked <u>slowly</u>.

She answered <u>correctly</u>.

But -*ly* is not completely reliable as a signaler of adverbs; it also occurs on nouns (*folly*) and on adjectives (*lovely, ugly*). But we are safe in saying that most -*ly* words are adverbs, simply because there are so many adjectives that we can turn into adverbs with this derivational morpheme.

There are some restrictions on this process, however: Not all adjectives can become manner adverbs. These restrictions are related to meaning. Some adjectives describe a state, such as *tall* and *old*, or a fixed or inherent characteristic, such as *Norwegian;* others describe characteristics that change, such as *weak, active,* and *industrious.* Another distinction can be drawn between objective characteristics, such as *tall* and *old,* and subjective ones, such as *nice* and *splendid.* The adjectives that refer to objective or stative or inherent qualities rarely become manner adverbs: *tall, old, fat, young, short, thick, large, flat, round, red.* When they do, they are likely to have a special-ized, often metaphorical, meaning: *shortly, hardly, flatly, squarely, widely.*

Besides -*ly,* two other derivational suffixes produce adverbs: -*ward* and -*wise.* Words ending in -*ward* signal direction: *homeward, forward, backward, upward, downward.* Words ending in -*wise,* which indicate manner, include both old usages, such as *otherwise, lengthwise,* and *crosswise,* and new ones that are considered by some writers as unneces-sary jargon, such as *budgetwise, weatherwise, moneywise,* and *profitwise.*

Investigating Language 12.4

One of our most reliable derivational suffixes is -*ly.* In most cases the mes-sage it sends is "adverb of manner": *Quickly* means "in a quick manner," and *slowly* means "in a slow manner." But, as with most rules in our lan-guage, there are exceptions to both parts of that message—both the "adverb" part and the "of manner" part.

Consider the -*ly* words in the following sentences. Are they adverbs? Are they adjectives? Could they be nouns or verbs?

1. We're leaving <u>immediately</u> and driving <u>directly</u> to Austin.
2. Bob will be leaving <u>directly</u>.
3. The natives around here are not always <u>friendly</u>.
4. One person I met tried to <u>bully</u> me.
5. He wasn't <u>particularly neighborly</u>.
6. Shedding tears is not considered <u>manly</u>.
7. That is <u>hardly</u> a universal belief, however.
8. My <u>belly</u> aches, but I <u>flatly</u> refuse to stay home.

Use your understanding of form to test these *-ly* words. Remember the inflectional paradigms for nouns and verbs; remember the adjective test frame. And is it possible that *-ly* adverbs have a meaning other than manner? Use your intuition, too!

Adverb Inflectional Suffixes. The comparative and superlative inflections, *-er* and *-est*, combine with adverbs as well as with adjectives, although in a much more limited way. The comparative form of *-ly* adverbs, usually formed by adding *more* rather than *-er*, is fairly common. The superlative degree—*most* suddenly, *most* favorably—is rare in both speech and writing; it invariably calls attention to itself and will often have the main focus of the sentence:

> The committee was most favorably impressed with the proposal.

> The crime was planned most ingeniously.

In the discussion of adjectives, we listed a few words that serve as both adjectives and adverbs: *early, late, hard, fast, long, high, low, deep,* and *near.* These are simply adverbs made from adjectives without the addition of *-ly*; they are referred to as **flat adverbs**. Except for a few others such as *soon* and *often*, they are the only adverbs that take *-er* and *-est;* most of the *-ly* adverbs take *more* and, occasionally, *most* in forming the comparative and superlative degrees.

A great many adverbs have neither derivational nor inflectional affixes that distinguish them as adverbs. Instead, we recognize them by the information they provide, by their position in the sentence, and often by their movability:

Time:	now, today, nowadays, yesterday
Duration:	already, always, still, yet
Frequency:	often, seldom, never, sometimes, always
Location:	there, here, everywhere, somewhere, elsewhere, upstairs, abroad, outside, nearby
Direction:	away, thence
Concession:	still, yet
Sequence:	afterward, next, then

There are also a number of words without form distinctions that can serve as either prepositions or adverbs: *above, around, behind, below, down, in, inside, out, outside, up.*

Exercise 53

Fill in the blanks with variations of the words shown on the chart, changing or adding derivational morphemes to change the word class.

	NOUN	VERB	ADJECTIVE	ADVERB
1.	grief	_____	_____	_____
2.	_____	vary	_____	_____
3.	_____	_____	_____	ably
4.	_____	defend	_____	_____
5.	economy	_____	_____	_____
6.	_____	_____	pleasant	_____
7.	type	_____	_____	_____
8.	_____	prohibit	_____	_____
9.	_____	_____	_____	critically
10.	_____	_____	valid	_____
11.	_____	appreciate	_____	_____
12.	beauty	_____	_____	_____
13.	_____	accept	_____	_____
14.	_____	_____	pure	_____
15.	_____	continue	_____	_____

CHAPTER 12
Key Terms

Absolute adjective

Adjective

Adjective complement

Adjective derivational suffix

Adjective inflectional suffix

Adverb

Adverb derivational suffix

Adverb inflectional suffix

Attributive adjective

Case

Collective noun

Common noun

Comparative degree

Countable noun

Flat adverb

Form classes

Functional shift

Indefinite pronoun

Noncountable noun

Noun

Noun derivational suffix

Noun inflectional suffix

Number

Plural

Plural-only noun

Positive degree

Possessive

Predicative adjective

Proper noun

Superlative degree

Verb

Verb derivational suffix

Verb inflectional suffix

QUESTIONS
?
for DISCUSSION

1. A government spokesperson used the following clauses in a discussion of the economy:

    When we were approaching crunch.

    When push comes to shove.

    What part of speech are *crunch, push,* and *shove?*

2. The traditional Latin term for possessive case is *genitive.*
    Consider the relationship between the possessive noun and its headword in the following noun phrases:

    the teacher's explanation

    the car's overhaul

    Explain what is meant by *subjective genitive* and *objective genitive.*
    Now consider the following ambiguous sentence:

    I was disturbed about Tom's punishment.

    What is the source of the ambiguity?

3. We often use verbs adjectivally, as noun modifiers, as you saw in Chapter 7. But many words that look like verbs—that were, in fact, originally verbs—now have the characteristics of adjectives.

We have said that we can identify a word as an adjective if it can fit into the adjective test frame (The _____ NOUN is very _____). We also have an inflectional test: Can the word be made comparative and superlative? Using these two tests, identify the underlined words in the following sentences: Are they adjectives or verbs?

> Joe took the <u>broken</u> chair to the dump.
>
> That <u>disgusting</u> movie wasn't worth five dollars.
>
> The football rally was <u>exciting</u>.
>
> I feel <u>tired</u>.
>
> Joe was <u>drunk</u> last night.
>
> Many <u>working</u> mothers have problems with day care.
>
> The <u>decorated</u> tree looks beautiful.

4. Sometimes verbs are used as nouns (gerunds), as you saw in Chapter 8. What test can you apply to the following -*ing* words to test their part of speech? Are they verbs or nouns?

> The <u>meeting</u> was boring.
>
> Julie looked lovely at her <u>wedding</u>.
>
> The committee's <u>finding</u> surprised everyone.
>
> <u>Jogging</u> is good exercise.
>
> We watch the news every <u>evening</u>.

5. Explain the ambiguity of the following sentences in terms of their possible sentence patterns and parts of speech:

> My mother is always entertaining.
>
> They are frightening people.

6. Shakespeare, as you know, used language in all sorts of original ways. Here are two lines from *Romeo and Juliet*. What has he done with word classes?

> Thank me no thankings nor proud me no prouds.
>
> O flesh, flesh, how art thou fishified!

7. The dictionary labels *today* as both an adverb and a noun. Are those labels based on form or function? How should we define *yesterday* and *tomorrow*? Are they also members of both classes? Examine the following passage from *Macbeth* to see how Shakespeare used the words:

> Tomorrow, and tomorrow, and tomorrow
>
> Creeps in this petty pace from day to day

To the last syllable of recorded time,

And all our yesterdays have lighted fools

The way to dusty death.

8. Here are two lines from Groucho Marx, who also had a way with words:

    Time flies like an arrow.

    Fruit flies like a banana.

    Use your understanding of both sentence patterns and word classes to explain the joke.

9. In meeting a very tall person, you might ask the question, "How tall are you?" Strangely enough, we would ask the same question of a short person: We don't usually ask, "How *short* are you?" In this pair of adjectives, *tall* is called the unmarked version. Think of other adjectives we use for quantity or size or age or speed: *old/young, big/little, heavy/light, fast/slow*. Does our usage suggest marked and unmarked versions? Under what circumstances would we use the unmarked version?

CLASSROOM APPLICATIONS

1. Here's a sentence with a message you may not understand:

    The frabous gricks were brocking my parmy dorfer very botly.

    As you see, it's filled with nonsense words. But even though the sentence has no semantic, or dictionary, meaning, it still sounds like English. It has structural meaning. In fact, you can probably figure out the classes of the separate words, as well as the sentence pattern. Identify the derivational and inflectional clues that enable you to do so.

    Noun(s):

    Verb(s):

    Adjective(s):

    Adverb(s):

    What other clues, in addition to the form of the nonsense words, helped you?

    The traditional definitions of *noun* ("the name of a person, place, or thing") and *verb* ("a word showing action") are of no help here. Write new definitions based on the clues you identified.

Noun: _____

Verb: _____

2. Here's another grammatical nonsense sentence for you to interpret:

> Stear, the frabous grick botly brocked my parmy dorfer in the alflit because the dorfer jilked the grick.

First, answer the following questions:

1. What happened to the dorfer?
2. Why did it happen?
3. Who or what did it?
4. Where did it happen?
5. Describe the grick and the dorfer.

Now diagram the sentence. Then write a version in which the main clause is in the passive voice. Write a version in which the subordinate clause is passive.

3. Here's an altered version of the sentence in 2:

> Stear, the frabous grick, botly brocked my parmy dorfer in the alflit because the dorfer jilked the grick.

Explain how the addition of one comma changed the syntax. Note that the class of one word has changed in the new version. Which word? Diagram the new version.

4. In his book *Words and Rules: The Ingredients of Language* (Basic Books, 1999), Steven Pinker discusses our ability to form new words with prefixes and suffixes:

> The psychologists Harald Baayen and Antoinette Renouf calculated that every time you open a newspaper you will be faced with at least one word with *un-* that you have never seen before, one with *-ness,* and one with *-ly:* words like *uncorkable, uncheesey, headmistressly, breathcatchingly, pinkness,* and *outdoorsiness.* (p. 122)

Check the front page of your daily paper or a current magazine article to test this calculation. See how many such words your class can find, words that do not appear in the dictionary.

CHAPTER 13

The Structure Classes

CHAPTER PREVIEW

In contrast to the large, open form classes, the categories of words known as structure classes are small and, for the most part, closed. Although new words regularly enter the language as nouns and verbs as the need arises for new vocabulary, the structure classes—conjunctions, prepositions, auxiliaries, and the like—remain constant from one generation to the next. As native speakers, we pay little attention to the structure words. Until we notice a nonnative speaker omitting a determiner or using the wrong preposition, we probably don't appreciate the importance of the grammatical sense the structure words contribute.

Part of that grammatical sense comes from the stress-unstress pattern of speech, the rhythm of the language. Most structure words have weak stress: They have the lowest volume, providing valleys between the peaks of loudness that fall on the stressed syllables of the form-class words.

The first three structure classes we will look at are those that signal specific form classes: determiners, the signalers of nouns; auxiliaries, the signalers of verbs; and qualifiers, the signalers of adjectives and adverbs. Then we will look at prepositions and conjunctions, both of which have connective roles; interrogatives, the signalers of questions; expletives, which serve as structural operators of various kinds; and particles.

DETERMINERS

The **determiner** class is one of the structure classes that straddle the line between a word class and a function. On the one hand, our most common determiners, the articles, do indeed constitute a small, closed structure class. At the other end of the spectrum are the possessive nouns, which function as determiners while retaining their membership in the open class "noun." In between are the subclasses of determiners that belong to the pronouns, a closed class: Demonstrative, possessive, and indefinite pronouns all function as determiners; and, of course, as pronouns they also function as nominals (in fact, "pronominal" would be a more accurate label than "pronoun").

Determiners signal nouns in a variety of ways: They may define the relationship of the noun to the speaker or listener (or reader); they may identify the noun as *specific* or *general;* they may *quantify* it specifically or refer to quantity in general. Because determiners have an important role in the noun phrase, as signalers, we also include them under the umbrella term *adjectival,* as you learned in Chapter 7. Following are the most common classes of determiners, many of which have appeared in our sample sentences:

ARTICLES	POSSESSIVE NOUNS	DEMONSTRATIVE PRONOUNS	NUMBERS
the	John's	this/these	one
a(n)	my son's	that/those	two
	etc.		*etc.*

POSSESSIVE PRONOUNS		INDEFINITE PRONOUNS			
my	its	several	few	each	all
your	our	little	fewer	every	both
his	their	many	more	either	some
her	whose	much	most	neither	any
		no	enough	less	

We should note that possessive nouns as determiners may have their own determiners: *my daughter's* teacher; *the week's* groceries; *our cat's* fur.

Many of the features of nouns in the hierarchy shown on page 252 affect our selection of determiners. A noun appearing in the lowest, left-hand branch of the diagram, for example—a singular, countable noun—rarely appears without a determiner:

This cookie tastes good.

*Cookie tastes good.

John is my friend.

*John is friend.

There are certain exceptions to this rule. For example, the nouns *town, school,* and *car* are singular, countable nouns; nevertheless, in some prepositional phrases they appear without determiners:

the other side of <u>town</u>

going to <u>school</u>

the best kind of <u>car</u>

These exceptions present no problems for native speakers, of course. We're used to the sometimes arbitrary nature of the determiner:

We say, "I walked to town," but not "I walked to city."

We say, "I have a cold," but not "I have a flu."

We say, "I attend college," but not "I attend university."

We say, "I'm going into town," but not "I'm going into hospital."

(The British and Australians, incidentally, do "go into hospital," "attend university," and "look out of window.")

The difficulty for the nonnative speaker comes with learning which nouns are countable nouns and which are not. Other complications arise because determiners have built-in restrictions. Some will signal only plural nouns *(these, those, many, few, several),* some only singular nouns *(a, one, each, every),* some only noncountables *(much, less),* and others only countables *(few, many, a, one).*

Another fairly regular rule concerns the limitation of determiners with certain noncountable nouns, sometimes called mass nouns, such as *luggage, furniture, beer, cake, sugar, rice, coal, steel, water.* When mass nouns are used as noncountable, they cannot be plural, so they do not combine with determiners that have either the "plural" or "countable" feature: *a, one, two, these, several, many.*

*<u>These furnitures</u> are sturdy.

*<u>Many furnitures</u> are expensive.

*<u>Each furniture</u> has its own charm.

Some determiners have both countable and noncountable features built into them *(this, some, most, all),* so they can combine with both kinds of nouns:

<u>This furniture</u> is lovely.

<u>This chair</u> is comfortable.

<u>Some furniture</u> is expensive.

<u>Some chairs</u> are expensive.

<u>Most chocolate cake</u> is high in calories.

<u>Most coconut macaroons</u> are delicious.

<u>All polluted water</u> is undrinkable.

<u>Not all rules</u> are necessarily good rules.

The nonnative speaker must consciously learn these features of both nouns and determiners. But a further complication arises when these mass nouns take on countable meanings:

<u>These</u> whole-grain <u>flours</u> are popular now.

<u>The</u> light <u>beers</u> are getting better all the time.

Abstract nouns also present problems for the nonnative speaker because they may appear either with or without determiners:

I have finally regained <u>peace</u> of mind.

I have finally regained <u>my peace</u> of mind.

In some cases the determiner is tied to the presence of a modifier, such as a *that* clause:

*<u>The peace</u> of mind is hard to acquire in these insecure times.

<u>The peace of mind that comes with financial security</u> is my goal.

Even a proper noun may require a determiner when it has certain kinds of modifiers:

<u>The Altoona of my childhood</u> was a railroad town.

And for some inexplicable reason, the article *a* changes the meaning in sentences with *few* and *little:*

I have few friends.   I've had little trouble with my car.

I have a few friends.   I've had a little trouble with my car.

Finally, some determiners are extremely versatile. The **definite article**, *the*, can signal all classes of nouns that can take determiners when the definite meaning is called for—unlike the **indefinite** *a*, which is restricted to countables. The possessives, too—both nouns and pronouns—are wide-ranging, without built-in distribution restrictions.

Exercise 54

Identify the determiners in the following sentences.

1. My sister doesn't have enough money for her ticket.
2. John's roommate went home for the weekend.
3. Every course I'm taking this term has a midterm exam.

4. Bill spent more money on the week's groceries than he expected to.

5. I spend less time studying now than I did last term.

6. I haven't seen either movie, so I have no preference.

The Expanded Determiner. A determiner is not always a single word. In fact, we can think of the determiner slot itself as a series of slots with optional pre- and postdeterminers. The following formula will account for some fairly common **expanded determiners**, although a description that accounted for all the possibilities would be far more complex. This simplified scheme, however, should help you appreciate the intricacies of the grammar rules built into your linguistic computer:

(predeterminer) + DETERMINER + (postdeterminer)

		ORDINAL NUMBERS	CARDINAL NUMBERS
all (of)	the	first	one
both (of)	a	second	two
half (of)	my	*etc.*	*etc.*
only	these	next	
especially	*etc.*	last	
just			
double			

The pre- and postdeterminers are, of course, optional, so they are shown in parentheses in the formula.

In the following sentences, the pre- and postdeterminers are underlined; the determiner is written with capital letters:

All of THE cookies disappeared.

Only MY pretzels disappeared.

THE first ten students in line were chosen.

Only THE next two students complained.

Both (of) THESE students wrote A papers.

Half (of) THE class took part in the demonstration.

I have just ENOUGH gas for the trip.

Another type of expanded determiner is the phrasal quantifier; it can occur with either countable or noncountable nouns:

a lot of classes

a lot of homework

a great many friends

a large number of people

In terms of **subject–verb agreement**, it is the number of the noun—whether singular or plural—that determines the verb: homework *is*; classes (friends, people) *are*.

AUXILIARIES

Like the determiners and the other structure classes, the auxiliary class is limited in membership and closed to new members. Counting the forms of *have* and *be*, the modals, and the forms of *do*, the list of regular auxiliaries numbers around two dozen:

have	be	can	do
has	is	could	does
had	are	will	did
having	am	would	
	was	shall	
	were	should	
	been	may	
	being	might	
		must	
		ought to	

The following modal-like verbs also function as auxiliaries; they are sometimes referred to as semi-auxiliaries or marginal modals:

have to   be going to   used to   be to

We have to leave soon.

We're going to take the bus to Iowa City today.

We used to live there.

The bus is to leave at noon.

(We should note that *ought to* is sometimes classified with this group as a marginal modal rather than as a major modal. But because it patterns freely with the auxiliaries *have* and *be* and can also act as an operator in forming negatives and questions without *do* support, *ought to* meets the criteria for major modals.)

The marginal modals are diagrammed just as other auxiliaries are, on the main line:

There are a number of other phrasal modals that are often listed with the marginal modals shown here. In fact, we could make the case to include them with the four listed above: *be able to, be due to, be meant to, be obliged to, be supposed to, had better.* Even though many traditional grammarians do not recognize the marginal modals as a category, it's clear that in some cases the meaning is very close to that of a major modal: *be able to = can; be obliged to = should; had better = must.*

Two other modal-like verbs, *dare* and *need,* commonly appear in negative sentences and in questions:

She <u>need not</u> go.   <u>Dare</u> we go?

I <u>don't dare</u> go.   <u>Need</u> you go?

In function, the auxiliaries are perhaps more intimately connected to verbs than are determiners to nouns, because they alter the verb's meaning in important ways and often determine the form that it takes. Another important difference between the auxiliaries and the other structure classes lies in their systematic distribution. Determiners and qualifiers are somewhat arbitrary in distribution; but with few exceptions every verb can be signaled (preceded) by every auxiliary. The modals, *have,* and *do* combine with every verb; only *be* is restricted in any way, as we saw in Chapter 4, where we noted a few verbs, such as *seem,* that rarely appear with *be + -ing.*

Exercise 55

Underline the auxiliaries in the following sentences. Circle the main verb.

1. I have been having problems with my car.
2. I used to use two different brands of motor oil, one for summer and one for winter.
3. I should not have eaten those tomatoes.
4. Apparently some people can't even look at tomatoes.
5. Sally will be helping us with the party.
6. Margie has to leave early.
7. The kids are really frustrating me today.

8. The teens can be frustrating years for some adolescents.
9. The gymnasts should continue practicing their balance-beam routines.
10. I am keeping my opinions to myself.

ELL Issues   **Would**

There are a great many variations and subtleties in the use of modal auxiliaries, one of the most problematic areas of English grammar. Like all the modals, *would* has many uses.

To express a wish about a present condition or a future happening:

I wish it would stop raining.

I wish the teacher would speak more slowly.

To express a past or unrealized possibility:

I would help you if I could. (I'd help you . . .)

I would have helped, but I wasn't asked. (I'd have helped . . .)

(When the contracted *'d* is followed by the base form of the verb, it's short for *would*.)

For polite requests:

Would (could, will) you help me with this math problem?

(Of the three choices, *will* is somewhat less polite than *could* or *would*.)

To express exasperation or surprise:

She **would** say that, wouldn't she!

Who would have believed she was that old?

QUALIFIERS

As the following lists demonstrate, many words can act as **qualifiers** or **intensifiers** to alter the meaning of adjectives and adverbs. (In the adjective test frame the word *very* is used to represent all the possible qualifiers.) On the diagram the qualifier is attached to the adjective or adverb:

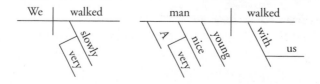

The diagrams illustrate that *very* says something about *slowly* and *nice*; it is the whole adverb phrase *very slowly* that modifies *walked* and the whole adjective phrase *very nice* that modifies *young man.*

The following list of qualifers can be used with the positive form of most adjectives, such as *good* and *soft*, and with adverbs of manner, such as *rapidly*:

very	really	fairly
quite	pretty	mighty
rather	awfully	too

A second group of qualifiers can be used with the comparative degree of adjectives, such as *better* and *nicer*, and with comparative adverbs, such as *sooner, later, nearer,* and *farther:*

still	some	no
even	much	

A number of others have a limited distribution:

<u>right</u> now   <u>just about</u> there

<u>wide</u> awake   <u>almost</u> there

<u>just</u> so

Many others are used in colloquial expressions:

<u>right</u> nice   <u>darn</u> right

<u>damn</u> sure   <u>real</u> pretty

Some of the adverbs of manner, the *-ly* adverbs, are themselves used as qualifiers with certain adjectives:

<u>dangerously</u> close   <u>politically</u> expedient

<u>particularly</u> harmful   <u>technically</u> possible

<u>absolutely</u> true   <u>especially</u> difficult

Because of the *-ly* adverbs in their ranks, the qualifier class, like that of the determiners, is not a closed class. In fact, the qualifier, like the determiner, can be thought of as both a word class and a sentence function. It has attributes of both.

Investigating Language   13.1

You may recall that the title of Chapter 6 includes a definition of *adverbial*: "Modifiers of the Verb." The discussion in that chapter takes you through the various forms that modify verbs—adverbs, prepositional phrases, noun phrases, verb phrases, and clauses. Note that the form-class "adverb" is one of five structures that function adverbially.

Now compare that definition with the traditional definition of *adverb*—one you may be familiar with: "a word that modifies a verb, an adjective, or another adverb." This definition clearly includes what we are calling qualifiers—that is, words that modify adjectives and adverbs.

Consider what you have learned about the form classes—nouns, verbs, adjectives, and adverbs; add to that what you know about structures that modify verbs—the adverbials. Then examine the following sentences, two of which are marked as ungrammatical:

> Quite slowly the old man climbed the stairs.

> *The old man quite climbed the stairs.

> The girl is very young.

> *The girl will very come over to babysit.

At this point you probably agree that these sentences suggest a difference between adverbs and the qualifiers *quite* and *very* that justifies their membership in separate word classes. Three other words in the earlier list of qualifiers—*really, fairly,* and *rather*—are traditionally classified as adverbs. Try to come up with sentences that would justify their membership in both classes, adverb and qualifier.

In their relationship to the form classes, the qualifiers are different from the determiners and auxiliaries in that they are optional; all the adjectives and adverbs they modify can appear without them. This is not true of the relationship of nouns and verbs to their signal words: Many nouns cannot appear without a determiner; and two of our verb forms—the *-en* and the *-ing* forms—require auxiliaries to function as the main verb. But like the other structure words, the qualifiers signal the form classes; they provide a useful test to differentiate adjectives and adverbs from other parts of speech.

PREPOSITIONS

The **preposition** (meaning "placed before") is a structure word found in pre-position to—preceding—a noun phrase or other nominal. Prepositions are among our most common words in English; in fact, of our twenty most frequently used words, eight are prepositions: *of, to, in, for, with, on, at,* and *by.*[1] Prepositions can be classified according to form as simple (one-word) or phrasal (multiple-word).

[1.] This frequency count, based on a collection of 1,014,232 words, is published in Henry Kuçera and W. Nelson Francis, *Computational Analysis of Present-Day English* (Providence, RI: Brown University Press, 1967).

Simple Prepositions. The following list includes the most common simple prepositions:

aboard	below	in	since
about	beneath	into	through
above	beside	like	throughout
across	between	near	till
after	beyond	of	to
against	but (except)	off	toward
along	by	on	under
amid	concerning	onto	underneath
among	despite	out	until
around	down	outside	up
as	during	over	upon
at	except	past	with
atop	for	per	within
before	from	regarding	without
behind			

Note that we label these words as prepositions only when they are followed by a nominal—that is, only when they are part of prepositional phrases. In the following sentence, for example, *up* functions as an adverb, not a preposition; *up* holds membership in both classes.

The price of sugar went <u>up</u> again.

Words like *up* also function as particles in two-word, or phrasal, verbs, such as *hold up*:

A masked gunman <u>held up</u> the liquor store.

But in the following sentence, *up* is a preposition, part of a prepositional phrase:

We hiked <u>up the steep trail</u>.

Investigating Language   **13.2**

Speaking of *up*, a "Dear Abby" correspondent sent in the following passage, which he had clipped from the *Reader's Digest* many years ago:

It's easy to understand UP, meaning toward the sky or toward the top of a list. But when we waken, why do we wake UP? At a meeting, why does a topic come UP? And why are participants said to speak UP? Why are officers UP for election? And why is it UP to the secretary to write UP a report?

The little word is really not needed, but we use it anyway. We brighten UP a room, light UP a cigar, polish UP the silver, lock UP the house and fix UP the old car.

At other times, it has special meanings. People stir UP trouble, line UP for tickets, work UP an appetite, think UP excuses and get tied UP in traffic.

To be dressed is one thing, but to be dressed UP is special. It may be confusing, but a drain must be opened UP because it is stopped UP.

We open UP a store in the morning, and close it UP in the evening. We seem to be all mixed UP about UP.

In order to be UP on the proper use of UP, look UP the word in the dictionary. In one desk dictionary, UP takes UP half a page; and the listed definitions add UP to about 40.

If you are UP to it, you might try building UP a list of the many ways in which UP is used. It may take UP a lot of your time, but if you don't give UP, you may wind UP with a thousand.

Try your hand at writing a similar passage using DOWN or OUT or OFF.

Phrasal Prepositions. Two-word, or **phrasal**, **prepositions** consist of a simple preposition preceded by a word from another category, such as an adverb, adjective, or conjunction:

according to	because of	next to
ahead of	but for	out of

along with	contrary to	prior to
as for	except for	thanks to
aside from	instead of	up to

Most three-word prepositions consist of preposition + noun + preposition:

by means of	in charge of	in spite of
in accordance with	in front of	on account of
in back of	in lieu of	on behalf of
in case of	in search of	

In a traditional diagram, we usually treat these phrases as we do the simple prepositions:

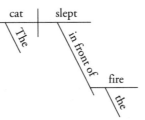

Because *in front of the fire* can also be analyzed as one prepositional phrase embedded in another, we can diagram it another way:

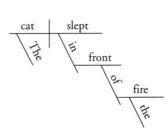

The foregoing lists include the most common, although certainly not all, of the prepositions. We use prepositions automatically, as we do the other structure words, in spite of the sometimes subtle differences in meaning they can express: *below* the stairs, *beneath* the stairs, *under* the stairs, *underneath* the stairs; *in* the room, *inside* the room, *within* the room. As native speakers we understand these distinctions, and, except for a few idioms that sometimes cause problems of usage, we rarely hesitate in selecting the right preposition for the occasion.

Exercise | 56

Identify the prepositions in the following sentences.

1. The Renfords have lived in San Diego since 1985.
2. They like it there because of the climate.
3. I like Minnesota in spite of the cold winters.
4. Prior to 1985, the Renfords lived in Baltimore.
5. According to some economists, the financial health of the Social Security System is in jeopardy.
6. I look on such predictions with skepticism.
7. Except for eggs, which rarely go up in price, the cost of groceries is going out of sight.
8. Between you and me, my grocery money may not hold out until payday.

CONJUNCTIONS

We use **conjunctions** to connect words and phrases and clauses within the sentence and to connect the sentences themselves. Within the sentence our most common connectors are the simple *coordinating* conjunctions and the *correlative* conjunctions. For joining sentences we use, in addition, the *subordinating* conjunctions, also called subordinators, and *conjunctive adverbs.* The relative pronouns and relative adverbs also function as connectors, joining relative, or adjectival, clauses to nouns.

Coordinating Conjunctions. We can use a coordinate structure for any slot in the sentence by using a coordinating conjunction (*and, or, but, yet, nor, for*):

> Riley <u>and</u> Tim worked out on Saturday.
>
> I'll meet you at the ticket window <u>or</u> in the grandstand.
>
> The dessert was simple <u>yet</u> elegant.
>
> Eager to start her new job <u>but</u> sad at the thought of leaving home, Kris packed the car <u>and</u> drove away from the familiar house on Maxwell Avenue.

The coordinating conjunctions also join complete sentences:

> I disapproved of his betting on the horses, <u>and</u> I told him so.
>
> He claims to have won fifty dollars, <u>but</u> I suspect he's exaggerating.
>
> She won't come to the party, <u>nor</u> will she explain why.

Notice that the clause introduced by *nor* requires a subject–auxiliary shift.

The coordinating conjunction *for* joins only complete sentences, not structures within the sentence. Even though it is close in meaning to *because*, it differs from the subordinating conjunctions: The *for* clause cannot open the sentence.

We should also mention that well-respected writers use both *and* and *but* as sentence openers (in spite of what you may have read or been told to the contrary). They are even used to open paragraphs. In Chapter 15, you'll find an example of *but* as a paragraph opener on page 339, the *Time* paragraph about the Vikings. And the opening of the passage that introduces the paragraph is *and* (as is the opener of this sentence!).

Correlative Conjunctions. Like the coordinating conjunctions, the **correlative conjunctions** (*both–and, either–or, neither–nor, not only–but also*) connect both complete sentences and elements within the sentence. Within the sentence *either–or* and *neither–nor* are used alike:

I will $\begin{Bmatrix} \text{either} \\ \text{neither} \end{Bmatrix}$ meet you in the lobby $\begin{Bmatrix} \text{or} \\ \text{nor} \end{Bmatrix}$ come to your room.

As a connector of sentences, *neither–nor* requires the subject–auxiliary shift; *either–or* does not:

Neither <u>will</u> I meet you in the lobby, nor <u>will</u> I come to your room.

Either <u>I will</u> meet you in the lobby, or <u>I will</u> come to your room.

Not only–but also can be used both within and between sentences:

<u>Not only</u> the coaches and players <u>but also</u> the fans had high hopes of defeating the Crimson Tide.

<u>Not only</u> did the government's experts underestimate the mortgage crisis that 2008 would bring, <u>but</u> they <u>also</u> delayed in taking action to change its course.

This sentence would be equally grammatical with either *but* or *also*, rather than both.

Both–and does not connect complete sentences; it connects elements within the sentence only:

Franco is a good sport, <u>both</u> on <u>and</u> off the playing field.

<u>Both</u> Jeanne <u>and</u> Marie worked hard to get their manuscript finished on schedule.

Conjunctive Adverbs (Adverbial Conjunctions). As their name suggests, the **conjunctive adverbs** join sentences to form coordinate structures as other conjunctions do, but they do so with an adverbial emphasis.

The following list also includes some of the most common simple adverbs and adverbial prepositional phrases that function as sentence connectors:

Result:	*therefore, consequently, as a result, of course*
Concession:	*nevertheless, yet, at any rate, still, after all, of course*
Apposition:	*for example, for instance, that is, namely, in other words*
Addition:	*moreover, furthermore, also, in addition, likewise, further*
Time:	*meanwhile, in the meantime*
Contrast:	*however, instead, on the contrary, on the other hand, in contrast, rather*
Summary:	*thus, in conclusion, then*
Reinforcement:	*further, in particular, indeed, above all, in fact*

Conjunctive adverbs differ from other conjunctions in that, like many other adverbials, they tend to be movable within their clause; they need not introduce the clause:

> My tax accountant is not cheap; <u>however</u>, the amount of tax she saves me is far greater than her fee.

> My tax accountant is not cheap; the amount of tax she saves me, <u>however</u>, is far greater than her fee.

The punctuation of coordinate sentences with conjunctive adverbs is explained on page 221. Their rhetorical effects are discussed on page 334.

Subordinating Conjunctions. The subordinators are conjunctions too, although their function is not to connect independent ideas as equals but rather to show a relationship between two ideas in which one of them is a *dependent* or *subordinate clause*. Like the conjunctive adverbs, the **subordinating conjunctions** are both single words and phrases:

Time:	*when, whenever, after, as, before, once, since, till, until, now that, while, as long as, as soon as*
Concession:	*though, although, even though, if, while*
Contingency:	*if, once*
Condition:	*if, in case, as long as, unless, provided that*
Reason:	*because, since, as long as*
Result:	*so that*

Comparison: *as, just as, as if*
Contrast: *while, whereas*

Most subordinate clauses come both before and after the main clause. This movability feature provides a test to differentiate between subordinators and coordinators. The coordinators—the conjunctive adverbs as well as the coordinating conjunctions—introduce only the second clause:

We decided to walk because we had missed the last bus.

Because we had missed the last bus, we decided to walk.

We decided to walk, for we had missed the last bus.

*For we had missed the last bus, we decided to walk.

We missed the bus, so we decided to walk.

*So we decided to walk, we missed the bus.

When set off by commas, subordinate clauses can also come between the subject and the predicate, where they will get added emphasis:

The City Council members, <u>before they adjourned their meeting</u>, voted to give a special award to the recycling center.

None of the players, <u>as they sat in the dugout</u>, heard the fans fighting in the stands just above them.

In addition to these simple and phrasal subordinators, we have a small group of correlative subordinators—two-part structures, one of which is part of the main clause: *as–so, the–the, no sooner–than.*

<u>As</u> General Motors goes, <u>so</u> goes the nation.

<u>The</u> more I go on fad diets, <u>the</u> more weight I seem to add.

He had <u>no sooner</u> arrived <u>than</u> he started to give orders.

Another two-part subordinator occurs in the clause of comparison:

There were <u>more</u> people at the political rally <u>than</u> we expected.

The governor gave a much long<u>er</u> speech <u>than</u> the program called for.

Adverbial subordinate clauses are discussed in Chapter 6. Subordinate clauses that are more clearly sentence modifiers and elliptical clauses are discussed in Chapter 9.

Relatives. Relative pronouns—*who* (*whose, whom*), *which*, and *that*— and **relative adverbs**—*where, when, why*—perform a dual function in the noun phrase: They introduce the relative, or adjectival, clause, connecting the clause to the noun it modifies; and they play a part in the clause, the pronouns as nominals and the adverbs as adverbials.

The price *that* <u>we pay for sneakers</u> keeps going up.

The man *who* <u>lives next door</u> rides a bicycle to work.

Nothing exciting ever happens in the small town *where*
<u>I was born</u>.

Adjectival clauses are also introduced by the **indefinite relative pronouns**, such as *whoever* (*whomever, whosever*), *whichever, whatever,* and *what* (meaning "that which"). These pronouns are called "indefinite" because they have no specific referent; instead, they have a general, indefinite reference. (See page 303.)

Adjectival clauses are discussed in detail in Chapter 7.

INTERROGATIVES

As their name implies, the interrogatives—*who, whose, whom, which, what, how, why, when, where*—introduce questions:

<u>What</u> are you doing here?

<u>How</u> did you get here?

<u>When</u> are you leaving?

The function of such questions, of course, is to elicit particular information.

The interrogatives also introduce clauses that fill NP slots in the sentence patterns. Such clauses are sometimes referred to as *indirect questions:*

Tell me <u>why he came</u>.

I wonder <u>who came with him</u>.

<u>Whose car he drove</u> is a mystery to me.

These clauses, which function as nominals, are discussed in Chapter 8. (We should note that the interrogatives are the same words that in other contexts are classified as relative pronouns or relative adverbs. For that reason the term *interrogative* more accurately labels a function than a word class.)

EXPLETIVES

Rather than providing a grammatical or structural meaning as the other structure-word classes do, the **expletives**—sometimes defined as "empty words"—generally act simply as operators that allow us to manipulate sentences in a variety of ways. In the diagrams of these sentences, the expletives are independent of the basic sentence.

There. The *there* transformation, as we saw in Chapter 5, enables us to delay the subject in certain kinds of sentences, thus putting it in the position of main stress, which generally falls in the predicate half of the sentence:

An airplane is landing   There's an airplane landing
    on the fréeway.   →   on the freeway.

The expletive *there* plays no grammatical role in the sentence. To analyze the sentence, you have to discover its underlying form by eliminating the expletive and shifting the subject in front of the *be.*

    The *there* transformation as a rhetorical tool is discussed in Chapter 15.

That. One of our most common expletives, *that,* introduces a nominal clause:

I hope <u>that our exam is easy</u>.

Unlike the relative pronoun *that,* which introduces adjectival clauses, the expletive *that* plays no part in the clause.

    "Expletive" is not the only label given to this use of the word *that;* it is sometimes called a "nominalizer" because its function is to turn a clause into a nominal, that is, a noun phrase substitute. And sometimes it is called a "subordinator." The label "expletive" is used by traditional grammarians to emphasize the "empty word" quality of *that,* in that it serves strictly as an operator; it plays no role in the clause itself. The use of *that* in nominal clauses is taken up in detail in Chapter 8.

Or. The expletive *or* introduces an explanatory appositive:

The study of sentences, <u>or</u> syntax, helps us appreciate how much
    we know when we know language.

The African wildebeest, <u>or</u> gnu, resembles an ox.

This *or* should not be confused with the conjunction *or,* which indicates an alternative (as in coffee <u>or</u> tea). The expletive introduces an equivalent in an appositive role. The diagram shows its expletive role:

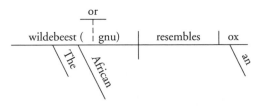

As. Another fairly common expletive introduces certain object complements in Patterns IX and X:

We elected him <u>as</u> president.

The diagram shows the role of *as* outside of the grammatical structure of the sentence:

Leaving out the *as* does not change the meaning of this sentence; whether to choose it or not is usually a matter of emphasis or rhythm. With verbs like *refer to, think of,* and *know,* however, *as* is required with the object complement:

> I refer to Professor Buck <u>as</u> a woman of character.
>
> I think of her <u>as</u> a woman of many talents.
>
> I think of her <u>as</u> exceptionally clever.
>
> I know her <u>as</u> a friend.

If **and *Whether (or not).*** These two expletives serve as nominalizers, turning yes/no questions into nominal clauses:

> I wonder <u>if the test will be easy</u>.

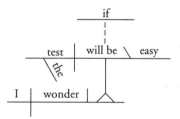

> It doesn't matter <u>whether I study or not</u>.

(You'll recall that for the other kind of questions—the information, or *wh-*questions—interrogative words act as nominalizers: I wonder <u>what I should study</u>.)

PARTICLES

The particle, which combines with a verb to produce a phrasal verb (look *up,* find *out,* turn *in,* look *into*), can be thought of as an alternative function that prepositions and adverbs perform rather than a word class of its own. Both transitive and intransitive verbs combine with particles:

We <u>turned in</u> at midnight. (intransitive)

The police <u>looked into</u> the allegations. (transitive)

Phrasal verbs are discussed on pages 44–45 and 47–48.

Exercise | **57**

Label the class of each underlined word.

1. I found some rare stamps <u>and</u> postmarks <u>on</u> <u>an</u> old envelope <u>in</u> the attic.

2. <u>Four</u> friends of mine <u>from</u> the dorm waited in line <u>for</u> sixteen hours, <u>for</u> they were determined to get tickets <u>for</u> the World Series.

3. <u>As</u> the experts predicted, the Republicans chose <u>an</u> ultraconservative <u>as</u> their party's candidate <u>at</u> the convention.

4. We should <u>be</u> arriving <u>by</u> six, <u>but</u> don't wait for us.

5. Our group <u>of</u> tourists will take <u>off</u> at dawn <u>if</u> the weather permits.

6. We <u>are</u> now studying the structure <u>of</u> sentences, <u>or</u> syntax, in <u>our</u> English class.

7. We <u>will</u> warm up <u>with</u> a game of one-on-one <u>while</u> we wait for the rest of the players.

8. We had <u>too</u> many problems with our <u>two</u> new puppies, so we gave them both <u>to</u> the neighbors.

CHAPTER 13
Key Terms

Adverbial conjunction	Conjunctive adverb
Article	Coordinating conjunction
Auxiliary	Correlative conjunction
Conjunction	Definite article

Demonstrative pronoun

Determiner

Expanded determiner

Explanatory appositive

Expletive

Indefinite article

Indefinite pronoun

Intensifier

Interrogative

Mass noun

Modal-like verb

Number

Particle

Phrasal preposition

Possessive noun

Possessive pronoun

Postdeterminer

Predeterminer

Preposition

Qualifier

Relative

Semi-auxiliary

Subject–verb agreement

Subordinating conjunction

QUESTIONS **?** for DISCUSSION

1. Prepositions and particles are among the most difficult words in the language for foreign speakers to master. Why do you suppose this is so? Look at the following sentences. How would you explain the selection of prepositions to a learner of English?

> Be sure to fill out the form carefully.
> Be sure to fill in the form carefully.

> I like to jog in the early morning.
> I like to jog on a sunny morning.

> Our house burned down last week.
> All of my books burned up.

> I'm working on my math.
> I'm really working at it.

2. In what sense are *dare* and *have to* modal-like? How do they differ from modals? In thinking about this question, consider their place in the verb-expansion rule.

In what sense are these verbs *not* like the other modals? Consider the following examples:

He has to work this afternoon.

Does he have to work this afternoon?

Do I dare walk alone?

You dare not walk alone around here at night.

3. In answering an interviewer's question, an economist recently said, "I do not foresee any improvement in the economy, absent any change in the elements that are driving it." What part of speech is *absent*?

4. In an article entitled "The Big Nine" (*Atlantic*, March 1988), Cullen Murphy reports on a 1923 study in which the lexicographer G. H. McKnight identified nine words in our language that account for one-quarter of all spoken words. (A list of forty-three accounts for one-half.) Here are the nine: *and, be, have, it, of, the, to, will,* and *you*. Identify their word classes.

   Murphy did his own research of written texts, ranging from an IRS document to the "Wizard of Id" comic strip and came up with similar results. You might find it interesting to evaluate your own writing. Then write a paragraph in which you use none of the nine—just to see if you can do it. Describe the difference— perhaps in tone or in rhythm—if any.

5. The *New Yorker* reported an apology printed by a Sydney, Australia, newspaper for inadvertently changing a word in a reader's letter to the editor. The correspondent had written, "The number of speakers became unmanageable." The paper changed *the* to *a*. How can one little structure word make such a difference?

6. One difference between the form-class words and the structure words, in addition to the size of their separate vocabularies, is the size of the words themselves. We can cite a few nouns that have fewer than three letters (which seems to be the requirement for crossword puzzles!)—*ox, ax* (also spelled *axe*), *ex* (obviously an abbreviation), *ma,* and *pa*. And here are three verbs—*be, do,* and *go* (the first two of which also fill the auxiliary function). Maybe you can think of others. But certainly most two-letter words are members of the structure classes or pronouns. Interestingly, some of those little ones have homophones in the form classes. Which of the following have homophones that qualify for the crosswords?

in   an   or   so   to   we   no   I   do   be

CLASSROOM APPLICATIONS

1. Sometimes the source of ambiguity in headlines and telegrams is the lack of structure words. Demonstrate the double meaning of the following ambiguous passages by adding structure words:

   PENTAGON REQUESTS CUT

   SHIP SAILS TODAY

   UNION DEMANDS CHANGE

   POLICE PATROLS STRIP

   Now come up with headlines of your own that have more than one meaning.

2. One of the assessment tools commonly used in the field of English as a Second Language (ESL) is the "Cloze" test, which consists of a prose passage with deletions at regular intervals. Language proficiency is then judged on the student's ability to fill in the blanks correctly. Here are two Cloze passages with every fifth word deleted. The first is from the opening paragraph of Shelby Foote's first volume of *The Civil War: A Narrative.* The second is the last paragraph in a *Time* article about weather on the occasion of the 1993 Mississippi flood. Fill in each blank with what you think has been deleted; then compare your answers with those of your classmates. Is there more agreement among you on the form-class words or on the structure words? Which blanks do you think would be the most difficult for a nonnative speaker?

   1. It was a Monday _____ Washington, January 21;

      Jefferson Davis _____ from his seat in _____

      Senate. South Carolina had _____ the Union a month

      _____, followed by Mississippi, Florida, _____

      Alabama, which seceded at _____ rate of one a

      _____ during the second week _____ the new

      year. Georgia _____ out eight days later;_____

      and Texas were poised _____ go; few doubted that

      _____ would, along with others._____ more

      than a decade _____ had been intensive discussion

      _____ to the legality of _____, but now the

      argument _____ no longer academic.

2. What is new about _____ weather is that, for
_____ first time, some of _____ factors that help
shape _____ may be man-made. Experts _____ it
may be decades _____ we are certain what _____
the buildup of greenhouse _____ or the depletion of
_____ ozone layer has had _____ the global climate. Last _____ flooding and heat wave _____
as a warning that _____ we wait for the _____ to
tell us what's _____ with the weather, it _____ be
too late to _____ anything about it.

CHAPTER

14

Pronouns

CHAPTER PREVIEW

Pronouns are among our most common words. You will rarely encounter a passage of two or more sentences that doesn't contain several pronouns. In fact, the sentence you just finished reading contains three.

We looked briefly at pronouns in earlier chapters when we substituted them for noun phrases in order to demonstrate where the subject ended and the predicate began:

> The county commissioners (they) have passed a new ordinance.
>
> The mayor's husband (he) spoke against it.
>
> The mayor (she) was upset with him.

These substitutions—*they*, *he*, and *she*—are among the personal pronouns, the kind you probably recognize most readily. But there are many other classes of pronouns as well—reflexive, demonstrative, relative, indefinite, and others. In this chapter we will look at all of the pronouns, pointing out places where a conscious understanding of the system can be helpful to you as a writer.

As their name suggests, **pronouns** are words that stand for nouns. Perhaps a more accurate label would be *pronominal*, because they actually stand for any construction that functions as a nominal in the sentence. We refer to the noun or nominal that the pronoun stands for as its **antecedent**.

Most pronouns replace an entire noun phrase:

The pistachio nut ice cream at Meyer's Dairy is delicious.

It   is delicious.

My friend Jan, who lives in Houston, is coming to visit.

She   is coming to visit.

Pronouns also substitute for other nominals, such as verb phrases and clauses:

The judge warned my brother to stay out of trouble.

He told me   that,   too.

Where you spend your time is none of my business.

$\begin{Bmatrix} \text{That} \\ \text{It} \end{Bmatrix}$ is none of my business.

Not all pronouns are alike. The label *pronoun* actually covers a wide variety of words, many of which function in quite different ways. A brief description of the main classes of pronouns follows.

PERSONAL PRONOUNS

The **personal pronouns** are the ones we usually think of when the word *pronoun* comes to mind. We generally label them on the basis of person and number:

PERSON	NUMBER		
	Singular	*Plural*	
1st	I	we	[person(s) speaking]
2nd	you	you	[person(s) spoken to]
3rd	$\begin{cases} \text{he} \\ \text{she} \\ \text{it} \end{cases}$	they	[person(s) spoken about]

For example, we refer to *I* as the "first-person singular" pronoun and *they* as the "third-person plural." In addition, the third-person singular pronouns include the feature of **gender**: masculine *(he)*, feminine *(she)*, and neuter *(it)*.

   The term **pronoun-antecedent agreement** describes our selection of the pronoun in reference to the noun or noun phrase (or nominal) it replaces: The personal pronoun "agrees with" its antecedent in both number and, for third-person singular, gender. Note that the second person (*you*) has neither gender nor number distinctions.

Case. The forms given in the preceding set are in the subjective (traditionally called "nominative") case; this is the form used when the pronoun serves as the subject or subject complement. The personal pronouns also inflect for the **possessive** case, as nouns do, and the **objective** case, an inflection that nouns do not have.[1]

Subjective:	I	we	you	he	she	it	they
Possessive:	my	our	your	his	her	its	their
	(mine)	(ours)	(yours)	(his)	(hers)		(theirs)
Objective:	me	us	you	him	her	it	them

The possessive forms of pronouns function as determiners. The objective case is used for pronouns in all the object slots: direct object, indirect object, and object complement. A pronoun as object of the preposition is also in the objective case, with one exception: The preposition *of* usually takes the possessive case, producing a structure called the "double possessive":

Tim's friend = a friend <u>of Tim's</u>

his friend = a friend <u>of his</u>

my class = a class <u>of mine</u>

With common nouns we often use the *of* prepositional phrase in the place of the possessive noun:

the car's engine = the engine <u>of the car</u>

the day's end = the end <u>of the day</u>

Alternative forms of the possessive case, shown in parentheses in the previous chart, are used when the headword of the noun phrase is deleted:

This is <u>my book</u>.   This is <u>mine</u>.

This is <u>her book</u>.   This is <u>hers</u>.

---

[1] In traditional grammar, the case labels often used are those of Latin: **nominative** (subjective); **genitive** (possessive); and **accusative** (objective). In addition to these three, Latin has separate cases for indirect objects (dative) and objects of prepositions (ablative). For most Latin nouns, these five categories mean at least four different case endings, along with several more for plural nouns.

Possessive nouns can also be used without headwords:

This is <u>John's book</u>.   This is <u>John's</u>.

<u>Mary's book</u> is missing.   <u>Mary's</u> is missing.

The third person singular *it*, the most neutral of the personal pronouns, is sometimes used as an "anticipatory" subject, as we saw in the discussion of cleft sentences (p. 103) and nominals (p. 188). In some cases it has clear pronoun status, as in this passage from Robert Frost's poem "Stopping by Woods on a Snowy Evening":

My little horse must think <u>it</u> queer

<u>To stop without a farmhouse near</u>.

In other cases the *it*, while acting as a grammatical subject, remains essentially an empty word:

It is raining

It's a nice day.

The plural pronoun *they* can also have neutral status:

They say best men are moulded out of faults. [Shakespeare]

Gender. We should also note that our system of personal pronouns—or, to be more accurate, a gap in the system—is the source of a great deal of the sexism in our language. Missing from the system is a singular third-person pronoun that refers to either gender. Our plural pronoun (*they*) includes both male and female; but when we need a pronoun to refer to an unidentified person, such as "the writer" or "a student" or "the doctor," the long-standing tradition has been to use the masculine (*he/his/him*):

The writer of this news story should have kept <u>his</u> personal
opinions out of it.

Attempts to promote *s/he* in recent years have been unsuccessful. Perhaps someday the plural pronoun will be accepted for both singular and plural, a usage known as the "singular *they*," which has become quite common in speech:

Someone broke into our car last night; <u>they</u> stole our tape deck and
all our tapes.

(This issue is discussed further on pages 341–345.) The topic is covered in great detail in Haussamen's *Revising the Rules*, found in the reference list on page 14 (at the end of Chapter 1).

Exercise | 58

Substitute personal pronouns for the underlined nouns and noun phrases in the following sentences.

1. <u>Luis and Maria</u> have bought a new house.
2. <u>Bev and I</u> will be going to the game with <u>Otis</u>.
3. Betsy bought <u>that beautiful new car of hers</u> in Charlotte.
4. Both of <u>her cars</u> are gas guzzlers.
5. There have always been uneasy feelings between <u>the neighbors and my husband</u>.
6. I want <u>Tony</u> to approve of <u>the project</u>.
7. The kids gave <u>their father and me</u> a bad time.
8. <u>My brother, who works for the Navy in California</u>, spends <u>his weekends</u> in Las Vegas.

Investigating Language | 14.1

The difference between *who* and *whom* is identical to the difference between *I* and *me* or between *she* and *her* or between *he* and *him* or *they* and *them*. We say

| I know him. | *and* | He knows me. |
| She helps them. | *and* | They help her. |

We also say

The man <u>who loves me</u> is coming to visit,

where *who* is the subject in its own clause, the subject of the verb *love*, and

The man <u>whom I love</u> is coming to visit,

where *whom* is the direct object of *love*.

The topic under discussion here, as you have probably guessed, is that of **case**. If you are a native speaker of English, nothing in the previous discussion comes as a surprise. Chances are you've never been tempted to say,

*Him knows I.   *or*   *Them helps she.

However, you may have been tempted to say—you may even have heard yourself say—

The stranger <u>who I helped this morning</u> was very grateful,

even though *who* functions as the direct object in its clause.

For some reason, that *who* doesn't sound as strange, or as ungrammatical, as

*Amy knows I.   *or*   *They help she.

If you consider the position of *who* in its clause, you can probably figure out why that sentence about the stranger is so easy to say—and why it sounds o.k.

The point is that we do *say* it. The fact that we do is one of the differences between speech and writing. But in writing, you'll want to figure out the appropriate case for the object position:

The stranger <u>whom I helped this morning</u>...

You can use your understanding of case to edit yourself.

Objects of prepositions. The direct object slot, of course, is not the only object slot in our sentences. The slot following prepositions—the object of the preposition—is probably even more common than the direct object. And except for the preposition *of* (noted on page 295), this slot too requires the objective case when the object of the preposition is a pronoun:

I bought this <u>for him</u>.   Pam bought this <u>for me</u>.

I gave it <u>to them</u>.   They came <u>with her</u>.

Again, you're probably not tempted to say "for he" or "to they" or "for I" or "with she." You automatically use the objective case of personal pronouns after prepositions. And native speakers are probably never tempted to say,

*This secret is just <u>between we</u>.

So why do you suppose it's so common to hear,

*This secret is just <u>between Joe and I</u>

        and

*This secret is just <u>between he and I</u>?

It's a question worth considering.

REFLEXIVE PRONOUNS

Reflexive pronouns are those formed by adding *-self* or *-selves* to a form of the personal pronoun:

PERSON	SINGULAR	PLURAL
1st	myself	ourselves
2nd	yourself	yourselves
3rd	himself herself itself	themselves

The reflexive pronoun is used as the direct object, indirect object, and object of the preposition when its antecedent is the subject of the sentence:

John cut <u>himself</u>.

I glanced at <u>myself</u> in the mirror.

I cooked dinner for Shelley and <u>myself</u>.

Joe cooked dinner for Gary and <u>himself</u>.

Investigating Language   14.2

For each of the italicized noun phrases in the following sentences, substitute either a personal pronoun or a reflexive pronoun. Assume that a name or noun phrase appearing more than once in a sentence refers to the same person or people in each instance:

1. Randall cut *Randall* while *Randall* was shaving.
2. The Kim sisters threw a party for *the Kim sisters*.
3. Although Selma ran a good race, two other runners finished ahead of *Selma*.
4. The wardrobe mistress gave *the wardrobe mistress* all the credit for the play's success.
5. The students said that *the students* understood the assignment.

Formulate a rule to explain the system you used to choose the class of pronoun. In what way do the following sentences depart from the system you described:

6. Joe cooked dinner for Gary and myself.
7. We decided that Gary and myself would do the dishes.

The rule you formulated for the first five sentences probably explains that the reflexive pronoun is used only when those identical noun phrases appear in the same clause, as in sentences 1, 2, and 4. In sentences 3 and 5, the repeated noun phrase appears in a second clause. However, in the last two examples, those requirements are absent: In 6 there is no antecedent for *myself* in the sentence; in 7, *Gary and myself* and its antecedent *we* are in separate clauses. While sentences like the last two are fairly common in speech, the written standard calls for personal pronouns:

Joe cooked dinner for Gary and me.

We decided that Gary and I would do the dishes.

Both versions are unambiguous; both forms of the first-person pronoun, *me* and *myself,* can refer only to the speaker. However, with third-person pronouns different forms produce different meanings:

Joe cooked dinner for Gary and <u>himself</u> (Joe).

Joe cooked dinner for Gary and <u>him</u> (someone else).

Exercise   59

Fill the blanks with the appropriate reflexive pronouns.

1. Gabrielle gave _____ a black eye when she fell.
2. Li and Mei-Ling cooked _____ salmon for dinner.
3. The ceramic figurine sat by _____ on the shelf.
4. We sat by _____ in the front row.
5. Paulo cooked a delicious Mexican feast for Rosa and_____.
6. Wearing our new designer jeans, Sheila and I admired
   _____ in the mirror.

ELL Issues   **Reflexive verbs**

Certain transitive verbs require that the direct object be a reflexive pronoun:

> Juan *prides himself* on his hat collection.
>
> The witness *perjured herself.*
>
> All the children *behaved themselves.*

Other verbs that sometimes take reflexives have a different meaning with nonreflexive direct objects:

> The hikers *found themselves* in an unknown part of the woods.
>
> The hikers *found* a cave where they could take refuge.

> Maggie took time to *compose herself* before answering the judge.
>
> Maggie *composed* a poem about snakes for her writing class.

INTENSIVE PRONOUNS

Also known as the *emphatic reflexive pronouns*, the **intensive pronouns** have the same form as the reflexives. The intensive pronoun serves as an appositive to emphasize a noun, but it need not directly follow the noun:

> I <u>myself</u> prefer chocolate.
>
> I prefer chocolate <u>myself</u>.
>
> <u>Myself</u>, I prefer chocolate.

Because *myself* is in apposition to *I* in all three versions, the diagram will not distinguish among them:

I (myself)	prefer	chocolate

RECIPROCAL PRONOUNS

Each other and *one another* are known as the **reciprocal pronouns.** They serve either as determiners (in the possessive case) or as objects, referring to previously named nouns. *Each other* generally refers to two nouns; *one another* to three or more.

> Juan and Claudia help <u>each other</u>.
>
> They even do <u>each other's</u> chores.
>
> All the students in my study group help <u>one another</u> with their
> homework.

DEMONSTRATIVE PRONOUNS

In our discussion of determiners we noted that the selection of a determiner is based on certain inherent features, such as definite or indefinite, countable or noncountable. The **demonstrative pronouns**, one of the subclasses of determiners, include the features of "number" and "proximity":

PROXIMITY	NUMBER	
	Singular	*Plural*
Near	this	these
Distant	that	those

> <u>That</u> documentary we saw last night really made me think, but <u>this</u> one is simply stupid.
>
> <u>Those</u> trees on the ridge were almost destroyed by gypsy moths, but <u>these</u> seem perfectly healthy.

Like other determiner classes, the demonstrative pronoun can be a substitute for a nominal as well as a signal for one:

> <u>These old shoes and hats</u>   will be perfect for the costumes.
>
> <u>These</u>   will be perfect for the costumes.

To be effective as a nominal, the demonstrative pronoun must replace or stand for a clearly stated antecedent. In the following example, *that* does not refer to "solar energy"; it has no clear antecedent:

> Our contractor is obviously skeptical about solar energy. <u>That</u> doesn't surprise me.

Such sentences are not uncommon in speech, nor are they ungrammatical. But when a *this* or *that* has no specific antecedent, the writer can usually improve the sentence by providing a noun headword for the demonstrative pronoun—by turning the pronoun into a determiner:

> Our contractor is obviously skeptical about solar energy. <u>That attitude</u> (or <u>His attitude</u>) doesn't surprise me.

A combination of the two sentences would also be an improvement over the vague use of *that:*

> Our contractor's skepticism about solar energy doesn't surprise me.

The vague reference of *this* and *that* has the same fuzzy quality as the broad-reference relative clause, which you read about in Chapter 9:

> Our contractor is skeptical about solar energy, <u>which doesn't surprise me</u>.

A singular demonstrative pronoun can also function as a qualifier:

I can't imagine being <u>that</u> rich.

I can't believe I weigh <u>this</u> much.

RELATIVE PRONOUNS

The **relative pronouns** are *who, which,* and *that;* they introduce clauses that modify the nouns that are the antecedents of these pronouns. *Who* inflects for both possessive and objective cases: *whose* (possessive) and *whom* (objective). The case of *who* is determined by the part it plays (its function) in its own clause:

The man <u>who lives across the street</u> sold me his car.

In this sentence *who* renames *man,* its antecedent, and plays the part of subject in the relative (adjectival) clause. In the next sentence the relative pronoun is in the possessive case form, *whose:*

The man <u>whose car I bought</u> was not very honest about the gas mileage.

Here *whose,* the possessive relative pronoun, again stands for *man;* in its own clause it acts as the determiner for *car,* the role that possessives normally play.

Whose also acts as the possessive form of *which:*

The wooded ridge across the valley, <u>whose trees were infested by gypsy moths</u>, turned brown in mid-June.

The relative pronoun *that* is generally subjective or objective, never possessive:

I lost the backpack <u>that I bought yesterday</u>.

That renames *backpack* and acts as the object within its own clause. In object position, *that* can be omitted:

I lost the backpack <u>I bought yesterday</u>.

When *that* is the subject of the clause, however, it cannot be omitted:

The route <u>that will get us there fastest</u> is straight across the mountain.

The *wh-* relative pronouns also have an expanded form with the addition of *-ever,* known as **indefinite relative pronouns:** *whoever, whosever, whomever,* and *whatever.* The expanded relatives have indefinite referents rather than specific ones as the simple relatives do:

I will give a bonus to <u>whoever works the hardest</u>.

I will pay you <u>whatever you deserve</u>.

I will call <u>whomever the doctor recommends</u>.

What is also considered an indefinite relative pronoun when it introduces adjectival clauses and means "that which":

I will pay you <u>what you deserve</u>.

The relative (adjectival) clauses are also discussed in Chapter 7.

INTERROGATIVE PRONOUNS

The list of **interrogative pronouns** is similar to that of the relatives: *who* (*whose, whom*), *which*, and *what*. The interrogatives, as their name suggests, are among the question words that produce information questions (in contrast to yes/no questions):

<u>What</u> do you want for lunch?

<u>Whose</u> car is that?

<u>Which</u> section of history did you get?

As we saw in Chapter 3, the interrogative word plays a part in the sentence. For example, in the first preceding sample sentence, *what* fills the direct object slot: "You do want *what* for lunch." In a sentence such as "What flavor do you prefer?" the interrogative *what* acts as a determiner for the noun *flavor*. In the other two examples listed, *whose* and *which* also act as determiners: *whose car, which section*. Because of this modifying function, *which*, *what*, and *whose* are sometimes classified as **interrogative adjectives.**

The interrogative pronouns also introduce nominal clauses and, like the relative pronouns, play a part in the clause. There is an indirect question involved in such clauses—either implied or stated, asked or answered:

Tell me <u>what you want for lunch</u>.

I know <u>who gave you that black eye</u>.

Nominal clauses are discussed in Chapter 8.

INDEFINITE PRONOUNS

The **indefinite pronouns** include a number of words listed earlier as determiners:

enough	many	all	either
few	much	both	neither
fewer	several	every	none

less	more	each	some
little	most	any	

One is also commonly used as a pronoun (as are the other cardinal numbers—*two, three,* etc.) along with its negative, *none*. As a pronoun, *one* often replaces only the headword, rather than the entire noun phrase:

> *The blue <u>shoes</u> that I bought yesterday* will be perfect for the trip.

> *The blue <u>ones</u> that I bought yesterday* will be perfect for the trip.

The personal pronoun, on the other hand, would replace the entire noun phrase:

> <u>*They*</u> will be perfect for the trip.

The pronouns *every, any, no,* and *some* can be expanded with -*body*, -*thing,* and -*one:*

some	{ body / thing / one }	every	{ body / thing / one }
any	{ body / thing / one }	no	{ body / thing / one (two words) }

(Note that *every* and *no*, which function as determiners, do not function as pronouns except in the expanded forms shown here.)

These pronouns can take modifiers in the form of clauses:

> <u>Anyone</u> *who wants extra credit in psych class* can volunteer for tonight's experiment.

They can also be modified by verb phrases:

> <u>Everyone</u> *reporting late for practice* will take fifteen laps.

And by prepositional phrases:

> <u>Nothing</u> *on the front page* interests me anymore.

Unlike most nouns, they can be modified by single adjectives in postheadword position:

> I don't care for <u>anything</u> *sweet*.

> I think that <u>something</u> *strange* is going on here.

And unlike other pronouns, when the expanded indefinite pronouns are used in the possessive case—as they are when functioning as determiners—they require an apostrophe + *s:*

> <u>Somebody's</u> books are in the back seat.

> The teacher ignored <u>everyone's</u> complaints about the exam schedule.

ELL Issues The "some/any" rule

Although the restrictions are not apparent in their forms, the choice of *some* and *any*, as well as their expanded versions with *body*, *thing*, and *one*, is usually determined by the presence or absence of *not* or another negative, such as *never*, *rarely*, *seldom*, and the like:

> Do you want <u>some</u> dessert?

> No, I do<u>n't</u> want <u>any</u>.

> I saw <u>someone</u> you know at the concert.

> I did<u>n't</u> see <u>anyone</u> I know.

The adverbs *somewhere* and *anywhere* carry the same restriction:

> My sister is <u>somewhere</u> in the mall.

> I'm <u>not</u> going <u>anywhere</u> until she shows up.

We should emphasize that while these examples follow the standard rule, it is not unusual to hear variations. In the first example, for instance, the response "No, I don't want some" would sound a bit odd—but would probably not be judged ungrammatical.

Exercise 60

Underline the pronouns in the following sentences. Identify the subclass to which each pronoun belongs.

1. When Roberto ordered a pizza with everything, I ordered one too.

2. Millie and Bev shopped at almost every store in the mall but couldn't find any shoes they liked.

3. Someone was standing in the shadows, but we couldn't see who it was.

4. All that I had for lunch was that overripe banana.

5. Booker and Marcus didn't eat much either, but they both ate more than I did.

6. I myself will go along with whatever you decide.
7. One hour of studying was enough for me.
8. Quarreling among themselves, the committee members completely disregarded one another's suggestions.
9. At the end of most months, I find myself without funds.
10. The employment office will find a job for whoever wants one.

CHAPTER 14
Key Terms

Antecedent

Case

Demonstrative pronoun

Emphatic reflexive pronoun

Gender

Indefinite pronoun

Indefinite relative pronoun

Intensive pronoun

Interrogative adjective

Interrogative pronoun

Number

Objective case

Person

Personal pronoun

Plural

Possessive case

Pronoun

Pronoun–antecedent agreement

Proximity

Reciprocal pronoun

Reflexive pronoun

Relative pronoun

Sexism

Singular

Subjective case

QUESTIONS
?
for DISCUSSION

1. The relative pronoun agrees with its antecedent in person and number but not necessarily in case. How do the following sentences illustrate that statement?

    I don't know the women who live next door.
    It was I whom you spoke with on the phone.

2. Comment on the choice of pronouns in the following sentence. Are they correct?

    I didn't know who felt worse: him or me.

3. In Chapter 3, Discussion Question 8 (page 66), we looked at the following ambiguous sentence:

> Rosa called her mother.

What is the source of the ambiguity? Would a sentence about Mario and father instead of Rosa and mother be equally ambiguous? What's the difference?

4. What is the difference in the meaning of *one* in the following sentences?

> <u>One</u> farmer told me there hadn't been rain in eight weeks.
> <u>One</u> can only hope that the weather changes soon.

5. The following sentences include clauses introduced by expanded, or indefinite, relative pronouns:

> I will give a bonus to whoever works hardest.
> I will pay you whatever you deserve.
> I will call whomever the doctor recommends.

Explain why a traditional diagram of such sentences would look like this:

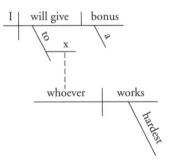

How should we diagram the sentences with *whatever* and *whomever?*

6. How do you explain the use of *we* and *us* in the following sentences?

> We graduates lined up to go into the gym.
> The speaker told us graduates that we were the hope of the future.

Is *we* used correctly in the following sentence?

> It wasn't a good idea for we dishwashers to go on strike.

7. Here's a statement with a single, straightforward meaning:

> I invited everyone in the class to my party.

The follow-up sentence is not quite as clear; in fact, it's ambiguous:

> Everyone didn't come.

Here's another ambiguous sentence:

> Everything doesn't cause cancer.

Paraphrase the two negative sentences in two ways to demonstrate their meanings. Then consider the meaning of *everyone* and *everything* and explain why their use with the negative should produce ambiguity.

8. An English language learner might find the following sentences ungrammatical:

> Anyone can have seconds on dessert.
> I haven't given some of the volunteers their assignments yet.

What would happen to the meaning of those two sentences if the writer had followed the "*some/any* rule"?

CLASSROOM APPLICATIONS

1. In this chapter you have seen eight subclasses of pronouns. Although they are all words you commonly use, you may not have realized they are all pronouns. Write a passage with as few sentences as possible using at least one pronoun from each of the eight subclasses: personal, reflexive, intensive, reciprocal, demonstrative, relative, interrogative, and indefinite.

2. The following passage, from "The Winter of Man," an essay by Loren Eiseley, was published in 1972, a time when the masculine pronoun was accepted as a generic singular. Note too the use of *man* in reference to humans in general.

> Students of the earth's climate have observed that man, in spite of the disappearance of the great continental ice fields, still lives on the steep edge of winter or early spring. The pulsations of these great ice deserts, thousands of feet thick and capable of overflowing mountains and valleys, have characterized the nature of the world since man, in his thinking and speaking phase, arose. The ice which has left the marks of its passing upon the landscape of the

Northern Hemisphere has also accounted, in its long, slow advances and retreats, for movements, migrations and extinctions throughout the plant and animal kingdoms. Though man is originally tropical in his origins, the ice has played a great role in his unwritten history. At times it has constricted his movements, affecting the genetic selection that has created him. Again, ice has established conditions in which man has had to exert all his ingenuity in order to survive. By contrast, there have been other times when the ice has withdrawn farther than today and then, like a kind of sleepy dragon, has crept forth to harry man once more. For something like a million years this strange and alternating context has continued between man and the ice.

Revise the passage in gender-neutral language.

Grammar for Writers

For some of you, this book has been your introduction to the study of grammar. Terms like *noun* and *adjective* and *predicate* and *participle* were completely new to you or, at best, distant echoes from a long-ago classroom. Others of you brought a fairly substantial understanding of parts of speech and sentences from grammar classes that may have begun in the fifth grade and continued through the twelfth, very likely starting every year with parts of speech and ending with complex sentences. The majority of you are probably somewhere in between, with memories of a grammar unit for a year or two, perhaps in the seventh and eighth grades.

Those differing backgrounds reflect actual differences in the way in which grammar is taught throughout this country. Grammar is not a subject area that curriculum experts agree on; it is, in fact, an area fraught with controversy and misunderstanding. Part of that misunderstanding lies in the problem of definition.

In Chapter 1 we looked at three definitions of *grammar:*

1. The rules in our heads that enable each of us to produce language.
2. The subject matter of books like this one, with its description of sentences and the rules that produce them.
3. The do's and don't's of usage, known as "linguistic etiquette."

For many people, it is only this third definition—the social rules of usage, those traditional rules about correctness—that they remember from their grammar classes. Grammar brings to mind red marks on essays pinpointing comma splices and spelling errors; it recalls warnings about ending sentences with prepositions or beginning them with conjunctions. It's understandable for people to assume that the purpose of studying grammar is to avoid error. This definition and this purpose—and the methods of teaching that reflect such a definition and purpose—contribute to the misunderstanding.

If the purpose of studying grammar is to avoid error, then it should follow that learning the "rules of grammar" will make you a better writer because you will avoid errors in your compositions. There are two problems with this assumption: First, the purpose for studying grammar goes far beyond that of avoiding error; and, second, composition teachers realized long ago that error-free writing is not necessarily effective writing. To write effectively, you must be sensitive to your readers, to take into account what they already know, what they expect, what they need to know. You must think about how the words and the structures you choose will accomplish your purpose.

Unfortunately, methods of teaching grammar have been slow to change. The traditional view of language as a set of rules to be memorized ignores all of the insights of modern linguistics. Instead, teachers should help their students recognize and explore their own innate competence and then help them use that knowledge when they write.

Composition teachers know that students who understand the structure of their language are in a position to recognize their own weaknesses and strengths as writers, to revise and edit their own writing; further, they can offer helpful evaluations in peer-review sessions. Students who have explored their own language expertise, who have acquired a vocabulary for discussing language, hold a decided advantage over those who have not.

We firmly believe that understanding English grammar—the title and theme of this book—does make a difference for writers and teachers of writing: It does so by enhancing a writer's confidence, by giving the writer control, by illuminating all the choices that are available. That control and those choices are the subject matter of Chapter 15, "Rhetorical Grammar." And because punctuation is such an important skill for both writing competence and writing confidence, we have pulled together punctuation lessons from throughout the book into Chapter 16, "Purposeful Punctuation."

CHAPTER
15

Rhetorical Grammar

CHAPTER PREVIEW

Although the term *rhetorical* and its noun form, *rhetoric*, have not been used up to now, you'll find a description of rhetoric in Chapter 1 under the topic of Language Variety:

> In the written language, too, what is appropriate or effective in one situation may be inappropriate or ineffective in another. The language you use in letters to your family and friends is noticeably different from the language you use in a letter when applying for a job. Even the writing you do in school varies, depending on the situation. The language of the personal essay you write for your composition class has an informality that would be inappropriate for a business report or a history research paper. As with speech, the purpose and the audience make all the difference.

If this description of rhetoric sounds to you like plain old common sense, you're absolutely right. You've always understood that the person you're talking to or writing to—in other words, your audience—will have an effect on what you say and the way you say it.

In terms of writing, then, rhetoric means that the situation—the topic, the purpose, and the audience—will make a difference in the way you write. And to a great extent that rhetorical situation will determine the grammatical choices you make, choices about sentence structure and vocabulary, even about punctuation. Rhetorical grammar is about those choices.

In this chapter we will discuss the ways you can use the grammar knowledge you have gained in the preceding chapters, the ways in which that knowledge can make a difference to you as a writer and, perhaps, as a teacher of writing. We will begin, as the book began, by considering sentence patterns; we will see how the features of those patterns, including their transformations and the choice of verbs, can heighten your awareness of the effect your writing has on your audience. We will then take up the grammatical choices and rhetorical effects of other sentence features.

SENTENCE PATTERNS

Basic Sentences. In Chapter 2 we recognized that such simple two-word sentences as "Mary laughed" and "Cats fight" rarely show up in actual prose. However, it's fairly common to see bare-bones sentence patterns just a bit longer than two words used both as topic sentences and as attention-getters. Here, for example, are two passages, both of which include a basic sentence that stands out and calls attention to itself. We have added the underlining.

The first, from Steven Pinker's *Language Instinct*, begins the discussion of his case for calling language an instinct:

> The trail begins with the study of how the particular languages we find in the world today arose. Here, one would think, linguistics runs into the problem of any historical science: no one recorded the crucial events at the time they happened. Although historical linguists can trace modern complex languages back to earlier ones, this just pushes the problem back a step; we need to see how people create a complex language from scratch. <u>Amazingly, we can.</u> (p. 32)

The second is from Stephen E. Ambrose's *Undaunted Courage*, his book about the Lewis and Clark expedition:

> Fewer than one out of ten Americans, about half a million people, lived west of the Appalachian Mountains, but as the Whiskey Rebellion had shown, they were already disposed to think of themselves as the germ of an independent nation that would find its outlet to the world marketplace not across the mountains to the Atlantic Seaboard, but by the Ohio and Mississippi river system to the Gulf of Mexico. <u>The threat of secession was quite real.</u> The United States was only eighteen years old, had itself come into existence by an act of rebellion and secession, had changed its form of government just twelve years earlier, and thus was in a fluid political situation. (p. 52)

In both of these cases, the underlined sentence is functioning as the topic sentence. The first one is an elliptical sentence, with an understood verb, which we can recover from the previous sentence: *Amazingly, we can see that.* Perhaps this doesn't qualify as bare bones, but by truncating it, the author has made it an attention-getter.

The Linking *Be* and Metaphor. It's fairly common, in discussions about verb choice, to play up the importance of action verbs and downplay the importance of *be*, with special attention to its overuse, a topic you'll read about later in this chapter. But there is one use of the linking *be* that deserves more attention: its role—and its power—in **metaphor**. When *be* links a subject complement to its subject in an unexpected way—that is, when the two referents are not, in reality, the same—the statement is anything but weak.

A successful Broadway musical was based on a metaphor:

> Life is a cabaret.

In several plays Shakespeare used the stage metaphor for life. This is Macbeth speaking:

> Life's but a walking shadow, a poor player
>
> That struts and frets his hour upon the stage.

and this one is from *As You Like It:*

> All the world's a stage.

Charles Schulz, the creator of "Peanuts," used metaphor for two popular titles to express the philosophy of his characters:

> *Happiness Is a Warm Puppy*
>
> *Happiness Is a Thumb and a Blanket.*

These Pattern 3 sentences are anything but weak.

Cohesion. An important concept for helping you to understand sentence patterns back in Chapter 3 was the recognition that sentences consist of a series of slots, some required and some optional, filled by structures of various forms. Your understanding of the slots can be helpful in thinking about sentence **cohesion**, the ties that connect each sentence to what has gone before—the glue that gives a paragraph and an essay unity. Part of that glue is provided by information in the sentence that the reader knows or expects, information that has already been mentioned.

Let's look at the paragraph you just read as an example of that cohesive glue and reader expectation. The first sentence introduces the topic of sentence slots, with a brief description. You can be fairly certain that the next sentence will say something further about sentence slots. And, yes, it does: The subject of the next sentence is *Your understanding of the slots.* In other words, the sentence opens with old, or known, information. You don't expect to get to the new information, the purpose of the sentence, until you get to the predicate slot. And there it is in the predicate—new information, even a new term, *cohesion*, and the descriptive *glue*. And the third sentence? Again, you're not surprised to see known information—this time, *glue*—in the subject slot.

This known-to-new sequence is fairly typical for cohesive paragraphs, where the new information of one sentence becomes the known information of the next. In fact, the known–new sequence is so pervasive a feature of our prose that it is sometimes referred to as the **known–new contract**. The writer has an obligation, a contract of sorts, to fulfill expectations in the reader—to keep the reader on familiar ground. The reader has every right to expect each sentence to be connected in some way to what has gone before, to include a known element.

One of our most common known elements, certainly as strong as the repeated noun or noun phrase, is the pronoun. Consider how often the subject slot of the second sentence in a passage is filled by a pronoun, such as *she* or *he* or *it* or *they*. That pronoun is automatically tied to its antecedent, a previously mentioned nominal that it stands for. If there is no obvious antecedent, then the pronoun is not doing its cohesive job.

In the following passage, part of the opening paragraph of an essay by Annie Dillard, the first sentence introduces the topic, *a weasel*, in the subject slot—another basic sentence pattern. And, as you can see, the subject slots of the next three sentences are filled by the pronoun *he:*

> A weasel is wild. Who knows what **he** thinks? **He** sleeps in his underground den, his tail draped over his nose. Sometimes **he** lives in his den for two days without leaving. Outside, **he** stalks rabbits, mice, muskrats, and birds, killing more bodies than **he** can eat warm, and often dragging the carcasses home.

The pattern of known and new information in this passage, which is fairly common in descriptive writing, has a different schema from the earlier paragraph discussed. The earlier one, where the new information in one sentence becomes the known information of the next, might be diagrammed in this way:

$$A—B, B—C, C—D$$

In the weasel paragraph, where succeeding sentences repeated the subject, the schema would look like this:

$$A—B, A—C, A—D$$

Cohesion can also be enhanced by the information in an opening adverbial slot. For example, the opening of the fifth sentence in the weasel passage, *Outside*, provides a cohesive tie by contrasting with the "inside" designation *in his den* of sentence four. In narrative writing, adverbials of place or time often serve as the glue that connects sentences and paragraphs.

How can the known–new principle of cohesion help you as a writer? Are you supposed to stop after every sentence and estimate the cohesive power of your next subject? No, of course not. That's not the way writers work. But when you are revising—and by the way, revision goes on all the time, even during the first draft—you will want to keep in mind the issues of the known–new contract and reader expectation. You can learn to put yourself in your reader's shoes to see if you've kept your part of the bargain.

SENTENCE RHYTHM

One of the most distinctive features of any language—and one of the most automatic for the native speaker—is its sense of rhythm. Our language has a rhythm just as surely as music does—a regular beat. That sense of rhythm is tied up with the sentence patterns and with the known–new contract. If you read the opening sentence in this paragraph out loud, you'll hear yourself saying "one of the most" in almost a monotone; you probably don't hear a stressed syllable, a beat, until you get to *distinctive*:

one of the most disTINCtive

And you probably rush through those first four words so fast that you pronounce "of" without the *f*, making "one of" sound like the first two words in "won a prize."

The rhythm of sentences, what we call the **intonation** pattern, can be described as valleys and peaks, where the loudest syllables, those with stress, are represented by peaks:

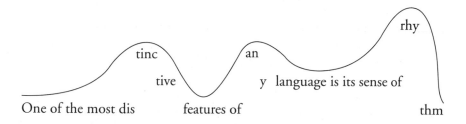

Not all the peaks are of the same height—we have different degrees of stress—but they do tend to come at fairly regular intervals. As listeners we pay attention to the peaks—that's where we'll hear the information that the speaker is focusing on. As speakers, we manipulate the peaks and valleys to coincide with our message, reserving the loudest stress, the highest peak, for the new information, which will be our main point of focus.

End Focus. The rhythm of a sentence is closely tied both to its two-part subject–predicate structure and to the known–new contract. The topic, or theme, stated in the subject will usually be a valley or low peak in the intonation contour, especially if it is known information. The prominent peak of stress, the focus on the new information, will come in the predicate; it will be close to the end of the sentence. Linguists describe this common rhythm pattern as **end focus**. It is a rhythm that experienced writers are sensitive to. Good writers, you can be sure, are tuned in to the rhythm of their own inner voice as they write; they understand how to manipulate sentences in order to control the way the reader reads them and to prevent misreading.

Read the following passage aloud and listen to the intonation pattern you give to the underlined sentence:

> Did you hear what happened? <u>Barbara wrecked her motorcycle yesterday</u>. She was on her way to work when the car in front of her stopped suddenly—and she didn't.

You probably read that second sentence with the stress on *motor*. In a different context, however, the rhythm could change if the purpose of the sentence has changed. In the following passage, the known information has changed. Again, read it aloud and listen to the intonation:

> Sue told me that Barbara had an accident this morning on her way to work. But I think she got her facts wrong. <u>Barbara wrecked her motorcycle yesterday</u>.

This time you probably put the main stress on *yesterday;* in this context it would make no sense to stress *motorcycle*. Try reading the passage that way, and you'll easily recognize the problem: All the information in the last sentence up to the word *yesterday* is already known. In this context it is old information: "Barbara wrecked her motorcycle" is a repetition, albeit more specific, of "Barbara had an accident." As a reader, you know intuitively that it's not time to apply stress until you get beyond that old information, until you get to *yesterday*, the new focus.

You'll note, however, that the principle of end focus is still operating, with the main stress on the last sentence element. But imagine how awkward the sentence would be if the adverb *yesterday* were shifted to the beginning of the sentence. It would certainly be grammatical from a structural point of view; as you know, adverbials are movable, especially adverbials of time. Even in opening position the reader might recognize *yesterday* as the new information and give it main stress. But the sentence would certainly have lost its natural rhythm. Read the passage aloud and you'll hear the problem:

Sue told me that Barbara had an accident this morning on her way to work. But I think she got her facts wrong. Yesterday Barbara wrecked her motorcycle.

While sentence variety is certainly commendable, you won't want to shift an adverbial to the opening slot just for the sake of variety—certainly not if that adverbial is the new information.

Investigating Language 15.1

Read the following passages, listening carefully to the intonation contour of each sentence. Indicate the words (or syllables) that get main stress. Compare your reading with that of your classmates. Identify the new information in each sentence. Does its position and emphasis fulfill the known–new contract?

1. Never invest in something you don't understand or in the dream of an artful salesperson. Be a buyer, not a sellee. Figure out what you want (be it life insurance, mutual funds or a vacuum cleaner) and then shop for a good buy. Don't let someone else tell you what you need—at least not if he happens to be selling it. [Andrew Tobias, *Parade*]

2. Plaque has almost become a household word. It is certainly a household problem. But even though everyone is affected by it, few people really understand the seriousness of plaque or the importance of controlling it. Plaque is an almost invisible sticky film of bacteria that continuously forms on the teeth. Plaque germs are constantly multiplying and building up. Any dentist will tell you that controlling plaque is the single most important step to better oral health. [Advertisement of the American Dental Association]

3. To simulate chance occurrences, a computer can't literally toss a coin or roll a die. Instead, it relies on special numerical recipes for generating strings for shuffled digits that pass for random numbers. Such sequences of pseudorandom numbers play crucial roles not only in computer games but also in simulations of physical processes. [I. Peterson, *Science News*]

4. Frank evaluation of its [caffeine's] hazards is not easy. There is a vast literature on the effects of caffeine on the body, and for every study reaching one conclusion, seemingly there is another that contradicts it. Although most major health risks have been ruled out, research continues at a steady clip. [Corby Kummer, *Atlantic Monthly*]

SENTENCE TRANSFORMATIONS

Because end focus is such a common rhythm pattern, we can think of it as a part of the contract between writer and reader. The reader expects the main sentence focus to be in the predicate unless given a signal to the contrary. And we do have several such signals at our disposal.

Several of the sentence transformations we looked at in Chapter 5 allow the writer to shift the focus of the sentence, pointing the reader to a particular slot. The *it*-cleft transformation is one of the most versatile. Here are three variations of the sentence about Barbara, each of which guarantees that the reader will put the emphasis exactly where the writer intends for it to be:

1. It was Barbara who wrecked her motorcycle yesterday.

2. It was her motorcycle that Barbara wrecked yesterday.

3. It was yesterday that Barbara wrecked her motorcycle.

If sentence 3 had been included in that earlier passage about the accident, it would have been impossible for the reader to miss the new information; in the cleft transformation the emphasis is clearly on *yesterday*.

The *it*-cleft is not a structure you will want to overuse, but it certainly is useful—and almost foolproof—when it comes to controlling the rhythm of a sentence and directing the reader's focus.

Another cleft transformation, also described in Chapter 5, uses a *what* clause to direct the reader's attention. In the following sentence you will probably put the emphasis on *bothers:*

> Mike's cynical attitude toward the customers really bothers me.

Here are two variations using the *what*-cleft:

> What bothers me is Mike's cynical attitude toward the customers.
>
> What bothers me about Mike is his cynical attitude toward the customers.

While all three versions mean essentially the same thing, the choice in a particular context will be determined in part by what the reader already knows—and consequently expects.

Another common sentence variation you saw in Chapter 5 is the *there* transformation, which allows the writer to focus on the subject by shifting it to the slot following *be*—either the predicating *be* or the auxiliary *be:*

> Several hundred people were crowding the courtroom.
>
> There were several hundred people crowding the courtroom.
>
> Another big crowd was in the hallway.
>
> There was another big crowd in the hallway.

The last paragraph in the previous Investigating Language exercise includes two *there* transformations in the second sentence:

> There is a vast literature on the effects of caffeine on the body, and for every study reaching one conclusion, seemingly there is another that contradicts it.

Here the author undoubtedly wants the reader to put main stress on *vast literature* and on *another.*

Do writers consciously call up such focusing devices from their grammar tool kits as they write? Do they tell themselves, "Time to use my trusty *it*-cleft, or should I delay this subject with the *there* transformation?" No, they probably don't. They may not even know labels like "transformation" and "cleft." But as experienced writers and readers, they're tuned in to sentence rhythm as they compose—especially as they revise. And you can be sure that in reading their own prose, whether silently or aloud, they are paying attention to the way in which the reader will read the sentence.

CHOOSING VERBS

Most writing teachers would probably agree that choosing verbs is one of the writer's most important jobs. The verb, after all, occupies the central, pivotal slot of the sentence pattern. A well-chosen verb not only heightens the drama of a sentence and makes its meaning clear; it can send a message to the reader that the writer has crafted the sentence carefully, that the idea matters.

Sometimes the culprit that keeps a sentence from sending that message is the phrasal verb, the verb + particle combination we saw in Chapter 3, known as an idiom: *turn down, bring about, put up with, take up, do away with, get on with, give up.* There's nothing wrong with these common idioms—and they certainly are common, part of our everyday speech. But the single-word synonym may be more precise—and it's always tighter:

> The legislature turned down the governor's compromise proposal.
>
> The legislature rejected . . .

> The lawyer turned down the prosecutor's offer of a plea bargain.
>
> The lawyer refused . . .

> The police are looking into the rumors about corruption.
>
> The police are investigating . . .

> The police are looking into the evidence.
>
> The police are analyzing . . .

Certainly another difference between the phrasal verb and its one-word counterpart is the level of formality: *To investigate* and *to analyze* sound more formal than *to look into.* In informal contexts, the idiom may be the best choice—for example, in a personal essay or narrative, or for a general audience, such as you might address in a letter to the editor of a newspaper. But for research papers or technical reports—and certainly for résumés and letters to prospective employers—the single-word version might be more effective. So one step in your revision process is to look carefully at (to *scrutinize*) the verbs that you have chosen—and recognize that you have a choice.

You may also have introduced some flabbiness simply by selecting a common garden-variety verb. In Chapter 4, you saw a list of the ten most frequently used verbs in English: *be, have, do, say, make, go, take, come, see,* and *get.* In many cases these are the verbs that take part in idioms. And because they have so many nuances of meaning, you can often find a more precise one.

Exercise 61

Revise the following passages by finding more precise alternatives to the italicized verbs. In some cases you will have to make changes other than just the verb substitution.

1. The small band of rebels *fought off* the army patrol for several hours, then *gave up* just before dawn. News reports about the event did not *give any specific details about* how many troops were involved.

2. The majority leader *has* a great deal of influence in the White House. He or she can easily *find a way around* the established procedures and go directly to the president.

3. Several economists are saying that they *look forward to* an upturn in the stock market during the second half of the year. Others, however, maintain that interest rates must *stop their fluctuating* if the bull market is to prevail.

4. The night-shift workers took their complaints to the shop steward when the managers tried to *force* them into *giving up* their ten-cent wage differential.

5. The chairman of the Senate investigating committee *spoke against* the practice of accepting fees for outside speeches. He said that the new rules will *put a stop to* all such questionable fund raising. To some observers, such practices *are the same thing as* bribery. Several senators have promised to *come up with* a new compromise plan.

6. Dorm life changed drastically when colleges *did away with* their traditional "in loco parentis" role. In the old days, of course, there were always students who *paid no attention to* the rules. At some schools, where the administration would not *put up with* violations, students were routinely *kicked out.*

The Overuse of *Be.* Another major culprit contributing to flabbiness is the overuse of *be* as the main verb. *Be* sentences commonly serve not only as topic sentences (as in the paragraph you're now reading), but also as supporting sentences throughout the paragraph. You might be surprised, in checking a paragraph or two of your own prose, at how often you've used a form of *be* as the link between the known and the new information. An abundance of such examples—say, more than two or three in a paragraph—may constitute a clear "revise" message.

Sometimes you can eliminate *be* simply by substituting a different verb. We used this technique in rewriting the second sentence of the previous section:

Most writing teachers would probably agree that choosing verbs

is one of the writer's most important jobs. The verb, after all, ~~is~~ occupies

the central, pivotal slot of the sentence pattern.

You may have noticed *be* in the first sentence too, which we didn't change. We could have written, "choosing verbs *constitutes* one of the writer's most important jobs," but that sounds a bit forced; it interferes with the natural rhythm.

Another technique for eliminating the flabbiness that *be* often brings with it is [Oops! There it is again!] to make use of appositives and absolute phrases and other kinds of modifiers to combine sentences, to combine ideas. For example, in the following passage the second and third sentences can become appositives, nominals that rename another nominal, which you studied in Chapter 8.

Last year scientists announced the discovery of the smallest known primate. It is one of several species of Eosimias (dawn monkey). This extinct animal was no longer than a human thumb.

Revision: Last year scientists announced the discovery of the smallest known primate, one of several species of Eosimias (dawn monkey), an extinct animal no longer than a human thumb.

In combining the following sentences, we have turned the subject complement of the second one, where *be* is the main verb, into a sentence appositive, punctuated with a dash:

The play opened to rave reviews and standing-room-only crowds; it was a smashing success.

Revision: The play opened to rave reviews and standing-room-only crowds—a smashing success.

The sentence appositive acts as a summary statement that gives special focus to the idea of the main clause.

The Passive Voice. In Chapter 5 you learned how to transform a sentence in the active voice into the passive voice by adding *be* + *-en* to the verb and shifting the object to subject position; the active subject can become the object of a preposition:

Active: *The committee discussed the report.*

Passive: *The report was discussed by the committee.*

It's certainly possible that everything you've read in other books or heard from teachers about the passive voice has been negative—admonitions to avoid it because of wordiness or vagueness.

The typical caution against the passive voice goes back at least as far as 1907, when the following passage appeared in a handbook of rules by one Edwin Woolley. [Boldface type has been added in this and the passages that follow.]

Do not use the passive voice when such use makes a statement clumsy and wordy. . . . Do not, by using the passive voice, leave the agent of the verb vaguely indicated, **when the agent should be clearly identified**. (Quoted in Haussamen, p. 55. See reference list, p. 14)

One of the most influential books on the subject of voice is *The Elements of Style* by Strunk and White, first published in 1957, a book that continues to influence handbooks and textbooks. Here is the summary of the section entitled "Use the Active Voice":

Many a tame sentence of description or exposition can be made lively and emphatic by substituting a transitive in the active voice for some such perfunctory expression as *there is* or *could be heard*. (p. 18)

This passage is followed by several passive examples and their active revisions—and another summary statement:

Note in the examples above, that **when a sentence is made stronger**, it usually becomes shorter. Thus, brevity is a by-product of vigor. (p. 19)

You have no doubt figured out that the clauses in bold type are all in the passive voice.

It's true, of course, that some passive sentences could be improved by being revised into the active (including, perhaps, the one you are now reading!)—*but not because they're passive.* The reason lies elsewhere: perhaps because they have the wrong focus. In that case, it's the focus that's the problem—not the mere fact of their being passive.

As with cleft sentences and the *there* transformation, the passive voice enables the writer to shift emphasis in the sentence, so that the reader will put the focus where it should be—on the new information. That passive shift can also provide transition between sentences. When the object of the action is the known information—when it is the topic under discussion—the passive transformation can shift that information to the subject slot, where we generally find the topic.

In the earlier discussion of cohesion, on page 315, we looked at the pattern of known and new information in the paragraph about sentence slots. The subject of the third (and last) sentence includes the word *glue,* the known information from the previous sentence and the topic of the new one:

> Part of that glue is provided by information in the sentence that the reader knows or expects, information that has already been mentioned.

Part of that glue functions as the subject—but it's not the agent. We put the agent, the "doer" of the verb *provided,* in end-focus position because it is the new information. We used the passive transformation to do so.

Here's another example, the opening of a paragraph from *Time* about the destruction of the Brazilian rain forests. Note that in the second sentence, which is passive, the known information of the subject provides transition:

> If Americans are truly interested in saving the rain forests, they should move beyond rhetoric and suggest *policies* that are practical—and acceptable—to the understandably wary Brazilians. *Such policies* cannot be presented as take-them-or-leave-them propositions. If the U.S. expects better performance from Brazil, Brazil has a right to make demands in return. [emphasis added]

MICHAEL D. LEMONICK

In the first sentence, *policies* is new information in object position; in the second it is known and it has become the topic—and the subject.

THE ABSTRACT SUBJECT

As you know from your study of the passive voice, the agent—the perpetrator—is not always the subject of the sentence; in some passive sentences it doesn't appear at all. However, the more concrete and active the sentence, the more likely the agent will function as the subject—or at least make an appearance. The more abstract and passive the sentence, the more likely the agent will be missing.

One common cause of abstraction is **nominalization**, verbs that have been turned into nouns. We saw the process of nominalization in Chapters 11 and 12 in connection with derivational affixes, the word endings that change the class of the word. Remember that a verb is an action word. A verb *shows* the action; but a noun simply *names* the action:

> The governor's <u>opposition</u> to abortion has caused many pro-choice organizations to work against his reelection.

> There is a growing <u>recognition</u> that forests are more valuable when left standing.

Our language, of course, is filled with nominalized verbs—most of which are useful, legitimate ways of expressing ideas. In this paragraph, for example, you have seen *action* and *connection*, both of which began as verbs (*act, connect*) and are now ordinary, everyday nouns.

But because nominalized verbs are so common and so easy to produce, they can become a trap for the unwary writer, introducing abstraction where concrete ideas belong. It's during the revision stage of writing that you'll want to be on the lookout. Ask yourself, Is the agent there and, if so, is it functioning as the subject? In other words, does the sentence explain *who is doing what?* If the answer is no, your sentence may be a prime candidate for revision.

Another source of abstraction and flabbiness is the sentence with a verb phrase or a clause as subject, rather than the usual noun phrase. You learned in Chapter 8 that these structures are grammatical, common substitutes for noun phrases. But because they are abstractions, they too may be pitfalls for the unwary writer. Again, the source of the problem may be that of the missing or misplaced agent:

> <u>The canceling of the after-school drama program by the school board</u> caused the community to raise strong objections.

> With the opening of China to certain aspects of capitalism, <u>what is happening</u> is that American companies are looking for ways of expanding their markets and their product lines to take advantage of the situation.

> <u>Analyzing the situation in the Far East</u> has shown that opportunities for investment are growing.

Although we need context to tell us the best way to revise these sentences, we can see and hear a problem. The sentences seem to be about actions—but they can't show the action in a strong and concrete way because the agents of those actions are not there in subject position. This kind of agentless sentence should send up a red flag—a signal that here's a possible candidate for revision.

Exercise 62

Here are some sentences that might sound familiar—that is, you may write like this yourself. Try to achieve a more direct style and tone as you revise the sentences. Be especially alert to nominalizations and passives. The first three items are the examples from the preceding discussion. Remember to ask yourself, "Who is doing what?"

1. The canceling of the after-school drama program by the school board caused the community to raise strong objections.

2. With the opening of China to certain aspects of capitalism, what is happening is that American companies are looking for ways of expanding their markets and their product lines to take advantage of the situation.

3. Analyzing the situation in the Far East has shown that opportunities for investment are growing.

4. In the biography of Lyndon Johnson by Robert Caro, an account of the Senate election of 1948 is described in great detail.

5. When Julie filled out an application for a work-study job, she was surprised to learn that a detailed financial statement would have to be submitted by her parents.

6. Getting his new pizza parlor to finally turn a profit has meant a lot of hard work and long hours for Tim.

7. The broadening of one's view of life and the establishment of worthy goals are both important aims of education.

8. The encouragement of the thinking process is also an important educational aim. Strategies should be developed by students for the understanding of problems and for their solutions.

THE SHIFTING ADVERBIALS

One of the writer's most versatile sentence elements is the adverbial, in terms of both form and position. As you recall from Chapter 6, the adverbs and prepositional phrases and noun phrases and verb phrases and clauses that add adverbial information can open the sentence or close it, or they can interrupt it somewhere in the middle. Sentence variety by itself is, of course, not a reason for opening or closing a sentence with an adverbial structure. Rather, you should understand the effects on cohesion and reader expectation that adverbials will have in different positions.

In Chapter 3 we labeled the adverbial function as "optional," but that label is somewhat misleading. Even though an adverbial is rarely needed from a grammatical point of view, the adverbial information is often the main idea—the new information of the sentence. For example, in the sentence,

> I got up <u>early</u> <u>to study for my Spanish test</u>,

the two adverbials are optional in terms of the sentence pattern: *I got up* is a grammatical Pattern VI sentence. But the person saying or writing that sentence probably does so to convey time or purpose. It's the information in one or both adverbials that actually provides the main focus of the sentence.

The decision about placement of adverbials, then, is connected to sentence focus and to the concept of known and new information. If the adverbial is the main focus, it probably belongs at or near the end of the sentence. We saw an example of this situation earlier in this chapter with the sentence "Barbara wrecked her motorcycle yesterday," where the adverb *yesterday* supplied the new information. In opening position, the adverbial will usually tie the sentence to what has gone before, either because it is the known information or because it is providing a cohesive element, such as time sequence, with an adverbial like *then* or *later that day* or *on the following afternoon*.

The opening adverbial in the sentence you just read provides that cohesive tie: *In opening position* contrasts with the discussion in the previous sentence about closing position. In a sense it is known information, even though opening position had not been discussed in the paragraph up to that point: Common sense tells us that a sentence has an opening as well as a closing position.

The versatility of adverbials lies not only in the variety of positions they can occupy; it lies also in the variety of their forms. They can be short and brisk, or they can be long and relaxed, changing the tone and pace of the sentence.

> I haven't been feeling well <u>lately</u>.
>
> I haven't been feeling well <u>since September</u>.
>
> I haven't been feeling well <u>since the beginning of the semester</u>.
>
> I haven't been feeling well <u>since September, when the semester started</u>.

The Adverbial Clause. In Chapters 6 and 9 we emphasized the movable nature of adverbial and subordinate clauses. They are both movable and versatile: Our long list of subordinators enables us to connect ideas for a wide variety of reasons. Certainly subordinate clauses are common structures in our language: In speech we use them often and automatically. In writing, of course, they are not automatic, nor are they always used as effectively as they could be. Two problems that show up fairly often are related to the meaning of the sentence: (1) The wrong idea gets subordinated; and (2) the meaning of the subordinator is imprecise.

Here, for example, are two related ideas that a writer might want to combine into a single sentence:

> We worked hard for the candidates.
>
> We suspected they didn't stand a chance.

Here are some possibilities for connecting them:

> <u>While</u> we worked hard for the candidates, we suspected they didn't stand a chance.
>
> <u>Although</u> we worked hard for the candidates, we suspected they didn't stand a chance.
>
> We worked hard for the candidates, <u>even though</u> we suspected they didn't stand a chance.

We need context, of course, to know precisely what the connection between the two ideas should be, but given no other information, the last version expresses what would appear to be the logical relationship.

Perhaps an even more common problem than the imprecise subordinator is the compound sentence with no subordination—the sentence with two independent clauses, two equal focuses, that would be more accurate and effective with a single focus. The most common culprit is the compound sentence connected by *but:*

> The prime rate went down two percentage points during the last quarter, but government economists are still worried about high inflation and low productivity.

Because *but* is a coordinating conjunction, just as *and* is, the sentence has two ideas that, by reason of the structure, can be considered only as equals. But are they? Probably not.

Here's another compound sentence with *but,* a paragraph opener in an article about sleep. The paragraph preceding this one gives examples of accidents on the job connected with work schedules:

> The biological clock is flexible enough to adjust to slight changes in a person's work schedule, *but* in many industries rotations in shift work are so drastic that they play havoc with body rhythms, leaving employees unable to sleep at home and impairing their productivity at work. [emphasis added]

> Erik Eckholm, *New York Times Magazine*

Here the two clauses are clearly not equal: The main idea is the second clause. The idea in the first clause, although it has not previously appeared in the article, is presented as understood, as information the reader is assumed to know—the known information. The new information is in the second clause. Making the first clause subordinate will help the reader focus on the new idea:

> *Although* the biological clock is flexible enough to adjust to slight changes in a person's work schedule, in many industries rotations in shift work are so drastic that they play havoc with body rhythms, leaving employees unable to sleep at home and impairing their productivity at work.

Remember that a compound sentence has two points of focus that, in terms of structure, are equal. The compound sentence is effective only when that structure accurately reflects the relationship of the two ideas. If a single point of focus would be more accurate, then a subordinating conjunction should introduce one of the two ideas.

Investigating Language 15.2

The paragraph by Stephen E. Ambrose quoted on page 314 begins with a 70-word compound–complex sentence. The second independent clause is connected by *but*, exactly like the Eckholm sentence about the biological clock, which we just revised. Consider revising Ambrose's sentence, as we did Eckholm's, by turning that opening independent clause into a subordinate clause with *although* or, perhaps, another subordinator. Does your revision improve the focus?

Can you suggest other possible changes for that sentence? Would breaking those 70 words into shorter sentences be an improvement?

Exercise 63

Combine each of the following groups of sentences into a single sentence by using subordination. In some cases you will want to reword the sentence. Remember that the subordinator you select will signal the relationship between the two ideas. You can probably come up with more than one possibility for each.

1. The famous Gateway Arch is in St. Louis.
    Kansas City claims the title "Gateway to the West."

2. Our spring semester doesn't end until the second week of June.
    Many students have a hard time finding summer jobs.

3. Thomas Jefferson acquired the Ozark Mountains for the United States in 1803.
   That was the year of the Louisiana Purchase.
   We bought the Louisiana Territory from Napoleon.

4. Many attorneys are unacquainted with oil and gas laws.
   They are unable to offer advice concerning oil and gas leases to their clients.

5. The neighbors added a pit bull to their pet population, which now numbers three unfriendly four-legged creatures.
   We have decided to fence in our backyard.

6. The human circulatory system is a marvel of efficiency.
   It is still subject to a wide variety of degenerative diseases.

7. Carbohydrates—starches—are the body's prime source of energy.
   Fad diets that severely restrict the intake of starches are nearly always ineffective.
   Such diets can also be dangerous.

8. Our congressman knows that the majority of voters in this district are upset with their tax rates.
   They also don't like the way their tax dollars are being spent.
   He has made "No New Taxes" the main theme of his reelection campaign.

9. Auto companies offered enticing cash rebates to buyers of new cars last January.
   Car sales increased dramatically.

10. By 1890 the buffalo population of the West had been nearly wiped out.
    It now numbers about 60,000.
    About 400 ranchers in Colorado are raising buffalo for meat.

The Adverbs of Emphasis. As you know, the adverbials are versatile structures. They provide their information of time, place, manner, and the like in a variety of shapes; and they give the writer special flexibility because they can fill so many different slots—at the beginning, the middle, and the end of sentences. But there's another group of adverbials, mainly single-word adverbs, whose purpose is to emphasize a particular structure and thus control the pace and rhythm of the sentence.

Read the following sentences and note where you apply the main stress:

I hardly slept last night.

I slept hardly at all last night.

My roommate never has trouble sleeping.

Some people are always looking for trouble.

Joe tells me that he rarely stays awake past midnight.

You probably put the emphasis on *hardly, all, never, always,* and *rarely.*

Given these examples, you can think of other words that you use for emphasis: other negatives, such as *seldom, barely, scarcely;* other time and frequency words, such as *afterwards, finally, sometimes;* and others expressing duration, such as *already, no longer, still.*

It's possible, of course, to write sentences in which these words would not have main stress, where the principle of end focus, for example, would still be in effect. But certainly these are words that you, as a writer, need to recognize; they often wield the power in a sentence, controlling its intonation contour and making a difference in the message.

The Common *Only.* One of our most versatile—but also most frequently misused—adverbials of emphasis is the common *only.* Like other emphasizers, *only* can change the focus of the sentence by directing the reader's attention to a particular word:

I'm taking <u>only twelve</u> credits this semester.

The car <u>only looks</u> old; it's really quite new.

Joe isn't <u>only handsome</u>; he's rich too.

Paul cleans house <u>only on Saturdays</u>.

When you read these sentences, you'll find yourself putting nearly equal emphasis on both *only* and the word that follows it.

But there's also a common problem with *only:* It's frequently misplaced—and most of the time we don't even notice!

I'm only taking twelve credits this semester.

Paul only cleans house on Saturdays.

We're only going to be gone for two or three days.

Jane refuses to watch the Super Bowl; she only likes baseball.

A well-placed *only* can strengthen the sentence focus. It sends a message to the reader that the writer has crafted the sentence carefully.

METADISCOURSE

In our discussion of sentence modifiers in Chapter 9, we contrasted the use of *clearly* in two sentences:

Mark did not explain the situation clearly.

Clearly, Mark did not explain the situation.

In the first, *clearly* is an adverbial modifying *explain;* in the second it adds emphasis, indicating the writer's commitment to the truth of the statement. This kind of attitude message is called **metadiscourse**, or discourse about discourse. Here are some further sample sentences from Chapter 9 that include sentence modifiers as attitude markers:

> <u>Frankly</u>, I didn't expect sailing to be so much work.

> <u>To our amazement</u>, the driver of the Corvette walked away from the accident.

> <u>To my regret</u>, I have never seen the Grand Canyon.

These words and phrases add a feeling of informality that may not be appropriate in a formal paper; and, in fact, examples like these are probably more common in speech than in writing. But, certainly, attitude statements like these (and like the "certainly" in this sentence) make a difference in the writer's voice, the sense of connection to the reader.

Here are some examples from the text itself. The first one is from the introduction to Part V (page 312):

> <u>Unfortunately</u>, methods of teaching grammar have been slow to change.

And this one is from the section in this chapter called Choosing Verbs (page 321):

> The verb, <u>after all</u>, occupies the central, pivotal slot of the sentence pattern.

Neither *unfortunately* nor *after all* contributes to the truth of its sentence; neither alters the fact of the statement in any way, so we certainly can't call them adverbials. Then why add those extra words? In both cases they are sending a message to you, the reader, from us, the authors of your grammar book. And don't assume that they are "extra" words: They're important.

In the first example, the word *unfortunately* tells you what we think about the grammar-teaching situation; it tells you what side we're on, in case you didn't know.

The signal in the second example, *after all,* is even more important. Without it, if we had written, simply,

> The verb occupies the central, pivotal slot of the sentence pattern,

you might have become indignant, at least momentarily, to think that we think that after fourteen chapters of studying sentences you still haven't figured out that verbs occupy an important place! The phrase *after all* is there to tell you that we are well aware that you do indeed already know the importance of verbs.

Here's another example from the text. This one opens the section in Chapter 2 on the noun phrase (page 21):

> The term *noun phrase* <u>may</u> be new to you, although you're <u>probably</u> familiar with the word *phrase* . . .

Think of what the words *may* and *probably* are doing in that sentence: Their purpose is called **hedging**. We don't know for sure that the term *noun phrase* is new to you, but we suspect it is; we do think you're familiar with the more common term *phrase*. In both cases, however, we're hedging our bets; *may* and *probably* allow us to do that. Writers have a fairly large repertoire of hedging words: *fairly* is one of them, along with *could, might, perhaps, at times, sometimes, almost, usually,* and many other such words and phrases that qualify our statements, that add a note of probability to what otherwise might come across as certainty, when certainty may not be appropriate or possible.

Another important purpose of metadiscourse is cohesion. Cohesive signals act as guideposts that clarify the purpose or direction of a passage and connect it to what has gone before. For example, when a sentence begins, as this one does, with the phrase "for example," you know the sentence will discuss an example of the concept just mentioned. The phrase may not be necessary—many examples go unmarked because they are expected—but sometimes that specific signal is very important.

Other connectors you're familiar with, such as *first, in the first place, second, next,* and *finally,* clearly add to the ease of reading, the flow of the text. Those that signal contrasting pairs of ideas—*on the one hand/on the other hand*—are also especially helpful to keep the reader on course. These are among the connectors called *conjunctive adverbs* that you studied in Chapter 10 on Coordination and in the Conjunction section of Chapter 12, The Structure Classes.

STYLE

Everything we write, we write "with style," in one sense of the word—when the word refers simply to an individual's way of writing. You have your own style of writing, just as you have your own style of walking and whistling and wearing your hair. We also use the word *style* to characterize the overall impression of a piece of writing, such as the plain style, the pompous style, the official style. When you follow advice about being brief and using simple words, the outcome will be a plain style; words that are too fancy will probably result in a pompous style.

The word *style* is also used in connection with variations in sentence structure, with the structural and punctuation choices that you as a writer can use to your advantage. For example, in the second sentence of the previous paragraph, three verb phrases in a series are connected with two *ands* and no commas:

> walking and whistling and wearing your hair

It could have been written with two commas and only one *and*:

> walking, whistling, and wearing your hair

Or only commas:

> walking, whistling, wearing your hair

Such stylistic variations have traditionally occupied an important place in the study of rhetoric. In fact, the Greeks had names for every deviation from ordinary word order and usage, and Greek orators practiced using them. Some of the more common ones you're familiar with, such "figures of speech" as simile, metaphor, and personification. But many of them, you probably don't even notice—such as the shift, in both this sentence and the previous one, of the direct object to opening position. In this section we will examine the rhetorical effects that these and other variations in sentence structure and punctuation can have.

Word Order Variation. Variation from the standard subject–verb–object word order is fairly common in poetry; it can be effective in prose as well, partly because it is uncommon. In the following sentence, Charles Dickens made sure that the reader would hear the contrast between *has* and *has not:*

> Talent, Mr. Micawber has; money, Mr. Micawber has not.

Another fairly common rearrangement occurs when a clause as direct object opens the sentence, as you saw in the previous paragraph.

> Which of these calls seemed more mysterious, it is not possible
> to say.

> JAMES AGEE

Robert Frost used this variation, too, in the first line of his famous poem "Stopping by Woods on a Snowy Evening":

> Whose woods these are, I think I know.

Notice that all these variations put special emphasis on the verb, the slot that would normally be in a valley when the sentence has a direct object.

With certain adverbs in opening position, the subject and the auxiliary can be reversed:

> Never before had I seen such an eerie glow in the night sky.
>
> Rarely do I hear such words of praise.

You'll notice that the opening adverbial is a peak of stress.

The following sentence, written by Winston Churchill, illustrates another kind of shift in word order. Here the very last noun phrase in the sentence is the grammatical subject:

> Against Lee and his great Lieutenant [Stonewall Jackson], united for a year of intense action in a comradeship which recalls that of Marlborough and Eugene, were now to be marshaled *the overwhelming forces of the Union.* [emphasis added]

When you read this sentence aloud, you can hear your voice building to a peak of stress on *overwhelming forces,* just as Churchill planned. In fact, it's hard to read the sentence without sounding Churchillian.

Ellipsis. Another fairly common stylistic variation is the use of ellipsis, where part of the sentence is simply left out, or "understood," usually for the purpose of avoiding repetition. In the following description of Stonewall Jackson, Churchill used ellipsis in both sentences. In the first, he left out the linking verb in all but the first clause. The tightness of the sentence actually reflects the description of Jackson's character:

> His character was stern, his manner [was] reserved and usually forbidding, his temper [was] Calvinistic, his mode of life [was] strict, frugal, austere.

> Black-bearded, pale-faced, with thin, compressed lips, aquiline nose, and dark, piercing eyes, he slouched in his weather-stained uniform a professor-warrior; yet [he was] greatly beloved by the few who knew him best, and [he was] gifted with that strange power of commanding measureless devotion from the thousands whom he ruled with an iron hand.

Notice also in the last sentence that in the clause after the semicolon both the subjects and the verbs are understood.

The Coordinate Series. Many of the structural variations that writers use for special effects occur in connection with coordinate structures—pairs and series of sentences and sentence parts. One effective way of changing the emphasis in coordinate structures entails a small deviation from the usual way of using conjunctions, as you saw in the example about "walking, whistling, and wearing your hair." In a series of three or more structures, we generally use commas between the parts of the series, and we use a conjunction before the final member. Here's another example:

> At the class reunion, we laughed, reminisced, and sang the old songs.

Here are two variations. Read them aloud and listen to the differences.

> At the class reunion we laughed and reminisced and sang the old songs.

> At the class reunion we laughed, reminisced, sang the old songs.

The differences are subtle, but meaningful. The first variation puts emphasis on each verb with a fairly equal beat: / and / and /. It also puts a lilt in your voice. The second variation, the one without conjunctions, has an open-ended quality, as though the list were incomplete. The writer seems to be saying, "I could go on and on; I could tell you much more."

The following sentence, from Churchill's description of Stonewall Jackson, includes that second technique. The phrases themselves have no conjunctions, as a regular series would, nor does the final series of adjectives:

> His character was stern, his manner reserved and usually forbidding, his temper Calvinistic, his mode of life strict, frugal, austere.

The omission of the conjunction contributes to the strictness and frugality of style that echo the words themselves. With conjunctions, the sentence would lose that echo:

> His mode of life was strict and frugal and austere.

The Introductory Appositive Series. In the following passages, the sentence opens with a series of noun phrases that act as appositives to the subject. In the first example, Churchill describes Queen Victoria:

> High devotion to her royal task, domestic virtues, evident sincerity of nature, a piercing and sometime disconcerting truthfulness—all these qualities of the Queen's had long impressed themselves upon the mind of her subjects.

The following description is from a *Time* article on the Vikings, written by Michael D. Lemonick and Andrea Dorfman:

> Ravagers, despoilers, pagans, heathens—such epithets pretty well summed up the Vikings for those who lived in the British Isles during medieval times.

Often the noun phrase series is in apposition to a pronoun as subject, as in this example from William Golding:

> Political and religious systems, social customs, loyalties and traditions, they all came tumbling down like so many rotten apples off a tree.

Notice, too, in these examples that the series does not include a conjunction before the last member.

The Deliberate Sentence Fragment. The sentence fragments that composition teachers flag with a marginal "frag" are the unintentional kind, usually the result of punctuation errors, the most common being the subordinate clause punctuated as a full sentence. But not all fragments are errors. Experienced writers know how to use them effectively—noun phrases or verb phrases that invariably call attention to themselves. The first two examples are from novels of John le Carré:

> They remembered the tinkling of falling glass all right, and the timid brushing noise of the young foliage hitting the road. <u>And the mewing of people too frightened to scream.</u>

The Little Drummer Girl

> Our Candidate begins speaking. <u>A deliberate, unimpressive opening</u>.

A Perfect Spy

In the following paragraph, which opens "Geraldo No Last Name" by Sandra Cisneros, we are hearing fragmented thoughts—ideal candidates for sentence fragments.

> She met him at a dance. Pretty too, and young. Said he worked in a restaurant, but she can't remember which one. Geraldo. That's all. Green pants and Saturday shirt. Geraldo. That's what he told her. And how was she to know she'd be the last one to see him alive. An accident, don't you know. Hit and run.

Repetition. Repetition has come up before in these pages—in both a positive and a negative sense. On the positive side, repetition gives our sentences cohesion: The known–new contract calls for the repetition, if not of words, then of ideas. It is part of the glue that holds sentences together. But we also have a negative label for repetition when it has no purpose, when it gets in the reader's way: Then we call it redundancy. If you've heard warnings about redundancy, if you've seen "red" in the margins of your essays, you might hesitate to use repetition deliberately. But don't hesitate. It's easy to distinguish redundancy from good repetition, from repetition as a stylistic tool.

The Greek rhetoricians had labels for every conceivable kind of good repetition—from the repetition of sounds and syllables to that of words and phrases in various locations in the sentence. We'll confine our discussion to repetition in coordinate structures that will make the reader sit up and take notice.

Consider the Gettysburg Address. Which of Lincoln's words, other than "Fourscore and seven years ago," do you remember? Probably "government of the people, by the people, and for the people." It's hard to imagine those words without the repetition: "Of, by, and for the people" just wouldn't have the same effect. And think about President Kennedy's stirring words, with his repetition of *any*:

> [W]e shall pay any price, bear any burden, meet any hardship, support any friend, oppose any foe to assure the survival and the success of liberty.

Notice, too, that the conjunction has been omitted before the last member of the series. He seems to be saying, "I could go on and on with my list."

You don't have to be a president to use that kind of repetition, nor do you have to reserve it for formal occasions. Whenever you use a coordinate structure, there's an opportunity for you to add to its impact with repetition, simply by including words that wouldn't have to be included. The following sentence, from an essay in *Time* by Charles Krauthammer, could have been more concise, but it would have lost its drama:

> There is not a single Western standard, there are two: what we demand of Western countries at peace and what we demand of Western countries at war.

And here is the second paragraph of the *Time* article about the Vikings by Michael D. Lemonick and Andrea Dorfman, with four repetitions of *they were*. The first paragraph began with that opening appositive series we saw earlier:

> But that view is wildly skewed. The Vikings were indeed raiders, but they were also traders whose economic network stretched from today's Iraq all the way to the Canadian Arctic. They were democrats who founded the world's oldest surviving parliament while Britain was still mired in feudalism. They were master metalworkers, fashioning exquisite jewelry from silver, gold and bronze. Above all, they were intrepid explorers whose restless hearts brought them to North America some 500 years before Columbus.

In the following one-sentence paragraph from *Undaunted Courage*, Stephen E. Ambrose describes the birthplace of Meriwether Lewis with repeated *where* clauses:

> Lewis was born in a place where the West invited exploration but the East could provide education and knowledge, where the hunting was magnificent but plantation society provided refinement and enlightenment, where he could learn wilderness skills while sharpening his wits about such matters as surveying, politics, natural history, and geography.

Notice, too, the parallelism of the *where* clauses, each including a contrasting pair of descriptors.

ANTITHESIS

In his book on classical rhetoric, Edward P. J. Corbett defines **antithesis** as "the juxtaposition of contrasting ideas, often in parallel."[1] Among his examples are the words of Neil Armstrong as he stepped on the moon in 1969:

> That's one small step for a man, one giant leap for mankind.

Benjamin Franklin included this example in a letter he wrote in 1783:

> There never was a good war, or a bad peace.

As you see, the contrasting ideas in these sentences come from opposites: *small/giant, good/bad.* In his book *The Discoverers*, Daniel Boorstein provides antithesis with the simple *not from—but from* in discussing the origin of clocks:

> The first steps toward the mechanical measurement of time, the beginnings of the modern clock in Europe, came not from farmers or shepherds, not from merchants or craftsmen, but from religious persons anxious to perform promptly and regularly their duties to God.

Note the opposite word meanings in the following passage from a *New York Times* book review by Martha Bayles:

> Precise detail adds texture, but profuse detail adds tedium . . . .

And here the contrast is a pair of adverbials:

> The surprise isn't how often we make bad choices; the surprise is how seldom they defeat us.

---

[1] *Classical Rhetoric for the Modern Student,* 2nd ed. (New York: Oxford University Press, 1971), p. 464.

We should also note in all of these examples, in both this and the previous section on repetition, the importance of **parallel structure**.

The use of the stylistic devices we have taken up in this chapter will invariably call attention to themselves. For that reason, you will reserve these structures for important ideas, for those times when you want your reader to sit up and take notice. Like the gourmet cook who knows that too many spices can overwhelm a dish, you won't want to overwhelm your reader. But you will want to recognize that, like the spice that turns a bland sauce into fine cuisine, these stylistic tools can make the difference between ordinary and powerful prose.

USING GENDER APPROPRIATELY

As you learned in Chapter 14, the system of personal pronouns has a gap. And it is that gap—the lack of a gender-neutral pronoun in the third-person singular slot—that is responsible for a great deal of the sexism in our language. You'd think that *he* and *she* and *it* would be up to the task of covering all the contingencies, but they're not. When we need a pronoun to refer to an unidentified person, such as "the writer" or "a student" or just "someone," our long-standing tradition has been to use the masculine:

> The writer of this news story should have kept <u>his</u> personal opinion out of it.

> Someone left <u>his</u> book on the table.

But that usage is no longer automatically accepted. Times and attitudes change, and we have come to recognize the power of language in shaping those attitudes. So an important step in reshaping society's view of women has been to eliminate the automatic use of *he* and *his* and *him* when the sex of someone referred to could just as easily be female.

In a paragraph we looked at earlier in this chapter in connection with sentence rhythm, the writer has made an effort to avoid sexism with the generic *salesperson*, a title that has all but replaced the masculine *salesman*. But notice the pronoun in the last sentence:

> Never invest in something you don't understand or in the dream of an artful salesperson. Be a buyer, not a sellee. Figure out what you want (be it life insurance, mutual funds or a vacuum cleaner) and then shop for a good buy. Don't let someone else tell you what you need—at least not if <u>he</u> happens to be selling it.
>
> ANDREW TOBIAS

In speech we commonly use *they* for both singular and plural:

> Don't let someone else tell you what you need—at least not if <u>they</u> happen to be selling it.

Eventually, perhaps, the singular *they* will become the accepted form in both speech and writing; after all, in the second person (*you/your/you*), we make no distinction between singular and plural, so it's not unreasonable to do the same in the third person. But such changes come slowly. What should we do in the meantime?

One common, but not necessarily effective, way to solve the problem of the pronoun gap is with *he or she:*

> . . . at least not if <u>he or she</u> happens to be selling it.

An occasional *he or she* will work in most situations like this one, but more than one in a paragraph will change the rhythm of the prose, slow the reader down, and call attention to itself when such attention is simply uncalled for.

The awkwardness of *he or she* in a passage becomes even more obvious when the possessive and objective case pronouns are also required. Avoiding sexist language by using *his or her* and *him or her* as well as *he or she* will quickly render the solution worse than the problem. Here, for example, is a passage from a 1981 issue of *Newsweek:*

> To the average American, the energy problem is mainly his monthly fuel bill and the cost of filling up his gas tank. He may also remember that in 1979, and way back in 1974, he had to wait in long lines at gasoline stations. For all of this, he blames the "Arabs" or the oil companies or the government, or perhaps all three. Much of the information that he gets from the media, as well as his own past experience, tells him that energy prices will continue to go up sharply and that gas lines are going to come back whenever a conflict flares up in the Middle East.
>
> FRED SINGER, "Hope for the Energy Shortage"

Now imagine a version in which the problem of sexism has been solved with *he or she:*

> To the average American, the energy problem is mainly his or her monthly fuel bill and the cost of filling up his or her gas tank. He or she may also remember that in 1979, and way back in 1974, he or she had to wait in long lines at gasoline stations. For all of this, he or she blames the "Arabs" or the oil companies or the government, or perhaps all three. Much of the information that he or she gets from the media, as well as from his or her own past experience, tells him or her that energy prices will continue . . . *Enough!*

That's only one short paragraph. Imagine reading a whole essay! Clearly, there are better solutions to the problem.

Because we do have a gender-neutral pronoun in the plural, often that singular noun can be changed to plural. In the *Newsweek* article, for example, the writer could have started out by discussing "average Americans":

> To average Americans, the energy problem is mainly their monthly fuel bills and the cost of filling up their gas tanks.

That revision, of course, has changed the relationship of the writer to the reader: The writer is no longer addressing the reader as an individual— a change the writer may not want. Often, however, the plural is an easy and obvious solution. For example, in the following passages from books about language, the change to plural does not affect the overall meaning or intent:

Of all the developments in the history of man [the human race], surely the most remarkable was language, for with it he was [our ancestors were] able to pass on his [their]

cultural heritage to succeeding generations who then did not have

to rediscover how to make a fire, where to hunt, or how to build

another wheel.

CHARLES B. MARTIN and CURT M. RULON

It has been said that whenever a person [people] speaks, he is [they are] either

mimicking or analogizing.

CHARLES HOCKETT

We should emphasize that these three examples of sexist language were written several decades ago, when the masculine pronoun was the norm. Chances are, none of them would have been written in this way today. All of us who are involved with words, who are sensitive to the power of language, have gone through a consciousness-raising in the matter of sexist language.

Let's assume that Fred Singer, the *Newsweek* writer, insists on maintaining the singular "average American." What other means would he have for eliminating the sexism of the masculine pronouns? In some cases, he could use different determiners. For example, he needn't write "*his* monthly fuel bill" and "*his* gas tank"; *the* will do the job. And in the last sentence, "his own past experience" could become "past experience" or, simply, "experience" without losing any information; "tells him" could become "says" or "suggests." He could probably get by with a single *he or she*, to replace the *he* of the second sentence; the other sentences with *he* can be revised with different subjects. Here's one possibility:

> To the average American, the energy problem is mainly the monthly fuel bill and the cost of filling up the gas tank. He or she may also remember in 1979, and way back in 1974, waiting in long lines at the gasoline stations. Who gets the blame for all of this? The "Arabs" or the oil companies or the government, or perhaps all three. The media, as well as the consumer's past experience, suggest that energy prices will continue to go up sharply and that gas lines are going to come back whenever a conflict flares up in the Middle East.

In the last sentence we've substituted "the consumer" for "the average American."

Here, then, are some of the ways in which you can make up for the pronoun gap when you write and/or revise your own sentences:

1. USE THE PLURAL:
   Every writer should be aware of the power of language when <u>he</u> chooses <u>his</u> pronouns.
   Revision: Writers should be aware of the power of language when <u>they</u> choose <u>their</u> pronouns.

2. USE *HE OR SHE* IF YOU CAN USE IT ONLY ONCE:
   Revision: Every writer should be aware of the power of language when <u>he or she</u> chooses pronouns.

3. TURN THE CLAUSE INTO A VERB PHRASE, THUS ELIMINATING THE PROBLEM SUBJECT:
   Revision: Every writer should be aware of the power of language when <u>choosing pronouns</u>.

This third method of revision is often a good possibility because the offending pronoun nearly always shows up in the second clause of a passage, often as part of the same sentence. In our example, we have turned the complete subordinate clause into an elliptical clause—that is, a clause with something missing. In this case what's missing is the subject. (The elliptical clause, which has some hidden pitfalls, is discussed in Chapter 9.)

4. AVOID *HIS* AS A DETERMINER, EITHER BY SUBSTITUTING ANOTHER ONE OR, IN SOME CASES, DELETING THE DETERMINER:
   The writer of the news story should have kept <u>his</u> opinion out of it.
   Revision: The writer of the news story should have kept (<u>all</u>) opinion out of it.

5. REWRITE THE ADVERBIAL CLAUSE AS A RELATIVE (WHO) CLAUSE:
When <u>a person</u> buys a house, <u>he</u> should shop carefully for the lowest interest rate.

Revision: <u>A person who</u> buys a house should shop carefully for the lowest interest rate.

The relative clause with its neutral *who* eliminates the necessity of a personal pronoun to rename *a person*.

6. CHANGE THE POINT OF VIEW:
Revision 2nd person: As a writer <u>you</u> should be aware of the power of language when you choose (your) pronouns.

Revision 1st person: As writers, <u>we</u> should be aware of the power of language when we choose (our) pronouns.

Exercise 64

1. Rewrite the *Newsweek* passage (page 342) using the second person. (Note: You might begin with "If you are an average American . . .")

2. The following passage was written in 1944, a time when the masculine pronoun was accepted as the generic singular. Revise it to reflect today's concerns about sexism in language.

Of all born creatures, man is the only one that cannot live by bread alone. He lives as much by symbols as by sense report, in a realm compounded of tangible things and virtual images, of actual events and ominous portents, always between fact and fiction. For he sees not only actualities but meanings. He has, indeed, all the impulses and interests of animal nature; he eats, sleeps, mates, seeks comfort and safety, flees pain, falls sick and dies, just as cats and bears and fishes and butterflies do. But he has something more in his repertoire, too—he has laws and religions, theories and dogmas, because he lives not only through sense but through symbols. That is the special asset of his mind, which makes him the master of earth and all its progeny.

SUSANNE K. LANGER, "The Prince of Creation"

CHAPTER *15*
Key Terms

Absolute phrase

Abstract subject

Adverbial clause

Adverbs of emphasis

Antithesis

Appositive

Cleft transformation

Cohesion

Coordinate series

Ellipsis

End focus

Gender

Hedging

Intonation

Introductory appositive series

Known-new contract

Metadiscourse

Metaphor

Nominalization

Parallel structure

Passive voice

Repetition

Rhetorical grammar

Rhythm

Sentence fragment

Sentence rhythm

Sexist language

Shifting adverbial

Style

Word-order variation

Purposeful Punctuation

CHAPTER PREVIEW

As you know, the purpose of punctuation is to indicate the grammatical structures in a written text. It makes the writer's meaning clear to the reader by marking boundaries, signaling levels of importance, and indicating linkages. Our summary here is organized according to these purposes.

Throughout the previous chapters we have explained punctuation in the context of the sentence patterns and their expansions. The first highlighted punctuation rule you saw—or, more accurately, nonpunctuation rule—came in Chapter 3 after the description of the basic patterns:

> Do not put single commas between the required slots.

In describing the various expansions of the required and optional slots, we have discussed the standard punctuation conventions, fully recognizing that many of those conventions are simply general guidelines. We strongly believe, however, that students—indeed, all of us who write—should know the standard punctuation conventions thoroughly and follow them as closely as possible, always with the reader in mind.

Our purpose in this chapter is not to answer all of your punctuation questions. A handbook will explain single quotes and footnotes and ellipses points and question marks within quotations and such. Rather, our purpose throughout the chapters—and summarized here—is to help you understand how punctuation contributes to meaning and to give you confidence as you express your meaning in prose.

MAKING CONNECTIONS

Compounding Sentences (see pp. 219–222)

1. Use a comma between the independent clauses of a compound sentence when they are joined by a coordinating conjunction (*and, but, or, nor, for, yet*):

> *There is a difference between the music of Bach and Mozart, and it is a difference worth discovering.*

> *The trial lasted for almost three months, yet it took the jury only three hours to render a verdict.*

The comma may be omitted if the clauses are very short and closely connected:

> *Meg played the piano and Thom sang.*

To use the comma without the conjunction produces a nonconventional connection called the **comma splice**. Writers do use comma splices on certain occasions, especially when combining two or three short sentences for special attention:

> *They graduated on Friday, they got married on Sunday, they moved to Alaska on Monday.*

2. Use a semicolon between independent clauses not joined by a coordinating conjunction:

> *There is a difference between the music of Bach and Mozart; it is a difference worth discovering.*

The semicolon sends a message to the reader: Notice the tight connection.

3. Use a semicolon between the clauses of a compound sentence when a conjunctive adverb (such as *nonetheless, however, therefore*) or an adverbial phrase (such as *in that case, as a result, on the other hand*) introduces the second clause (see pp. 220–221):

> *The issues were difficult to sort out; however, the judges had to make a decision.*

> *The contract negotiations lasted for two years; as a result, many workers quit their jobs and found other ones.*

The movability of the conjunctive adverb, set off by commas, enables the writer to change the focus in the second clause: The word just preceding it gets the main stress.

4. Use a semicolon between clauses joined by a coordinating conjunction if one or both of the clauses includes commas:

> *During the Italian Renaissance the inside of the pomegranate, which is divided into compartments containing colorful seeds, was*

> *the basis for a popular fabric design; and in the Middle East this*
> *beautiful fruit figured prominently in the decorative arts.*

The reader knows immediately on reaching the semicolon that another complete sentence is coming; that immediacy would be missing with only a comma as the signal.

5. Use a colon between the clauses of a compound sentence when the second clause explains or amplifies the first clause (see pp. 221–222):

> *After reading the letter, he did something that surprised me: He*
> *laughed and tore it up.*
>
> *My uncle was not wasteful: he was uncommonly thrifty.*

You have the choice of using either a capital or a lowercase letter on the second clause. Notice how the first clause sets up an expectation in the reader. The colon says, "Here comes the information that you're expecting" or "Here's what I promised." In the second example, the *not* in the first clause sets the reader up for a contrast in the second.

Compounding Structures Within Sentences (see pp. 213–215)
For compound pairs of words, phrases, and clauses that occur within the sentence, do NOT use a comma with the conjunction:

> *High ceilings and cathedral windows are two features that I look for*
> *in a house.* (compound subject)
>
> *The skiers cleaned their boots and sprayed them with a water*
> *repellent.* (compound predicate)
>
> *The new citizens promised that they would obey the laws of the country*
> *and that they would uphold the principles of the Constitution.*
> (compound direct object)

Exceptions:

> You may use a comma with compound elements when the
> conjunction is *but:*
>
>> *I love mangos and peaches, but not apricots.*
>
> You may also use a comma to give special emphasis to the
> second element in a compound:
>
>> *The judge listened to our side of the story, and then ruled*
>> *against us.*
>
> A dash would give the second element even more emphasis:
>
>> *The judge listened to our side of the story—and then ruled*
>> *against us.*

Connecting More Than Two Parts: The Series (see pp. 214–215)

1. Use commas to separate three or more items in a series or list:

> *Tacos, cheeseburgers, and low-carb salads are the most popular foods served in the cafeteria.*

> *The subway carries children going to school, adults going to work, and tourists going to the next historic site on their itinerary.*

Note that the serial comma, the comma before the conjunction in a series, is left out by some writers and in some publications:

> *Tacos, cheeseburgers and low-carb salads are the most popular foods served in the cafeteria.*

You can read about the importance of the serial comma on page 215.

2. Use semicolons to separate items in a series or list when one or more of the items already includes a comma:

> *The estate included lands and buildings; a portfolio of stocks, IRAs, and government bonds; and an extensive collection of art works.*

SEPARATING PRENOUN MODIFIERS (see pp. 135–137)

1. Use a comma to separate two or more coordinate modifiers that describe the same noun. Coordinate modifiers, which describe the noun independently, require commas if they could be joined with *and*. Another way to test the need for the comma is to reverse their order. If this is possible, the comma is necessary. These adjectives are opinions, subjective qualities.

> *The film was censored for its raucous, vulgar language.*

> *A friendly, sensitive, intelligent counselor helped us with the complicated paperwork.*

Note that no comma comes between the final modifier and the noun.

2. Do NOT use a comma between cumulative modifiers. Cumulative modifiers, which describe the combination of the next modifier plus the noun it modifies, cannot be joined with *and;* and their order cannot be changed.

> *We gave her a crystal perfume bottle.*

> *A set of large shiny new brass pots hangs over the stove.*

In contrast to the coordinate modifiers, the cumulative modifiers will generally follow a set order: size, shape, condition or age, color, origin or material:

> *large shiny new brass pots*

Any coordinate adjectives will precede the cumulative modifiers in the string:

> *beautiful large shiny new brass pots*

3. Use a hyphen to join the elements of compound modifiers when the first modifier applies to the second modifier, not to the headword:

> *Everybody needs a home-cooked meal now and then.*

> *They attended a four-hour seminar on long-range planning.*

Also use hyphens in a complete phrase that fills the modifier slot:

> *The results from this study are based on out-of-date statistics.*

But do not use hyphens in compound modifiers containing an -*ly* adverb:

> *The senator presented his proposal in clearly defined terms.*

IDENTIFYING ESSENTIAL AND NONESSENTIAL STRUCTURES (see pp. 154–156)

1. Use commas to set off phrases or clauses that merely comment on the nouns they modify, rather than defining or restricting their meaning. In other words, a nonessential phrase or clause could be omitted without changing the meaning of the sentence.

Adjective clause:

> *A popular concept in today's corporate world is time management, which has four distinct phases.*

Participial phrase:

> *The line judge, blocked by the player's movement, could not tell whether the ball was in or out.*

Appositive:

> *Richard Wagner, the composer of* Tristan and Isolde, *was a leading exponent of German romanticism.*

2. Do NOT set off phrases or clauses that are needed to identify the nouns they modify. Omitting an essential phrase or clause would alter the meaning of the sentence.

> *Time management is a concept that has become popular in today's corporate world.*

> *A line judge who is blocked by the player's movement cannot tell whether the ball is in or out.*

> *The composer Richard Wagner was a leading exponent of German romanticism.*

3. Use commas to set off transitional phrases and parenthetical comments that interrupt the flow of the sentence (see p. 127):

> *Honesty, in my opinion, should always be tempered with kindness.*

> *Being totally honest is, after all, sometimes an excuse for being cruel.*

4. Use commas to set off nouns of direct address (see p. 197):

> *The fact is, my friends, we have no choice in this matter.*
>
> *Mr. Ortiz, can you send us a copy of the accident report?*

5. Use a comma to set off the reporting tag (e.g., *she said, he replied, Darwin observed)* from a direct quotation:

> *Eleanor Roosevelt said, "No one can make you feel inferior without your consent."*
>
> *"No one can make you feel inferior," Eleanor Roosevelt said, "without your consent."*
>
> *"No one can make you feel inferior without your consent," Eleanor Roosevelt observed.*

Note that the comma between the verb (*said*) and the quotation constitutes an exception to the highlighted rule mentioned in the chapter preview (see p. 347).

SIGNALING SENTENCE OPENERS

Put a comma after the following introductory structures:

A long prepositional phrase:

> *After a heavy downpour with lightning and high winds, the yard was littered with branches.*

A single-word sentence modifier:

> *Surprisingly, the roof was still intact.*

Adverbial clause or verb phrase:

> *Just to be thorough, my roommate checked the basement.*
>
> *As he feared, he found an inch and a half of water down there.*

Absolute phrase:

> *The electricity having gone out, our sump pump had quit working.*

Participial phrase:

> *Sighing heavily, we got out the wet-vac and went to work.*

SIGNALING EMPHASIS

1. Use a colon to introduce a list of appositives renaming a noun:

> *The study of grammar includes three areas: phonology, morphology, and syntax.*
>
> *For this class students need the following equipment: a laptop computer, a spiral notebook, a pen, colored pencils, and a calculator.*

Note that a complete sentence precedes the colon. Do not use a colon when the list of items fills a complement slot:

> *The equipment needed for this class includes a laptop computer, a spiral notebook, a pen, colored pencils, and a calculator.*

2. Use dashes to highlight explanatory or amplifying structures, such as appositives, modifiers, and parts of compounds:

> *Foods high in protein—meats, fish, eggs, and cheese—should be part of everyone's daily diet.*
>
> *This provision will prevent corporations—large and small—from buying influence with campaign contributions.*
>
> *The stores were filled with holiday shoppers—even more so than last year.*
>
> *The soloist had a lean face, a long nose—and cold blue eyes.*

Note that no punctuation precedes or follows a dash.

3. Use parentheses to downplay explanatory or amplifying material:

> *Foods high in protein (meats, fish, eggs, and cheese) should be part of everyone's daily diet.*
>
> *The stores were filled with holiday shoppers (even more so than last year).*

USING APOSTROPHES FOR CONTRACTION AND POSSESSIVE CASE (see pp. 246–248)

1. Use an apostrophe to show where a letter or letters are missing in a contraction:

> *doesn't* =does not
>
> *won't* =will not
>
> *class of '75* =class of 1975

2. Use an apostrophe plus *s* to form the possessive of a singular noun or an irregular plural noun:

> *the soldier's uniform* =the uniform of the soldier
>
> *a year's lease* =a lease for one year
>
> *the boss's daughter* =the daughter of the boss
>
> *my children's clothes* =the clothes of my children

Note: Exceptions include certain words with more than one sibilant (*s* or *z*) sound in the last syllable (Jesus', Moses') and proper nouns ending in an –*eez* sound: Aristophanes' plays, Ramses' tomb.

3. Use an apostrophe alone to form the possessive of a regular plural noun:

> *the soldiers' uniforms* =the uniforms of more than one soldier
>
> *the Mendozas' house* =the house of the Mendozas

4. Use an apostrophe plus *s* to form the possessive of indefinite pronouns:

> *someone's bright idea*
>
> *nobody's business*

5. Do NOT add an apostrophe to the possessive forms of personal pronouns: *ours, yours, his, hers, its, theirs.*

Exercise 65

The following passages are punctuated according to our conventional rules. However, the proliferation of commas tends to detract from their readability. Revise the punctuation with the reader in mind:

1. During the second two-year stretch of a president's term in office, he may find himself on the defensive, even with his own party, and, when, as frequently happens, his party loses a number of Senate and House seats in the midterm election, that second stretch can become even more defensive.

2. In recent years, the public attitude toward smoking, except perhaps in the tobacco-growing states, has changed so fast, with smoke-free zones everywhere, including restaurants, office buildings, and shopping malls, it could almost be called a revolution, and even outdoor stadiums, such as Oriole Park at Camden Yards and Jacobs Field in Cleveland, have established a no-smoking policy.

Exercise 66

Experiment with commas, colons, and dashes as you revise and/or combine the following sentences.

1. The cost of repairs to the nation's public transportation facilities is an expenditure that cannot be delayed much longer if the system is to survive. Roads, bridges, and railroads are all in need of repair.

2. To many people, the mushroom is a lowly fungus. It has little food value. To other people, it is a gourmet's delight.

3. The Chinese banned the import of certain American goods, such as cotton, synthetic fibers, and soybeans. The restriction has had an adverse effect on the U.S. economy, especially on the farmers.

4. According to fashion experts, the crew cut will be back in style before long. That particular haircut was more or less the hallmark of the 1950s.

5. My favorite activities are skiing, playing golf, and bowling; unfortunately, they cost more than my budget can stand.

6. Alexander Graham Bell is remembered as the inventor of the telephone. Most people probably don't know that Bell succeeded his father-in-law as president of the National Geographic Society.

7. Many scientists believe that sightings of "cryptids" are mistakes. Cryptids include Big Foot, the Loch Ness monster, and Yeti, known as the Abominable Snowman. Mistaken sightings can be attributed to unfamiliarity with known animals, rather than to delusions.

8. Eugene Schiffelin was a New Yorker. In 1890 he decided to introduce all the birds mentioned in Shakespeare's works into America. The only mention of the starling in Shakespeare is a single instance in *Henry IV.* Schiffelin loosed 60 starlings in Central Park. Today millions of starlings live here. They are voracious and aggressive and smart. They have blanketed the United States. In many places they blacken the sky.

Glossary of Grammatical Terms

(For further explanation of the terms listed here, check the Index for page references.)

Absolute adjective. An adjective with a meaning that is generally not capable of being intensified or compared, such as *unique* or *perfect* or *square*. Careful writers avoid such usages as "very perfect" or "more unique."

Absolute phrase. A noun phrase related to the sentence as a whole that includes a postnoun modifier (often a participial phrase). One kind of absolute explains a cause or condition ("*The weather being warm,* we decided to have a picnic"); the other adds a detail or a point of focus to the idea in the main clause ("He spoke quietly to the class, *his voice trembling*").

Accusative case. The Latin term denoting the case of nouns and pronouns functioning as direct objects and as objects of certain prepositions.

Active voice. A feature of transitive verb sentences in which the subject is generally the agent and the direct object is the goal or objective of the action. Voice refers to the relationship of the subject to the verb. See also *Passive voice*.

Adjectival. Any structure, no matter what its form, that functions as a modifier of a noun—that is, that functions as an adjective normally functions. See Chapter 7.

Adjectival clause. See *Relative clause*.

Adjective. One of the four form classes, whose members act as modifiers of nouns; most adjectives can be inflected for comparative and superlative degree (*big, bigger, biggest*); they can be qualified or intensified (*rather big, very big*); they have characteristic derivational endings such as *-ous* (*famous*), *-ish* (*childish*), *-ful* (*graceful*), and *-ary* (*complementary*).

Adjective phrase. A modified adjective, such as an adjective with a qualifier (*very happy, extremely happy*), a comparative or superlative word (*more* *generous, most generous*), or with a complement (*happy to see you, happy that you could come*).

Adverb. One of the four form classes, whose members act as modifiers of verbs, contributing information of time, place, reason, manner, and the like. Like adjectives, certain adverbs can be qualified (*very quickly, rather fast*); some can be inflected for comparative and superlative degree (*more quickly, fastest*); they have characteristic derivational endings such as *-ly* (*quickly*), *-wise* (*lengthwise*), and *-ward* (*backward*).

Adverbial. Any structure, no matter what its form, that functions as a modifier of a verb—that is, that functions as an adverb normally functions. See Chapter 6.

Adverbial objective. The traditional label given to the noun phrase that functions adverbially: "Joe went *home*"; "It was cold *last night*."

Adverb phrase. A modified adverb, such as an adverb with a qualifier (*very quickly, rather quickly*) or with *more* or *most* (*more quickly, most anxiously*).

Affix. A morpheme, or meaningful unit, that is added to the beginning (prefix) or end (suffix) of a word to change its meaning or its grammatical role or its form class: (prefix) *un*likely; (suffix) unlike*ly*.

Agent. The initiator of the action in the sentence, the "doer" of the action. Usually the agent is the subject in an active sentence: "*John* groomed the dog"; "*The committee* elected Pam." In a passive sentence the agent may be the object of the preposition *by*: "Pam was elected by *the committee*."

Agreement. (1) Subject-verb. A third-person singular subject in the present tense takes the *-s* form of the verb: "*The dog barks* all night"; "*He bothers* the neighbors." A plural subject takes the base form: "*The dogs bark*"; "*They bother* the neighbors." (2) Pronoun–antecedent. The number of the pronoun (whether singular or plural) agrees with the number of its antecedent: "*The boys* did *their* chores"; "*Each girl* did *her* best."

Allomorph. A variation of a morpheme, usually determined by its environment. For example, the three allomorphs of the regular plural morpheme are determined by the final sound of the nouns to which they are added: /s/ *cats*; /z/ *dogs*; and /əz/ *churches*.

Ambiguous. The condition in which a structure has more than one possible meaning. The source may be lexical ("She is *blue*") or structural ("*Visiting relatives* can be boring") or both ("The detective looked *hard*").

Antecedent. The noun or nominal that a pronoun stands for.

Anticipatory *it*. The use of the pronoun *it* in subject position in order to delay the actual subject: "It was Mary who had the accident in Phoenix." See also *Cleft sentence.*

Antithesis. The juxtaposition of contrasting ideas: "I come to bury Caesar, not to praise him."

Appositive. A structure, often a noun phrase, that renames another structure: "My neighbor, *a butcher at Weis Market,* recently lost his job." Clauses ("It is nice *that you could come*") and verb phrases ("My favorite hobby, *collecting stamps,* is getting expensive") can also function as appositives.

Article. One of the determiner classes, including the indefinite *a,* or *an,* which signals only countable nouns, and the definite *the,* which can signal all classes of nouns.

Aspect. The perfect (*have + en*) and progressive (*be + ing*) auxiliaries, which denote such features of verbs as completion, duration, and repetition—time elements not related to past, present, or future.

Attributive adjective. The adjective in prenoun position: "my *new* coat"; "the *big* attraction." See also *Predicative adjective.*

Auxiliary. One of the structure-class words, a marker of verbs. Auxiliaries include forms of *have* and *be,* as well as the modals, such as *will, shall,* and *must,* and the "stand-in auxiliary" *do.*

Base form of the verb. The uninflected form of the verb. In all verbs except *be,* the base form is the present tense: *go, help.* The base form also serves as the infinitive, usually preceded by *to.*

Base morpheme. The morpheme that gives a word its primary lexical meaning: *help*ing, re*flect.*

Be **patterns.** The sentence patterns in which a form of *be* is the main verb: Patterns I, II, and III.

Bound morpheme. A morpheme that cannot stand alone as a word. Most affixes are bound (help*ing;* *re*act); some base morphemes are also bound (con*cise;* *leg*al).

Case. A feature of nouns and certain pronouns that denotes their relationship to other words in a sentence. Pronouns have three case distinctions: subjective (e.g., *I, they, who*); possessive (e.g., *my, their, whose*); and objective (e.g., *me, them, whom*). Nouns have only one case inflection, the possessive (*John's,* the *cat's*). The case of nouns other than the possessive is sometimes referred to as common case.

Catenative verb. A transitive verb that can take another verb as its object: "I *like* to jog"; "We *enjoy* jogging."

Clause. A structure with a subject and a predicate. The sentence patterns are clause patterns. Clauses are either independent or dependent.

Cleft sentence. A sentence variation that provides a way of shifting the stress or focus of the sentence: "A careless bicyclist caused the accident" → "It was a careless bicyclist who caused the accident"; "What caused the accident was a careless bicyclist."

Cohesion. The grammatical, lexical, and semantic connections between sentences. Cohesive ties are furnished by pronouns that have antecedents in previous sentences, by adverbial connections, by known information, and by knowledge shared by the reader.

Collective noun. A noun that refers to a collection of individuals: *group, team, family.* Collective nouns can be replaced by both singular and plural pronouns, depending on the meaning.

Command. See *Imperative sentence.*

Common case. See *Case.*

Common noun. A noun with general, rather than unique, reference (in contrast to proper nouns). Common nouns may be countable (*house, book*) or noncountable (*water, oil*); they may be concrete (*house, water*) or abstract (*justice, indifference*).

Comparative degree. See *Degree.*

Complement. A structure that "completes" the sentence. The term includes those slots in the predicate that complete the verb: direct object, indirect object, subject complement, and object complement. Certain adjectives also have complements—clauses and phrases that pattern with them: "I was *certain that he would come*; I was *afraid to go.*"

Complementary infinitive. An infinitive that functions as the main verb. "I'm going *to move* next week"; "I have *to find* a new apartment." There is a modal-like quality in "going to" and "have to."

Complex sentence. A sentence that includes at least one dependent clause.

Compound-complex sentence. A sentence that includes at least two independent clauses and one dependent clause.

Compound sentence. A sentence with two or more independent clauses.

Compound word. A word that is a combination of two or more free morphemes acting as a unit. Some compound words are closed (*highlight*), some are hyphenated (*high-handed*), and some are open, written as separate words (*high school*).

Conditional mood. The attitude of probability designated by the modal auxiliaries *could, may, might, would,* and *should.*

Conjunction. One of the structure classes, which includes connectors that coordinate structures of many forms (e.g., *and, or*), subordinate sentences (e.g., *if, because, when*), and coordinate sentences with an adverbial emphasis (e.g., *however, therefore*).

Conjunctive adverb. A conjunction that connects two sentences with an adverbial emphasis, such as *however, therefore, moreover,* and *nevertheless.*

Coordinating conjunction. A conjunction that connects two or more sentences or structures within a sentence as equals: *and, but, or, nor, for,* and *yet.*

Coordination. A way of expanding sentences in which two or more structures of the same form function as a unit. All the sentence slots and modifiers in the slots, as well as the sentence itself, can be coordinated. See Chapter 10.

Correlative conjunction. A two-part conjunction that expresses a relationship between the coordinated structures: *either-or, neither-nor, both-and, not only–but also.*

Countable noun. A noun whose referent can be identified as a separate entity; the countable noun can be signaled by the indefinite article, *a*, and numbers: *a house; an experience; two eggs; three problems.*

Declarative sentence. A sentence in the form of a statement (in contrast to a command, a question, or an exclamation).

Deep structure. A term from transformational generative grammar that refers to the underlying semantic and syntactic relationships of the sentence, in contrast to surface structure, which is the sentence as it is actually written or spoken.

Definite article. The determiner *the*, which generally marks a specific or previously mentioned noun: *"the* man on *the* corner."

Degree. The variations in adjectives that indicate the simple quality of a noun, or positive degree ("Bill is a *big* boy"); its comparison to another, the comparative degree ("Bill is *bigger* than Tim"); or to two or more, the superlative degree ("Bill is the *biggest* person in the whole class"). Certain adverbs also have degree variations, usually designated by *more* and *most*.

Demonstrative pronoun. The pronouns *this* (plural *these*) and *that* (plural *those*), which function as nominal substitutes and as determiners. They include the feature of proximity: near (*this, these*); distant (*that, those*).

Dependent clause. A clause that functions as an adverbial, adjectival, nominal, or sentence modifier (in contrast to an independent, or main, clause).

Derivational affix. A morpheme that is added to a form-class word, either to change its class (*friend* → *friendly*; *act* → *action*) or to change its meaning (*legal* → *illegal*; *boy* → *boyhood*).

Determiner. One of the structure-class words, a marker of nouns. Determiners include articles (*a, the*); possessive nouns and pronouns (e.g., *Chuck's, his, my*); demonstrative pronouns (*this, that*); quantifiers (e.g., *many, several*); indefinite pronouns (e.g., *each, every*); and numbers.

Dialect. The shared linguistic features of a group of people, often one from a particular region or of a particular ethnic or social background.

Direct address. See *Vocative.*

Direct object. A nominal slot in the predicate of the transitive sentence patterns. The direct object names the objective or goal or the receiver of the verb's action: "We ate *the peanuts*"; "The boy hit *the ball*"; "I enjoy *playing chess.*"

Do support. The addition of the stand-in auxiliary *do* to a verb string that has no other auxiliary. The question, the negative, and the emphatic transformations all require an auxiliary. *Do* also substitutes for a repeated verb phrase in compound sentences: "Bryan liked the movie, and I *did* too."

Dynamic. Words that exhibit features related to qualities capable of change. Dynamic verbs can combine with the progressive aspect, *be* + *-ing*: "I *am leaving* now"; dynamic adjectives can follow the progressive form of *be*: "He is being *silly.*" See also *Stative.*

Edited American English. The variety of English usage that is widely accepted as the norm for the public writing of school essays, newspapers, magazines, and books. It is sometimes referred to as EAE.

Elliptical clause. A clause in which a part has been left out but is "understood": "Chester is older *than I (am old)*"; "Bev can jog farther *than Otis (can jog)*"; "*When (you are) planning your essay,* be sure to consider the audience."

Emphatic sentence. A statement in which the main stress has been shifted to the auxiliary: "I AM trying." When there is no auxiliary, the stand-in auxiliary *do* is added to carry the stress: "I DO want to go."

End focus. The common rhythm pattern in which the prominent peak of stress falls on or near the final sentence slot.

Exclamatory sentence. A sentence that expresses excitement or emotion. It may include a shift in the word order of a basic sentence that focuses on a complement: "What a beautiful day we're having!" It is characterized by heightened pitch and stress and is usually punctuated with an exclamation point.

Expanded determiner. The determiner, together with pre- and postdeterminers that qualify and quantify and in other ways alter its meaning.

Expletive. A word that enables the writer or speaker to shift the stress in a sentence or to embed one sentence in another: "A fly is in my soup → *There* is a fly in my soup"; "I know *that* he loves me." The expletive is sometimes called an "empty word" because it plays a structural rather than a lexical role.

Flat adverb. A class of adverb that is the same in form as its corresponding adjective: *fast, high, early, late, hard, long,* etc.

Form. The inherent features, the shapes, of words and phrases and clauses, as distinguished from their function in the sentence—characterized in words by prefixes and suffixes, in phrases by headwords and their objects or complements or modifiers, and in clauses by subjects and predicates.

Form classes. The large, open classes of words that provide the lexical content of the language: nouns, verbs, adjectives, and adverbs. Each has characteristic derivational and inflectional morphemes that distinguish its forms. See Chapter 12.

Free modifier. A nonrestrictive, nondefining modifier that is set off by commas and can usually occupy a position at the beginning, at the end, or in the middle of the sentence: "He spoke quietly to the class, *his voice trembling*"; "*Looking pale and nervous,* she stood at the podium"; "New England in the autumn, *because of the brilliant maples and birches,* has become a tourist destination."

Free morpheme. A single morpheme that is also a complete word (in contrast to a bound morpheme, which is not).

Function. The role that a particular structure plays, or the slot that it fills, in a sentence (or in any larger structure). In "The book on the table is mine," "table" functions as the *object of a preposition* in the prepositional phrase "on the table"; the prepositional phrase functions as an *adjectival,* modifying book. The entire noun phrase "the book on the table" functions as the *subject* in its sentence.

Functional shift. The conversion of one word class to another, simply by changing its function: "He *bottled* the wine" (noun to verb); "She *lowered* the curtain" (adjective to verb); "We took a s*wim*" (verb to noun).

Gender. A feature of personal pronouns and certain nouns that distinguishes masculine (*he*), feminine (*she*), and neuter (*it*). Nouns with gender distinctions include *waiter, waitress, actor, actress, girl, boy, man, woman, ewe, ram.*

Genitive case. The Latin term for possessive case.

Gerund. An *-ing* verb functioning as a nominal: "I enjoy *jogging*"; "*Running* is good exercise."

Gerund phrase. A gerund together with all of its complements and modifiers.

Grammatical. Usage that conforms to the rules that native speakers follow or that native speakers would find acceptable in a given situation. See also *Ungrammatical.*

Headword. The word that fills the noun slot in the noun phrase: "the little *boy* across [the *street*]." The verb is the headword of the verb phrase; the preposition is the headword of the prepositional phrase.

Hedging. A metadiscourse signal that helps readers interpret the writer's degree of certainty: *perhaps, possibly, might, seems,* etc.

Helping verb. See *Auxiliary.*

Heteronyms. Words that are spelled the same but differ in both meaning and pronunciation: *bass/bass; wound/wound; Polish/polish.*

Homonyms. Words and morphemes that have the same sound and the same spelling but have different meanings: *saw/saw;* farm*er*/bright*er.*

Homophones. Words that have the same sound, but with both different meanings and different spellings: *sale/sail*; *to/too/two*.

Idiom. A combination of words, a set phrase, whose meaning cannot be predicted from the meaning of the individual words.

Imperative sentence. The sentence in the form of a command. The imperative sentence includes the base form of the verb and usually an understood subject (*you*): "*Eat* your spinach"; "*Finish* your report as soon as possible"; "You *go* on without me."

Indefinite article. The determiner *a*, or *an*, which marks an unspecified count noun. See also *Definite article*.

Indefinite pronoun. A large category that includes quantifiers (e.g., *enough, several, many, much*), universals (*all, both, every, each*), and partitives (*any, either, neither, no, some*). Many of the indefinite pronouns can function as determiners.

Indefinite relative pronoun. The relative pronouns with *-ever* added, which have indefinite referents; they introduce adjectival clauses: "I will give a bonus to *whoever* works the hardest" (i.e., to the person who works the hardest).

Independent clause. The main clause of the sentence; a compound sentence has more than one independent clause.

Indicative mood. The expression of an idea as fact (as opposed to probability). Verb phrases without modal auxiliaries and those with *will* and *shall* are considered the indicative mood: "We *will* go soon"; "We *are going* tomorrow." "When *are* you *going?*" See also *Subjunctive mood* and *Conditional mood*.

Indirect object. The nominal slot following the verb in a Pattern VIII sentence. In a sentence with a verb like *give*, the indirect object is the recipient; the direct object is the thing given: "We gave *our friends* a ride home." The indirect object can be shifted to the slot following the direct object with the preposition *to* or *for*: "Joe gave a message to Kim"; "Sam bought a ticket for his dad."

Infinitive. The base form of the verb (present tense), usually expressed with *to*, which is called the "sign of the infinitive." The infinitive can function adverbially ("I stayed up all night *to study* for the exam"); adjectivally ("That is no way *to study*"); or nominally ("*To stay up* all night is foolish"). The only verb with an infinitive form separate from the present tense is *be*.

Infinitive phrase. The infinitive together with all of its complements and modifiers.

Inflection. See *Inflectional suffix*.

Inflectional suffix. Morphemes that are added to the form classes (nouns, verbs, adjectives, and adverbs) to change their grammatical role in some way. Nouns have two inflectional suffixes (*-s* plural and - *'s* possessive); verbs have four (*-s*, *-ing*, *-ed*, and *-en*); adjectives and some adverbs have two (*-er* and *-est*).

Intensifier. See *Qualifier.*

Intensive pronoun. A pronoun that serves as an appositive to emphasize a noun or pronoun. It is formed by adding *-self* or *-selves* to a personal pronoun: "I *myself* prefer chocolate."

Interjection. A word considered independent of the main sentence, often punctuated with an exclamation point: " *Ouch!* My shoe pinches"; " *Oh!* Is that what you meant?"

Interrogative. One of the structure classes. Sometimes referred to as " *wh-* words," the interrogatives— *where, when, who, what,* and *how*—introduce questions and nominal clauses, filling the roles of nouns, adjectives, and adverbs in their clauses: " *Where* is she going?" "I wonder *who* is going with her."

Interrogative sentence. A sentence that is a question in form: "Are you leaving now?" "When are you leaving?"

Intonation. The rhythmic pattern of a spoken sentence, affected by its stress and pitch and pauses.

Intransitive verb. The verbs of Pattern VI sentences, most of which require no complement to be complete.

Irregular verb. Any verb in which the *-ed* and *-en* forms are not that of the regular verb; in other words, a verb in which the past tense and past participle forms are not simply the addition of *-d*, *-ed*, or *-t* to the base form.

It-cleft. See *Cleft sentence.*

Known-new contract. A common feature of prose in which the known information opens the sentence and the new information occupies the point of main focus at or near the end of the sentence.

Linking verb. The verbs of Patterns IV and V, which require a subject complement to be complete.

Main verb. The verb that fills the last slot in the verb-expansion formula. See also *Predicating verb.*

Manner adverb. An adverb that answers the question of "how" or "in what manner" about the verb. Most manner adverbs are derived from adjectives with the addition of *-ly*: *quickly, merrily, candidly.*

Mass noun. See *Noncountable noun.*

Metadiscourse. Any words that are included in a message beyond the subject of the message itself: such connectors as *for example, finally, in the first place*; attitude markers, such as emphatic words (*clearly, certainly*), hedges (*possibly, perhaps*), and other comments of the author directed to the reader.

Metaphor. A figure of speech in which an attribute is applied to something or someone that is literally untrue but that expresses a sense of connection. When we call Superman *a man of steel,* we are using the term "steel" metaphorically, to attribute the qualities of steel to Superman. Many common expressions are based on metaphor: *the eye of the hurricane, a carpet of grass, a movie that bombed.*

Modal auxiliary. The auxiliary that occupies the opening slot in the verb-expansion rule and may affect what is known as the mood of the verb, conveying probability, possibility, obligation, and the like.

Mood. A quality of the verb denoting fact (indicative), a condition contrary to fact (subjunctive), and probability or possibility (conditional).

Morpheme. A sound or combination of sounds with meaning.

Morphology. The study of morphemes. See Chapter 11.

Nominal. Any structure that functions as a noun phrase normally functions. See Chapter 8.

Nominal clause. A clause that fills a noun phrase (NP) slot.

Nominalization. The process of producing a noun by adding derivational affixes to another word class, commonly a verb: *legalize-legalization; regulate-regulation; friendly-friendliness.*

Nominative case. The Latin term for subjective case.

Noncountable noun. Nouns referring to what might be called an undifferentiated mass—such as *wood, water, sugar, glass*—or an abstraction—*justice, love, indifference.* Whether or not you can use the indefinite article, *a,* is probably the best test of countability: If you can, the noun is countable.

Nonfinite verb phrase. A verb phrase that functions other than as a predicate. Verbs and verb phrases acting as adjectivals, adverbials, and nominals within the sentence are nonfinite.

Nonrestrictive modifier. A modifier in the noun phrase that comments about the noun rather than defines it. Nonrestrictive modifiers following the noun are set off by commas.

Noun. One of the four form classes, whose members fill the headword slot in the noun phrase. Most nouns can be inflected for plural and possessive (*boy, boys, boy's, boys'*). Nouns have characteristic derivational endings, such as *-tion* (*action, compensation*), *-ment* (*contentment*), and *-ness* (*happiness*). Nouns can also function as adjectivals and adverbials (The *neighbor* children went *home*).

Noun clause. See *Nominal clause.*

Noun phrase (NP). The noun headword with all of its attendant pre- and postnoun modifiers.

Number. A feature of nouns and pronouns, referring to singular and plural.

Object complement. The slot following the direct object, filled by an adjectival (Pattern IX) or a nominal (Pattern X). The object complement has two functions: (1) It completes the idea of the verb; and (2) it modifies (if an adjective) or renames (if a nominal) the direct object: "I found the play *exciting*"; "We consider Pete *a good friend.*"

Object of preposition. The nominal slot—usually filled by a noun phrase —that follows the preposition to form a prepositional phrase.

Objective case. The role in a sentence of a noun phrase or pronoun when it functions as an object—direct object, indirect object, object complement, or object of the preposition. Although nouns do not have a special form for objective case, many of the pronouns do; personal pronouns and the relative pronoun *who* have separate forms when they function as objects. See Chapter 14.

Optional slot. The adverbial information that can be added to all the sentence patterns; such information is not required for grammaticality.

Parallel structure. A coordinate structure in which all the coordinate parts are of the same grammatical form.

Participial phrase. A participle together with all of its complements and modifiers.

Participle. The *-ing* and *-en* verb (or verb phrase) functioning as an adjectival or adverbial. See also *Present participle* and *Past participle.*

Particle. A word that combines with a verb to form a phrasal verb: look *up*, look *into*, put *up with*.

Passive voice. A feature of transitive sentences in which the direct object (the objective or goal) is shifted to the subject position and *be* + *-en* is added to the verb. The term *passive* refers to the relationship between the subject and verb: "Ed ate the pizza" → "The pizza *was eaten* by Ed."

Past participle. The *-en* form of the verb.

Past tense. The *-ed* form of the verb, usually denoting a specific past action.

Person. A feature of personal pronouns that distinguishes the speaker or writer (first person), the person or thing spoken to (second person), and the person or thing spoken of (third person).

Personal pronoun. The pronoun that refers to a specific person or thing. In the subjective case the personal pronouns are *I, you, he, she, we, you, they,* and *it.* The personal pronouns have variant forms for objective and possessive case.

Phoneme. The smallest unit of sound that makes a difference in meaning.

Phonology. The study of phonemes.

Phrasal preposition. A preposition consisting of two or more words, a simple preposition preceded by a word from another category, such as an adverb or adjective: *according to, aside from, because of, prior to.*

Phrasal verb. A verb-particle combination that produces a meaning that cannot be predicted from the meaning of the parts: *look up, put up with, make up.*

Phrase. A word or group of words that functions as a unit within the sentence.

Plural. A feature of nouns and pronouns denoting more than one, usually signaled in nouns by the inflectional ending *-s* (or *-es*).

Positive degree. See *Degree.*

Possessive case. The inflected form of nouns (*John's, the dog's*) and pronouns (*my, his, your, her, their,* etc.) usually indicating ownership.

Predicate. One of the two principal parts of the sentence, the comment made about the subject. The predicate includes the verb, together with its complements and modifiers.

Predicate adjective. The adjective that functions as a subject complement.

Predicate nominative. The noun or nominal that functions as a subject complement.

Predicating verb. The function of the verb slot in the sentence patterns, consisting of the main verb together with its auxiliaries. The verb-expansion rule in Chapter 4 accounts for the auxiliary-verb combinations of the predicating verb.

Predicative adjective. The adjective that occupies a complement slot in the sentence as subject complement or object complement.

Prefix. An affix added to the beginning of the word to change its meaning (*un*likely, *il*legal, *pre*scribe, *re*new) or its class (*en*able, *be*little).

Preposition. A structure-class word found in pre-position to—that is, preceding—a nominal. Prepositions can be classed according to their form as simple (*above, at, in, of,* etc.) or phrasal (*according to, instead of,* etc.).

Prepositional phrase. The combination of a preposition and a nominal, which is known as the object of the preposition.

Prescriptive grammar. An approach to teaching grammar, the purpose of which is to prescribe "proper" usage, rather than to describe how the language is actually used. It is sometimes referred to as "linguistic etiquette."

Present participle. The *-ing* form of the verb.

Present tense. The base form and the *-s* form of the verb: *help, helps.* The present tense denotes a present point in time ("I *understand* your position"), a habitual action ("I *jog* five miles a day"), or the "timeless" present ("Shakespeare *helps* us understand ourselves").

Pronoun. A word that substitutes for a noun—or, more accurately, for a nominal—in the sentence.

Pronoun-antecedent agreement. See *Agreement.*

Proper noun. A noun with individual reference to a person, a historical event, or other name. Proper nouns are capitalized.

Qualifier. A structure-class word that qualifies or intensifies an adjective or adverb: "We worked *rather* slowly"; "The work was *very* difficult."

Reciprocal pronoun. The pronouns *each other* and *one another,* which refer to previously named nouns.

Referent. The thing (or person, event, concept, action, etc.)—in other words, the reality—that a word stands for.

Reflexive pronoun. A pronoun formed by adding *-self* or *-selves* to a form of the personal pronoun, used as an object in the sentence to refer to a previously named noun or pronoun: "I gave *myself* a haircut."

Regionalism. A characteristic feature of the pronunciation or structure of the language spoken in a particular region of the country.

Regular verb. A verb in which the *-ed* form (the past tense) and the *-en* form (the past participle) are formed by adding *-ed* (or, in some cases, *-d* or *-t*) to the base. These two forms of a regular verb are always identical. "I *walked* home"; "I have *walked* home every day this week."

Relative adverb. The adverbs *where, when,* and *why,* which introduce adjectival clauses.

Relative clause. A clause introduced by a relative pronoun (*who, which, that*) or a relative adverb (*when, where, why*) that generally modifies a noun. The broad-reference *which* clause functions as a sentence modifier.

Relative pronoun. The pronouns *who* (*whom, whose*), *which,* and *that* in their role as introducers of a relative clause.

Restrictive modifier. A modifier in the noun phrase whose function is to restrict the meaning of the noun. A modifier is restrictive when it is needed to identify the referent of the headword. The restrictive modifier is not set off by commas.

Retained object. The direct object of a Pattern VIII sentence that is retained in its original position when the sentence is transformed into the passive voice: "The judges awarded Mary the prize" → "Mary was awarded *the prize.*"

Sentence. A word or group of words based on one or more subject-predicate, or clause, patterns. The written sentence begins with a capital letter and ends with terminal punctuation—a period, question mark, or an exclamation point.

Sentence modifier. A word or phrase or clause that modifies the sentence as a whole. See Chapter 9.

Sentence patterns. The simple skeletal sentences, made up of two or three or four required elements, that underlie our sentences, even the most complex among them. Ten such patterns will account for almost all the possible sentences of English. See Chapter 3.

Serial comma. The comma that is used before the conjunction in a series: "On our fishing trip to Alaska, we caught salmon, halibut, and the elusive Arctic grayling." Some publications, as a matter of policy, omit the serial comma.

Simple preposition. A one-word preposition. See also *Phrasal preposition.*

Singular. A feature of nouns and pronouns denoting one referent.

Standard English. See *Edited American English.*

Stand-in auxiliary. The auxiliary *do* (*does, did*), which we add to sentences when we transform them into questions, negatives, and emphatic statements when there is no auxiliary in the original.

Stative. Words that exhibit features relating to an unchanging state, in contrast to those that change. Stative verbs do not pattern with the progressive aspect: *"I am *resembling* my mother." Stative adjectives generally do not follow the progressive form of be: *"He is *being* tall." See also *Dynamic.*

Structuralism. An approach to analyzing grammar, associated with mid-twentieth-century linguists, in which the purpose is to describe how the language is actually used in its various dialects, not to prescribe a "correct" version.

Structure classes. The small, closed classes of words that explain the grammatical or structural relationships of the form classes. See Chapter 13.

Subject. The opening slot in the sentence patterns, filled by a noun phrase or other nominal, that functions as the topic of the sentence.

Subject complement. The nominal or adjectival in Pattern II, III, IV, and V sentences following the verb, which renames or modifies the subject. The passive version of a Pattern IX or X sentence will also have a subject complement, the nominal or adjectival that in the active voice functions as the object complement.

Subjective case. The role in the sentence of a noun phrase or a pronoun when it functions as the subject of the sentence. Personal pronouns have distinctive forms for subjective case: *I, he, she, they,* etc.

Subject-verb agreement. See *Agreement.*

Subjunctive mood. An expression of the verb in which the base form, rather than the inflected form, is used (1) in certain *that* clauses conveying strong suggestions or resolutions or commands ("We suggest that Mary *go* with us"; "I move that the meeting *be* adjourned"; "I demand that you *let* us in"), and (2) in the expression of wishes or conditions contrary to fact ("If I *were* you, I'd be careful"; "I wish it *were* summer"). The subjunctive of the verb *be* is expressed by *were* or *be*, even for subjects that normally take *is* or *was*.

Subordinate clause. A dependent clause introduced by a subordinating conjunction, such as *if, since, because*, and *although*.

Subordinating conjunction. See *Subordinator*.

Subordinator. A subordinating conjunction that turns a complete sentence into a subordinate clause and expresses the connection between the subordinate clause and the main clause.

Substantive. A structure that functions as a noun; a nominal.

Suffix. An affix added to the end of a form-class word to change its class (act → act*ion;* laugh → laugh*able*) with derivational suffixes or to change its grammatical function (boy → boy*s;* walk → walk*ing*) with inflectional suffixes. See also *Derivational affix* and *Inflectional suffix*.

Superlative degree. See *Degree*.

Surface structure. A term used by transformational grammarians to designate the sentences of the language as they are spoken and written. See also *Deep structure*.

Syntax. The structure of sentences; the relationship of the parts of the sentence.

Tense. A grammatical feature of verbs and auxiliaries relating to time. Three verb forms indicate tense: the base form and the *-s* form (present) and the *-ed* form (past). Note that "tense" in relation to the modal auxiliaries refers only to form, not to time.

Tensed verb. A verb string that includes T(tense). In contrast, gerunds, infinitives, and participles have no tense marker.

***There* transformation.** A variation of a basic sentence in which the expletive *there* is added at the beginning and the subject is shifted to a position following *be*: "A fly is in my soup" → "There is a fly in my soup."

Third-person singular. The personal pronouns *he, she*, and *it*. The term is also used in reference to the *-s* form of the verb.

Transformational grammar (also called Transformational Generative, or T-G). A theory of grammar that attempts to account for the ability of native speakers to generate and process the sentences of their language.

Transitive verb. The verbs of Patterns VII through X, which require at least one complement, the direct object, to be complete. With only a few exceptions, transitive verbs are those that can be transformed into the passive voice.

Ungrammatical. Usage that does not conform to the rules that native speakers follow. Usage that varies from one dialect or speech community to another is not necessarily ungrammatical. "I ain't coming" is an unacceptable usage to many, although it follows the "rules." However, it is not part of the prestige, or standard, dialect and would be inappropriate in most formal and business situations. See also *Grammatical* and *Edited American English.*

Verb. One of the four form classes, traditionally thought of as the action word in the sentence. A better way to recognize the verb, however, is by its form, its *-s* and *-ing* endings. Verbs also have an *-ed* and an *-en* form, although in the case of some irregular verbs these forms are not readily apparent. And every verb, without exception, can be marked by auxiliaries. Many verbs also have characteristic derivational forms, such as *-ify* (*typify*), *-ize* (*criticize*), and *-ate* (*activate*).

Verb phrase (VP). A verb together with its complements and modifiers; the predicate of the sentence is a verb phrase. See also *Gerund phrase, Infinitive phrase,* and *Participial phrase.*

Verb-expansion rule. The formula that describes our system for expanding the verb with auxiliaries to express variations in meaning. See Chapter 4.

Vocative. The noun or noun phrase of direct address, considered a sentence modifier: *"Mike,* is that you?"

***What*-cleft.** See *Cleft sentence.*

***Wh*-question.** A question that is introduced by an interrogative, such as *who, which, when, where, why,* or *how,* that asks for information of content, in contrast to a yes/no question.

Yes/no interrogative. The words *if* and *whether* (*or not*) that introduce nominal clauses that ask or suggest a *yes/no* question: "I wonder *if Kim is coming*"; "I wonder *whether or not she's coming."*

Yes/no question. A question that calls for a *yes* or *no* response. It is characterized by the opening auxiliary, in contrast to the interrogative that opens the *wh*-question: *"Are* you being served?" *"Did* the Orioles win?"

Appendix:
Sentence Diagramming

Our use of sentence diagramming to teach grammar reflects the purpose described by Alonzo Reed and Brainerd Kellogg, who created this system of illustrating sentences well over a century ago: "to picture the complete analysis of the sentence, with principal and subordinate parts in their proper relation" (p. vi).[1]

We would extend that statement of purpose to emphasize the role of a visual method for helping students recognize and differentiate the sentence patterns as well. We believe that the sentence patterns, introduced in Chapter 3, provide a practical framework for organizing the details of clauses, along with their modification and subordination and coordination.

Reed and Kellogg acknowledge the criticism that diagramming alters the order of sentence parts. They maintain, however—and we agree—that this alternation "is a merit, for it teaches the pupil to look through the literary order and discover the logical order" (p. vii). We also agree that engaging in "the logical analysis of the sentence ... is to learn to think" (p. v).

We would add that, in conjunction with diagramming, the sentence patterns provide an organized set of tools for thinking. The ten diagrams on page 59 make clear the basic structure of the patterns, as well as their similarities and differences. For example, there is only one pattern, the intransitive Pattern VI, in which the predicate requires no structure beyond the verb; the diagrams also clarify that only transitive patterns include the vertical line that identifies a direct object; and the slanted lines in Patterns II and III explain why *be* qualifies as a linking verb.

When you can see so clearly that it's the verb that determines the sentence pattern, you can then understand—and visualize—that the same features apply when the verb form is no longer that of predicating verb, when it functions as a modifier or a nominal within another clause.

---

[1] Alonzo Reed and Brainerd Kellogg, *Higher Lessons in English* (New York: Maynard, Merrill & Co., 1902.) Between 1877 and 1913, 25 editions were published.

Throughout the text we have included diagrams to illustrate the various sentence expansions. You will find them listed in the Index under the name of the structure. We are including in this Appendix a few diagrams for structures not covered in the book. However, we do not assume that every sentence is amenable to diagramming. And we would also note that many teachers using the text consider diagrams optional for their students; the sentence patterns and their formulas can easily be understood without them.

VARIATIONS FROM REED & KELLOGG

1. One major change from the R&K system occurs in Patterns IX and X, the two transitive patterns that include object complements. The R&K diagram locates the object complement between the verb and the direct object:

$$ \mathrm{S} \mid \mathrm{V} \diagup \mathrm{OC} \mid \mathrm{DO} $$

They explain that the line separating the verb from the object complement slants toward the OC to show that the complement belongs to the object. In our version, too, the OC line slants toward the object, but our diagram also maintains the linear order of the sentence:

$$ \mathrm{S} \mid \mathrm{V} \mid \mathrm{DO} \diagdown \mathrm{OC} $$

This version also illustrates that the connection between the direct object and its complement is similar to the connection between the subject and the subject complement in linking verbs.

2. Another difference, fairly minor, concerns the line that connects a subordinate clause with the main clause. We show it as a dotted line; the R&K system uses a line that is half solid and half dotted when the word expresses both an adverbial and a connective purpose, such as *when, where, after*, etc.; we make no distinction based on meaning.

EXCEPTIONS TO R&K DIAGRAMS

Not all structures are amenable to diagramming. One example is the noun phrase in which the headword has an expanded determiner, as discussed on pages 272–273:

> *All of the **cookies** are gone.*

In this sentence, *cookies* is the headword, preceded by an expanded determiner. However, the traditional diagram would show *All* as the headword:

In this case, a tree diagram would make the relationship clear:

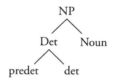

ADDITIONAL DIAGRAMS

In the diagram of the **noun phrase**, no matter where in the sentence it appears and no matter how many modifiers it includes, the headword is on a horizontal line with the determiner, adjective(s), and modifying noun(s) slanting down from it:[2]

---

[2] The relationship of prenoun modifiers is not always represented accurately by the diagram. For example, the first diagram does not indicate that *new* modifies *kitchen table*, not just *table*; in the second example, the adjective *important* modifies *career decision*, not just *decision*.

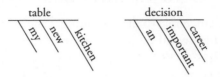

When the modifiers themselves have modifiers, either qualifiers or other nouns, the diagram will make that clear:

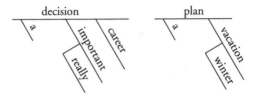

When the determiner is a possessive noun, it may have a determiner of its own: my daughter's car, the car's electrical system:

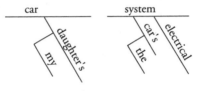

As the diagrams illustrate, the whole phrases "my daughter" and "the car" have been made possessive. You can show that *my daughter's* and *the car's* constitute a single modifier of the headword by substituting a possessive pronoun: *her* car, *its* electrical system.

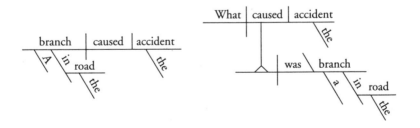

In Chapter 5 we saw the ***what-*cleft**, a way of changing sentence focus; the result is a nominal clause, like those you saw in Chapter 8:

A branch in the road caused ⟶ What caused the accident was
the accident.   a branch in the road.

Elliptical **clauses of comparison** were discussed in the chapter on Sentence Modifiers (page 200–202):

I'm a year older than my sister.

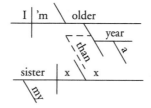

My roommate studies harder than I do.

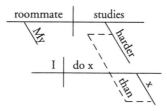

Some elliptical sentences we saw were ambiguous:

The Packers beat the Patriots worse than the Panthers.

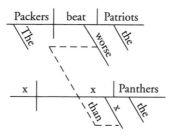

Answers to the Exercises

CHAPTER 2

Exercise 1, page 22

   1. The students   their long trip
      d   H   d   H

   2. our new neighbors   the hall   our best friends
      d   H   d H   d   H

   3. Mickey's roommate   the library   every evening
      d   H   d H   d   H

   4. A huge crowd   the streets   the big parade
      d   H   d H   d   H

   5. This new lasagna recipe   an enormous crowd
      d   H   d   H

   6. Jessica   her new boyfriend   some cookies
      H   d   H   d   H

Exercise 2, page 24

   1. They   2. He   3. She   4. They   5. They   6. It

Exercise 3, page 29

   1. adv   2. adv   3. adj, adv   4. adj   5. adv

CHAPTER 3

Exercise 4, page 38

1. Brian's problem | is | serious. (II)
    NP   be   adj
    subj   pred   subj comp
              vb

2. The workers | are | on the roof. (I)
    NP   be   prep phr
    subj   pred   ADV/TP
           vb

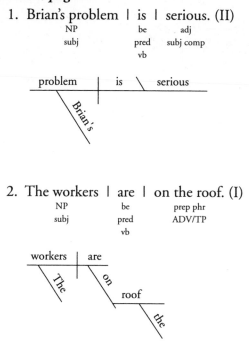

3. The excitement of the fans | is | really contagious. (II)
    NP   be   adj
    subj   pred   subj comp
          vb

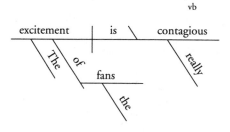

4. Brevity | is | the soul of wit. (III)

    NP₁ ... be ... NP₁
    subj ... pred ... subj comp
    ... vb

5. The final exam | was | at four o'clock. (I)

    NP ... be ... prep phr
    subj ... pred vb ... ADV/TP

6. The kids | are | very silly. (II)

    NP ... be ... adj
    subj ... pred vb ... subj comp

7. The Bunkers | were | noisy neighbors. (III)

    NP₁ ... be ... NP₁
    subj ... pred vb ... subj comp

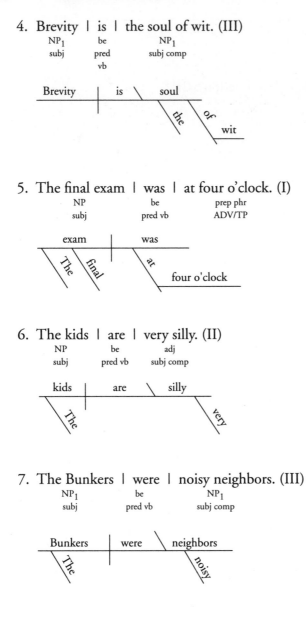

8. Those joggers | are | out of shape. (II)

       NP   be   prep phr
      subj   pred   subj comp
                vb

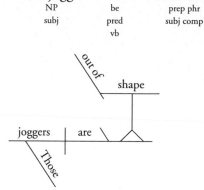

9. The basketball team | is | on a roll. (II)

       NP   be   prep phr
      subj   pred   subj comp
                vb

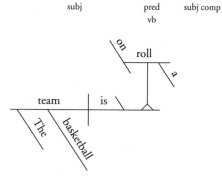

10. A foolish consistency | is | the hobgoblin of little minds. (III)

     NP$_1$ be   NP$_1$
     subj   pred   subj comp
                vb

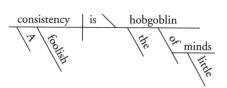

Exercise 5, page 40

1. The baby | looks | healthy. (IV)

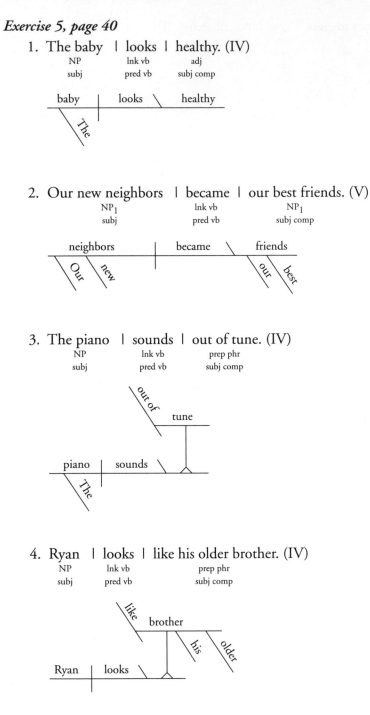

2. Our new neighbors | became | our best friends. (V)

3. The piano | sounds | out of tune. (IV)

4. Ryan | looks | like his older brother. (IV)

5. You | look | a mess! (V)
   pro   lnk vb   NP₁
   subj   pred vb subj comp
  (NP₁)

6. That spaghetti | smells | wonderful. (IV)
     NP   lnk vb   adj
     subj   pred vb   subj comp

7. Your idea | seems | sensible. (IV)
    NP   lnk vb   adj
    subj   pred vb subj comp

idea | seems \ sensible
Your

8. Cyberspace | remains | a complete mystery. (V)
    NP₁   lnk vb   NP₁
    subj   pred vb   subj comp

Cyberspace | remains \ mystery
a \ complete

9. The monkeys | acted | silly. (IV)
    NP   lnk vb   adj
    subj   pred vb subj comp

10. The discussion | was | over my head. (II)

NP   be   prep phr

subj   pred vb   subj comp

Exercise 6, page 43

1. The rug in the dining room is dirty.   (II)

      adj

2. On sunny days we lounge on the lawn between classes.   (VI)

   adv   adv   adv

3. The break between classes seems very short on sunny days.   (IV)

       adj   adv

4. At the diner on Water Street, we chatted aimlessly until midnight.   (VI)

        adj   adv

      adv

5. Daylilies grow wild in our backyard.   (VI—or, perhaps, IV)

         adv

6. In 1638 a young philanthropist of Puritan background became the

  adv   adj

founder of the oldest university in the U.S.   (V)

                       adj

        adj

7. The name of that young man was John Harvard.   (III)

        adj

8. My cousin <u>from Iowa City</u> works for a family <u>with seven children</u>.   (VI)

Exercise 7, page 45

1.

2.

3.

4.

5.

6.
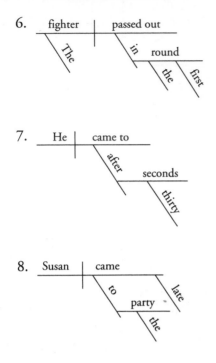

7.

8.

Exercise 8, page 48

1. The boys | prepared | a terrific spaghetti dinner. (VII)
   NP₁   tr vb   NP₂
   subj   pred vb   dir obj

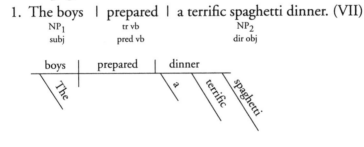

2. An old jalopy | turned | into our driveway. (VI)
   NP   int vb   prep phr
   subj   pred vb   opt ADV

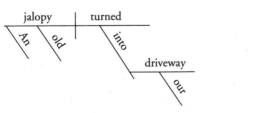

3. The ugly duckling | turned into | a beautiful swan. (V)

      NP₁ — lnk vb — NP₁

      subj — pred vb — subj comp

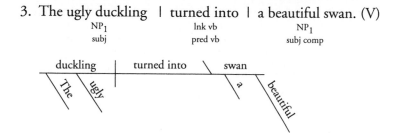

4. The fog | comes | on little cat feet. (VI)

    NP — int vb — prep phr

    subj — pred vb — opt ADV

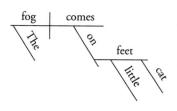

5. On Sundays | the neighbor across the hall | walks | his dog |

    prep phr — NP₁ — tr vb — NP₂

    opt ADV — subj — pred vb — dir obj

  at 6:00 A.M. (VII)

    prep phr

    opt ADV

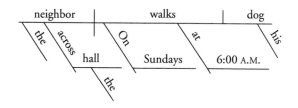

6. Betsy | often | jogs | with her dog. (VI)

   NP — adv — int vb — prep phr

   subj — opt ADV — pred vb — opt ADV

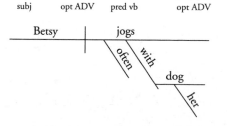

7. After two months | the teachers | called off | their strike. (VII)
    prep phr   NP₁   tr vb   NP₂
    opt ADV   subj   pred vb   dir obj

8. The whole gang | reminisced | at our class reunion |
    NP   int vb   prep phr
    subj   pred vb   opt ADV

    about the good old days. (VI)
    prep phr
    opt ADV

9. My best friend from high school | arrived | on Friday |
    NP   int vb   prep phr
    subj   pred vb   opt ADV

    for the weekend. (VI)
    prep phr
    opt ADV

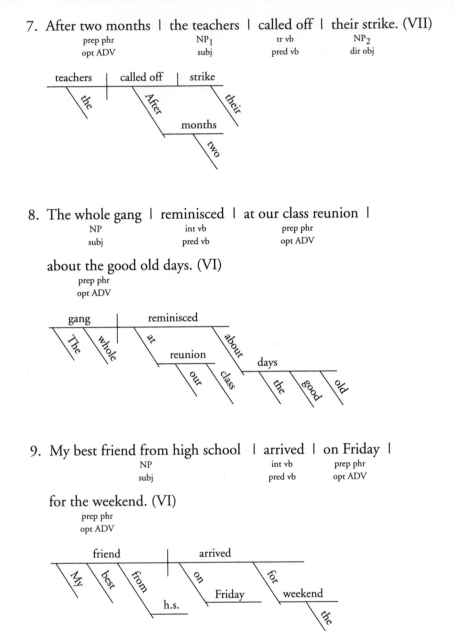

10. The mass of men | lead | lives of quiet desperation. (VII)

       NP₁   tr vb   NP₂
       subj   pred vb   dir obj

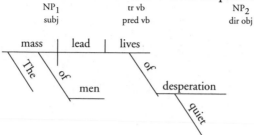

Exercise 9, page 50

1. Jessica | made | her new boyfriend | some cookies. (VIII)

    NP₁   tr vb   NP₂   NP₃
    subj   pred vb   ind obj   dir obj

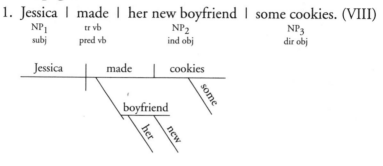

2. I | made | an A | on my research paper. (VII)

   pro   tr vb   NP₂   prep phr
   subj   pred vb   dir obj   opt ADV
   (NP₁)

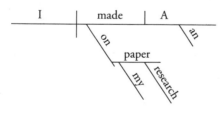

3. For lunch | Manny | made | himself | a humongous sandwich. (VIII)

   prep phr   NP₁   tr vb   pro   NP₃
   opt ADV   subj   pred vb   ind obj   dir obj
                                (NP₂)

4. The kids | made up | a story about Pokemon monsters. (VII)

   NP₁   tr vb   NP₂

   subj   pred vb   dir obj

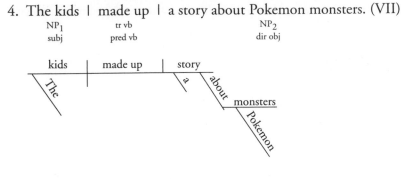

5. The teacher | wrote | a lot of comments | in the margins. (VII)

   NP₁   tr vb   NP₂   prep phr

   subj   pred vb   dir obj   opt ADV

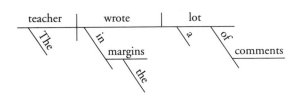

6. My advisor | wrote | a letter of recommendation | for me. (VIII)

   NP₁   tr vb   NP₂   prep phr

   subj   pred vb   dir obj   ind obj

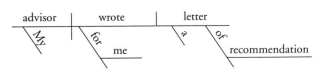

7. I | wrote down | the assignment | very carefully. (VII)

   pro   tr vb   NP₂   adv phr

   subj   pred vb   dir obj   opt ADV

   (NP₁)

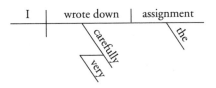

8. My roommate | always | writes | in her diary | after dinner. (VI)

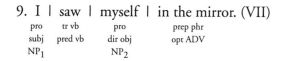

NP   adv   intr vb   prep phr   prep phr

subj   opt ADV   pred vb   opt ADV   opt ADV

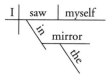

9. I | saw | myself | in the mirror. (VII)

pro   tr vb   pro   prep phr

subj   pred vb   dir obj   opt ADV

NP_1 NP_2

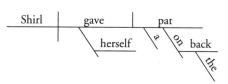

10. Shirl | gave | herself | a pat on the back. (VIII)

NP_1 tr vb   pro NP_3

subj   pred vb   indir obj   direct obj

                          NP_2

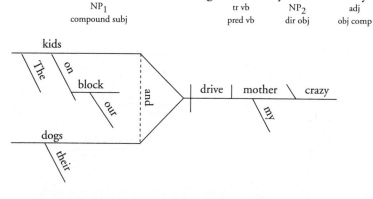

Exercise 10, page 54

1. The kids on our block and their dogs | drive | my mother | crazy. (IX)

             NP_1 tr vb NP_2 adj

       compound subj   pred vb   dir obj   obj comp

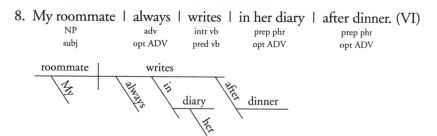

2. She | calls | them | a menace to the neighborhood. (X)

pro	tr vb	pro		NP$_2$
subj	pred vb	dir obj		obj comp
(NP$_1$)		(NP$_2$)		

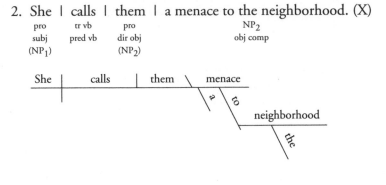

3. On Friday | the weather | suddenly | turned | cold and blustery. (IV)

| prep phr | NP | adv | lnk vb | compound adj |
| opt ADV | subj | opt ADV | pred vb | subj comp |

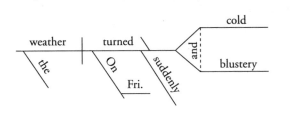

4. Yesterday | Luis | bought | himself | an expensive leather coat |

adv	NP$_1$	tr vb	pro	NP$_3$
opt ADV	subj	pred vb	ind obj	dir obj
			(NP$_2$)	

at Nordstrom. (VIII)

prep phr
opt ADV

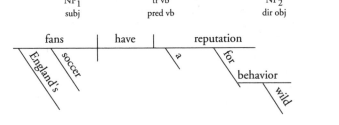

5. England's soccer fans | have | a reputation for wild behavior. (VII)

| NP$_1$ | tr vb | NP$_2$ |
| subj | pred vb | dir obj |

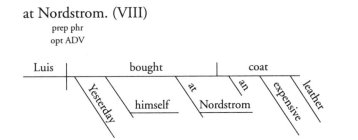

6. My boss at the pizza parlor | promised | me | a raise. (VIII)

              NP₁   tr vb   pro   NP₃

              subj   pred vb   ind obj   dir obj

                                              (NP₂)

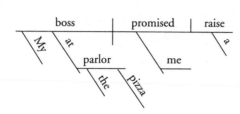

7. Hector's party | broke up | at midnight. (VI)

           NP   int vb   prep phr

          subj   pred vb   opt ADV

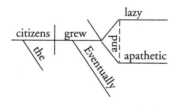

8. Eventually | the citizens | grew | lazy and apathetic. (IV)

      opt ADV   NP   lnk vb   compound adj

        adv   subj   pred vb   sub comp

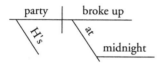

9. Joe | cut | himself | a huge piece of cake. (VIII)

     NP₁   tr vb   pro   NP₃

     subj   pred vb   ind obj   dir obj

                    (NP₂)

10. Alaska | became | the forty-ninth state | in 1959. (V)
     NP₁   lnk vb   NP₁   prep phr
     subj   pred vb   subj comp   opt ADV

11. According to the latest census, | Wyoming | is |
     prep phr   NP₁   be
     opt ADV   subj   pred vb

our least populous state. (III)
     NP₁
     subj comp

12. Some people | consider | Minnesota's winters | excessively long. (IX)
     NP₁   tr vb   NP₂   adj phr
     subj   pred vb   dir obj   obj comp

13. Our team | plays | Indiana | in the HIT | on Saturday night. (VII)
     NP₁   tr vb   NP₂   prep phr   prep phr
     subj   pred vb   dir obj   opt ADV   opt ADV

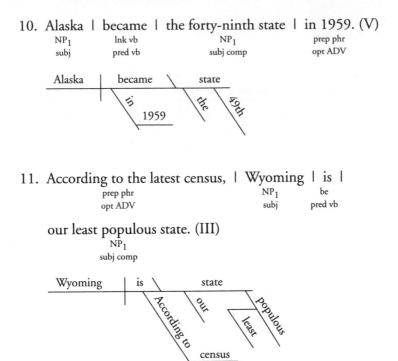

14. I | ordered | you | a large Coke and a cheeseburger with onions. (VIII)

pro   tr vb   pro   NP₃

subj   pred vb ind obj   compound dir obj

(NP₁)   (NP₂)

15. Emily | selected | peach and lavender |

NP₁   tr vb   compound NP₂

subj   pred vb   dir obj

as the color scheme for her wedding. (X)

NP₂

obj comp

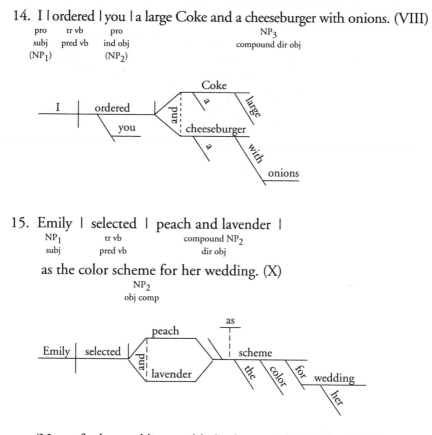

(Note: *for her wedding* could also be considered adverbial.)

CHAPTER 4

Exercise 11, page 69

1. have	has	had	having	had
2. do	does	did	doing	done
3. say	says	said	saying	said
4. make	makes	made	making	made
5. go	goes	went	going	gone
6. take	takes	took	taking	taken
7. come	comes	came	coming	come
8. see	sees	saw	seeing	seen
9. get	gets	got	getting	got, gotten
10. move	moves	moved	moving	moved

11. prove	proves	proved	proving	proved, proven
12. put	puts	put	putting	put
13. think	thinks	thought	thinking	thought
14. beat	beats	beat	beating	beat, beaten
15. meet	meets	met	meeting	met

Exercise 12, page 75

A.

1. has worked
2. was working
3. will be playing
4. was being
5. is having

6. should have had
7. had had
8. could have been
9. may have been trying
10. might have been being

B.

1. past + be + -ing + study
2. pres + have + -en + find
3. past + lose
4. pres + have + -en + be + -ing + skip
5. past + can + be
6. past + crash
7. pres + seem
8. pres + will + be + -ing + have
9. pres + may + be + -ing + graduate
10. past + shall + have + -en + study

CHAPTER 5

Exercise 13, page 93

1. The Emancipation Proclamation was signed by President Lincoln in 1862.
2. Several sensational news stories have been published by the campus paper this semester.
3. A run-off election will be held in two weeks.
4. The victim's remains were found in the woods by volunteer searchers.
5. The suspect is being kept in solitary confinement.

6. A new tax collection system will be discussed by the county commissioners at their next meeting.
7. I am pleased by your positive attitude.
8. Bill was being teased about his new mustache by his fraternity brothers.
9. Your room should be cleaned at least once a week.
10. Power lines have been knocked down by heavy thunderstorms in three counties.

Exercise 14, page 96

1. *No Country for Old Men* was given rave reviews by many critics.
2. Some citizens are made nervous by certain parts of the Patriot Act.
3. The third graders are being given too much homework.
4. Three finalists have been chosen for the science award.
5. The staircase walls have been turned into an art museum by these colorful murals.
6. Roger Federer is often referred to as the greatest tennis player of all time.
7. Our kitchen cupboards should be painted bright red.
8. Some of our most intricate fugues were composed by Bach.

Exercise 15, page 97

1. The cheerleading squad led the football team onto the field. (VII)
2. A committee chooses the cheerleaders in the spring. (VII)
3. The managing editor had warned the new reporters about late submissions. (VII)
4. Someone has burglarized several apartments in our building recently. (VII)
5. Someone stole our neighbor's new computer last weekend. (VII)
6. Someone manufactured dental floss for the first time in 1882. (VII)
7. People in financial circles are talking about the possibility of recession. (VII)
8. The bank must have granted Gabrielle an extension on her loan payment. (VIII)
9. The critics called the play a smashing success. (X)
10. Someone has rendered the poison harmless. (IX)

Exercise 16, page 102

1. expletive (VII)
2. adverb (I)
3. expletive (I)
4. expletive (I)
5. adverb (I)
6. adverb (VI)
7. expletive (I)
8. adverb (VI)

CHAPTER 6

Exercise 17, page 117

5. (VII)

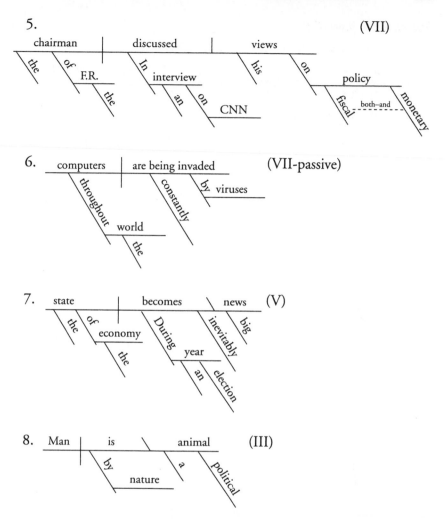

6. computers | are being invaded (VII-passive)

7. state | becomes \ news (V)

8. Man | is \ animal (III)

Exercise 18, page 118

1. I'm going to wax the car parked in the garage.
   I'm going into the garage to wax the car.

2. We watched the game from the porch.
   We watched the game being played on the porch.

3. Fred tripped his teammate who was holding the bat.
   Fred stuck the bat out and tripped his teammate.

4. Susan washed the stones she found in the riverbed.
   Susan went to the river to wash the stones she found.

Exercise 19, page 120

1. Pete is working <u>nights</u> <u>this week</u>. (VI)
    N   NP

2. I was awake <u>the whole night</u>. (II)
    NP

3. I'll see you <u>soon</u>. (VII)
    adv

4. <u>This morning</u> Pam threw away the leftover spaghetti. (VII)
    NP

5. George will do dishes <u>next time</u>. (VII)
    NP

6. I love weekends. (VII)

7. Bill works <u>weekends</u>. (VI)
    N

8. <u>At the first sign of winter</u> the birds flew <u>south</u>. (VI)
    prep phr   adv

Exercise 20, page 123

1. Our cat <u>often</u> jumps <u>up</u> <u>on the roof</u> <u>to reach the attic window</u>.
   (main clause: VI; infinitive: VII)

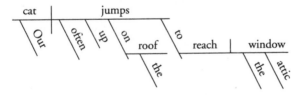

2. <u>Sometimes</u> she <u>even</u> climbs the ladder <u>to get there</u>. (main clause:
   VII; infinitive: VI)

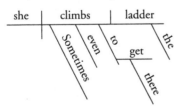

3. <u>Last night</u> my computer blinked <u>ominously</u> <u>during an</u> <u>electrical storm</u>. (VI)

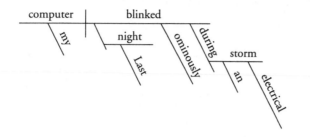

4. I <u>immediately</u> turned it off. (VII)

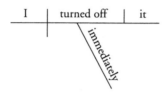

5. We went <u>to the mall</u> <u>last Saturday</u> <u>to check out the big sales</u>. (main clause: VI; infinitive: VII)

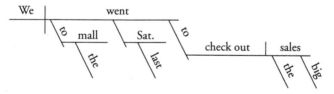

6. <u>Afterwards</u> we stayed <u>home</u> <u>to watch the playoff game with Uncle</u> <u>Dick</u>. (main clause: VI; infinitive: VII)

Exercise 21, page 125

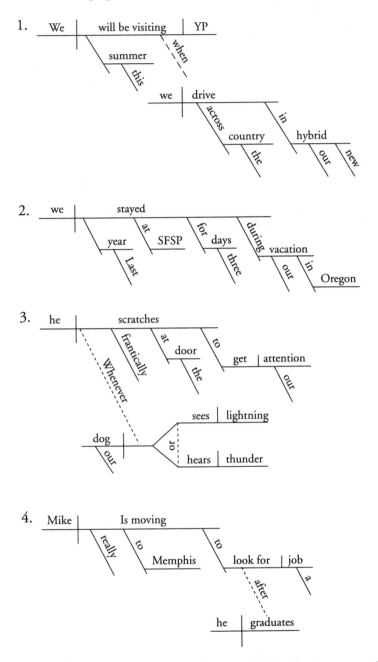

(Note: The adverbial clause could also be interpreted as a modifier of the main verb.)

5.

6.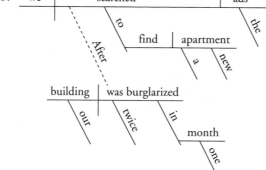

CHAPTER 7

Exercise 22, page 138

A. 1. <u>a</u> highly successful land <u>speculator</u>
      (D)   (qualified adj)   (n)   (H)

   2. <u>today's</u> <u>standards</u>
       (D)   (H)

   3. <u>his</u> entire <u>fortune</u>
       (D)   (adj)   (H)

   4. <u>This</u> financial <u>disaster</u>
       (D)   (adj)   (H)

   5. <u>a</u> local <u>newspaper</u>
       (D) (adj)   (H)

   6. <u>their</u> newly discovered <u>eccentric</u>
       (D)   (modified part)   (H)

   7. <u>an</u> old blue military <u>uniform</u>
       (D) (adj) (adj)   (adj)   (H)

   8. <u>every</u> public <u>function</u> and <u>meeting</u>
       (D)   (adj)   (H)   (H)

9. <u>a</u> large upholstered <u>chair</u>
   (D) (adj)   (part)   (H)

10. <u>the</u> state <u>legislature</u>
    (D)   (n)   (H)

11. <u>his</u> own imperial <u>bonds</u>
    (D)   (adj)   (adj)   (H)

12. <u>each</u> <u>note</u>
    (D)   (H)

13. <u>the</u> face <u>value</u>
    (D)   (n)   (H)

14. <u>a</u> scientific <u>conference</u>
    (D)   (adj)   (H)

15. <u>His</u> lavish <u>funeral</u>
    (D)   (adj)   (H)

B. 1. <u>The</u> department's personnel <u>committee</u>
       (D)   (n)   (H)

       <u>the</u> main <u>office</u>   <u>this</u> <u>morning</u>
       (D)   (adj) (H)   (D)   (H)

    2. <u>Our</u> whole <u>family</u>   <u>the</u> new Sunday brunch <u>menu</u>   <u>the</u> <u>cafeteria</u>
       (D)   (adj)   (H)   (D)   (adj)   (n)   (n)   (H)   (D)   (H)

    3. <u>Serena's</u> <u>daughter</u>   <u>an</u> expensive-looking copper-colored <u>bracelet</u>
       (D)   (H)   (D)   (adj)   (part)   (n)   (part)   (H)

       <u>the</u> subway <u>station</u>
       (D)   (n)   (H)

    4. <u>The</u> bicycle-safety <u>commission</u>   <u>the</u> new <u>regulations</u>
       (D)   (n)   (n)   (H)   (D)   (adj)   (H)

       <u>their</u> regular <u>meeting</u>   <u>this</u> <u>noon</u>
       (D)   (adj)   (H)   (D)   (H)

    5. <u>Her</u> lovely, gracious <u>manner</u>   <u>the</u> <u>start</u>
       (D)   (adj)   (adj)   (H)   (D)   (H)

    6. <u>Any</u> <u>mother</u>   <u>the</u> <u>job</u>   <u>several</u> air-traffic <u>controllers</u>
       (D)   (H)   (D)   (H)   (D)   (n)   (n)   (H)

    7. <u>The</u> rising interest <u>rates</u>   <u>a</u> serious <u>concern</u>
       (D)   (part)   (n)   (H)   (D)   (adj)   (H)

       <u>every</u> cost-conscious <u>citizen</u>
       (D)   (n)   (adj)   (H)

Exercise 23, page 141

1. <u>with a cast on his left foot</u>

2. <u>of the museum</u> (*near the visitors' information booth* could modify either *museum* or *meet*)

3. <u>after the game</u> (*at Bob's house* could modify either *party* or *game*)

4. <u>of computer viruses</u>

5. <u>from within</u>

6. <u>for my science course</u>, <u>from Stanford</u>

7. (*of any size* could modify either *loans* or *businesses*)

8. <u>with the weakest qualifications</u>, <u>about the selection process</u>

Exercise 24, page 144

1. <u>that doesn't bite</u>; modifies *rattlesnake; that* = subj; VI

2. <u>who plays alone</u>; modifies *A person; who* = subj; VI

3. <u>that the jazz club is sponsoring</u>; modifies *concert; that* = dir obj; VII

4. <u>[that] she gave the bride and groom</u>; modifies *gift; [that]* = dir obj; VIII

5. <u>whose virtues . . . discovered</u>; modifies *plant; whose* = det; VII (passive)

6. <u>who have everything but good sense</u>; modifies *kids; who* = subj; VII

7. <u>whom she had not seen in years</u>; modifies *people; whom* = dir obj; VII

8. <u>in which the connection . . . explained</u>; modifies *article; which* = obj of prep; VII (passive)

9. <u>which was damp and drafty</u>; modifies *shed; which* = subj; II

10. <u>that killed the rat</u>; modifies *cat; that* = subj; VII
    <u>that ate the malt</u>; modifies *rat; that* = subj; VII
    <u>that lay in the house</u>; modifies *malt; that* = subj; VI
    <u>that Jack built</u>; modifies *house; that* = dir obj; VII

Exercise 25, page 148

Here are some possibilities; you will think of others.

1. Bill owns <u>that expensive sports car standing in the driveway</u>. (Note that the indefinite *an* becomes definite with *that*.)

2. I am babysitting for <u>the baby sleeping upstairs in the crib</u>.

3. Some of <u>the fans lining up at the ticket office</u> will probably be disappointed.

4. <u>The students searching the Internet</u> want to find material for their research projects.

5. The defense could not stop <u>the fullback charging through the line</u>.

6. <u>The teachers walking the picket line</u> have been on strike for eight days.

Exercise 26, page 151

1. The award <u>given every year to the outstanding volunteer</u> has
(VIII passive)
been announced.

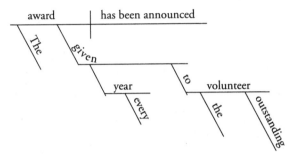

2. <u>Being a philosopher</u>, she can propose a problem for every solution.
(III)

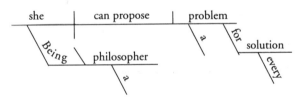

3. He has all the gall of a shoplifter <u>returning an item for a refund</u>.
(VII)

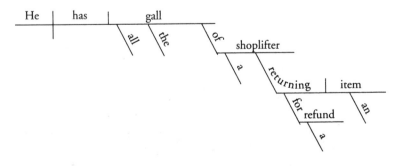

4. The hostess gave the <u>departing</u> guests some leftover food for
(VI)

their pets.

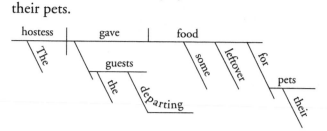

(The prepostional phrase could also be interpreted as adverbial.)

5. <u>Finding the price reasonable</u>, they rented the apartment on the spot.
(IX)

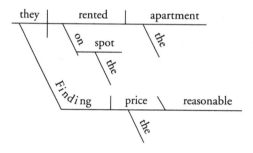

6. Congress shall make no law <u>abridging the freedom of speech or</u>
(VII)

<u>of the press</u>.

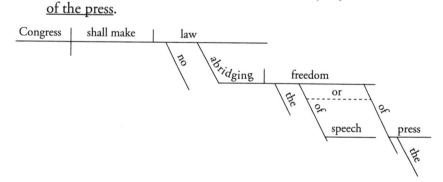

7. They planned the class picnic for Saturday, <u>hoping for good weather</u>.
   (VI)

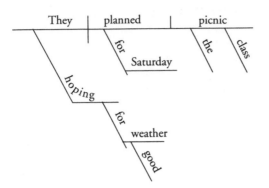

8. The university will not fund research <u>involving genetic manipulation</u>.
   (VII)

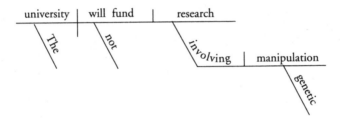

9. The special computer workshops <u>held on campus last weekend</u>
   (VII passive)
   were designed for students <u>majoring in business</u>.
   (VI)

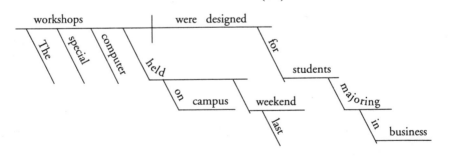

10. The teachers' union has finally approved the last two <u>disputed</u>
                                                    (VII passive)
      sections of the contract <u>offered by the school district</u>.
                                            (VII passive)

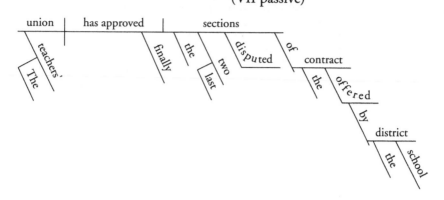

Exercise 27, page 153

Here are some possibilities; you will probably think of others.

1. Because the house needed considerable repair, my parents were able to buy it for little money.

2. When installing a new program, you should turn off all other applications.

3. Having misunderstood the assignment, I got a low grade on my paper.

4. The archeologists could not decipher the inscription, which was covered with the grime of centuries.

5. The bus left without the woman who was still searching for change in her purse.

6. The patient spent four hours on the operating table while doctors performed a double bypass on her (or his) severely blocked arteries.

7. Once considered only an average player, Chris has greatly improved his game in the last three months.

8. The dean of men surprised several members of the football team as they were breaking in through the window of the girls' dormitory.

9. I'll eat anything that's pickled.

10. Seen from miles away, the mountain might be mistaken for a cloud.

Exercise 28, page 157

1. Samuel Johnson, who published his famous dictionary in 1755, defined . . .
2. The town where I was born, which has a population of 3,000, offers . . .
3. standing . . . window—*restrictive*, no comma
4. Naphtha, which is highly flammable, is . . .
5. that are . . . employees—*restrictive*, no comma
6. printed before 1501—*restrictive*, no comma; . . . is called an incunabulum, which literally means "swaddling clothes."
7. bearing down on Florida—*restrictive*, no commas; who live . . . coast—*restrictive*, no comma
8. who . . . sing—*restrictive*, no comma
9. who are . . . foolish—*restrictive*, no comma
10. Derek Jeter, leaping high in the air, speared . . .; that would . . . game—*restrictive*, no comma

Exercise 29, page 160

1. in which players . . . target (relative clause)
2. which originated . . . Netherlands (relative clause); of bowling and shuffleboard (prep phrase); of billiards and chess (prep phrase)
3. that is 42 . . . wide (relative clause); of four players to a side (prep phrase); to a side (prep phrase)
4. that is . . . away (relative clause)
5. called Blue Hone (participial phrase); which is . . . resiliency (relative clause)
6. of the wrist (prep phrase); imparting . . . named (participial phrase); for which . . . named (relative clause)
7. on a team (prep phrase); to knock . . . bounds (infinitive phrase)
8. of curling equipment (prep phrase); used by players . . . stone (participial phrase); of a teammate's stone (prep phrase)
9. whose stones . . . target (relative clause); of the target (prep phrase); that is closer (relative clause)
10. where there are . . . circuit (relative clause); who play . . . circuit (relative clause)

CHAPTER 8

Exercise 30, page 170

1. <u>simple ballads sung to guitar music</u>
2. <u>son of the legendary songwriter Woody Guthrie</u>
3. <u>An offbeat film about illegal trash dumping</u>
4. <u>the search for personal freedom</u>
5. <u>a contemporary folk singer and songwriter;</u> *<u>Soul Journey</u>* <u>and</u> *<u>Time (The Revelator)</u>*
6. <u>Casey</u>

Exercise 31, page 174

A.
1. Flying a supersonic jet—VII, subject; main clause: III
2. playing practical jokes on his players—VII, direct object; main clause: VII
3. telling a few jokes—VII, object of preposition; main clause: VI
4. staying awake in my eight o'clock class—IV, subject complement; main clause: III
5. Leaving the scene of the accident—VII, subject; main clause: III
6. seeing the suspect near the entrance of the bank—VII, direct object; main clause: VII
7. winning eight gold medals at the Beijing Olympics—VII, appositive; main clause: VI
8. swimming . . . day—VI, object of preposition; main clause: VI
9. going to college—VI, object of preposition; main clause: VI
10. Thinking a problem through—VII, subject; main clause: VII

1.

2.

3.

4.

5.

6.

7.

8.

9.

10.

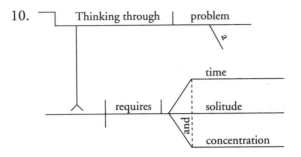

B. Here are some possibilities; you will probably think of others.

Taking grammar tests makes some people nervous. (subj)

Other people like taking grammar tests. (direct obj)

Being punctual is a rare virtue. (subj)

My father has pointed out to me the advantages of being punctual. (obj of prep)

Giving people a helping hand makes me feel useful. (subj)

There are many good reasons for giving people a helping hand. (obj of prep)

Lying on the beach is not everyone's idea of the best way to spend a vacation. (subj)

I enjoyed lying on the beach last summer. (direct obj)

Exercise 32, page 176

Here are some possibilities; you may come up with others.

1. After we had finished the decorations, the ballroom looked beautiful.

2. You will reduce your revising time by following a few helpful pointers.

3. In making a career decision, you will find your counselor a big help.

4. By signing this waiver, the tenant gives up any right to make claims against the owner.

5. Our backpacks got really heavy after we hiked up that steep mountain trail.

Exercise 33, page 179

1. to give . . . Christmas—VIII, direct obj
2. To side with the truth—VI, subj
3. to beg for mercy—VI, subj comp
4. To walk . . . night—VI, subj
5. to become president—V, direct obj
6. never to take . . . lunch—VII, appositive
7. to shock . . . views—VII, direct obj
8. to distract . . . nest—VII, direct obj
9. to be . . . friendship—II, subj comp
10. To know him—VII, subj; to love him—VII, subj comp

1.

2.

3.

4.

5.

6.

7.

8.

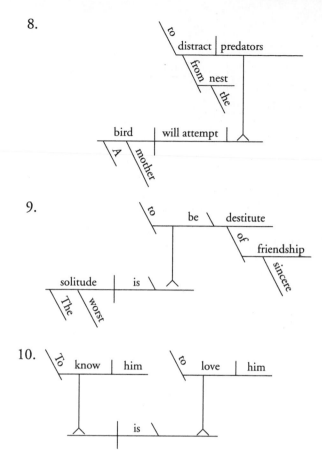

9.

10.

Exercise 34, page 181

1. <u>for you to tell the truth</u>, infinitive (subj comp)
2. <u>remaining silent</u>, gerund (obj of prep)
3. <u>To ignore . . .order</u>, infinitive (subj)
4. <u>to welcome . . . company</u>, infinitive (direct obj)
5. <u>to buy up . . . stocks</u>, infinitive (appositive)
6. <u>Raising . . . profile</u>, gerund (subj)
7. <u>to write . . . assignment</u>, infinitive (direct obj)
8. <u>your proofreading . . . me</u>, gerund (direct obj)
9. <u>to watch . . . morning</u>, infinitive (direct obj)
10. <u>The baby's crying</u>, gerund (subj)

1.

6.

7.

8.

9.

10.
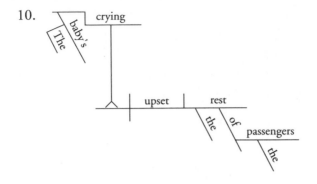

Exercise 35, page 183

Here are some possibilities; you will undoubtedly think of others.

1. You should know <u>that this flight has been cancelled</u>. (dir obj)

2. <u>That the airlines overbook their flights</u> makes everyone angry. (subj)

3. My parents are expecting <u>that I will call them from the airport</u>. (dir obj)

4. <u>That my flight will be late</u> has not occurred to them. (subj)

5. The truth is <u>that they never asked me about my travel plans</u>. (subj comp)

6. The fact <u>that I might keep them waiting</u> disturbs me. (appositive)

Exercise 36, page 185

1. Main clause: VII; nominal *where* clause (dir obj): VII

2. Main clause: VII; adverbial *when* clause: VII

3. Main clause: IV; adverbial *when* clause: VI

4. Main clause: III; nominal *when* clause (subj): VI

5. Main clause: VI; adverbial *where* clause: VI

6. Main clause: VIII; adverbial *when* clause: VII; nominal *where* clause (dir obj): VII

7. Main clause: VII; adverbial *when* clause: VII; nominal *where* clause (dir obj): VI

8. Main clause: VII; nominal *where* clause (dir obj): VII (passive)

9. Main clause: VII; adverbial *when* clause: III

10. Main clause: VII; nominal *where* clause (dir obj): I; adverbial *when* clause: VI

Exercise 37, page 186

1. <u>how awesome a redwood tree could be</u> (dir obj)
2. <u>that it was too short</u> (subj comp)
3. <u>What Carlos said about his cousin</u> (subj)
4. <u>why people fear intimacy</u> (obj of prep)
5. <u>that they could have a dog</u> (dir obj)
6. <u>Who invented calculus</u> (subj)
7. <u>which twin was Elaine</u> (dir obj)
8. <u>if we could come for the weekend</u> (dir obj)
9. <u>he would explain his explanation</u> (dir obj)
10. <u>that they should replay the point</u> (appositive)

1.

2.

3.

4.

5.

6.

7.

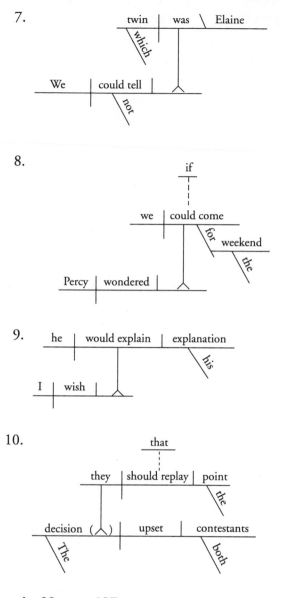

8.

9.

10.

Exercise 38, page 187

1. <u>clipping . . . magazine</u>, gerund (obj of prep)
2. <u>To search . . . scores</u>, infinitive (subj)
3. <u>that we . . . house</u>, nom clause (dir obj)
4. <u>when he would arrive</u>, nom clause (dir obj)
5. <u>to raise their fares</u>, infinitive (dir obj)
6. <u>that they . . . fares</u>, nom clause (dir obj); <u>to raise their fares</u>, infinitive (dir obj)

7. <u>falling asleep at the wheel</u>, gerund (subj comp)

8. <u>Why reality shows . . . popular</u>, nom clause (subj)

9. <u>that the semester is almost over</u>, nom clause (appositive)

10. <u>to make . . . class</u>, infinitive (dir obj)

11. <u>getting . . . want</u>, gerund (subj comp); <u>what you want</u>, nom clause (dir obj); <u>wanting . . . get</u>, gerund (subj comp); <u>what you get</u>, nom clause (dir obj)

12. <u>I had studied the wrong chapters</u>, nom clause (dir obj)

CHAPTER 9

Exercise 39, page 198

1. <u>Amazingly</u>

2. (none)

3. <u>Well</u>

4. (none)

5. <u>Strangely</u>

6. (none)

7. <u>Without a doubt</u>

8. <u>no doubt</u>

9. (none)

10. <u>my friend</u>

Exercise 40, page 200

1. (no commas)

2. us, although

3. over, we

4. coffee, since (optional)

5. rent, even

6. (no commas)

7. apartment, even (optional)

8. heat, get

Exercise 41, page 202

A. 1. When you are late for work, the subway is better than the bus.

2. If bread is kept too long in hot weather, mold will grow on it.

3. While we were driving to the game on Saturday, an accident tied up traffic for over an hour.

B. 1. I picked up a Midwestern accent while *I was* living in Omaha.

2. My accent is not as noticeable as Carlo's *accent is* [noticeable].

3. Holmes hit Ali harder than Norton *hit Ali* (or *Holmes hit Norton*).

4. If *it is* necessary, strain the juice before adding the sugar.

5. While *I was* waiting . . .

6. If *your paper is* handed in late . . .

7. Love goes toward love, as schoolboys *go* from their books. But love *goes* from love, *as schoolboys go* toward school with heavy looks.

8. The weather in Little Rock is not as humid *as it is in* New Orleans.

Exercise 42, page 205

1. <u>her tail . . . metronome</u> (part)

2. <u>their arms . . . shoulders</u> (part)

3. <u>The rain having . . . hour</u> (part)

4. <u>her book . . . floor</u> (adj phr); <u>her eyes . . . flames</u> (adj phrase)

5. <u>the streets . . . light</u> (NP); <u>the planet . . . edges</u> (part); <u>the sky . . . infinity</u> (NP)

6. <u>his bunched shirt . . . blades</u> (prep ph); <u>his toes . . . floor</u> (part); <u>the aunt's arms . . . shoulders</u> (prep. phrase)

Exercise 43, page 207

1. Cleaning the basement this morning wasn't very much fun.

2. It surprised me that Otis didn't want to stay for the second half of the game.

3. The president criticized the Congress rather severely in his press conference; some observers considered his criticism quite inappropriate.

4. Contrary to the prediction of the weather service, the first snowstorm of the season in Denver was both early and severe.

5. Our having company for dinner three times this week probably means hot dogs for the rest of the month.

CHAPTER 10

Exercise 44, page 215

1. (no commas)

2. now, I

3. tires, shock absorbers, and brake linings

4. 1970s, a 1959 Chevy, required

5. (no commas)

6. Corvette, the car

Exercise 45, page 219

There's more than one possibility in each case.

1. I can't decide which activity I prefer: swimming . . . or jogging . . .

2. I almost never watch television. Either there is nothing on that appeals to me or the picture . . .

3. I don't enjoy flying, and I don't feel like taking the train.

4. Either the superintendent or the members of the school board make the final decision.

5. Either the recipe was printed wrong, or I misread it.

6. I was unhappy with what he said and how he said it.

7. The coach announced an extra hour of drill on Saturday and no practice on Sunday.

8. My history class, as well as both English classes, requires. . .

9. For my birthday dinner, Aunt Rosa has promised to fix her famous lasagna and to bake my favorite cake.

10. For the picnic we brought lemonade and baskets of chicken.

CHAPTER 11

Exercise 46, page 233

nov | a

re | nov | at | ion

in | nov | ate

nov | ice

nov | el | ist

   nov = new

dur | able

en | dure

dur | ation

dur | ing

en | dur | ance

   dur = hard

aud | it | or

aud | ience

in | aud | ible

aud | it | or | ium

aud | io

   aud = hear

con | ceive

cap | able

sus | cept | ible

cap | ture

inter | cept

   cap (cept) = take

Exercise 47, page 234
Check your answers with the dictionary and/or your instructor.

Exercise 48, page 239

1. pre cis ion (bound + bound + bound; affix, base, affix)
   d   d

   (Note: d = derivational; i = inflectional)

2. candid ate (free + bound; base, affix)
   d

3. de tour ed (bound + free + bound; affix, base, affix)
   d   i

4. ex cess ive ly (bound + bound + bound + bound; affix, base, affix, affix)
   d   d d

5. un a ware (bound + bound + free; affix, affix, base)
   d d

6. money (free; base)

7. side walk s (free + free + bound; base, base, affix)
   i

8. pro mot ion (bound + bound + bound; affix, base, affix)
   d   d

9. il leg al (bound + bound + bound; affix, base, affix)
   d   d

10. weal th y (free + bound + bound; base, affix, affix)
    d d

11. tele vis ion (bound + bound + bound; affix, base, affix)
    d   d

12. re vis es (bound + bound + bound; affix, base, affix)
    d   i

CHAPTER 12

Exercise 49, page 245

1. pleasure
2. regulation, regulator
3. stealth
4. health, healer
5. derivation, derivative
6. inflection
7. formula, formation
8. revival
9. seizure
10. retirement, retiree

Exercise 50, page 246

1. teacher's, teachers'
2. horse's, horses'
3. sister's husband's, sisters' husbands'
4. son's, sons'

Exercise 51, page 248

1. Price's
2. Hedges'
3. James's
4. Massachusetts'
5. Linus's

6. neighbor's
7. neighbors'
8. Miss Piggy's
9. women's
10. Confucius'

Exercise 52, page 258

friendly	friendlier	friendliest
helpful	more helpful	most helpful
wise	wiser	wisest
awful	more awful	most awful
rich	richer	richest
mellow	mellower	mellowest
expensive	more expensive	most expensive
valid	more valid	most valid
pure	purer	purest
able	abler (more able)	ablest (most able)

Exercise 53, page 263

1. grief	grieve	grievous	grievously
2. variation	vary	variable	variably
variance		various	variously
variety			
3. ability	enable	able	ably
4. defense	defend	defensive	defensively

5. economy	economize	economical economic	economically
6. pleasure	please	pleasant	pleasantly
7. type	typify	typical	typically
8. prohibition	prohibit	prohibitive	prohibitively
9. critic criticism	criticize	critical	critically
10. validation validity	validate	valid	validly
11. appreciation	appreciate	appreciative	appreciatively
12. beauty	beautify	beautiful	beautifully
13. acceptance	accept	acceptable	acceptably
14. purity	purify	pure	purely
15. continuation continuity	continue	continuous continual	continuously continually

(Note: You may think of other possibilities.)

CHAPTER 13

Exercise 54, page 271

1. my, enough, her
2. John's, the
3. Every, this, a
4. more, the week's
5. less, last
6. either, no

Exercise 55, page 274

1. <u>have been</u> (having)
2. <u>used to</u> (use)
3. <u>should have</u> (eaten)
4. <u>can't</u> (look)
5. <u>will be</u> (helping)
6. <u>has to</u> (leave)
7. <u>are</u> (frustrating)
8. <u>can</u> (be)
9. <u>should</u> (continue)
10. <u>am</u> (keeping)

Exercise 56, page 281

1. in, since
2. because of
3. in spite of
4. Prior to, in
5. According to, of, in
6. with (on = particle)
7. Except for, in, of , out of
8. Between, until

Exercise 57, page 288

1. <u>and</u>—coordinating conjunction; <u>on</u>—preposition; <u>an</u>—determiner; <u>in</u>—preposition
2. <u>Four</u>—determiner; <u>from</u>—preposition; <u>for</u>—preposition; <u>for</u>—coordinating conjunction; <u>for</u>—preposition
3. <u>As</u>—subordinating conjunction; <u>an</u>—determiner; <u>as</u>—expletive; <u>at</u>—preposition
4. <u>be</u>—auxiliary; <u>by</u>—preposition; <u>but</u>—coordinating conjunction
5. <u>of</u>—preposition; <u>off</u>—particle (part of verb); <u>if</u>—subordinating conjunction
6. <u>are</u>—auxiliary; <u>of</u>—preposition; <u>or</u>—expletive; <u>our</u>—determiner
7. <u>will</u>—auxiliary; <u>with</u>—preposition; <u>while</u>—subordinating conjunction
8. <u>too</u>—qualifier; <u>two</u>—determiner; <u>to</u>—preposition

---

CHAPTER 14

Exercise 58, page 297

1. They
2. We, him
3. it
4. them
5. them *or* them and him
6. him, it
7. us
8. He, them

Exercise 59, page 300

1. herself
2. themselves
3. itself
4. ourselves
5. himself
6. ourselves

Exercise 60, page 306

1. <u>everything</u>—indefinite; <u>I</u>—personal; <u>one</u>—indefinite
2. <u>every</u>—indefinite; <u>any</u>—indefinite; <u>they</u>—personal
3. <u>Someone</u>—indefinite; <u>we</u>—personal; <u>who</u>—interrogative; <u>it</u>—personal
4. <u>All</u>—indefinite; <u>that</u>—relative; <u>I</u>—personal; <u>that</u>—demonstrative
5. <u>much</u>—indefinite; <u>they</u>—personal; <u>both</u>—indefinite; <u>more</u>—indefinite; <u>I</u>—personal
6. <u>I</u>—personal; <u>myself</u>—intensive; <u>whatever</u>—indefinite relative; <u>you</u>—personal
7. <u>enough</u>—indefinite; <u>me</u>—personal
8. <u>themselves</u>—reflexive; <u>one another's</u>—reciprocal
9. <u>most</u>—indefinite; <u>I</u>—personal; <u>myself</u>—reflexive
10. <u>whoever</u>—indefinite relative; <u>one</u>—indefinite

---

CHAPTER 15

There is no one correct answer for any of the exercise items in this chapter. The answers given here are simply suggestions.

Exercise 61, page 322

1. The small band of rebels *resisted* the army patrol for several hours, then *surrendered* just before dawn. News reports . . . did not *specify* . . .
2. The majority leader *wields* a great deal of influence in the White House. He or she can easily *circumvent* . . .
3. Several economists are saying that they *anticipate* an upturn . . . Others, however, maintain that interest rates must *stabilize* if . . .
4. The night-shift workers . . . tried to *compel* them to *relinquish* . . .
5. The chairman . . . *denounced* the practice . . . He said that the new rules will *eliminate* . . . To some observers, such practices *signify* [or *constitute*] bribery. Several senators have promised to *formulate* . . .
6. Dorm life changed drastically when colleges *abrogated* [or *abolished*] . . . In the old days . . . students who *defied* [or *disregarded, disobeyed*] the rules. At some schools . . . would not *tolerate* . . . routinely *expelled.*

Exercise 62, page 327

1. The community objected strongly when the school board cancelled the after-school drama program.
2. Now that China has opened its doors to certain aspects of capitalism, American companies are looking for ways to expand their markets and their product lines.
3. Analysts of the situation in the Far East agree that opportunities for investment there are growing.
4. In his biography of Lyndon Johnson, Robert Caro describes the 1948 Senate election in great detail.
5. When Julie applied for a work-study job, she was surprised to learn that her parents would have to submit a detailed financial statement.
6. Tim worked long and hard before his new pizza parlor finally turned a profit.
7. Two important aims of education are to broaden one's view of life and to establish worthy goals.
8. Another important aim of education is to help students learn to think: to develop strategies for understanding and solving problems.

Exercise 63, page 330

1. Even though the famous Gateway Arch is in St. Louis, it is Kansas City that claims the title "Gateway to the West."
2. Many students have a hard time finding summer jobs because our spring semester doesn't end until the second week of June.
3. Thomas Jefferson acquired the Ozark Mountains for the United States when he negotiated the Louisiana Purchase with Napoleon in 1803.
4. Many attorneys are unable to offer advice to their clients concerning oil and gas leases because they are unacquainted with the relevant laws.
5. When the neighbors added a pit bull to their pet population, which now numbers three unfriendly four-legged creatures, we decided to fence in our backyard.
6. Even though the human circulatory system is a marvel of efficiency, it is still subject to a wide variety of degenerative diseases.
7. Because carbohydrates are the body's prime source of energy, fad diets that severely restrict them are not only ineffective, they are often dangerous.

8. Because our congressman knows that the majority of voters are upset with both their tax rate and the way their taxes are spent, he has made "No New Taxes" the main theme of his reelection campaign.

9. When the auto companies offered cash rebates last January, sales of new cars increased dramatically.

10. Although the buffalo population of the West had nearly been wiped out by 1890, it now numbers about 60,000, with some 400 Colorado ranchers raising buffalo for meat.

Exercise 64, page 345

1. If you are an average American, the energy problem is mainly your monthly fuel bill and the cost of filling up the gas tank. You may also remember that in 1979, and way back in 1974, you had to wait in long lines at gasoline stations. For all of this, you may have blamed the "Arabs" or the oil companies or the government, or perhaps all three. Much of the information in the media, as well as your past experience, probably tells you that energy prices will continue to go up . . .

2. Of all born creatures, we humans are the only ones that cannot live by bread alone. We live as much by symbols as by sense report . . . For we see not only actualities but meanings. We have, indeed, all the impulses and interests of animal nature; we eat, sleep . . . That is the special asset of the human mind, which makes Homo sapiens the master of earth and all its progeny.

CHAPTER 16

Exercise 65, page 354

1. During the second two-year stretch of a president's term in office, he may find himself on the defensive, even with his own party; when—as frequently happens—his party loses a number of Senate and House seats in the midterm election, that second stretch can become even more defensive.

2. In recent years, the public attitude toward smoking (except perhaps in the tobacco-growing states) has changed so fast, with smoke-free zones everywhere, including restaurants, office buildings, and shopping malls, it could almost be called a revolution; even outdoor stadiums, such as Oriole Park at Camden Yards and Jacobs Field in Cleveland, have established a no-smoking policy.

Exercise 66, page 354

1. The cost of repairs to the nation's public transportation facilities—roads, bridges, and railroads—is an expenditure that cannot be delayed much longer if the system is to survive.

2. To many people, the mushroom is a lowly fungus with little food value; to others, it is a gourmet's delight.

3. A Chinese restriction on importing certain American goods, such as cotton, synthetic fibers, and soybeans, has had an adverse effect on the U.S. economy—especially on the farmers.

4. According to fashion experts, the crew cut—the haircut that was more or less the hallmark of the 1950s—will be back in style before long.

5. Unfortunately, my favorite activities—skiing, playing golf, and bowling—cost more than my budget can stand.

6. Most people probably don't know that Alexander Graham Bell, the inventor of the telephone, succeeded his father-in-law as president of the National Geographic Society.

7. Many scientists believe that sightings of "cryptids"—including Big Foot, the Loch Ness monster, and Yeti, the Abominable Snowman—are simply mistakes, attributable to unfamiliarity with known animals, rather than to delusions.

8. Eugene Schiffelin, a New Yorker, decided to introduce all the birds mentioned in Shakespeare's works into America. In 1890—because of a single mention in *Henry IV*—he loosed 60 starlings into Central Park. Today millions of aggressive and smart and voracious starlings have blanketed the United States; in many places they blacken the sky.

Index

Notes